My Life Most Memoirable

The collected memoirs of
Paige Krystal Wilcox

Copyright © 2020 Paige Krystal Wilcox
All rights reserved.
Second Edition: July 2020

This book or any portion thereof may not be reproduced or used in any manner whatsoever without the express written permission of the author except for the use of brief quotations in a book review, scholarly journal, or other non-commercial uses. For permission requests, write to the author (email@homepaige.com.au).

First Edition: December 2018
This Edition: July 2020

Changes since the previous edition include:
Condensed Formatting, Minor Edits, and Added Content Note

ISBN: 9798665845807

This book is dedicated to the many who didn't make it.

Special thanks to each and every person I can call friend, and the countless individuals who provided feedback on the stories in this book.

AUTHOR'S CONTENT NOTE

EVERY TALE CONTAINED WITHIN THIS BOOK is based on my perception of events that I experienced first-hand. Aside from the narrator, all other characters are fictional, as are many locations. Not just to protect privacy, this choice was made to allow readers to focus on what mattered most; how it felt to experience various situations. Each volume begins with more specific detail about this writing choice.

The Memoirable series began, in part, as a way to reclaim my personal story that had been told without my consent, in a way that hurt me deeply. It was also to counter the underrepresentation and misrepresentation of people like me in media, which is something I perceived to be a cause of mistreatment. Spending several years serving the community as a volunteer across Australia, I was compelled to continue the series to counter additional problems faced by me, as well as other members of the community.

Throughout my writing process I have always consulted a combination of trusted individuals, relevant support groups, as well as the most current content and language guides available to me. This means that I have the best possible version of my story at the time of producing a final draft. However, as we continue to learn more about ourselves and each other globally, language and storytelling is evolving.

To allow readers a deeper understanding of the situations explored, it was important that these books include some mistakes made by myself and other characters. I must acknowledge that there are also likely to be incidental terms, phrases, and stories that have been deemed inappropriate, unhelpful or hurtful since final edits. Publishing revised editions was considered, however this would imply that there is global consensus regarding appropriate language and storytelling. There is not. It would also imply that any consensus is unchanging. It is not.

So what is the best way forward?

As you travel back and forth in time through my life experiences, there is something you should keep in the back of your mind. The best way to learn is to seek information from a variety of sources. Despite aforementioned consultation, this book ultimately contains the intimate perspective of a single person, at specific times of their life. If anything should be assumed, it is that by the time you are reading this book, I have since grown beyond the perspective depicted. I do, after all, identify with the label *life-long learner*.

Volume I
1982 - 2016

Over the course of a single month in 2015, the 33 posts of a two-timeline episodic blog were published under the title *Version 33*. With the addition of a third timeline, these posts were reworked to become the Memoirable trilogy.

Spanning four books, the trilogy allowed readers to either take a linear journey through three novellas (*Outer Shell, Inner Demons,* and *Synthesis*) or travel back and forth through three timelines in the one book (*The Synthesis of Outer Shell and Her Inner Demons*).

This volume is that book.

PROCEED WITH CAUTION

THIS VOLUME IS MY PERCEPTION of events that occurred around me from the age of 5, winding up 30 years later. I didn't think I would make it to the ripe old age of 35, and by the final chapter you will understand why. Should you dare to, you are about to embark on a journey composed of three intersecting adventures, each occurring in a different place and time:

1. *Outer Shell*, an awkwardly dramatic tale of unlikely survival into adulthood;
2. *Inner Demons*, a sordid, cautionary tale of denial, with a dash of romance; and
3. *Synthesis*, a gruelling tale of courage, sacrifice, and triumph over adversity.

For those who need it to reduce feelings of disorientation, chapters from *Outer Shell* are identifiable by two hollow circles (see: ○○), *Inner Demons* by a single hollow circle (see: ○), and *Synthesis* by a single black circle (see: ●).

Consent is important to me, so I must warn you of content that may unsettle some readers. Throughout this book the following themes are explored, the level of detail steadily progressing:

Sexuality
Addiction
Suicide
Mental illness
Surgical procedures
Religion
Cancer

The thoughts and ideas expressed in these books are my own and have absolutely nothing to do with any of my employers, past or present, unless stated explicitly. No character descriptions should be considered as accurate representations of real people. To protect the privacy of the players in my life—and because it's not feasible to write about thousands of individuals in detail—in parts I have:

1. Written collectively about people;
2. Reordered timelines; and
3. Chosen feeling over detail.

By turning the page, you acknowledge that you have read and understood the words above.

Do we have an agreement?

Let us begin.

Chapter Two

○○ **IMPERCEPTIBLE**

WE HAVE TRAVELLED BACK IN TIME to the late 1980s. We are in regional Queensland, Australia, where the air is hot and dry. At this point in time, I exist as virtually nothing but inner monologue; unvoiced thoughts. Picture all-consuming blackness. Got it? We're now on the same page. That was an intentional pun, and you need to know that I am not at all sorry; puns are a big part of my life. I digress. If I squint with my brain, I can see little more than abstract details this far back. I am somewhere in my fifth year of life and there seems to be a lot of darkness. Is there actually an absence of light? Or is that just the way my memory is processing the lack of available information? Ahah! I see something. A long hallway with a step, and the colour green. Linoleum? Lime green laminate. And there are hand puppets!

I can't remember why, but unlike most Australian kids, I didn't go to kindergarten or preschool. Instead, The Visitor would come to my house, I think on a weekly basis. The Visitor is only a vague shadowy human shape to me, devoid of any specific characteristics, but I remember the puppets. Well, at the very least I remember the idea of the puppets. Each week The Visitor would bring the puppets for me to play with. There were other objects—toys—but it was the puppets that I loved. They were my first hobby, and the first of many forms of escapism. The puppets were also my introduction to storytelling, and something to use to give my physical situation context.

Back then my name was Sarah, but that is not what anyone called me because I was hidden, protected under an outer shell where nobody could see me. Outer Shell (see: the name of my physical form) was skinny, pale, short, with hair more accurately described as white than blonde and bright green eyes that would occasionally turn dull. At five years of age, the meagre Outer Shell was almost as invisible as I was.

One day, utilising Outer Shell as a means of transport, I was taken to a new place by Parental Being. There was an adult stranger and lots of children who were also strangers. The surrounds were colourful and overwhelmingly busy with new objects to look at. I was scared so I held Parental Being's hand tightly. It became apparent that Parental Being was going to leave, and I was to stay. My fear intensified.

Inner Monologue: You can't leave me; you are my only constant. I don't know anything or anyone in this place. I don't like it here. Who are these people? Why can't I stay at home with the puppets? I want to go back to playing with the puppets. Don't leave.

Body Language: Shaking.

I saw the situation like a scene that I would play out with The Visitor and the puppets. In this scene, I could see three players that were not me.

The Classroom Players:
1. The Anchor (see: Parental Being's arm)
2. The Storm (see: the adult stranger)
3. The Ocean (see: room of unfamiliar children and objects)

Sobbing and crying out in anguish, I clung on to The Anchor. I refused to allow The Storm to pluck me from safety and hurl me into The Ocean. Poor Parental Being must have been in agony on my first day of school. Eventually I conceded, and for the first time of many, I sat completely alone in a room full of people. For the first time that I could remember, I was in a place I didn't know, without Parental Being. It was my first experience with the feeling that I had been betrayed.

Later in life, this ability to be alone while surrounded by people would become something I loved about the city. I would actively seek out new places and experiences. I would come to cherish the associated feelings, the rush of adrenaline, sense of anonymity. But not yet. In this moment I just felt frightened.

Within these initial memories, I already knew that I was very different to those around me. There was a distinct disconnect between Outer Shell and me. I could see that other people were one connected being, but Outer Shell was a completely separate entity to me. I had to concentrate to move Outer Shell, and was convinced that together we did not make a whole person. I watched the children around me and tried to work out why I was different to them.

I used the puppets as context to understand the unique situation I was in. Although I could seek refuge in Outer Shell and control it like a puppet in order to communicate with the outside world, I didn't feel powerful. It didn't evoke the same feelings as the puppets that could be taken off and put away. I felt trapped; the seed of feelings that later developed to become claustrophobia. I had to find a way out, but I knew that I had to keep this knowledge secret. From this point forward in life, I considered myself to be completely alone.

○ INAUDIBLE SCREAMS

"I GOOGLED YOU," SHE TOLD ME, immediately killing anything positive I had been feeling.

Skipping back a few hours, I had a slight wine buzz; my entire face infected with a ridiculous grin as I looked around at my colleagues in an unusually relaxed social setting. I was perched in a specific position that allowed me to gaze up at the red wall at one end of the old Renaissance architecture style building I worked in. The Medical College Building had been part of a State Public Works building program undertaken by the Queensland Government to counter the effects of the Great Depression. Men could just turn up in the morning, and they would be assigned a task for that day.

I considered myself fortunate to work in such a beautiful old building, able to admire the red face brick, white flat-arched windows, and majestic tan columns and dome as I approached every weekday and some weekend mornings. I felt less fortunate about the cage lift that was frequently out of action, sometimes for weeks at a time because replacement parts were so difficult to source. During assessment periods, long hours were required, so I would often find myself wandering the corridors at night. They were lined with dark stained wooden panels, with equally dark flooring and every few metres hung a white sphere that emitted dull light. I listened to the building moan, windows rattling from the wind, and considered it to be the perfect setting for a supernatural thriller.

As delightful as it was to look at, our workplace had been particularly stressful for a prolonged period due to the looming restructure that would follow the review currently being carried out. Nobody felt particularly safe; the rumour mill churning out all sorts of material to cause unrest to everyone from the highest ranking down to the lowest. Right now though, nobody was giving any thought to that. We were all in a happy little bubble of disregard.

Inner Monologue: Life is great!
Body Language: Life is great!

A small group of us had stayed back after work to drink at the local café, and although I had promised just one drink, I was already several glasses of wine in. The first glass was my favourite white at the time, Pinot Gris. The second was something red and really I was just drinking it to help my colleague finish the bottle. I shouldn't have been drinking red wine at all, but I wasn't far from a hospital and those places are great at dealing with life-threatening allergic reactions. I continued to alternate between wine I had purchased, and whatever wine I was able to acquire without spending any money. Over the course of a few hours, the number of colleagues present dwindled, but I stayed on and continued to drink until it was just me and a woman, also in her early thirties. At the time I didn't know her well, and for reasons that will become apparent in the following paragraphs, I will refer to this woman as The Instigator.

The Instigator requested that before we part ways, we take a short walk, and get to know each other a bit better. I had enjoyed interacting with her, and I was well-lubricated from the wine, so I gladly accepted. Her accent intrigued me, with hard 'r' sounds I usually associated with people from the United States and Canada, but I knew she was from somewhere else. I liked listening to her speak, however the positive feelings I was relishing while communicating with her changed abruptly, as once we were alone and had engaged in some light chit chat, she admitted to searching for me on the internet. My internal reaction was similar to what you experience when someone unexpectedly hits you.

Wine buzz turned sour and my skin was rapidly flushed with a radioactive glow. My stomach turned at those words. *I Googled you.* I knew what was coming next, as over the three years prior, I'd heard them countless times from students, work colleagues and new acquaintances.

"I heard about that thing, you know what I'm talking about," a student had mentioned, cornering me in the hallway of The Medical College Building.

"I know about your history," a Work Colleague informed me, following up the comment with a wink and a nudge, as if that would make it less offensive.

"I was hoping you could clarify something I heard about you," a new friend pressed.

Inner Monologue: You're being presumptuous, Paige. This could be different.
Body Language: Raised eyebrows to simulate surprise.

"I was thinking about that work email we got," The Instigator told me. "The one about the additional options on the online forms."

Her eyes were too bright, an expression that would have been more appropriate for gushing over winning the lottery or speaking about her greatest passion in life. It was not appropriate for this conversation.

"I now know one," she squealed, literally bouncing with each step. "You are my first!"

Okay, so it wasn't different. This was exactly what I was expecting, what I had been hoping wasn't the case. For the quarter hour that followed, I politely listened as ignorantly hurtful words flowed from her mouth, her obnoxious excitement visibly growing with each word. I grasped tightly onto the feelings that were fighting to materialise, pulling my best poker face over the internal weeping.

I was something of a pro at this. While training as a film actor, I came to know it as the Social Self, which is not necessarily a lie to those around you, but one of a number of ways you can adjust how you represent yourself based on the physical situation you are in. It's pushing forward what's presently considered the best, letting characteristics deemed currently undesirable to take a back seat until a more appropriate time. It's not a lie, it's just remoulding the truth. It's not that much of a lie.

Inner Monologue: It's not her fault. It's not her fault. It's not her fault. It will be over soon. It will be over soon. It will be over soon.
Body Language: Tight lipped smile. Gentle nods of acknowledgement.

Unfortunately... No, not unfortunately. Considering what it prompted, that doesn't seem the right word choice now. Fortunately, wine tipped me over the edge, and in a recurring situation I had previously handled with utmost diplomacy, I decided on complete, ugly, brutal honesty. Not my finest hour, but as you'll soon learn, it was certainly not my worst.

Inner Monologue: I shouldn't have to be repeatedly subjected to this! I refuse to keep reliving this stupid scenario!
Body Language: Slouched posture, moist eyes.

Opening the floodgates (see: tears; see also: words), I coarsely spat whatever vocabulary I could think of at The Instigator to make it clear that I was upset by her comments, and that I didn't want to see her again. I made sure it was crystal clear that through her own doing she had reached a point of no return. She had crossed a line that she could never come back from! I returned to a level of social ineptitude I associated with childhood. We parted ways, both feeling hurt and confused.

To distract myself, I went immediately to the house of a version of Friendly Entity that was a male fiction writer, but I couldn't let it go. It wasn't just the specific conversation that haunted me, but what it meant. Was I destined to live this over and over, tortured until I eventually died? Died... I played the word over again in my head. In my drunken state, I saw two solutions.

Inner Monologue: Option 1, kill yourself. You won't have to endure this ever again if you are dead.

Hmmm.

Inner Monologue: Option 2, write. You can write.

Both options had been on my mind in recent times. The second option was something that had been on it quite a bit more, but fear had held me back, justified by a thousand other reasons people come up with to justify procrastination.

Furiously at first, I wrote down notes about the things I had been hurt by in the past, paying particular attention to those that had occurred most frequently. Furiously is how I start most projects, now that I have identified my consistent weakness of having trouble following through with any goal that—not unlike the end of this sentence—takes a considerable amount of time to reach.

The next morning I sat in one of my favourite cafés on James Street in Fortitude Valley. It was one of several fine dining establishments I had discovered were great for a modestly priced breakfast. I was on a stool looking through glass at a beautiful mess of green vines and leaves over grey, modern architecture. It had become a tradition to splurge and take myself out for breakfast every weekend, not only to indulge but to reflect on the events of the week. Using a notes app on my phone, I forged my thoughts into the form of an open letter, and sent the rough draft of it to The Instigator, along with an apology for my inappropriate reaction to her words.

Now that I'd had this idea to write and had started, I could think of little else. I obsessively spent every moment alone writing. After a few hasty rewrites to refine the letter, I broadcast it to a small, select audience on social media. This select audience consisted mostly of people I was confident would respond well. My intent was to progressively widen the audience until the letter was public, available to anyone, at any time, to stumble across.

The letter was my second attempt to come out of the closet on a mass scale via social media. Learning from the previous attempt that had left me burnt out and unable to talk about the experience for years, this time I was more cautious. I carefully considered the specific language I used and mentally prepared myself for possible backlash. I also gave thought to the boundaries I wanted to create and enforce.

○

Open Letter, 2015:
Dear Friends,
This post has been written in an attempt to further educate the people in my life on a current hot topic that directly affects me. Please, read this in its entirety before commenting or messaging me about it. I also ask that you be respectful if you do choose to say something. I've discussed this with thousands of people over the last 15 years and have received a considerable amount of hate from strangers and people who claimed to care about me. I've also received a lot of questions I shouldn't have.
I would like to stress that many women in my position have had a much more difficult time than me, and that makes me one of a few privileged individuals in an underprivileged minority group, that group being the T in LGBTIQ.
I think about having had sex reassignment surgery as I think about having had my wisdom teeth removed; I only think about it if it's specifically mentioned. Generally speaking, I do not think about either of these things from day to day because they do not get in the way of me doing anything I do. Something that separates the two is the social stigma and consequent trauma associated with sex reassignment surgery, and everything that came before that.
Usually I am able to live my life as a strong-willed wacky straight white female without

giving any thought to what I had to endure to get to this point. But with Caitlyn Jenner coming out, and the U.S. Supreme Court ruling on marriage, the word transgender is constantly in my feed; so I am currently thinking about it several times a day. This is why you may be a good friend and may not have known prior to reading this.

Back to teeth. Because there is no social stigma and psychological trauma with removal of wisdom teeth, if that topic comes up I can quickly chime in with, "I had mine out! All four, all at once. I looked so funny all swollen!" Transitioning from one gender to another however, history tells me that I have to be more cautious. That is why when this topic has come up recently, online and in person, I have not immediately sung, "I'm like her! I underwent psychological and hormone therapy and surgery to become female on the outside, as I always had been on the inside!" Instead, I have written this.

I may write more, but for now I would like to address a few things so that you do not cause offence in ignorance. The following list has come from the most commonly asked questions.

1. You may describe me as a woman, girl, lady, chick, or a woman who has had sex reassignment surgery. You may not refer to me as transgender or a transgender woman or person. Many women in my situation are fine with that label, but I am not. Just as I won't call someone with a mobility impairment disabled. We are people first, condition, disease, or syndrome second. I grew up with labels I hated enforced upon me and I will not tolerate it as an adult.
2. Sexual and reproductive function is none of your business, unless we are going to have sex or try to reproduce together. I do not exist to satisfy your curiosity. Because you didn't ask though, I will tell you that I never think about my past leading up to and during sex, and I would describe myself as 'infertile'.
3. An appropriate way to display support is to remain in my life. Telling me you saw something trans* related or sending me articles about trans* issues is not an appropriate way to display support, it's pointing out and reminding me that you see me as different to other women. I see as much of that stuff as I care to. It's not an interest of mine, it's just a part of my history.
4. Some of my partners have known/ been told before/ during/ after we were together. Some may be finding this out right now. I have had responses ranging from full support, to violent anger. It's none of your business who those people are.
5. It is never appropriate to point out my appearance or behaviour and how feminine or masculine it is. I am confident in who I am and do not need you to convince me of my legitimacy or illegitimacy.
6. Any questions about 'before' are off limits (name, physical attributes etc).
7. I am not ashamed of my past.

Thank you for taking the time to read this. I am aware that I have taken a risk in sharing this to such a wide audience (though as students and colleagues have repeatedly shown, this information is already accessible). My hope is that this post provides a more positive response than information gained through 'whispers' and Google searches.

This is not something that should be shocking or taboo, but for many it is.

About time that changed.

• TESTING THE WARRIOR

IN THE FUTURE, upon reading the phone message notification, an electric panic zips through every cell of my body. My skin is set alight in an instant as if to compliment the artificially vibrant red curls that gently lick at my neck and shoulders in time with the fluctuations of the lazy afternoon breeze. I gruffly push against the strong urge to offload to L2.

I thought I'd have more time, I think.

Rather rapidly, the perimeter of the leafy western suburb of Brisbane where I sit is transformed into the outer edges of the world. Everything beyond the small metal table at the al fresco café dissolves, and I shrink into a more intimate reality. Before long, everything ceases to exist, bar three objects:

Me

My phone

The café table

Picking up the phone, I read the full message, and as I assess the words within the context of the present situation, pure dread sets in. Proof again that the only best laid plans are the plans you can immediately adapt when the unexpected arises. Here, in the future, the unexpected has in fact arisen. Again I fight the urge to reach out to L2.

"I'm sorry, Paige. I've been detained and you might need to do this alone."

Might. A deliberate incorrect use of the word to soften the blow.

Moisture forms on my warm, charged skin, and a slight hand tremor reverberates through to the phone I am holding, preventing me from obsessively rereading the sentences that have caused me such horror. Realising the pointlessness of staring trance-like at a phone I cannot read, I drop the phone back to its resting place on the table so that the tremor isn't so evident. This slows the progression of the powerful physical reaction to my circumstances, but rumination seeks to return a dash of urgency and arms my tear ducts, lightly lubricating my eyes, ready to release with full fury the moment instinct deems necessary.

Almost every moment of the year leading to this day has been meticulously planned out to prepare myself to face this invisible monster, who I've run from since childhood. The metaphorical cliffs I have thrown myself off in the past year have been progressively higher, strengthening me so that today I can stand up, fight past the fear, and charge forward. I've slain countless demons to get here and have a fighting chance. But this moment—a final test—has come much sooner than I had expected, and perhaps childishly, my expectation was that there would be someone with me, holding my hand.

Don't message L2, I tell myself.

Then, *Can I do this on my own?*

At first I am tempted to reach out to Imbibidy Bob, who, since invading my life when I was a young adult, has been my consistent crutch for any situation requiring false bravado. Proof of an equally unhealthy attachment who could also be considered a substance, I contemplate fishing for some distracting content from L2. Instead, I choose an action that requires no substance use, or indeed anything external at all.

Following a deep breath, oxygenating my brain for enhanced function, I release the air slowly, separating myself from the instinctive reaction that is telling me to take flight rather than confront my childhood affliction. The café begins to rematerialize. I repeat the purposeful breathing, and the leafy suburb reappears. Breathing once more, I allow the rest of the world to return. I congratulate myself for this small win, that win being the choosing anything over Imbibidy Bob and L2.

With respect to public speaking, the current version of myself that is thirty-four years old has a solid base of experience. Said experience however, is largely the delivery of technical information to accounting graduates, medical students, and doctors. I've also developed a skillset that allows me to be confident telling adult strangers—individually and in small groups—about the past I've kept buried for the majority of my adult life. At least online, I have grown to be assertive in most instances when people respond disrespectfully, be it purposefully or in ignorance by accident. What I don't have experience with—and in this moment the thought consumes me—is speaking to an auditorium full of teenage students and high school teachers.

Taking myself back to mentally revisit my adolescence, I recall the countless times I've fallen ill with anxiety caused by the mere thought of having to give a presentation to my peers. I remember how cruel teenagers can be, especially when in a pack. Especially when they know I am different to them. The teenagers I will soon stand in front of will definitely know that I am different, because it's my whole purpose for being there.

Wow, I'm really doing this.

As the ultimate authority on the subject, I am preparing to speak to them about my deepest insecurities, and talk through the major plot points of my life, leaving myself completely open to ridicule.

The preceding year—or perhaps even my whole life—has prepared me for speaking openly to a group of adults about something deeply personal. And these days I wouldn't find it laborious speaking to an audience of children or teenagers about a topic once removed from my painful personal life experience. But this personal-teenager-stranger combo? That terrifies me.

I do not feel prepared at all.

In my head, I try to create a list of three reasons that will make this a necessary evil. I just need three solid reasons to force myself forward.

●

<u>*Reasons I Must Push On:*</u>
1. It is a selfless act that will help one or more of the students.
2. It is a selfish act that will keep me alive for much longer.
3.
3..
3...

●

Crap.
I can't think of a third reason, but surely those two are enough?
You're not a scared little child anymore. It's time to grow up.
With no way of knowing what is on the other side, I force myself to cross the final threshold of my journey.

Chapter Three

○○ **IGNOMINY**

DISGUSTING, SHRIVELLED PEAS. Through the eyes I shared with Outer Shell, I looked down at the green objects with disdain. They were the only food still remaining on a previously full plate. The ceramic plate was mostly sand coloured, with large, deep brown rings. It looked striking against the table surface that had a mottled pastel design. I screwed up Outer Shell's nose to clearly indicate to those around me that I was repulsed. I was sitting in the dining room with my immediate family who, for the purpose of de-identification and to make a point, will be known in this book as three collective, genderless characters.

The Family Players:
1. The Family (see: any combination of mother, father, older brother, sister, and younger brother)
2. Parental Being / My Parent / Your Parent (see: mother, father, or both)
3. My Sibling / Your Sibling / Sibling (see: older brother, younger brother, brothers, sister, or all three)

The name Parental Being assigned to Outer Shell is ▇▇▇. For future reference, the correct way to pronounce ▇▇▇ is Blank.

"▇▇▇ (Blank), if you don't finish your dinner, you can't have dessert," Parental Being asserted. I noted frustration, the feeling evident in the way the words made their way out of Parental Being's mouth. This removed all intended authority, placing me in control of the situation. Anyway, Parental Being was addressing Outer Shell, not me. In my not-so-humble opinion, I was completely off the hook.

Inner Monologue: I know what you're doing. You think that by threatening to take away the offer of a treat, I will do something I don't want to do. The offer or removal of the offer of dessert doesn't change the taste and texture of the peas, and I don't need dessert. I feel satisfied with how much food I have eaten and dessert might even make me feel sick.
Body Language: Stiff posture.

Indignantly silent, I sat watching The Family eat dessert, Outer Shell's scrawny arms dangling by its side. Stubbornness was a personality trait inherited from Parental Being, passed down through many generations of strong-willed people. Realising negative punishment hadn't worked,

Parental Being tried a new tactic to modify my behaviour. After what seemed like an eternity, Outer Shell was seated at the table in darkness, by itself. I used the power of my mind to make Outer Shell prod the peas with a fork. I found this situation—my introduction to the notion of boredom—to be undesirable, so I considered my options.

Inner Monologue: I'm tired. I don't want to sit here anymore. If I don't eat the peas, I will have to continue to sit here. If I eat the peas, I can leave the table.
Body Language: Slouched posture.

Defeated, I forced the peas into Outer Shell's mouth one by one, each time triggering its gag reflex. I hated those peas, with their confusing dusty but moist texture beneath the firm, wrinkled exterior. The tactile experience was important. It didn't actually matter to me how the peas tasted because the way they felt was enough to elicit disgust. Excuse me a moment; I think I need to go throw up.

In the bathroom, I examined the naked body of Outer Shell. I wondered why I had been put inside it, instead of being paired with something that looked more like the girls in my class. The eyes, those we shared, and sometimes I saw a look in people that told me, I can see you in there. I could never be sure though, so I kept these ideas to myself. To be hidden was to be safe. Hiding was a good thing.

Not everything seemed inappropriate, I noted, toying with the idea that in the future maybe Outer Shell would magically transform and we would become one. Perhaps everyone went through this, and they just didn't talk about it. The nose and ears of Outer Shell were smaller and cuter than some of the girls at school. My host also had delicate hands and slender, elegant feet, but down below the navel, that wasn't right at all. I could never feel at home in here while that thing was dangling there. Yuck!

It crossed my mind that I might be able to use a knife to correct the issue, but that sounded dangerous, painful and could get in the way of the magical change that might happen later. Better to just leave it be for now. On examination, I discovered that there was something else wrong down there. Something that was wrong with Outer Shell's form. It occurred to me that I didn't just get given the wrong body; it was also a defective one. I would leave it for now. It did warrant further investigation, but at that time I had no way to access the required information.

"I have an idea," Parental Being announced later in the evening, responding to my disappointment that The Visitor no longer brought puppets each week since I had started attending primary school.

"What is it?" My eyes were bright and wide.

Parental Being, grinning, presented me with a sock, some wool, a needle, and some thread.

"I'm going to show you how to make one."

"With a sock?" I screwed up Outer Shell's face to communicate my disbelief.

Smiling down at me, Parental Being produced two small craft eyes from a pocket.

"And these."

Together, we discussed how we would approach the craft project, and then Parental Being talked me through each step so I could carry it out.

To begin with, I put the sock on Outer Shell's hand so that the fingers were where the toes would normally go, and the thumb was where the heel would usually go. Parental Being pushed against the area of the sock where the arch of the foot would normally reside, and showed me how to make it look like a mouth. We marked where the eyes looked best, and, using the needle and thread, sewed them on. I cut several pieces of wool the same length, gathered the pieces together, and wound another piece of wool around the middle to keep the pieces all together to mimic hair. This was glued on. I now had my very own, handmade hand puppet! I felt empowered, but not for long.

The next day our class went to the swimming pool. To my horror, I had to remove my clothes and expose Outer Shell, naked, to a room full of boys. Initially I refused to do so, but then I was forced. I can't remember if I wailed, because the rest of those memories are missing and I have no desire to attempt retrieval. A tough lesson I have learned is that some memories disappear because my mind is not yet in an appropriate place to process them.

My memories resume when we are in the pool, all being asked to put our heads under water by The Chief (see: a very scary teacher).

Inner Monologue: Why would I put Outer Shell's head under water? It's perfectly fine above water. If water gets up the nose, I will feel it and I know that it's not a nice feeling.
Body Language: Shaking.

The situation I was in prompted a memory flashback. I was falling into a pool, water forcing its way into my nostrils. There was silent footage of My Sibling rescuing me, just in time to save my life, but not quick enough to spare me the incredibly painful sensation of breathing in water. Back in the present time, The Chief looked directly at me. I shrank back inside Outer Shell, silent, as I was most of the time now. "▇▇▇▇, put your head under the water."

I manipulated Outer Shell's head to communicate my refusal to follow the command. This was not something I would consent to.

Unimpressed, The Chief looked around at everybody else. "Class, form a circle around ▇▇▇▇."

Inner Monologue: What is happening? Why is everybody surrounding me? Why am I in the middle of a circle of people? This water is cold. Maybe I should put Outer Shell's head under the water. No, I can't. No. Please.
Body Language: Shivering.

"Now splash him, and laugh!" No sooner had the order been issued, Outer Shell was hit with water from all directions. I was also hit, the chlorinated water stinging my eyes. It became impossible to tell the difference between tears from my eyes and water from the pool.

Inner Monologue: Why would you do this? How can you just follow directions like that? What is wrong with you all? I hate you all. I hate you!
Body Language: Sobbing with whole body.

Although time has caused the details of this memory to fade, I still carry the intense pain of that day with me now. I'm sitting in a dark café as I write this, eyes a little too wet, lump in my throat. I want to cry, but I won't let myself because even in the dark, I am aware that people surround me. The last thing I need right now is more public humiliation. That day—the day I first felt shame—I decided to blindly follow anyone in a position of authority, no matter how I felt.

○ **SEX XP**

STANDING TALL, ARM RESTING on the shovel that had been used to create the large hole in the ground before me, I looked down at the fresh grave with contempt. I ripped the shovel from its steady position, stabbed the nearby mound with as much force as I could muster, and in a quick manoeuvre, thrust a small portion of dirt onto Outer Shell's face, obscuring it completely. I repeated the motions, covering the traumatic childhood memories I'd endured while confined to the prison I'd finally escaped from, the prison named Outer Shell. Behind piles of dirt, I hid the shame of my failed suicide attempts, the awkward social interactions of my young adult self, and the considerable amount of uncomfortable sexual experiences that had felt more like POV pornography than something I'd actively participated in. Following the final thrust, I flipped the shovel, and scraped it along the surface to smooth it out.

"Excellent."

I smiled, hurling the shovel at the nearby shrubbery, before promptly turning my back, ready to commence life as a cisgender woman with no past history living in a male body. It occurred to me, quite suddenly, that I was now an adult virgin. This caused immediate panic, because apart from not being all that familiar with the ins and outs of my newly adjusted outer shell, I had spent years surrounded by people who did not know about my past, and this had put me back in a closet of sorts. It had at first been an accident that I was able to go back into hiding, able to pass as someone assigned the correct gender at birth, but I liked the feeling of being regarded as cisgender, so made the decision to actively deny everything that had come before.

I gave a lot of thought to how I would tackle the virginity situation and concluded that the best person to lose my virginity with would be a stranger that I would never see again. I can't remember how I came to that conclusion, but that was what birthed The Virginity Project. In hindsight, it probably should have been called something like The Deflowering Project or The Losing My Virginity Project, but that's too long anyway.

o

The Virginity Project – Purpose:
To have sexual intercourse with a man for the first time.

o

Meeting new people was still something I found difficult, even without the added pressure of intent to have sexual intercourse. Then there was the additional pressure because it would be the first time, and still more pressure because I would be using a body with features that were relatively new to me. This caused my anxious brain a lot of grief, and I decided that the best way to ensure a positive first impression was to make that impression online. Had I been in this situation prior to the digital age, I could very well still be a virgin today.

To get it over with, I took to an adult dating site that had no focus on heading into a relationship. They called it 'adult matchmaking' and we were all there for the same reason more or less; sex without any strings attached. We didn't need or want to know anything about each other. We could just come together, get enjoyment from the way our bodies were able to connect, and then part. It was that simple.

I created a fictional character to play, choosing the name Violet, because it felt stronger and sexier than my real name and I needed all the help I could get. After taking some photos of myself that didn't include my face, I created a profile. There was no way I wanted anyone I knew to stumble across a photo of my face and realise what I was up to. From the planning phase through to completion, I considered the project to be an especially scandalous affair. Why did I view it that way? I was being purposefully dishonest.

Aware that it was against my moral code, I deliberately withheld two pieces of information from my candidates: the fact that this would be my first time, and the fact that I'd lived most of my life in a male body. In addition to being behaviour that I considered to be immoral, keeping the second bit of information to myself was a very stupid, dangerous thing to do. Women have been murdered as a reaction to less. No, I am definitely not blaming the victim, but I am reflecting on how lucky I am to have avoided becoming one.

It didn't take me very long to choose a candidate because there were so few prerequisites on my list.

○

The Virginity Project - Candidate Prerequisites:
The successful candidate will make the introductory move. This is to reduce my feelings of guilt.
The successful candidate will be young. This is so that he isn't too much more experienced than me.
The successful candidate will have a full photo of his face. This is to ensure I am not meeting anyone I already know.
The successful candidate will be attractive to me, though he is not required to boast traditional good looks.

○

One of the first messages I received was from Frenchie (see: successful candidate). As he had initiated contact, the first box was immediately ticked. Frenchie was a 19-year-old exchange student, visiting from some place in France I'd never heard of. Excellent, he was young enough to not have too much XP, and I didn't even need a photo to know that I didn't know him in person. I'd know if there was a French exchange student in my life, for reasons that are surely obvious. A combination of his photo and stats ticked the rest of the boxes (I found him cute; he was tall and slender with dark, curly hair). We exchanged the minimum acceptable number of messages, and then agreed to meet.

○

The Virginity Project - Interview Venue:
The initial meeting must take place in a relaxed, public setting.

○

We chose to meet in a café for a beverage to break the ice, and to lure me into a false sense of security, because that would totally mean that what I was doing wasn't at all dangerous. It still was. Our conversation was so superficial that at the end of it, all he knew about me was that I was in my 20s, knew a little of the French language from primary school studies, and was not experienced in bed. All that I knew about him was that he was a 19-year-old French exchange student—*Oh, that accent!*—which was information I already had.

○

The Virginity Project - Procedure Venue:
The procedure must take place somewhere that is completely disconnected from my own life.

○

Not too long after the successful interview, Frenchie and I met up at his apartment and did the deed. We started in the shower, then moved on to his bedroom. I found that during the act I didn't have to think much at all.

What a waste of anxiety! It was slightly awkward to begin with, but our proportions were quite well suited and he knew what he was doing well enough that I was able to just take his lead. Similar to ballroom dancing, but naked, and I assume without a room full of onlookers. I've not stumbled onto a video of the act, so...

o

The Virginity Project – Outcome:
A wondrous success!

o

It would not have been possible for me to be happier with the outcome, but I'd had my taste, liked it, and now I had an appetite for more of the same. My plan had originally been to close the dating profile after this encounter, hoping that my next time would be inside a committed relationship. As with most of the plans I've had in my life however, with new information I allowed them to change.

I don't actually know how many partners I had over the following months, but it was more than I've had in any other year of my life since. I went out of my way to get as much experience as possible until eventually, I no longer felt nervous when being intimate with a man for the first time. Through diligence, I had cured myself of all anxiety relating to sex! Just as quickly as I had begun, I stopped and returned to a more conservative lifestyle.

• JUST ADD WATER

EIGHTEEN MONTHS BEFORE THE FUTURE when I cross the final threshold, is a moment as precise as is possible for a moment to be, that moment being the one that causes The Year of Growth to commence. It begins shortly after some serious soul-searching to determine why I had unravelled to the point of drunkenly giving the now-estranged Friendly Entity a run-down of my specific plans for suicide. Just weeks after my trip to the doctor seeking help, where I bawled my eyes out as I told him how incredibly happy I was, I have produced a lengthy list of potential sources for my dissatisfaction with life. Choosing to ignore a deeper seeded issue with my toxic relationship with Imbibidy Bob, I first seek a hormone-related solution. I return to Nurture Essence, who I have not seen since my gender-affirming surgery.

It takes a little research to find the new clinic where Nurture Essence works for any trans-related medical issue, and I am surprised by how different a suburb it now resides in. In a word, affluent. On the day of my appointment the prosperous suburban sentiment is accentuated by petrichor. Once inside, though, I note that not much has changed in 15 years with regard to the chthonic atmosphere. Everything I see in the room is a reminder that the medical profession has not yet caught up with the reality of human diversity. If you aren't both heterosexual and cisgender, you need to see a specialist General Practitioner who stealthily operates some distance from the public eye.

The waiting room is littered with pamphlets that are all within a specific range. One is about unplanned adolescent pregnancy, and another provides information about transgender health. The walls are lined with posters about safe sex and HIV. I note that there are new preventative measures and treatments for previously prevalent, incurable ailments.

I hear footsteps and turn to my left.

"I don't need your file to remember you."

I gaze up at the radiant being that is Nurture Essence. Her black hair has turned grey, but she has few other signs of having aged. The overall package conjures up the words authentic and beautiful.

I would like to age that well, I think to myself. *But with all the sun damage I've sustained it's unlikely.*

There is still that energy that radiates from Nurture Essence that makes me feel safe around her, and I can't help but smile. She's the first to break the extended silence.

"How are you, Paige?"

"I'm well," I say as I stand up, ecstatic that she has remembered me from all those years ago.

"Come through."

"I was surprised to be coming somewhere new," I comment as I float behind her, looking around at the unfamiliar room. It could be any medical examination office if it weren't for more gay health posters.

"Yes, we were lucky," Nurture Essence tells me. "For quite a while after the Government closed our facility, we didn't have a home."

"I heard about that," I say, with sadness in my voice. The unfortunate business had all gone down during the years I had withdrawn. For quite some time there was nowhere local to provide adequate healthcare for transgender people.

"Fortunately a generous donation allowed us to open this place."

Nurture Essence swivels with her whole body, then uses her arms to gently lead my eyes around the room we're in.

"I'm glad," is all I can think to respond with.

We both sit.

"Are you still with Original Companion?"

"No," I answer, looking down at my feet. "That didn't work out."

Failure. Not the most recent.

"Good," she says. "If I recall correctly, he had a bad influence on you. Are you with anyone now?"

"No. But I don't feel bad about that. I'm not lonely."

Is the final statement true? It seems a little forced.

"And how is work? What are you doing now?"

"I work at The Medical College, supervising medical student exams and assessment feedback processes. I also do contract work as a corporate trainer, designing and facilitating workshops for international accounting graduates."

"You're happy, and you have solid employment. You're successful!"

I smile, but beneath my smile is sadness, for an unfortunate truth has been highlighted. Being successful in any sense means that I am far more privileged than the average transgender person. Amusingly, by cisgender standards a personal or professional appraisal certainly wouldn't lead to the word successful. The majority of people in my life who are in the dark about the demons I have slain, they probably think I'm quite lazy. They certainly wouldn't label me as anything synonymous with successful.

"Paige?"

There I go again.

"I guess I am."

"Good," she comments. "I'm glad."

We both smile. This is a nice reunion, and I've forgotten why I am even here. The analytical expression on her face tells me she's trying to figure something out. I remain silent, my eyes wandering around the room.

"What can I do for you today?"

Why am I here?

I continue to look around the room, searching for something that will trigger my memory. I didn't just come here to reminisce. Did I? No. I wouldn't waste a doctor's time without a good reason.

"I'm having trouble remembering," I finally voice.

"That's okay. Take your time," Nurture Essence reassures me with an incredibly soothing vocal quality.

"I mean to say, the reason I am here is because I'm having trouble remembering. Specifically, I need a solution regarding hormone replacement therapy."

"Yes?"

I pause to organise my thoughts. Random memories are flashing through my mind, prompted by our conversation.

Unhelpful, Paige. Focus!

"I keep getting moods," I tell her.

Wait, that's not enough information. Ugh, Paige, get out of your head!

I feel agitated because I'm having trouble adjusting to hormonal changes yet again. The mild head pain also isn't helping, a symptom of my umpteenth evening spent off the rails with Imbibidy Bob.

"I forget to take my pill," I clarify. "Each day, I can't remember if I've taken it. Sometimes I might take two or three in one day. Sometimes I don't think I take any. I realised recently that I'd been without for a month. Going back on them, I'm having a lot of trouble readjusting."

"I see."

"I am here to talk about an alternative hormone replacement therapy."

I put my hands together, and nod, pleased that I have finally managed to get my thoughts out in a coherent manner, albeit excessively wordy.

"Well, there are a few options. There's a cream that you rub in every day. You might find that easier to remember because you would spend a few minutes rubbing it in."

"I'd still forget," I say, my posture becoming terrible because I feel pathetic.

I'm too young for problems like this, but at least I've brought my own possible solution with me.

My posture improves with this thought.

"I read about an implant, but I couldn't find much information for my specific situation."

"For transgender women, the implant is an oestradiol pellet that's inserted into your abdominal fat. It needs replacing every 9 to 18 months, depending on how your body responds. It's more expensive up front, but cheaper long term. Each time you'll gain a new scar. That puts a lot of women off."

I laugh at the thought of concern over adding to my impressive collection of visibly scarred tissue. In the future this will be even more laughable, because all scars will overshadowed by a single, large, surgical scar that will be located below my navel. But I'm not aware of that yet.

"I don't have a problem with that," I tell Nurture Essence. "It's cheaper, and I'm free to forget for a year. I have lots of surgical scars now, so that doesn't bother me. Can I go with that option? That sounds like the best option for me."

Nurture Essence smiles in a way that says my response is unsurprising.

"Certainly. I'll write you a script."

"Excellent!"

I'm pleased with this outcome, but of course it isn't quite as simple as her comment suggests.

"You'll need to have the pellet put together by an interstate compounding pharmacy, because your required dose is not available in Queensland. I have the details of one in New South Wales who does it, or you can do some research on your own to find another. You'll have to order the pellet over the phone, and send them the script in the post. After they receive both the payment and the script, they'll mail you the pellet, then you can make an appointment with me to inset it."

Of course this isn't available in Queensland, I think. *In this part of Australia, many people still think we don't exist. Or they hate us. Some manage to hate us while also believing that we don't exist.*

One day maybe things will be different.

"Thank you," I say, feeling positive about this step. I'm hopeful that it will nudge me in the right direction so I can return to being the genuinely happy woman I'm certain I once was.

Reflecting on unfortunate debauched workplace shenanigans I can only vaguely remember, it doesn't turn out to be difficult to leave The Medical College Building behind. This is done in pursuit of work that is both more challenging and rewarding, and leads to life looking quite different skipping forward to twelve months before the future where I cross the final threshold.

As I near the end of the hour-long walk to work, my ears romanced by the latest pop music, my entire face is infected with a ridiculous grin. Cheeks glowing—a physical response to a combination of the music, the walk, and thoughts about the upcoming work day—I slow my walking pace and cast my eyes over the impressive building I am about to enter. As I take in the view, the words of Nurture Essence return and play in my mind.

You're successful.

Arguably, 'you're successful' are the two words that prompted me to seek a position with responsibilities at a higher level, leading to me standing in this precise spot, taking in this exact view.

I consider myself especially fortunate to now work at the Southern Teaching Hospital, a beautiful modern building, and the recipient of a prestigious architecture award. As I head up the stairs of the dark terracotta atrium that is densely populated with meticulously chosen vegetation to be soothing for patients, I note that I am being watched by a group of medical students at a table in the hospital cafe on the left.

What is it they're thinking, I wonder. But not in the paranoid way I would have thought in the past. This is a healthy curiosity. Are they themselves wondering?

Where does she walk from? Has she had a chance to read our email yet? How long should we wait before we approach her with our problem?

It's difficult to avoid feelings of self-consciousness when you notice people watching you.

I walk around the corner, smile and wave at The Bodyguard as I pass Security, then Lady Sadie as I move past the bathroom, and then at some of the more familiar students as I step through the first doorway. It occurs to me—having been greeted by each person by name—that I now have a reputation for being an expert networker; someone who knows and is known by almost everyone. These are all just superficial, friendly interactions, however. As far as I know, none of them are aware of what I have been through, and based on life experience, a good number of them would no longer be so friendly if they had such knowledge.

On my approach, in one smooth motion, a door on the left slides left and a door on the right slides right, allowing me to enter. As I cross into a part of the hospital that is reserved for medical students, I glance to my right and do a mental tally of the number of students scattered about the place. 40? 50? I smile sheepishly as I recall my naïve younger self setting the goal of knowing each student by name before the end of the first semester. Within two months I had happily removed the goal from my list.

The well-secured main office is locked, as indicated by a reddish LED that I can only just distinguish with my inconsistently colour-blind eyes. I swipe one of my proximity cards, listen to the musical tone, watch the light vanish and then return as green. I turn the handle, push against the heavy door, and enter the open area reserved for staff.

"Good morning," I sing, mimicking the melody Parental Being taught me as a child.

Professional Associate appears and laughs at me.

"Good morning, Paige! I love how upbeat you are in the morning."

I stretch my lips so that my smile is a little wider, and replay my two favourite words to make it more genuine.

You're successful.

Moments later, as I sit alone in my office waiting for the computer to start up, I check my phone and note a message from Bosom Buddy.

Sometimes male, and sometimes female, Bosom Buddy is one of several close friends who have me on suicide watch and I choose to view this as a reminder of my survival, rather than of the darkness that has been survived. This view alone is proof that true improvement has occurred.

Bosom Buddy: *Good morning, Paige. How're you travelling today?*

My fingers work quickly to type a reply.

Me: *I'm doing well. No plans to deliberately die.*

Bosom Buddy sends an immediate reply that begins with a smiling emoji, and ends with a love heart emoji.

Bosom Buddy: *Good to hear. Have a great day.*

And with that, I put away my phone for the day.

"I don't know if you can help me," Teaching Clinician states, as he barges in to my office, stuffing his face with some kind of pastry.

Entitled doctors, I think, hiding my annoyance behind a casually kind smile.

Teaching Clinician's statement isn't an indication that he's evaluated my abilities and judged them as poor. Rather, it's an acknowledgement that he teaches students who are studying a different part of the curriculum to the students who are under my supervision. If anything, this highlights the good reputation I have earned at the Southern Teaching Hospital in a relatively short space of time. People think it reasonable that I will be able to assist with something beyond the scope of my position description.

"I'll do my best," I say.

As Teaching Clinician tells me his problem, I have to concentrate to understand his words that are muffled by the pastry-munching. Following a long string of words by him and some deep thought by me, I reluctantly inform him that I do not have the answer he seeks, and he resigns to waiting for the relevant Professional Associate to return to the office.

So that I'm ready to provide immediate assistance to medical students and hospital staff throughout the day, I log into every online system I have access to.

Moments later, Professional Associate enters.

"What's the word, Ms Wordsmith?"

"I like words," I reply, smiling up at my female colleague.

"I'll give you some context. I can't think of the word I need."

She tells me her story.

"Tmesis," I tell her, pleased that the uncommon word has only recently been added to my vocabulary by means of a Word of the Day newsletter.

Professional Associate thanks me and rushes out of the room, allowing me to return my attention to the computer and start working my way through work emails. Throughout the morning I continue to alternate between completing my work and assisting with ad hoc problems. Eventually, it's time for lunch with Former Colleague, a young academic man I know from my days at The Medical College.

As I sit opposite Former Colleague in the hospital café, we are all smiles and laughter, occasionally sipping on the coffees before us. Although not much time has passed since our last meeting, his short patchy-grey hair has noticeably receded.

"You're like a completely different person," Former Colleague tells me. "I was worried about you last year. You were starting to look like a bitter, old hag like..."

"I'm in a really good place right now," I declare, deliberately cutting him off. Although I sometimes slip when tired and upset, I do my best to avoid engaging in conversation that could be labelled gossip. Goodness knows I've been the subject of enough of it in my time.

"I can see through all of this, though," Former Colleague comments.

"Sorry? I don't follow," I say.

"The constant jokes, not taking anything seriously. That's not who you are."

"Behaving in this way is how I've become popular," I argue.

"Paige, it's time to talk about something serious."

Former Colleague looks down at his coffee, before lifting his gaze to burn holes in my eyes. Few men dare to stare into them with such intensity, but Former Colleague doesn't shy away. It's refreshing, and something I've always admired about him.

I calmly stare back into his near-black eyes as I ponder the reason for the comment, guessing that he's read my blog. People from my past often reach out after reading it. Perhaps there is no need to come out after all.

"Abrupt," I laugh, before dropping my facial expression to neutral. "What's this about?"

"Why aren't you studying Medicine?"

A question I was confronted with numerous times back when I was employed by The Medical College. I have given serious consideration to training as a doctor. I've never pursued it, however, because...

"My memory is too poor."

"That's no excuse, Paige. I can see how many other things you're thinking about while actively participating in this conversation. You're certainly intelligent enough. Have you ever cogitated on studying Medicine?"

"Yes," I admit. It feels odd to acknowledge it aloud. "A few times. But I wouldn't be able to remember things. There's no point going after it, because I know I would fail."

"Medicine is more problem solving than remembering facts, and you've got those skills. You just have to cram before the exams. After that, you can look up anything you need to know."

I scrunch up my face. My days are already filled with problem solving, and I enjoy it a lot. Of course, most of that fulfilment I'm getting in the workplace is because the job is new. It might not be able to hold my interest for long after I've completed every task a handful of times.

"You should be aiming higher. It's great that you can tell your friends you have a nice big office to yourself now, but this job isn't going to stimulate you for long."

I shrug, marvelling at his intuitiveness. Former Colleague continues.

"What's your long term plan? Where do you see yourself in ten years? Five?"

Should I tell him about my blog?

"I don't know."

And I shrug again, as my inner monologue takes over. *What is my plan after my book? Do I know what I want from life on the other side of this? Arts? Academia?*

"Do you read?"

"Of course I read," I reply sternly. "Do I read," I mutter indignantly.

"What are you reading at the moment?"

I look down at my coffee, embarrassed, and answer quietly, "*Bram Stoker's Dracula*. It's for one of my book clubs."

Former Colleague laughs.

"Paige, no. That is high school trash. Can I recommend you some books? Something that's not a fairy tale?"

"Okay," I submit. I whip out my phone to make note of the books for later. Goodness knows I'm not going to be able to remember more than one title.

"Fyodor Dostoyevsky's *Notes from the Underground*, *Endgame* by Samuel Becket, and the Márquez book *One Hundred Years of Solitude*."

"Why these specific books?"

"Paige, this type of reading will help guide you to thinking more in a way that will be useful for academic pursuits. Like Medicine. Or whatever you choose. Probably Medicine. I can see you as a surgeon."

I chuckle at his persistence.

"I'll read the books," I compromise.

"Just give it some thought," Former Colleague insists. "It's better for you to pursue this before you have children."

Ouch.

I return to my desk, deep in thought.

Why do so many people approach me about this? Is it that they somehow know that it's something I've considered? I've actively sought to stamp down on any desire to study Medicine for fear of failure. A lot of my blog revolves around Medicine, and there's that single, throwaway line…

'Here began my strong, lifelong attachment to Medicine, a bond that would later cause me to hold on through difficult times so that I could remain a part of medical education.'

At the same time, what about all the other things I want to do with my life? I would have to sacrifice almost all of them to head in that direction. Is this a big life problem? Am I going in the right direction? Have I spent so much time considering an early death that I've become incapable of planning for a future? Is my fear of missing out an excuse that is limiting my options for a rewarding career?

I have too many questions, and no answers, but I have three books to read as a place to start. As soon as I get back to my desk, I start my new intellectual journey by downloading an audiobook version of the shortest of the three books, *Notes from the Underground* by Fyodor Dostoyevsky. I figure, the last thing I want to do is to scare myself off by jumping straight to the most challenging read.

Chapter Four

○○ **MARIONETTE**

I bent Outer Shell's left knee as I lifted the thigh, and pushed the lower leg forward while the foot was suspended in the air, then straightened the leg out, planting the foot back on the ground. I did the same with the equivalent body parts on the right, and then again on the left. This was how I would drive Outer Shell to walk forward and since it seemed like we might be together for a while, I hoped that it would start to feel more natural.

Making Outer Shell walk seemed to be a particularly difficult task to complete when I was aware of onlookers, so I focused on the world around me to distract myself. I purposefully started to avoid stepping on any definite lines. This started with the edge of each segment of pavement and the cracks between panels of wooden flooring. It evolved so that if the left foot made contact with the edge of a tile or a brick, I would ensure the right foot did the same to even things out.

As if I needed to intensify the academic struggle of this task, I also did my best to ensure that anyone watching was unaware of what I was doing. Working with Outer Shell to move about—avoiding, balancing, and hiding—became a craft that I worked on alone, slowly improving. Each time I took Outer Shell out in public, it was a test of whether or not true development had occurred.

Parental Being taught me how to use Outer Shell to ride a bike. This was much more difficult than walking to begin with. My inability to coordinate Outer Shell's movements caused us to fall, and then fall again. Outer Shell became superficially damaged. I wailed, an expression of physical and emotional discomfort, then got back on and tried again. Soon I was able to complete the activity without causing Outer Shell to fall off. I noted that focusing on steering gave me something to concentrate on, similar to how I would distract myself when taking Outer Shell for a walk (by stepping on an even number of cracks or edges). I became very good at riding the bike, and started to enjoy the sensation of wind against Outer Shell, blowing the blonde hair away from its face.

Weekly sessions with The Visitor long gone by, I was now required to settle for playing with my one sock puppet, and toys that were unfortunately not puppets at all. I developed a strong attachment to a dark brown teddy bear, and also a light blue fluffy blanket with a shiny, smooth, satin trim. These two items would accompany me wherever possible, and in my head I would take them to the places I had gone to in the stories with The Visitor. Faraway lands where plants and animals were different.

After only six months attending my first school, we had to leave. Once the initial shock wore off, I was all too happy about the arrangement. In my head, I made a list of the reasons.

> Why this is Good News:
> 1. The traumatic first day of school.
> 2. The traumatic first day of swimming.
> 3. A multitude of other, smaller traumatic experiences involving trying unsuccessfully to communicate with people.

We left the dark house dominated by the colour green and moved to a place tucked away in an even more rural part of Queensland. There were 54 students in my new school and, if I recall correctly, only three of us were my age. We were split into two classes and it was one kilometre from our house. Two classes that had too many students with too broad a range of development levels. These were the days before the internet opened up a whole new world of possibility for remote study. I'm sure they did the best they could with limited resources, but the environment wasn't exactly conducive to a quality education.

> *Inner Monologue: I get to start over! None of these people know about anything that happened at my old school! Excellent!*
> *Body Language: Shoulders back, head high, wide smile.*

With the exception of my first day, Parental Being, My Sibling and I would ride our bikes, saving money by not using the car. Sadly, starting over didn't work as well as I had hoped. When I met my new class (and you should keep in mind that although they could see Outer Shell, they could not see me) something weird happened. Outer Shell's heart started to beat faster and harder. It was uncomfortable and happened so rapidly that at first I thought I might die. I was so overwhelmed by the sensation that I couldn't voice the thoughts in my head.

> *Inner Monologue: Is this the end? What is happening to Outer Shell? Why can't I stop it? Am I losing control? Are we separating? Please, don't let this happen in front of strangers!*
> *Body Language: Rigid. Wide eyes.*

There were slight changes in the way the world around me looked, sounded and smelled. What started as dizziness escalated to become a severe throbbing pain that filled my skull, building in pressure as if its goal was to push the individual pieces of skull apart. It was inescapable. My thoughts became cloudy and I felt as though I was floating and tied down at the same time. The words anxiety and migraine were not yet in my vocabulary.

Inner Monologue: Is the change happening? Am I moving to a new body?
Body Language: Unknown.

It's quite possible that the only thing that came out was a whispered hello but as with almost every migraine since, I wasn't present enough to know for sure. Regardless of how it actually went down, I felt deeply agitated that although I'd been fortunate enough to get a second chance, I had mucked it up. I still didn't manage to make a good first impression. I was a complete failure as a social creature.

As the memory of that day faded, I found that I was particularly good at understanding new concepts and I started to feel more comfortable with learning than anything else in life, particularly when Outer Shell was not involved. Attempting to express myself through drawing and painting was something I found stressful, but I enjoyed regular visits to the principal's house to learn how to prepare and cook food based on a recipe. I loved being in the kitchen and was fortunate to never be asked to prepare a single pea. Learning to read and write was something I found equally exciting and terrifying; *excitrifying*, I thought to myself. While there was promise in a new way to communicate with the outside world, it was potentially also another way to fail at communicating with the outside world.

With my new ability to read, I found a book about the human body, and my earlier suspicion regarding an issue with Outer Shell's anatomy was confirmed. There was one of something where there should have been two. Great, the body I had incorrectly been assigned was faulty! It would be no good to anyone at all! Concerned that this could have an impact on the upcoming magical transformation that I was sure would happen any day now, I alerted Parental Being to the issue. Not long after, I woke up in hospital.

To my knowledge, there were five main complications that could arise from a testicle not being located where it was supposed to be.

<u>Possible Complications</u>:
1. Testicular cancer
2. Fertility problems
3. Testicular torsion
4. Trauma
5. Inguinal hernia

Outer Shell experienced the fifth complication, inguinal hernia, which is where the opening between the abdomen and the inguinal canal is too loose and a portion of the intestines pushes into the groin. Not great, but it's one of the better things on the list. The dressing that was on Outer Shell when I regained consciousness after the surgery was very bulky. It covered a scar of six or seven centimetres just above the groin, and the entire area below.

While in hospital, I was kept company by a teddy bear that reminded me of the one I had at home. Still not a puppet, but I could again make up stories with it to pass the time in a more enjoyable way. All healed well and Outer Shell was left with the first of many visible scars. Here began my strong, lifelong attachment to Medicine, a bond that would later cause me to hold on through difficult times so that I could remain a part of medical education.

Back at home, routines started to develop, and I found comfort in the consistency of the school week. The library became a sanctuary, as we would always go there at the same time to watch an educational program on the television. Outer space was involved, and the thought of beings in another universe with different customs to us intrigued me greatly. I fantasised about being a creature from Outer Space. Perhaps something had gone wrong and I would just be in this body until my friends from my home planet returned. While we watched, Outer Shell's mouth would hang open. I was too distracted to bother with puppetry, and I felt safe in this space while all eyes were glued to the small screen.

Quite suddenly, a male classmate tore away the sense of security I felt and it began with him sitting in the chair where The Watcher (see: librarian) would usually sit.

"You're not The Watcher," I called out, laughing. What a silly boy!

"How do you know?"

I gave the question some thought and announced, "You're not big enough. The Watcher is much bigger than you."

Moments after the classmate jumped off the chair and sat on the floor with the rest of us, The Watcher entered the room. There was laughter, so we were interrogated.

"▇▇▇▇▇ called you a big fat pig," one student stated.

I didn't fight the accusation, so it was assumed true. Another failure to be like other humans, but this time it didn't just affect me. The Watcher wept, hurt by something I hadn't even said, and although it was no longer considered appropriate to use a wooden ruler to hit us as punishment, I still received a stern talking to from the principal. I hated myself. Many years later The Watcher visited Parental Being and recounted the story, still hurt, still of the opinion that I was a terrible person.

So that I wouldn't find myself in so many social situations that made me feel horrible due to my inability to adequately perform, I developed a preference for being alone. I also created an effective mask to keep my real feelings hidden deep inside, externalising just enough to be seen to react to the world around me. As almost all situations required me to actively think about manipulating Outer Shell to convey feelings, I became a full-time liar and stopped feeling any associated guilt.

○ BOOT STRAP

"You're killing it," I whispered to nobody, winking and blowing a kiss into the cool morning air. With careless effortlessness, I let my hip fall to the left as I threw my lengthy, bent leg forward. I then allowed my red stiletto heel to collide with the pavement beneath me. I did the same with my right side to create a loose, mildly sexual strut, running my fingers through bleached-to-death-blonde, knotted curls to attempt a deliberate messy style. Think of the look made popular by Blake Lively's character Serena in *Gossip Girl*, but done on a budget of nearly zero.

The impossibly steep footwear dug into my skin and rubbed with each impact until, 6 kilometres into my 10-kilometre walk home, I could bear it no longer. Bending down to remove my shoes I winced. My ultra-toned abs were tender from thrashing around, committing murder on the dancefloor – something that had become one of my favourite pastimes. I noted the beginning of a bruise on my right knee and a weeping graze on the left as I slipped off the shoes. Worth it.

It was 5am by the time I reached my final destination, so I was not surprised to find that my housemate Quantum Cheshire (see: a male friend the same age as me) was a zombie, involuntarily groaning. I didn't feel like going straight to bed, so I tiptoed through the flat, over the loose, creaky floorboards covered with thin, torn linoleum, making my way to the balcony out the back where I rolled a death stick, set it on fire and sucked in. Deeply inhaling the smoke, I embraced the jittery calmness that washed over me. I leant against the metal railing and closed my eyes to focus more intently on the sensation. Heavenly, every, single, time...

It was the strong desire to repeatedly experience the feeling I obtained from smoking that had kept me mostly sober all night, drinking only what others paid for. The walk home had also saved me the few dollars of a train fare, and I was happy enough existing on small portions of Home Brand dim sims, hot potato chips, noodles (with powdered soup for flavouring) and baked beans. All of this kept me supermodel thin, with barely any flesh between the skin and the bone it was tightly wrapped around. I was a fox.

A few hours later Future Corpse (see: male neighbour) was standing at my front door, waiting for me to return from the kitchen. As I approached and presented him with a small plastic bag, he stretched his lips to create an impossibly wide smile, and he was now nothing but teeth.

"Thank you. It was nice to see you," Future Corpse said, wrapping his bony fingers around the plastic bag containing a fine white crystalline substance. I watched as he walked down the stairs.

"Thanks for the sugar," he called over his shoulder for the last time. Smiling, I waved and watched Future Corpse vanish into his apartment, where he would remain for the rest of his life.

Unable to explain the lack of proof of any formal qualifications or work experience, I found the search for a job quite challenging. I resorted to using an agency, and even then, the only interview I scored was for a casual cleaning job. The stench of my last cigarette was barely disguised by cheap spray-on deodorant, and although they must have known I had lied when I told them I didn't smoke, the interview landed me a job cleaning in a food court. To celebrate gaining employment, I purchased 12 cans filled with an unreasonably sweet alcohol premix.

"Can you smell that?" Quantum Cheshire asked, gulping down the last piece of red meat on his plate.

"I think so," I said, inhaling, then screwing up my nose. "Is it sewerage?"

I emptied another can.

"I'll call the real estate agent. There could be a leak, and those can get expensive if left untreated."

I shrugged to communicate how much I cared, threw the next empty can at the bin, missed, shrugged again, and wandered out to the back of the flat for another smoke.

"Yuck," I shuddered, spooked by how many flies were buzzing around Future Corpse's tiny bathroom window. "Yeah, there's definitely something wrong out here. There are so many flies."

I sniffed the air, then blew a puff of second-hand smoke into it.

"Smells like something died."

"Morbid much?"

A week later, I commenced work as a cleaner. My workmates consisted of misfits, immigrants, and individuals who had made an unfortunate life choice that had closed off every avenue of higher paid, more respectable work. Customers weren't subtle in the way they looked down on us. Most of the time we were a club of invisible people, but sometimes, just sometimes, we'd receive the gift of an expression of pity from a person who was clearly too privileged to ever stoop to making a living from cleaning up after people. It was as demoralising as the pay was terrible.

The food court where we worked was very busy, so we didn't get much time together to chat. This suited me perfectly. I was constantly scared of saying or doing something that would lead to disclosure of my past. That could be catastrophic!

o

Potential Dangers If Outed:
Verbal abuse
Humiliation
Physical violence
Loss of employment

o

"That is disgusting!"

My words were muffled by gagging from the sickly sweet stench I was met with when I got home from work. I quickly shrank back into the flat and closed the door. It helped a little.

"They couldn't find anything wrong," Quantum Cheshire updated me. "So they've just coated the area out back with something to mask the smell."

"What a lazy solution." I brushed a fly off the hot chips I was eating. "Ugh! So many flies!" I held the chips out to Quantum Cheshire, but he shook his head and started to move around the kitchen, opening all of the cupboards.

"It's pretty strong in here, actually," Quantum Cheshire called, his head stuck in a cupboard. "Maybe there's something rotting. Ahah!" Triumphantly, Quantum Cheshire held up a bag of shrivelled potatoes covered in tiny green shoots. Covering his face, Quantum Cheshire ran outside, returning quickly to wash his hands.

I frowned, shooing another fly away from my chips.

"It can't be just that," I said while chewing. "There's definitely a smell coming from outside."

The smell got worse, and the flies multiplied, but my money and social situation meant that I had to spend a lot of time at home. During this time in my life I had no family to speak of; the smoke from those burning bridges still causing me grief when I allowed myself to think about it. My social circle was miniscule and it took an expensive 3 to 4 hours riding the train to visit Best Friend. Because I needed to fund a smoking addiction, I limited trips to special occasions like birthdays. It was the quality of the time together that made our friendship great anyway.

Most hours outside of work were spent writing, equal parts fiction—predominantly scandalous modern film adaptations of plays by Shakespeare—and journals. I wrote down my darkest, most intimate thoughts, explored them, then packed them away and forgot about them.

It became clear to me that the way I was living was not sustainable. I longed to be loved by a man like in the books I read and films I watched. I wanted to be held, kissed, and to make love. My existence was a lonely one, and I decided that this just wasn't good enough. To get away from the horrid smell and to stave off the strong feelings of loneliness, I paced back and forth through the local shopping centre, taking advantage of the air conditioning and looking at all the pretty things I couldn't afford.

It was one day as I approached the flat after a long session of wandering through the shopping centre, munching on a piece of cold, sliced meat from the deli, that I saw something that caused me to slow my pace. There were cops everywhere. Well, at least three, which was a lot to see in one place back then. Although I couldn't think of anything I may have done to lead to an arrest, I felt immediate panic. Some of the cops were wearing what looked like gas masks. They looked over at me, and within moments of me stepping inside the flat, one of them was knocking on the door.

"Can you tell me when you last saw Future Corpse?"

I shrugged, masticating as I considered the question.

"It was about a month ago," I answered, swallowing. "He came over to borrow sugar."

The policewoman wrote something on a notepad.

"Oh my God," I exclaimed as the penny finally dropped. "That's about when the flies and the smell started."

I watched as the other police officers went in and out of the flat next door. The flat inhabited by Future Corpse—or rather Current Corpse—which was the flat where he had been rotting for a whole month. I was overcome with sadness, not so much because he had passed away, but because it had taken a month for his absence to be noticed. It was probably only because he hadn't paid his rent.

"Excuse me," I said, running to the toilet to empty my stomach.

The sad reality of Current Corpse made me consider my own lonely existence. My social circle was too small for anyone to notice my absence right away. What if I got hurt and couldn't get to a phone and wasted away over a period of... I wondered how long it would take die of starvation or dehydration. I would have to take action to improve my situation.

Through internet chat groups, I embarked on a journey to find new friends and true love. I chose to always mention my past before anything else and was surprised to find that the internet was host to a swarm of men who were not only okay with it, but who desired a woman like me, a woman who could never get pregnant. Sadly, I soon realised that they were mostly cheating husbands who considered me a risk-free place to wander.

Before long, I had fallen in with a group of transfolk, consisting mostly of men who liked to crossdress. Also in the group were women who had male body parts, with no desire to ever transition to a fully female form. A girl named Terminal reached out to me, and started to visit a lot. Terminal looked the way a masculine man looks when he puts on a dress, and I was certain that strangers assumed she was, in fact, a masculine man who was wearing a dress as a joke or to make some undeterminable statement. I'm ashamed to admit that I was embarrassed to be seen with her in public, so I arranged to always catch up with her at my flat.

Late night calls started to interrupt my sleep.

"I've just tried to kill myself," Terminal would inform me. "This is not a joke. This is a serious call for help."

And then she would be at my door, and then sleeping on the sofa, whimpering. Quantum Cheshire would be annoyed at me for letting Terminal invade our personal space. I walked on eggshells, afraid to be the thing that pushed Terminal over the edge. One day, she stopped calling. I felt an uncomfortable mix of relief and sorrow, so I decided to push myself to move forward with a distraction. If she was still around, I figured she would eventually call or turn up at my front door. She never did.

I went on date after date, never caring to see any of the men a second time. One was too short, which made me seem conspicuously tall. I didn't want to stand out in any way that might tip people off about my past. Another was too big, causing me to feel powerless. Most of the guys were just too difficult to converse with. I needed someone who could lead the conversation. Many were married, and those men offered nothing that interested me. The dates became less frequent as my frustration grew. One day, I gave up. And that is when I met Original Companion.

• EXHUMED AGAINST WILL

LEANING AGAINST A TREE on the sidewalk, one earpiece dangling freely to allow some awareness of the real world, I listen to the final words of Dostoyevsky. I'm feeling calm and introspective, my face touched gently by the warm afternoon breeze, the nearby sounds of traffic and chatter made more subtle by the audiobook, until...

"Oh! My! God! PAIGE!"

The expression on my face before I turn to face Basic Bee indicates that I'm annoyed, and also that I'm not sure of who the voice belongs to.

Ding!

I have a text message. The guy I'm meeting is running late.

"I can't believe it's you!"

"Basic Bee! Hey! What are you up to?"

I smile, and attempt jovial body language, but only an excessively inebriated person would be fooled by my artificial enthusiasm. Fortunate.

Basic Bee could be regarded as overdressed for a weeknight, and although I'm in no position to judge, she's definitely more intoxicated than most people would allow themselves to get on an evening that is followed by a workday. Presumably, she has the day off, or doesn't work Monday to Friday. I do work Monday to Friday, and do not have the following day off, so I am stone, cold sober; I'm in a responsible phase of life, having decided to trial limiting myself to only a standard portion of Imbibidy Bob per day. We'll see how it goes.

Basic Bee throws her arms around me, pulls me in tight, and kisses me on the cheek. The unwelcome embrace causes my body to become a plank of wood.

"There's a whole table of us here," Basic Bee informs me, pointing to the same bar my date has suggested as a meeting place.

Oh no. Can I not go anywhere in Brisbane without running into somebody I know?

"Paige, I can't believe it's you," Basic Bee remarks, and she turns to face her friends, so they can more easily hear her bellow. "Everyone! It's Paige!"

I give the table of people a rigidly polite wave. Only one of them is even vaguely familiar to me.

"Why are you in the street? Who are you waiting for?"

"A guy I haven't seen in a long time," I answer. "It's a date."

"Anyway," Basic Bee dismisses. "I'm so glad to run into you. We had so much fun at that party last year."

"I can't remember much of it, but I know I had a good time and the photos were really great."

There are a great deal of nights I can't remember participating in.

"I cannot believe how beautiful you are," Basic Bee compliments me. She runs her fingers along my jawline. This makes me feel even more uncomfortable, but you'd never know that from observation.

"When the guy at the party told me you used to be a man, I couldn't believe it."

I'm now especially uncomfortable, but I'm masking it well. Besides this being something I don't enjoy hearing, I'm also concerned about everyone in earshot. It is, after all, a public space.

"Thanks," I mutter, and I silently curse the man who outed me at whatever party it is that Basic Bee is remembering.

"Seriously, though. It's incredible. You're one of the most feminine women I know!"

I'm now thinking that Basic Bee needs to read my Open Letter.

"There's a reason I feel so close to you," Basic Bee admits.

Here we go.

"Oh?"

"My brother is a transsexual. He's doing a transition or whatever. He's just at the start of treatment at the moment, and we still love him anyway, even if he wants to be a woman. We'll still love him no matter what he decides he is."

The lack of sensitivity and incorrect gender pronouns make me too angry to speak. I try to focus on my breathing, to ensure adequate oxygen is making it to my brain.

"Anyway, that guy at the party was telling me about you, and I was so excited! I honestly had no idea. He told me who you were before, and I just couldn't believe it. What was your name again? Your name from before?"

My jaw drops involuntarily, but I'm no longer speechless.

"That's a really rude question," I whisper.

"Yeah, but sorry, I'm just saying what the guy was saying. I'm not being rude. What was your name? I can't remember. Michael?"

"No," I choke, actively cooling my temper. "And I'm not going to tell you. It's not okay to ask that."

"Oh, yeah, well he was saying how he knew you before you were Paige, and my brother is *just* like you."

Plastered people are the worst, I think. And then, in a somewhat sarcastic mental tone, *what fantastic timing!*

My date is approaching in the distance, and I have just noticed, causing me to panic. My date doesn't know about my past yet, and even if he was aware, I'd prefer he didn't hear it spoken about in this manner.

"I've got to go," I excuse myself. "It was lovely to see you."

I briefly congratulate myself on the ability to be so civil with someone who feels like an enemy in attack.

"Let's get together and get munted again soon!"

"Sure, love to," I lie, hurrying off in the direction of my date, as I type a message suggesting a different venue.

Very early on in the conversation, I realise that where I am is in front of the firing squad. Well, not really, but that's what it feels like. This isn't like the first coffee I shared with him. I cast my mind back to our first meeting.

Back then, I was an adult virgin, set on losing my virginity to the young French man in front of me. He was 19, and I was 20-something. We were making light conversation to get me comfortable enough to take my clothes off in front of him and do the deed. The deflowering or whatever. He was deliberately accentuating his accent because he knew I was attracted by it. Back then, he didn't know about my past, or even that I was a virgin.

Right now, I am far from a virgin. The conversation we are making is anything but light, and I doubt that there is any chance at all that I will be removing my clothes in front of him ever again. His French accent is subtle, and because of the words coming out of his mouth, I don't find it the least bit attractive. Right now, I realise that he knows almost everything about me, and has viewed the regrettable *Paige Uncensored* videos.

Almost everything isn't enough for Frenchie, though. He wants to know more. He demands to know every tiny little detail. Where you're joining us in the conversation, there is one more little bit of information he wants to pry out of me.

"What was your name?"

That old chestnut again so soon.

"I'm not telling you what my name used to be," I say firmly, silently grateful for the warm-up with Basic Bee.

"What did you say your name was? John? Matthew? Luke?"

Nice try.

"I'm just Paige."

"Really though, Paige. Tell me. Who were you? Before you were Paige?"

I shake my head.

"James? Michael?"

I've already given him so many details I'm not comfortable providing. This is too far. I don't even want to think about my former identity, and I regret answering the sneaky Direct Message with a secret agenda that I received from him several weeks ago.

Frenchie: *Hi Paige, I don't know if you remember me, but we got together when I was a student visiting in Australia. I stumbled onto your Twitter and I thought maybe you would like to catch up? I'm back in Australia to holiday. Best, Frenchie*

At the time I was feeling lonely, so I accepted. I guess I was also curious about how he had changed over the years. What is it that makes us want to revisit the past? What is it that makes people want to know about mine? Why couldn't he just accept and let go of the past, and join me in the present? Why the obsession with how things had been long before we had met? How did any of this even matter?

"Did you just get back in touch with me to humiliate me?" I narrow my eyes to show him that I'm displeased with him.

"Come on Paige, you owe me."

The comment cuts and I feel defensive. Yes, I agree that I did the wrong thing back then, but it was done, and it was a long time in the past. I'm living much more transparently now.

"Yeah, well," I spit. "If you don't tell someone what you don't want, it's not their fault if you end up with it."

It's a cop out and I know it, but it does make sense.

"You think you're pretty impressive, don't you?"

I've pissed him off. I remain silent.

"As a tranny," Frenchie comments, his tone deadly serious, his face like ice.

My face drains of blood as he continues.

"As a tr███ny, you're never really your birth gender, but you're never really your new gender either."

F███k you!

Frenchie smiles, pleased with his ultra-sick burn.

"Sticking scales all over your skin does not make you a mermaid."

Are you sure you want to block this user?

If only.

"Stop," I beg.

"Only if you tell me what your name was."

"It's not that difficult to find out! You can look it up on the f███cking internet!"

"I want to hear it from your lips," Frenchie presses. "I want to hear you call out your old name."

I could just walk away.

I should just walk away.

I could have left him in the past.

I should have left him in the past.

"It's ███████," I growl angrily.

And as I get up to leave, I trip and fall to the ground at his feet.

Chapter Five

○○ **INGRESS**

ON CHRISTMAS EVE, NEAR THE BEGINNING of the 1990s, I beamed as I looked down at the freshly unwrapped gift before me. In Outer Shell's hands were bobby pins!

> *Inner Monologue: Can they see me? Do they know? Is this an indication that my transformation will soon occur? How do I find out if this is a clue or a test?*
> *Body Language: Frozen.*

"Oh, sorry. I got the labels mixed up," Parental Being told me. The bobby pins were taken away, given to My Sibling, and I was presented with a different small parcel. Deflated, I opened it and voiced the obligatory thanks, trying not to let too much disappointment show. I can't even remember what the replacement gift was.

We, The Family and I, were on the floor of the lounge room in our new home. It was Christmas Eve, and we were partaking in our rather formal gift exchange ceremony. The reason we did this on Christmas Eve and not on Christmas morning like other families, was because Christmas Day was a very important work day for Parental Being.

Early on Christmas Day we rose, dressed in semi-formal attire, shared breakfast with a Bible reading at the dining room table, and left for The Church where, along with the rest of the congregation, we would listen to Parental Being talk about the Protestant version of the Christian God. Some of the tales I liked, but most of them didn't make logical sense to me, like the one we listened to on Christmas Day, about a child that was born without a father. This opinion was something I learned to keep to myself. It was important that I maintain a certain image for the sake of Parental Being's reputation. The Family was required to set an example for the wider community by keeping up appearances despite the truth. It was never appropriate to question anything about the religion.

Everywhere I regularly went, which was mostly either The Church or the Village of Old People of Gatton (see: the nearest town), I found little places to hide when I couldn't handle being around people anymore. In case you're wondering, it was often. On the rare occasion, I would emerge from a hiding place at The Church to find that The Family had gone home without me. If I waited around long enough, they would always realise I was missing and, unlike my Invisible Friends from outer space, they would return to collect me. Sometimes this would take quite a while.

Home was an elegantly decaying Queenslander, partway up a dusty brown hill. What surrounded the house wasn't a lawn so much as a desolate wasteland with the occasional weed, tree or shrub. We also had a corrugated iron water tank that would sometimes imprison a frog for life and we would have to hydrate with a very unfortunate-tasting product. The car garage and laundry were in a separate building, and a large mulberry tree provided shade and a means to climb onto the old wooden structures. With My Sibling, I would stain Outer Shell's feet and hands with mulberries. On my own, I would go adventuring.

My favourite places to explore were in-between the trees, and in the little burrow in the shrubbery I had helped My Sibling create. I would crawl through and hide, imagining that I was on a space ship far away, living an extraordinarily happy life, free to move beyond the confines of Outer Shell, never hindered by social ineptitude. The stories I invented and played out became increasingly elaborate as I learned to read and my knowledge of experiences outside of my own expanded. I fell truly, madly and deeply in love with fiction, where I was not limited by the truth of my immediate surrounds. I now deemed Sock Puppet too primitive for my original works of fiction, so on my own, I planned and created something new.

The new puppet I made from a combination of an old, decaying clown doll, scraps of fabric I'd stolen from clothing around the house, twine, and two sticks. I used twine to connect the two sticks to form a cross. I cut two short and two long pieces of twine and attached one to each of the four stick ends. The other end of each of the short pieces of twine were then attached to a hand of the doll, and I attached the free end of the long pieces of twine each to a foot. This type of puppet is called a marionette, and because I was wandering along the house steering Outer Shell to operate my new marionette, I was a marionettist, twice over. Yes, I was meta long before it was cool.

Even though the house we lived in was planted on arid land, many animals resided and thrived there. Goldy, an old pregnant dog we named because of the colour of her hair, was on the property when we moved in. She gave birth to puppies and we kept one, originally naming him Wombat because he looked like a wombat, and then Foxy because as he grew he started to look more like a fox. To save money, Parental Being built a chicken coop and populated it with one rooster and several hens. I don't remember if they had names, but the hens provided us with eggs, which I liked, so I was fond of them.

Parental Being built a pen in the backyard for a goat we had purchased. She soon gave birth to another goat. We used milk from the goat instead of buying cow's milk, and so that visitors wouldn't realise we were serving them goats milk with their tea, Parental Being would store it in an old plastic cow's milk bottle. This was until a rather astute visitor put an end to the deceit by checking the Best Before date on the milk that didn't quite taste the way it should.

Adding to our collection, My Sibling found a stray cat hiding in our yard. I noted that the cat was rather large, and suggested that maybe she was pregnant like the other animals.

"I'm going to call it Blacky," I announced weeks later, claiming the tiny black kitten I was instantly attached to. Blacky was one of three kittens produced by the stray cat that had taken refuge in our home. To my dismay, the two female kittens were given away because we didn't have enough money to have them desexed or to feed their potential offspring. Blacky was one of those two. The kitten we were allowed to keep was named Speedy Gonzales, after the mouse of the same name in the *Warner Brothers Loony Tunes* and *Merrie Melodies* cartoons. It is possible that I told My Sibling that it was a silly name because he was a cat, not a mouse.

As I developed, it became apparent to me that something wasn't right about Parental Being. I sensed sadness, but not about anything in particular that I could tell. It seemed odd to me to be sad without a reason. The only solution I could think of was to say, "Smile. I love you." This small gesture was well received and temporarily effective.

Outer Shell and I started to grow closer, reactions feeling almost natural enough for me to feel like we were one person, though we still weren't. The hope that I would one day be transformed, or be shifted into a body that was my own, kept me satisfied existing in the temporary prison. We learned to climb, and discovered the thrilling sensation of falling and swinging through the air, holding onto a rope tied to a tree. We experienced the pain of cuts, bruises and being covered in blisters caused by unprotected exposure to the harsh Australian sun. These blisters were a lot less fun to pop than bubble wrap, not just because of the pain, but also because of the messy clear liquid that was released.

Curiosity grew in me, so through practical experience, I started to teach myself about the world. I would ride my bike down the hill, and it was through this action that I learned that the brakes on the back wheel had a different function to the brakes on the front. Using the front brake to stop suddenly to avoid going over a cattle grid, I flipped the bike, did a somersault, and caused Outer Shell's face to violently collide with the ground. Its bottom lip became bloody and swollen. This was very painful.

I taught myself that plastic and rubber respond differently when exposed to high temperatures. I did this by putting rubber thongs (see: flip flops) in the oven. The smell was terrible and they did not melt like plastic things did. I wondered how effective the sun was for cooking, because it had done well to burn Outer Shell's skin to the point of painful blisters, but I discovered that leaving an egg in the sun for hours did not lead to something edible.

Beyond the house and the yard that had become overcrowded with animals, there was an unused farm with structures that were falling apart, and I dedicated a lot of time to investigating on my own and making up stories about being a professional explorer. Little by little, I adjusted to the new school, house and surrounds, but before I could call it home, I received the news that again we were to relocate. This time I wasn't as welcoming of the news. I didn't need a fresh start. All I foresaw was another opportunity to repeatedly fail miserably at making a good first impression. My ability to ever feel settled in one place died that with that news, and it wasn't the only thing.

Goldy was put down, I assume because she was very old. Wombat-Foxy, who had become very naughty by digging into the chicken coop and murdering hens, was injured badly when he was trying to cross the road. He also had to be killed. When we returned from visiting The Grandparent in Brisbane one day shortly after, I was informed that the goat had strangled herself by running around the tree she was tied to. She was now dead. My Sibling tried to teach the baby goat to swim. He couldn't, but he did live for a few more days, shivering until he drew his last breath. Parental Being wouldn't tell me where he was buried.

Preparing to move homes took a lot more effort this time. I watched Parental Being kill every last hen, so that we could eat them. Often, there was not enough force behind the motion for the axe to remove the head in one go, and the chook would spasm, neck broken, but still very much alive until the second blow. Most of them would run around headless for a short while, spraying blood everywhere, before collapsing, fatally exhausted, in a heap. My Sibling and I alternated between pulling out the internal organs and plucking out the feathers. I disliked both of these jobs, but I dutifully carried out each task as directed.

I felt quite displeased with how life was going, so I decided to spend more time in my fictional world, playing with the marionette, or just in my head. Speedy Gonzales must have also been displeased, because he disappeared. When we finally left that house, it was just as desolate as the landscape had suggested when I had initially looked upon it.

○ MR ANTECEDENT

"YOU WROTE ABOUT ME," HE ACCUSED in his authoritative tone. Great, so Original Companion was following what I was doing on the computer. In my defence, everything had been so dramatic that I couldn't resist writing about it. In his defence, he was just curious and wanted to read some of my writing. Perhaps we were both in the wrong, but I was probably the more villainous of the two in this particular situation.

His full name, Original Companion LongEuropeanSurname, entered my life before anything else. The introductory email vaguely mentioned how he had found me online and he dared me to try to pronounce his long European surname. After a handful of email exchanges, he drove to my flat in the Western suburbs of Brisbane, picked me up, and took me to a café that was hidden away in the hills of Mount Glorious. I impressed him with my ability to pronounce his name correctly, which I was only able to do because of years in the school band with a boy who had a similar surname.

We chatted over salad and drinks, and continued the conversation as we took a long walk in the sub-tropical rainforest. I felt as though I had always known him, so comfortable in his company. I liked his short blonde hair, bright blue eyes, soft tan, strong jawline and cheeky grin; he liked to make me blush. He wasn't as tall as me, but for once I wasn't actually bothered. It caused people to look at me as though I was a trophy, and that made me feel more physically attractive.

Although it went against all of the rules I had been taught about how to behave in order to gain a man's respect, I stayed at his place that first night and we slept together. To my horror, on that first night, I passed wind in front of him. He laughed hysterically about how it sounded more like a freight train passing close by than a fart. We stayed up late chatting and by morning, it already felt like we had been together for weeks.

"You don't smoke," he declared early on, taking a cigarette from my mouth.

"I don't date smokers," he continued, throwing the unwanted object in the trash. "So for this to continue, you've already had your last."

This was the first thing he changed about me, and rather than seeing it as the red flag that it was, I convinced myself that it was a good thing. He was helping me do something I couldn't have done without his guidance. He was improving me, and he continued the campaign by pushing me to look for employment that was more suitable for someone he was dating.

"I've bought you an expensive business suit," Original Companion told me one day. "So you can apply for a better job. It's embarrassing telling people that you're a cleaner."

This is why months later I found myself sitting in a treatment room of a cosmetic clinic. Mid-treatment, I was desperately trying not to see something that was in the room. Eventually it was impossible to ignore, so, through the stealthy darkness of thick safety goggles, I glanced at the left hand of my client, Tumescent. My eyes were confronted with the exact image I had hoped I hadn't seen out of the corner of my eye, and I blushed.

Tumescent was a tall, fair-skinned man of above-average build, with an extensive, thick coat of black hair that he wanted to shed, which was why he was in the room with me. We were in a treatment room that was an all-consuming white, giving an impression of sterility and utmost seriousness. He was lying naked on his back, and I was sitting on a stool beside him, holding the equipment. To clarify, I was holding the handle of the IPL equipment being used to take care of his hair issue. Tumescent was holding his own equipment, gently stroking it.

"I'm making it easier for you," he told me as he stroked himself, and then went on to offer an explanation without prompting. "It will be easier if you have a firm surface to work on."

"Three, two, one," I counted down as a warning. I pressed the button and there was an intense flash of light. Tumescent flinched, partly a reaction to the sudden burst of light, but also an involuntary pain response. I slid the handpiece along by 8mm, to an untreated area of his arm.

"Three, two, one."

I pressed the button, there was another flash of light, and Tumescent flinched again. Although clearly painful, the treatment did not have a negative impact on his relentless erection.

o

How IPL Works:
IPL (intense pulsed light) works on the same principles as laser. That is, light energy is absorbed into particular target cells with colour (chromophores) in the skin. The light energy is converted to heat energy, which causes damage to the specific target area. IPL targets "problems" in two main areas; hair (reduction) and skin (pigmentation and fine lines).

For hair reduction (not 'removal' because over time new hair can grow), this is most effective with a combination of thick, black hair, and pale skin, making Tumescent a perfect candidate. When the hair and skin are of a similar shade, or when the hair is lighter, the skin is also targeted (see: damaged) in the process. This side effect is how IPL is used to treat skin conditions such as unwanted pigmentation.

o

Back to Tumescent. After shaving the surface that he had so kindly hardened for me, I squirted ultrasound gel on and spread it around with a wooden spatula, trying to ignore the way his body was responding to the gentle touch. Unlike laser hair removal that doesn't require equipment to come into contact with the skin, for IPL to work the 'head' is pressed firmly against the skin. Ultrasound gel must be applied as a barrier between the head and the skin to reduce unwanted damage (see: burns). In the beginning this made it awkward for me when treating vaginas, anuses, penises and scrotums, as I felt like I was lubricating them in preparation of a sex act. Adding a hard-on to the mix made it disconcerting. It was okay though; he only had to come in so many times to reach his goal.

In order to fully understand the client experience, we (see: beauty therapists) were urged to practice treatments on each other. I can't imagine there are many professions where you get to become so intimately familiar with the people you work with. It was during one of these practice sessions that I decided I would like to permanently reduce the thickness of my eyebrows. It is important to note that for any treatment on the face you are required to wear eye pads that prevent the IPL from reaching your eyes. Just this once, my workmate and I decided to go against the safety procedure so that it was easier to access the hair underneath the eyebrows (sculpting should always be done from underneath, keeping to the natural curve above). I could just close my eyes, and that should be an adequate way of shielding myself from the light.

Wrong.

The pain was immediate, but I didn't lose vision until a few hours later. It's all a bit of a blur, but due to breaking that one rule, I was rushed off to emergency. As it happens, eyelids are too thin to offer protection and IPL will go right through, burning a hole in the back of your eye. This will require immediate treatment, and weeks of follow-up appointments to monitor the healing process.

On the first trip home from the Ophthalmology Department of the Royal Brisbane and Women's Hospital, Original Companion admitted to me that he had "kinda been seeing someone" when we first met. During the second drive back, he let it drop that he had started seeing her when he was near the end of his previous relationship, and on the third he confessed that he had been a friend of that woman while he was with his ex-wife and maybe there was overlap there too. But there were valid reasons and anyway, none of those women were me, so it was fine. He would never do that to me.

Things continued to progress and we lied to people about how we met. We made up a story about both going for a walk in the gardens of the Roma Street Parklands, in the Brisbane CBD.

"We struck up conversation," he would tell Friendly Entity, in their forms of various sexualities and genders. "We went for a drink, and then we started dating."

This was a difficult sell, because at the time there was no way that would have actually happened because I was far too shy.

It made perfect sense that, after a short time together, we should move into an apartment that was ours. I realised later, that this was more about escaping his ex-girlfriend, than it was about progressing things with me.

"I have a high sex drive," Original Companion told me. "I need sex at least every second day."

He also went into detail about particular things that he liked to do, the underlying message being that if I didn't attempt to satisfy this near-insatiable appetite, someone else would. I was appalled at the thought of our relationship becoming non-monogamous. He was mine, or he was someone else's. Like most things in life, I saw it as binary. If someone else took his fancy, I would be discarded, becoming the unwanted object thrown in the trash like my final cigarette.

Through fear, I learned to initiate and offer sex even when I didn't want to. Dread kept me forcing myself to engage in acts that made me feel so ill that I often spent the whole time focusing on not letting my disgust show, because that wouldn't have been sexy. As the woman in the relationship, it was my responsibility to be sexy.

"Family is important; you should reconnect with them."

So I swallowed my pride and reconnected with The Family. Some of them called me PK, a nickname I offered them because it didn't specify a gender, and at least they weren't calling me ▮▮▮▮▮. The Family ensured that there were no gender-specific pronouns used, making me a neutral object. Most of them started to refer to me as Paige, but using male descriptors. Some of them would refuse to call me anything but ▮▮▮▮▮. I was too scared to stand up for myself, and I convinced myself that I was asking too much of them. The Family had only had a few years to get used to the idea. I felt weak. I made sure that the time Original Companion and I spent with them was as brief as possible, and when they left I would sob until my tear ducts had dried up.

"You shouldn't do the dishes that way," he reprimanded.

But he would buy me a nice dinner I couldn't afford.

"Other women would be okay with this," he insisted.

He would pay for our trips into the countryside.

"Real women wouldn't think like that," he asserted.

The Grandparent died, and I received news that a former classmate incarnation of Friendly Entity had overdosed and did not survive.

"Sex would make me feel better in this situation. Come on, try it, you'll see."

And out of the goodness of his heart, he tried to teach me to drive, military style. The yelling and violent movements were helpful, for my own good.

"Your nipples are smaller than a real woman's nipples," he judged.

But he purchased a new suit for me, so I could apply for a respectable professional job in an office.

"Getting breast implants will make you feel more feminine."

And I drew the line there, choosing not to modify my body to meet someone else's expectations.

My self-esteem plummeted and it wasn't long before I truly believed that there was not another man on the planet who could possibly love me. I was so lucky. This amazing man somehow found it in himself to love me and wanted to marry *me*. The way I found out he wanted us to get married was that he accidentally called me by the name of his ex-wife. He now loved me as much as he had loved her. I was so lucky.

On our day trip into the hills where we had gone on our first date, I could see the outline of the small jewellery box through his trousers. After a short walk, we indulged in wine and cheese as we watched the sun set over the hills. Each time we did something new I waited for it to happen, but the proposal never came. Eventually we drove back to Brisbane to have dinner at one of the nice restaurants I could never have afforded to go to if paying my own way.

In the car, parked, we sat in silence for a while. Original Companion took the box from his pocket and shoved it into my hand. I opened the box, and there was a beautiful diamond ring looking up at me.

"Does this…" I trailed off.

"I want to marry you," he clarified.

"Can you put it on me?"

That night, decorated with my new engagement ring, I was silent and clearly unhappy, so Original Companion hesitantly asked me what was wrong. I confessed that I was unhappy because this didn't make for a delightful story. Proposals were all about the story, and I didn't want to make something up this time. Original Companion immediately demanded that I return the ring to him, promising that within the year, he would again propose.

Time all but ground to a halt. We slipped back into our regular routines, the temporarily reneged proposal becoming the elephant in the room. On a hike one day, as we stood at the top of a high cliff overlooking a valley, Original Companion turned to me and said, "You know, next time I should propose to you at the edge of a cliff. That way, if you decline, I can push you off."

We laughed; his maniacal, mine nervous.

The toxicity of our relationship continued to increase, and we played manipulative games with each other. I tried to find ways to sometimes get my way, often resorting to emotional blackmail. To give myself more reason to endure the hellish relationship, I started to write down things that had happened, turning them into works of fiction that Original Companion, on one unfortunate day, decided to read.

"You wrote about me," he yelled, throwing his arms into the air.

We fought, and with the help of a bisexual female Friendly Entity, I packed my bags and ran away during the night.

Original Companion found me, we reunited, and to prove our renewed dedication to and trust for each other, we made a sex tape that I later attempted to delete all copies of, something surely only possible in the days prior to the cloud.

Just short of a year, we travelled by car south through New South Wales to Victoria to visit his family. It was a scenic drive that took days, and on the day before I was to meet his family, we stayed at a beautiful old chalet on the top of Mount Buffalo. At the time I felt like it could have been a great set for a remake of *The Shining*.

Original Companion suggested we take a walk to check out the view before we had dinner. We walked to the edge of a cliff, overlooking a stark valley of recently burnt vegetation, and he dropped to his knee. I've no idea what he said as he pulled the little box out of his sock and flipped it open to reveal the diamond ring again, because I was far too preoccupied with the fact that he was asking me at the edge of a cliff.

Inner Monologue: Will he push me off if I decline? Is this really what I want? Can I make this decision when I am thinking about the possibility of being pushed off if I

give the wrong answer? There's clearly only one answer I can give.
Body Language: Shaking.

I accepted the proposal, however our downward spiral continued with more of the same behaviour, and I eventually grew to be unhappy enough to leave permanently. I dyed my hair black to help me feel stronger, returned the engagement ring, and left.

"You won't be alone for long," he told me. "You're easy to love."

As a parting gift, he handed me a piece of paper. On the paper was a nutritional plan for me to follow so I could lose weight.

• THE FINAL CALLING

EVERYTHING CHANGES RAPIDLY TODAY; the day I decide to become a role model. The anger and shame of the encounters with Basic Bee and Frenchie have faded thanks to Imbibidy Bob who now stares back at me, unflinching, from his perch on the coffee table. This isn't out of strength of character or anything, but because he lacks the physiological and anatomical features that allow one to blink. As far as I know, this goes for all glasses of alcohol, though I do acknowledge that things can exist without me having any knowledge of them.

Imbibidy Bob and I continue to stare at each other, me deep in thought, him slowly diluting by means of the ice cubes that have allowed me to start consuming him before adequate chilling of my bottle of Pinot Gris.

"Hmmm," I say, and I scoop Imbibidy Bob up, pull him against my lips, tilt him, and sip.

I allow my mind to briefly wander to the absent Friendly Entity and Bosom Buddy, both of whom have also been secretly pressed against my lips. One friendship has been strengthened by the boozy encounter; the other has not. How much of a role has Imbibidy Bob played in this? Best not ruminate for risk of creating an unnecessary issue. I plunge my mind an even greater distance back in time.

Fuelled by energy gained from the responses to my Open Letter—publicly outing myself as having gone through a gender transition and outlining boundaries for future discussions—I set to work on writing about my associated life experiences in more detail. This is mostly to satisfy people's curiosity without requiring me to sit down with hundreds of people individually to answer intrusive questions.

At first my writing takes the form of an autobiographical book, however I quickly feel uncomfortable being alone while wading through the murky waters of my past. I plan out the 33 major plot points I want to explore, and in the space of a single month, I blog my way to the finish line, engaging with the growing audience as I do so. Once complete, the blog becomes a crutch, helping me limit ignorantly hurtful comments while dealing with people who are curious; I can tell them to read my blog, and come back with any additional questions. Few feel the need to return for answers.

During the months that have followed, countless people from my past have resurfaced because of the blog, and I am repeatedly confronted with the pain of guilt over people I was not there for at the time they needed me. Although many experiences are quite positive, I become increasingly unhappy with the many responses that reinforce that my past—where I have come from and what I have endured to become the woman I am—is shameful.

"I'm deeply unhappy," I admit to Imbibidy Bob many months later, pulling out a mind map. "But I have a plan."

Imbibidy Bob waits silently for me to elaborate, giving details of the plan I've decided to keep even from Friendly Entity and Bosom Buddy.

"Well," I begin. "I was thinking about what Nurture Essence told me when I went back to get the hormone implant six or so months ago."

I bring Imbibidy Bob toward my mouth again, take a sip of his alcoholic essence, and place him back in front of me where he waits for me to follow up with more detail. In my altered state, I wait for him to remember what I'm sure I told him in the debrief that had immediately followed my appointment. He doesn't say a word. Alcoholic beverages can be so sassy.

"You never listen to me," I accuse, only half-joking. I'm half expecting that my liquid friend should remember our exchanges.

"I'm referring to her comment about me being successful. It didn't occur to me that I might now be viewed as successful, and that for women in my situation, that's not typical."

I take Imbibidy Bob's lack of movement as encouragement to continue. Clearly he finds my little epiphanies endearing.

"When I was a terrified little girl, I didn't have anyone to look up to. There was no public figure to serve as proof that if I survived, I could also achieve anything, let alone something above the average."

Imbibidy Bob's silent stare is really a tight-lipped smile, holding back the suggestion of a public transgender figure he knows I don't approve of as a representative for the community.

"That's quite recent, and also most of us are not rich and famous, and do not have those resources at our disposal."

I stop for a moment to think.

"And I know there are a few others now, but most of them are in entertainment, and in any case I don't identify with a single one of them, and, well, I have things to atone for."

Taking Imbibidy Bob's silence as a question, I point to a phrase on my mind map.

"I need to get there. I need to live completely in the open, proving that there is no shame in my past. But I can't just jump to that when I have a lifetime of negative experiences that have made me feel safer in the closet."

On the piece of paper, I run my finger over the path I plan to take.

"Each of these will progressively strengthen me, and ultimately prepare me for the final step."

I stare back at Imbibidy Bob.

"You think emotional resiliency is a bit vague? How will I go about that? How am I going to measure it?"

Squealing with glee, I jump off the couch, run into my bedroom, and return with another sheet of paper.

"I'm going to redesign my life!"

I swear Imbibidy Bob laughs, asks me to explain, and reminds me of the wonderful success that was The Virginity Project.

"Yes! Exactly like that!"

My eyes light up as I begin to talk about my newest project.

"I've identified the key areas of my life that need changing so that I'm farther from an emotional deficit and therefore more resilient when a new stress presents itself!"

•

The Resiliency Project – Purpose:
To prepare myself for future emotional stress by increasing the distance between me and the Red Zone.

•

The first target area is the first waking moments; those that have a strong effect on my mood for the rest of the day.

There are two different things I do to improve my first waking moments. The first is to set my alarm at a time on Friday—the last day of my working week—so that I can get ready for work at a slow pace, arriving at work on time, without rushing. I set Thursday's alarm one minute earlier, Wednesday a minute earlier than that, and so on and so forth. Basically, I am getting a sleep in of an additional minute every day, without it impacting my ability to get to work on time.

The second is to choose a different, relaxing song to wake me up each morning. The reason I have chosen a different song for each day is to reduce the association between particular songs and having to get up to go to work. Technically, it should take at least five times as long to form the negative attachment to each of the five songs and having to leave the comfort of bed.

The other items on the list take a little more effort to correct. Living in an apartment that the owner intends to sell has caused me distress, so I opt to take over a friend's place on a lease, which will give me a specific date to prepare for my next move. Because I feel unfulfilled and underpaid at work, I have secured a higher paid role, with a broader range of responsibilities that will allow me to develop the leadership skills I know I possess. It has become clear that my lifestyle has been inadequate in the areas of nutrition and exercise. I now walk to work each morning, and each Monday I stock the work fridge with enough groceries to make fresh salads for lunch every day. The only other issue I perceive is excessive alcohol intake, but I decide that I have enough issues to concentrate on and opt to deal with that later.

●

<u>The Resiliency Project — Outcome</u>:
A wondrous success!

●

Finally back to the present, as a more resilient human being, I am ready to jump off my first cliff and test my wings.

Chapter Six

○○ **AUSDRUCKSVOLL**

"▮▮▮▮, CAN YOU READ THE LETTERS above the red line for me?" The doctor spoke in a flat tone with a vocal quality containing so much bass that a minor vibration rattled the window. Between that and his sharp appearance, I knew that this was a man I must respect.

Sweat caused by the tropical air tickled the back of Outer Shell's neck as I studied the Snellen chart before me. We were in a tiny white and blue doctor's office and the chart, named after Herman Snellen who developed it in 1862, was being used to measure my visual acuity as part of an ongoing investigation into the frequent, severe headaches I was experiencing. The question confused me because there were clearly two red lines, not one as the doctor's word choice indicated. Each red line was under a series of letters, the lower red line under a much smaller set. As I considered the question, my eyes danced to an invisible staccato tune, searching for clues around the sterile room.

Inner Monologue: I don't get it. Can he not see properly? Is there another layer to this test? Am I being tested for psychological problems? I'm probably being tested for psychological problems! Have I given something away? Surely not. I've been silent for too long. I should just answer the question.
Body Language: Furrowed brow.

"Which red line?" I hesitantly asked, attempting the question with a casual pitch.

Inner Monologue: It doesn't really matter which line I read above anyway. I can clearly see every single letter on the chart, including the information at the base that identifies the chart as a product of the USA. A minor detail such as that could not be seen by someone with poor eyesight. Maybe I should just read the smallest letters to get this over with.
Body Language: Biting upper lip.

When I started paying attention again, I saw that the doctor had pulled out a book. On each page was a circle made up of dots of different colours and sizes. These are called Ishihara or pseudoisochromatic plates. There are four types of plates, each used for assessing type and severity of colour-blindness in a different way. Depending on whether or not you have a colour vision defect, you will see a different figure when viewing a Transformation plate. With Vanishing plates you should only see a figure if your vision is normal, as opposed to the Hidden Digit plates that only reveal a figure for people with a colour vision defect. The Diagnostic plates reveal different figures for people with different types of colour-blindness. I failed the colour vision test, and there is a reason I have provided you with this information.

How I Performed During The Test:
1. In some of the plates I saw figures that should only be visible to people who are not colour-blind.
2. I was unable to see some figures that should be visible to all people with red-green colour-blindness.
3. For some plates, instead of one or the other, I could see the figure designed to be visible to people who are colour-blind and the figure designed to be visible to people who are not colour-blind.
4. For a few plates, if I continued to stare, the figure would change, vanish, or appear over time.

My Identified Issues with Colour Perception:
1. I have difficulty differentiating between certain shades of green and red (see: the test revealed that I am red-green colour-blind). Some shades I can identify with confidence (see: the test revealed that I am not red-green colour-blind).
2. I have difficulty differentiating between almost all shades of purple and blue.
3. I have difficulty differentiating between certain shades of yellow and green, particularly dark yellows and light greens. Some shades I can identify with confidence.
4. I have difficulty differentiating between certain shades of red, orange and pink. Some shades I can identify with confidence.

Accidentally discovering that I had problems with the perception of colour was interesting, and I was quite fascinated by how inconsistently colour-blind I was. The investigation into my headaches, however, went nowhere and I soon became frustrated. So that the tedious, seemingly pointless appointments would stop, I chose to pretend that I was no longer getting headaches. It was just another lie that I decided would not harm anyone.

Our new home was in a small coastal town in North Queensland that somehow felt especially dry and humid at the same time. Parental Being drove us to our new home at night, so that when we entered the town, we wouldn't notice the huge hills made of salt that were considered an eyesore. The old Queenslander style house we moved into was so poorly constructed, that if you measured the distance between the floor and the ceiling, you would get a different measurement for every corner, in every room. I willed for a cyclone to wipe the house out, so that we could get a new house from the insurance company, like the neighbours did when their house burnt down. Parental Being didn't like it like when I voiced those desires.

Our house wasn't really ours, it was owned by The Church that Parental Being now worked at. Convenient for everyone but us, the house was located a short walk from The Church. This presented us with a new situation, making the house less of a home, and more of a drop-in centre. We didn't have any real privacy, because people from The Church would visit without notice every day of the week. So that I could escape Parental Being, My Sibling and the revolving door of visitors, finding a new hiding spot became a priority.

In the end I didn't even have to be creative to find a new hiding place, because again there was a tree with branches that draped over the car garage. It wasn't a proper garage, but rather just a few sheets of corrugated iron sloppily nailed to a wooden frame beside the house, designed to protect a car from sun and leaves, but not from rain. There were too many holes for that. For solitude, all I had to do was climb the tree, crawl along one of the branches, and I could hide on the roof. There were enough leaves on the branches that rested on the roof that I could be completely in the shade. Sometimes I would just lay back, close my eyes, and let my imagination run wild, but this was something I only did if I was especially tired; such inactivity made me very uncomfortable.

There were three active things I did when I was on the roof, listed below in order of frequency, from highest to lowest. It was the perfect space for these activities; nobody could interrupt me because nobody knew where I was.

Activities to Complete on the Roof:
1. Read a book.
2. Write a journal entry.
3. Complete homework assignments.

Of course, I couldn't spend all of my time by myself up on the roof, so I would position Outer Shell in the middle of the lounge room, surrounded by specifically placed materials for the purpose of crafting. Knees bent, reaching forward, I operated Outer Shell's arms to lay out each item on the floor before it. These particular materials would eventually become a hand puppet with a moving mouth.

Materials Required for Hand Puppet with Moving Mouth:
1. Corduroy, tan coloured
2. Cotton fabric, black
3. Felt, red

4. Ball of woollen yarn, yellow
5. Toy eyes (2)
6. Needle and thread
7. Scissors
8. Cardboard, from cereal box
9. Craft glue
10. Chalk

To begin, I folded the piece of cardboard in half, and cut a semicircle, choosing the radius based on the shortest edge. A previous attempt had led to a shape that was not a circle. The circle was to become the mouth of the puppet, and I created everything around it. I unfolded the semicircle, placed it on top of the black fabric, traced around it with the chalk, and cut it out. I put the black circle aside.

Grabbing the corduroy, I folded it in half and cut two square pieces with edges a little shorter than the circumference of the mouth, and cut 1 centimetre darts (v-shaped slits) along one edge of each piece, creating flaps that could be folded along a round edge without unsightly overlapping fabric. I took one of the squares, and one by one, folded and glued all of the flaps to one half of the mouth. I did the same with the other piece, but to the other half of the mouth. To cover the flaps and bare cardboard, I glued the black fabric over the top. I cut a small piece of red felt in the shape of a tongue and glued it to the fold, to mimic a tongue emerging from the throat.

The lips were made with more of the red felt, and glued on, as were the eyes. To make hair, I grouped long strands of the yellow woollen yarn and braided them, then used the needle and thread to sew them to the top of the head. It was an ambitious project and resulted in a blonde, feminine puppet with a flat head and no chin. It took several more attempts before I was able to work out how to give the puppet a more human figure, including arms with fingers, and clothing. When designing and sewing the clothing, I felt joy.

It was a good thing that I perfected the art of puppet making, because Parental Being presented me with a book. The book was filled with plays that all tied back to Christianity, and I could use it to put on plays for The Church. I enlisted fellow puppeteers, and we performed plays with appropriate themes for the children in Sunday School and The Church. I thoroughly enjoyed it, but I wished that I could create plays about things that I imagined, rather than always requiring a religious focus. I became annoyed by the responsibilities that came with being a child of someone who ran a church, but I persevered because I could see no satisfactory alternative.

There was a shift at school from a focus on learning new things, to merely memorising facts, recall becoming the most prevalent form of testing. I started to feel that I was less intelligent than those around me because my ability to remember things was very poor. I perceived my memory to be worse than every other student and most adults I knew. To this day, I feel that in this one instance, there was absolutely no disconnect between my perception and reality.

My cognitive flaw resulted in lower grades than I was accustomed to but I was, at least, always one of the best performers in the informal spelling bees we held in class. This was in part because I consumed so much written material, but also because The Grandparent would be quite stern with me whenever I made mistakes with English. The Grandparent was an accomplished linguist, and although The Grandparent and Parental Being had only moved to Australia in the 1970s, I was told, "We are living in Australia, and therefore we should speak and write Australian English correctly!"

The Grandparent was one of my favourites. There was never any guessing required with regard to motive or meaning behind The Grandparent's words and actions. The Grandparent would verbalise everything precisely as intended, even if it hurt people's feelings. One day a metal weight fell out of the car onto Parental Being's foot, splitting a toe open on the concrete driveway. "Have a good cry," The Grandparent said, looking from the mess of blood and broken nail to Parental Being's red, wet face. "You always were an emotional one."

Whenever we visited The Grandparent in Brisbane, we would go for walks through the inner Western suburbs of Brisbane. It was often just The Grandparent and me, because The Grandparent had a certain pace that would be maintained no matter what. If you couldn't match the pace you shouldn't ruin the walk by tagging along. One day The Grandparent took me down to Kayes Rocks in Toowong, overlooking the Brisbane River. I was told that when our family first moved to Australia, back when Parental Being was a child, there was a great flood. It wasn't like in the Bible story, and they were far enough up the hill to escape the water, but it was pretty bad. They were completely cut off until the floodwaters receded.

After a very long road trip back to North Queensland, my social circumstances started to change. Parental Being put me in situations to help me make friends, either because it seemed like I couldn't do it myself, or due to concern that I spent too much time alone. My preference was still to escape to fiction however, and at home I would crawl up onto the roof to hide from The Family and read. I developed a taste for the *Animorphs* series, and loved anything involving demonic possession. This was a topic I had to explore in the library at school, because Parental Being would look through anything I had at home to ensure messages didn't conflict with our religion. I imagined myself as a character that could transform at will, or move between bodies.

Now that we lived on the coast in North Queensland, learning to swim was an important part of the school curriculum. I again had issues with revealing Outer Shell in the change-room, but I had finally mastered submersion – a skill everyone else had moved far beyond. In the water it was difficult to move Outer Shell as required, so Outer Shell and I found ourselves in the Special Class for swimming. Because I had trouble remembering the rules, I was also put in the Special Class for mathematics.

School wasn't all bad, though. I met a teacher who had a positive impact on me and I am still in contact with him today. He taught me music, beginning with recorder, then, progressively, various instruments in the percussion family. Relative to everything else that was a struggle, rhythm didn't take me too long to master, but I had trouble letting go and playing with feeling. Parental Being purchased a second-hand drum kit and I spent hours by myself bashing away to my heart's content. I played in the school band and of course my new skill was used in The Church (playing to the modern songs, not the old hymns).

Slowly, over the course of a few years, I discovered the wonderful sensation of truly letting go and just feeling my way through the music. There was nothing else in my life quite like it, with the exception of singing. I had finally found something Outer Shell was useful for! I joined the school choir and sang at The Church. Outer Shell sounded great, and I felt fantastic, so I did it as often as possible. At lunchtime, I would sing as I walked to the library. Maybe it wasn't so bad being trapped in Outer Shell after all... Then, seemingly out of nowhere, puberty hit us like a tonne of bricks.

○ **THE LYCANTHROPE**

A FEW DAYS AFTER I HAD LEFT Original Companion and moved into an apartment on my own, Legitimate One stood next to my desk at work introducing himself.

"May I borrow your reddish pen?"

I gazed up at him, my awe hidden under an effective mask of casual indifference. The product of a man from South-Central Asia and a woman from Central Europe, his appearance was exotic to me; I had trouble looking away. His tan was darker than olive, but lighter than a chocolate Labrador, like a latte with an extra shot of espresso. This, along with the dark irides and hair, created a contrast that accentuated the whiteness of his teeth and sclera. Oh, those teeth, with prominent canines reminiscent of a wolf. No doubt I blushed as I handed him the red ballpoint pen that I used to autograph my work.

This was when I had moved on from three cleaning jobs and what turned out to be a fairly brief stint at the cosmetic clinic because they didn't have enough clients to justify keeping me on. I was now a medical typist in a laboratory. The reason I got the job was because Original Companion had prompted me to do a short course in medical typing. Thanks to Original Companion, I was slowly working my way up in the corporate world! Although we were not in contact, the Ghost of Original Companion continued to follow me into my next phase of life.

Legitimate One took the pen from me, signed his timesheet, then left. Every few days, near the end of my shift and at the beginning of his, he would return and I couldn't believe that he could forget to bring a pen every time when it was the only reason he came into our office. He told me that he was a scientist picking up casual late shifts to help him through medical college. Was it really possible for someone studying to be a doctor to be this disorganised and unable to learn from mistakes? I toyed with the idea that perhaps he didn't forget his pen at all. Maybe he just wanted an excuse to make contact with me. I laughed at the absurdity of my fantasy.

"Why do you go by Ms? Why not Miss, or Mrs?" he quizzed me one day, as part of a fleeting exchange.

"Why do I have to broadcast my marital status, when men do not?" I challenged.

"Your iris is moon-shaped," Legitimate One commented on another occasion. "It's irregular, like a waning gibbous."

I whipped out my compact mirror to see what he was talking about. My eyeliner was slightly smudged, so I corrected it before looking at my iris. "Oh my God, you're right!"

"You seem surprised. Was it not always like that?"

"No," I confirmed. "That must be from the IPL incident. Would you like to hear an awful story?"

Legitimate One listened intently as I told him about the injury I had sustained while attempting to improve the appearance of my eyebrows. Although the story was not a happy one, we smiled at each other for the duration of the retelling.

I knew that I liked him, and this increased with every ephemeral conversation, but I kept my distance, cautious, still feeling the multitude of painfully fresh wounds caused by Original Companion. The sensual subtext of the banter was just subtle enough to not necessarily mean anything. It could be in my head, a projection of my own, one-sided desires. But it was not one-sided. Each time it seemed like he was trying to suss out whether or not I was into him, I would try to be non-committal, keeping him on a leash with a maybe.

I can't remember who suggested it, but we started to write essays to each other. We began by each choosing a word. We would write an essay about our personal attachment to the word, send it to each other, and then write a response to the essay we received. It was through these essays that I began to fall in love, legitimately.

Concerned that I was falling in love with a man who didn't know about a past I denied, I jumped on a train, left the city and went into the countryside to visit Best Friend. I told her all about Legitimate One, and we put our heads together to brainstorm. We realised that we could use the essays to our advantage, to get a feel for how he might react to the news of my past. Pretending I had watched the film *Transamerica* with Best Friend, I chose 'transgender' as the next essay topic.

The essay I received from Legitimate One frustrated me. He'd had some experience with the word, as a family friend had gone through a gender transition. His wording however, was such that I could not determine how he would see me if I told him about my transition. I decided that for the moment, I would just have to leave it and see how things progressed.

Beginning with a group hike, and then over food and drink, I started to hang out with Legitimate One outside of work. Really, these were dates, but because I was so scared, I referred to the dates as hanging out. Colleagues would try to pry information out of me, but my lips would remain tight, unwilling to admit to anything more than a developing friendship. This didn't really help with Legitimate One feeling unsure of where he stood with me. I have no doubt that the friends he spoke to about me were telling him that I was just playing with him, that if I was serious, something physical would have happened by now.

"You could meet me downstairs for a kiss," he joked in a text on the way to work one day. He was trying to progress things in a playful way. I realised that it had been almost six weeks, and it was unfair for me to keep him in this holding pattern any longer.

"I would like to," I confessed. "But I have responsibilities that other people don't have," I continued.

I told him that I needed to discuss something with him, and that it should be in person. We had reached the point of no return. I was terrified of the reaction I might receive, but the emotional attachment was now far too strong for me to be cowardly and just walk away. Although I denied it, everyone at work knew something was going on between us. Any action I decided to take would have consequences, so I made my choice and we agreed to meet by the river in the evening the following day.

On the day of the talk, I spent extra time on my appearance. I plucked my eyebrows, perfected my make-up and chose to wear an elegantly sensual black lace ensemble with a lining the colour of my pale skin. I needed to look my best, to work against what I perceived to be a past so undesirable that I had spent years refusing to acknowledge it. Fearing that the stress would result in bad breath, I spent the day popping strong mint sweets in my mouth. This didn't help with the pain in the pit of my stomach, which growled noisily in the background.

In the distance I could see Legitimate One perched on a railing, looking out over the river, and I wanted to fly away. It would be so much easier to just turn back, and send a message with some excuse. I considered the six weeks that had led to this evening, from the light banter to the in-depth essays. So far, he was the most fantastic human I could imagine, and he seemed to really care for me. Tonight, that could all change.

In silence, we sat by the river, watching the city lights ripple in the reflection on the water. I couldn't do it. There was a lump in my throat more substantial than ever before. My chest felt tight, barely able to contain the fast, steady kick that was my heartbeat. Moisture was starting to build up around my eyes.

"Would a drink help?"

I took up his offer. We had some shots in a nearby bar, and we then wandered over to a wooden park bench under a tree. The drink gave me the strength to tell him that I did not always look and sound like this; that I had gone through a gender transition. After I had finished disclosing everything, we sat in silence.

Heartbeat.

Silence.

Heartbeat.

More silence.

Heartbeat.

SO MUCH SILENCE!

"That doesn't change the way I feel about you," he assured me. Cue the most intense, heartfelt first kiss of my life, salty streams flowing down my face.

What followed was like a tidal wave and tsunami. We spent as much time as we could together, and during the early weeks, kissing gobbled up a lot of that time. I would receive a text message when he was near work, and we would meet in the elevator to kiss briefly before he started. If we were meeting in the street, when we were close enough to see each other, we would pick up the pace to embrace just a few seconds earlier. There were fireworks and we would have done anything for each other.

Work became a much more enjoyable environment, and with our relationship finally out in the open, we were able to interact a little more without him using the excuse of forgetting to bring a pen to sign in. Sometimes Legitimate One would come up behind me, silently, and put his hand on my neck, trying to scare me. He was shocked and disappointed that I didn't react at all, a throwback to the times of disconnect between Outer Shell and me, the full details of which I had not shared.

Legitimate One started to visit me at home. The first time, he sent me a message to let me know he had arrived and was waiting outside on the footpath. When I came out to greet him, I was carrying a plastic bag filled with trash; it made sense to make the best use of the time, so I walked past him, threw out the trash, finally returning to welcome him with a kiss. He mentioned that at first he was offended that I had chosen to deal with the trash first. It took him a while to get used to this task-oriented side of me.

"There's something I would like to discuss with you," Legitimate One announced one day, patting the bed beside him; a signal that I should sit.

"What is it?"

"As you know, I leave soon for Central Europe as a part of a student exchange program, and I won't be back for over three months."

With sadness, I acknowledged his words with a subtle nod.

"I would like you to consider moving in with me when I return."

After seeing Legitimate One off at the airport, I went to his house and lay on his bed, overwhelmed by the conflicting feelings of sadness and promise. I would need to write a list of things to keep me occupied, so that I didn't have too much free time to focus on how much I missed him.

Fortuitously, I thought at the time, Work Colleague had their birthday that night. Fuelled by mixed feelings of sadness, bitterness, and confusion, I became exceptionally drunk, and woke up in my bed with no memory of the party. It was days later that Work Colleague approached me and gave me vague details of events that I couldn't remember (see: taking off bra; see also: unknown context).

Legitimate One somehow found it in his heart to forgive me for getting drunk and removing my bra at the work party, but it took a little more effort to redeem myself at work. Swearing that I would never again drink with people I worked with, and with the help of a list, I redesigned my life to avoid loneliness and repeats of the drunken misbehaviour.

o

Coping Strategies While Legitimate One is Overseas:
Learn Legitimate One's First Language. It seems like an interesting language, and as a bonus, you'll have an additional way to communicate with Legitimate One as it's one of the languages he speaks!
Handwrite letters to Legitimate One. This way, you will keep him up to date with everything, and it will be more personal than email. You can make it even more personal by adding a scent to the paper that reminds him of home!!
Purchase Phone Cards. Regularly rise at 4am to make overseas calls to Legitimate One before he goes to bed and before you commence work. This will really close the distance gap!!!

o

Three and a half months later, I sat anxiously at the airport. I watched the doors that Legitimate One was to appear through after surviving customs. I wondered how different he would look now, after so many weeks of living on a high carb European holiday diet. When I finally saw him, in some ways it felt as though I was gazing upon a stranger. His face and body were rounder, and his hair was longer. He smiled, flashing those wonderful teeth, and I was in love all over again.

It made sense for Legitimate One to move into my apartment, and when the lease came to an end, we moved into a nicer apartment that was new to both of us. Life together felt incredibly natural and although we didn't marry, we became like family. Together, we made trips to see his family and mine, but to avoid potential awkwardness, at my direction we never allowed the two families to meet.

A good six or seven years after emerging as Paige, most of my family were now actually calling me Paige and using the correct pronouns, however Parental Being and My Sibling continued to avoid any mention of gender. Instead of telling my family how hurt and uncomfortable I was, I quickly redirected the conversation if it seemed like they were going to talk about me while Legitimate One was present. When he wasn't there, I would just allow them to incorrectly refer to me as male or a genderless object.

Most dealings with Legitimate One's family were much more positive, and I even travelled overseas to stay with his grandmother in his hometown in Central Europe. While we were there, I was able to test out my language skills on the locals when he fell ill, and I was required to travel to the shops to obtain food and medication without assistance.

The flight back to Australia was painful. By the end of our stay, Legitimate One had managed to pass onto me whatever it was that had made him feel so unwell, so countless times I found myself running down the aisle of the plane to get to the toilet before I soiled myself. It reminded me of the night of my surgery, only on that occasion I had been in a private hospital, and had the privacy of my own bed- and bathroom. It was difficult enough to handle in that situation. I let the diarrhoea last about six weeks before I went to the doctor, hoping that it would just clear up on its own. Tests revealed parasites, so I was put on medication and soon returned to normal.

After Legitimate One graduated from Medicine, he started to teach me to drive. He was a calm teacher, and I loved that he didn't yell at me like Original Companion had when he'd tried to teach me. I returned to The Film School for Maintenance Class so that I didn't miss Legitimate One so much when he worked the night shift in the hospital. Maintenance Class involved learning a new scene every week, and having a teacher direct me to play the character a few different ways, with the expectation that we would apply everything previously learnt in Technique and Scene Class. On the weekends when Legitimate One wasn't rostered to work, we explored South East Queensland.

"Ugh, they're still wet," I called out to Legitimate One on one of these trips. We were at Agnes Waters.

Without giving it much thought, I threw my bikini in the microwave and set it for 10 seconds, and then another 10 seconds. I'd read every short story by Paul Jennings, so I figured the worst possible outcome was ending up with surprise super strength.

"Legitimate One, would you mind putting this in again while I take a shower?"

"Are you sure?"

"Yeah, I need to wear them today but they're still a bit too damp and will feel gross."

"Okay," Legitimate One hesitantly agreed.

I slipped out of my clothes and hopped in the shower. The warm water felt so good on my skin. I smiled as I immersed myself. I loved water.

"Paige, I've got some bad news for you."

"What?"

Legitimate One opened the microwave and pointed, unwilling to put into words what he was referring to. Inside the microwave I saw my bikini bottom. There was an area of black that hadn't been there before. Inside the area of black there was... nothing. I had accidentally created a crotchless bikini. I perceived my mistake being that I put the bikini in the microwave for too long, though others might claim that the mistake was putting it in the microwave at all. I opted to wear black knickers instead, and made a mental note that clothing probably shouldn't be dried in a microwave.

It took some time for me to realise that there was something missing from our life together. A contrast to my relationship with Original Companion, Legitimate One and I weren't having sex at all. Being the avoidant person that I was, instead of prompting a discussion, I tried, unsuccessfully, to initiate. Legitimate One had spoken negatively about women's lumps and bumps on a multitude of occasions, so I decided that I must be too fat. I reduced my food intake, and increased my exercise. I became more slender, but it didn't work as a way of securing his sexual attention.

I paid for a series of laser hair removal treatments on my legs so they would always be smooth. That didn't work either, so I purchased a range of expensive lingerie, and pranced around the apartment in them, trying desperately to gain attention and approval. No, not that either. My behaviour became increasingly overt, until one day, Legitimate One told me that we needed to talk.

"I feel like we are an old married couple," he confessed. "I love you, and I want to spend the rest of my life with you. I love our life together, but I don't have any desire to have sex with you."

This confused me, because all of the media I consumed told me that a sex life was of paramount important in a relationship. But I was also taught that this wasn't an acceptable issue to use to leave someone. Could I live without sex? Could I live without Legitimate One? Was there a middle ground?

I agreed to stay with him, but in the month that followed, I noticed every single man that wandered by. I noticed the soft appearance of their lips. I noticed the shape of their pecs and buttocks, the bulge in the crotch of their pants. Before long, the mere scent of a man that I couldn't see would arouse me. This was going to be a problem, and I needed a solution before irreparable damage to the relationship occurred.

"What if I have whatever the male version of a mistress is? Maybe I could go into sex work. It wouldn't be personal; I would always come home to you."

"I'm too proud for that," Legitimate One told me, and I was shocked that I had even considered something so unconventional.

In the wee hours of the morning a week later, I stared at the empty side of the bed where Legitimate One had slept for years. Although it had been my decision to leave and just be friends, I was hurting. A lot. I was surrounded by the scent of a random man, a reminder of a failed attempt to distract myself from the pain of the first night alone. Filled with feelings of loneliness for the first time in years, I comforted myself by making a list.

○

My Favourite Memories with Legitimate One:
We saw each other in the distance, and both picked up the pace to reduce the amount of time until our lips locked
We moved into our apartment together, so we wouldn't have to spend so much time apart
We took a bus, train, boat, car, plane and explored Queensland and then other parts of Australia
We introduced each other to different types of food, and proved our knowledge of each other with appropriate gifts
We met and became involved in each other's families
We travelled overseas, got sick, and nursed each other back to health
We provided emotional support during the diagnosis and treatment of My Sibling's brain tumour and the death of a dear friend

○

Tempted to reach out with text messages to try to lure him back, I reminded myself of how unsuited we were. My mind started to wander and I found myself ruminating on all the grief I had caused him, creating issues from his benign statements due to the unhealed wounds Original Companion had left me with. The wounds had never healed to become scars, because I had gone straight from one relationship to the next.

Inner Monologue: This is for the best. We've basically become friends anyway, and I need to be alone to find out who I am without a man by my side.
Body Language: Limp.

• PLEASE LIKE ME

THE PHOTO I'M CONFRONTED WITH in my social media feed is a direct link to my first relationship anniversary with Legitimate One. Our young adult faces gaze at the camera lens with satisfied smiles; his dark hair freshly cut, my lips adorned with a deep red lipstick. The blouse I'm wearing is a low-cut V-neck, drawing everyone's eyes to my exposed noticeably scarless, youthful décolletage. Where his dark fingers are wrapped around my pale arm, there is more contrast between our skin colours than usual because he's been spending a lot of time in the sun.

The photo itself provides a stark contrast to the lonely reality of the present, where I am touching my own arm in the precise location Legitimate One had all those years ago. Visibly aged and scarred, I'm feeling lonely and one thing I know I can't handle is another complete 180 from someone when they find out about my past gender transition. This—teamed with two other reasons because I live by a rule of three—prompts me to plan and embark on a new dating project!

It's the following day that I sit with Bosom Buddy, who is male for the occasion.

"I'm conflicted," I tell him, looking away. "I don't really feel lonely lonely, but I do desire a partner. It's not like I need one, just... I acknowledge that it is a life luxury that I would like to have again."

"I see."

"At the same time, I'm planning to move to Melbourne in a year, and I don't know what my life is going to be like after my book is released. Guys who date me won't know what they're signing up for. I already have strangers approaching me about my blog, and so many people from my past are coming out of the woodwork. And I'm in Brisbane now, but this isn't where I'm planning to stay. And I'll have big decisions to make. And I don't want a guy to influence my..."

"Paige, stop. Back up. Honestly, I have no idea where you're going with this. To be honest, you're annoying me."

"I'm ready to take it up a notch," I say, and turn my laptop to face him.

"Oh wow," he reacts to what he sees. "Are you sure?"

"Yes," I confirm, grinning.

I'd tell you what's on the screen, but it's going to be revealed through conversation anyway.

"Friends with benefits doesn't really seem like your MO," he remarks snidely. "You don't see this as immoral at all?"

"Nope, not at all," I fight, ignoring his earlier comment.

"Explain?"

"Eh, I'll explain my thought process to you later. For the moment, I want to run my profile by you before I post it."

"Okay."

I squeal as I turn the laptop back so only I can see the monitor.

"For the description, I have just put my standard. *Passionate writer, actress, educator, lifelong learner, adventurer, foodie, future leader, social media addict.*"

Bosom Buddy shrugs, probably regretting asking for context.

"Okay, well the next part is about what I'm doing with my life. I've written this: *Hi! I'm Paige, like in a book, but with an 'i' in the middle. Picture me saying that as I close and open my hands as if they are the covers of a book. Speaking of books, I've been busy writing one and am currently in the process of getting it into a publishable state while writing my second book, which is the end of the trilogy."*

"I like it," Bosom Buddy affirms, nodding. "Creates intrigue."

"And then, for what I'm good at, I've just written, *helping people to understand things outside their experience.*"

"I agree."

"The next few sections aren't that interesting, but regarding what I've been spending a lot of time thinking about, I've written, *My book (editing etc). If you search for 'Paige Version 33 Blog' you can find the condensed, blog version. Read at least the first three posts before messaging me about it.* And then I've put an emoji that's poking out its tongue."

Bosom Buddy sighs and rolls his eyes before he replies with, "Are you sure you want an emoji in there?"

"Yes," I confirm, unflinching.

"I'm not sure why you're even running any of this by me if you're just going to do your own thing anyway."

"So I can write about it in my next book."

"Huh. So I'll be in your next book?"

"Yep!"

"Cool. Can you make me into a superhero?"

"There aren't any superheroes in my book. Have you even read the first two drafts I sent you?"

"I keep meaning to finish them, but they're so long, you've written better versions and a third timeline since then, and I know your whole story anyway!"

"Good point."

"Okay, so we've established that you're returning to a dating site, and this time making reference to your book and blog. To me, it seems like you're just there to drive traffic to your blog, and elicit interest in your book."

A laugh through my nose leads to an amusing grunting sound, and I have to wait for Bosom Buddy to stop sniggering before I can respond.

"I admit, part of the reason I am there is to spread my message further, but I am also genuinely seeking to connect with new people. I'm not hopeful, but maybe someone will be open to being with me. You know, as a partner. The most important part of this whole thing, is that I don't have to come out to potential partners. It's all there before they make contact. If I hear from anyone, it's because they already know, and they're awesome!"

"I accept your explanation."

"You're too kind."

"Also, I just want to point out that I never had a problem with your past, and I'm not happy about you moving to Melbourne. Just so we're clear."

And with one click of the mouse, I commence my new journey.

The number of men I chat with is in excess of 50, but I only meet with a few, and all soon fall away when I get a message from Currently Nameless.

There's something intriguing about his beaming face and wispy hair in the profile photo he has chosen to sell himself, and I can tell that he is both well-educated and a deep thinker. The rosy-cheeked blonde man tells me he has read my blog, and also that it would be a shame not to meet the person behind a piece of writing he couldn't put down until he'd reached the end. A genuine compliment about my creative and intellectual endeavours sets him miles ahead of the multitude of men who compliment me exclusively on my appearance.

Conversation with Currently Nameless is fairly standard to begin with, and it soon becomes apparent that we share a lot of interests, one of those being that we are both immensely work-focussed, decidedly in the field of medicine. Naturally, he asks me what I do for a living, and I tell him that I coordinate teaching for medical students. I'm not a doctor, but maybe one day.

Which hospital?

An odd question. Most people don't even realise how much teaching occurs in hospitals. When I tell him that my employer is the Southern Teaching Hospital, he reacts with disappointment.

Conflict of interest, is the term he casually drops, and I ask for clarification.

What he tells me, is that he's a doctor who graduated from The Medical College several years earlier. Not only that, but the hospital I work at, and the hospital where he works? They are the same hospital. As if I've asked him to prove it, he even mentions a colleague by name. Academic Consociate, that is.

He then asks me, *does this make me less desirable, or more? Will a conflict of interest draw you in or turn you away?*

I take a moment to step back and assess the situation from a distance, and come to the conclusion that I don't perceive it as a legitimate conflict of interest. It's not like we're directly connected. We don't actually work together, neither is in a position of power above the other, and as far as I'm aware we've never even bumped into each other.

Instead of talking through these thoughts, I simply tell him that the information has not swayed me in one direction or the other. I tell him, *I'm as keen to meet and see what happens as I was prior to this revelation.*

It is Currently Nameless who decides we should move off the dating app, and he sends me his mobile number.

You could get this number from the hospital switchboard, he tells me. *But don't look me up*, he adds, as if to remind me that he perceives this situation as a conflict of interest. His comment makes me wonder, had I turned his question back on him, would he have told me that he now found me more desirable?

I'd like to keep this separate from work, if we can, he adds.

With each additional comment, I feel like I have a direct electronic link to his uncensored thought process. This increases his desirability, planting the seed that he's somebody I can trust.

What name shall I put it under, I ask, realising I never got his name.

Legitimate One.

Without him having done anything, my fondness of him immediately grows. I stare for a while at the name he shares with the ex that caused the feelings leading to me being on the dating app in the first place. Considering my options for entering his details into my phone, I laugh at the absurdity. It's quite important to have these two men clearly identifiable as separate entities, as a message to one would *not* be appropriate for the other. Both being doctors, I can't use profession as a way to differentiate them, so I decide to label him L2, a shortened form of Legitimate Two.

I try to organise to catch up with L2 to meet at a cafe or bar to see if we have chemistry in person, but he tries to convince me to just let him come straight to my apartment. He tells me he likes the idea of me opening the door to my apartment, and making the first move by grabbing him and pulling him inside. Chemistry aside, this doesn't sound like a safe thing to do with someone I don't know, even if Academic Consociate does apparently know him.

Having read my life story, as well as knowing precisely where I work, and who I work with, he definitely has the upper hand. Eventually—after quite a bit of written conversation—he convinces me to invite him over for wine and a board game that will probably end up with us both naked and engaging in activities that would make us sweaty.

The first time L2 and I attempt to organise the tryst is after his shift at the hospital that ends up becoming an extended shift due to a colleague calling in sick. We reschedule to a day when he has a family event that ends up drawn out for longer than he expects, so again he takes a raincheck. He also takes this opportunity to let me know that this would have been our last chance for a while, because he's doing a short stint out west to cover a doctor who is going away for 5 weeks. Rural relieving, he calls it.

I would still like to see you though, he confirms.

Although I decline his invitation to travel out to visit him during his rural term, we agree that we will keep communication lines open while L2 is away. We'll flirt and get to know each other through modern technology, and on his return, enter into physical territory.

Rural relieving isn't quite what he expects. Our conversations swing from heavy flirting as escapism, to talking through the increasingly stressful situations he's presented with in the rural hospital; counselling sessions, essentially. Both lines of communication escalate. On one side, we explore our sexuality, sending each other requests for specific explicit photos and video footage. On the other side, we talk through the issues at work that are causing us grief. One day, he stops responding. I send one follow-up message, and then allow communication to cease, of the understanding that if he wants things to continue, he will send me a message.

Chapter Seven

○○ **TERMINATION**

OUTER SHELL CONVULSED AGAIN, and another stream exited the mouth, adding one more layer of fluid and undigested pills to the already decimated sheets.

Spasm.
Vomit.
Repeat.

Similar to the disorientation I had felt when starting to drown, I didn't know which way was up. Unlike the experience of almost drowning, getting here was deliberate; I didn't wish for a saviour.

"What are you doing?" screamed Parental Being, rapidly approaching through a shower of tears. "███████!"

Outer Shell rattled violently, and I longed for it all to end. I wanted—needed—Outer Shell to expire as soon as possible, so I could be free. Being discovered by Parental Being in a moribund state added guilt to the cocktail of intolerable emotions. Even one minute more of this hell would be too much for me to bear. How did I get here?

By the end of Year 8, my first year of high school, I had managed to turn myself around to become one of the highest achieving students in mathematics, thanks to a great teacher who ensured I completed all homework assignments. In fact, I was doing well in most subjects, though whenever I was required to perform an oral presentation, I would become too sick with anxiety to attend school.

I started to become genuinely social, and moved about freely between the different school cliques and church groups, but not really committing to any of them. There wasn't a person on the planet who actually knew me, so loyalty couldn't hold me captive. I wasn't particularly liked or disliked, as far as I was aware, with the exception of The Abducted and Her Lemmings (they took delight in tormenting me because of Parental Being's religion). My favourite moments were still when nobody was around, and a lot of this time was now spent under a tree at the beach a short walk from our home. I craved the sensation of the breeze against Outer Shell, providing a little relief from the humidity I despised.

Using all of my savings, I purchased an electronic typewriter and I wrote a novel. Naturally, it was about demonic possession, and the main character was the girl I wished I could be. I put her through a series of tests, and allowed her to fail a few of them before a triumphant finale. So that Parental Being would allow me to continue with my writing, I ensured that the themes were consistent with those acceptable to The Church.

Surrounding the house and The Church was a large amount of land, covered in grass. Maintenance of the yard was a shared responsibility, and to make it easier, The Church owned a ride-on mower. It took a little coaxing, but I was eventually allowed to use it in place of the push mower that made the job much more tedious. This allowance was probably ill-advised. One day while mowing the lawn, I noticed rope on the ground ahead. In a panic, I tried to swerve to miss it but was unsuccessful and in addition to getting the rope stuck around the blades, I crashed into a tree. I could have prevented the accident with the simple act of using my foot to brake.

Because we were in a small town, with a fair amount of flat, empty land at our disposal, I was able to start learning to drive a car early. This was also ill-advised. It took three near misses to prompt me to put away the keys indefinitely.

Reasons I Stopped Driving:
1. I was driving the car at night, from the car 'garage' over to The Church, so that My Sibling could drive us to the Roadhouse with some other teenagers. I heard the shriek of a young child, and realised that the reason I couldn't see the child was because I had forgotten to turn on the lights. The child was physically uninjured. Physically.
2. I was driving the car on the roof of a shopping centre, and realised that the edge of the building was rapidly approaching, but instead of slowing, I turned suddenly and almost rolled the car.
3. I was driving at a campground, and, similar to the situation with the ride-on mower, I realised that there were a lot of tents in my path and instead of slowing down and coming to a complete stop, I tried to weave my way through the tents. Although nobody was harmed, this was the straw that broke the camel's back. I decided that my brain was too faulty to drive.

By the end of Year 9, I had managed to turn myself around yet again and become one of the lowest performing students in mathematics, and it had little to do with the quality of our teacher. I accomplished the same for every class that required any amount of concentration in order to succeed. Why did this occur? Adolescence.

With the onset of puberty, my childish dreams of magically transforming into an appropriate body were lost. Outer Shell was going in another direction, growing into a man. To make matters worse, my sexual thoughts about boys were causing Outer Shell to react involuntarily. Magic didn't exist. Life wasn't fair. I was to be stuck permanently in this horrible form that I could no longer fully control, and nobody would ever come to know or see me for who I really was.

I didn't just feel lonely now; I was devoid of hope. The world around me became a dark, suffocating cloud. I found it taxing to eat, which caused Outer Shell to become deathly thin. The food I took to school would often end up in the trash and even the simple act of getting out of bed in the morning became arduous. It took all of my energy and cognitive ability just to choreograph Outer Shell's movements in a way that hid how bad things really were.

"Um, ▇▇▇▇," one of my classmates in Home Economics said one day. "I think we have a problem."

The classmate pointed at my oven. It was on fire. I had drifted off inside my head and hadn't been paying attention to see all the warning signs leading up to it.

"What did you do?"

"I didn't do anything! I followed the recipe exactly!"

I looked at the flaming oven.

"If you followed the same directions as everyone else your oven would not be on fire," the teacher accused.

"But look, my tray is shallower than everyone else's! The fire has started because the mixture has dripped over the edge because the tray is too shallow," I argued, unwilling to accept responsibility for causing a fire in a classroom.

I became moody and withdrew from all extracurricular activities, including those involving the music that had previously brought me such joy. Burning bridges was executed in a spectacular fashion; snapping at people as if out of nowhere, making a fool of myself on a daily basis. Outer Shell became ill, and I spent months at home, missing too much content to ever recover my former grades.

Life became too hard, and I had nobody to talk to about what I was going through. A lifetime attending The Church taught me that any affiliated person would condemn me rather than assist, but I didn't know anyone outside The Church well enough to feel safe opening up about my struggles. My thoughts started to focus on something I had observed years earlier, just before My Sibling was sent away to live with The Grandparent.

It was night-time, and I was alone in my bedroom. I heard a loud human howl and then sobbing, so I went to investigate. My Sibling was in the kitchen, kneeling on the floor, their arms in the air, shaking, both hands wrapped tightly around the handle of a large knife. The sharp end of the knife was pointing back at their body. The intent to plunge the knife into itself was clear. I watched Parental Being intervene in silence. My Sibling didn't live with us for long after that.

It was now time for me to attempt the same thing, so I retrieved the memory and noted the perceived flaws in My Sibling's execution of the act. I would have a better chance of successfully achieving the desired outcome due to avoiding a public space, and choosing a method that didn't require an awkward act of physical violence by Outer Shell, against Outer Shell.

I selected a Sunday night, feigning a headache to leave The Church early, so that I could be alone in the house. I raided the medicine cabinet, and filled Outer Shell with as many tablets as possible, as quickly as I could, so that it was irreversible by the time any physical reaction began. Fortunately, although I wouldn't have used that word at the time, Parental Being came home early to check on me and no death occurred. Great, so I had absolutely no control at all.

Through conversation Parental Being uncovered that I was depressed, but I refused to disclose any of the reasons why. Mention of medication for mental illness was taboo, so the only action taken was to pray to the Christian God. If healing didn't occur, it wasn't meant to be. Days, weeks, months and then years passed, and I numbly went about doing the minimum that was required of me, until I was in Year 11, and my English teacher prompted change.

"███████, I need to meet with you and Parental Being," the teacher said after summoning me. A combination of the words and tone used indicated that I was in trouble.

The purpose of the meeting was to raise the issue of my diminished performance, and to collaboratively formulate a plan of attack for moving forward. It was a stunning failure for everyone involved. Instead of finding a way to improve my grades, I withdrew from school entirely. I was now a depressed teenage girl trapped in an emerging adult male body with no future prospects.

○ **NOW FLOURISH**

IN THE WAKE OF MY RELATIONSHIP with Legitimate One biting the dust, I felt nothing but unrest. Life was barren, and death was everywhere I looked, just like the arid landscape of my second childhood home. Work was mind-numbingly boring, and as it became clear that there was no corporate ladder to climb, my desire to remain with the company died. There were constant reminders of the failed romance that had begun and come to an end there; my ears polluted with frequent questions and condolences from curious and concerned colleagues. Outside of work, I now noticed that, without realising it, I had allowed years of my personal time to be swallowed up almost exclusively by Legitimate One. Any friendships that weren't in a state of advanced decay had already permanently passed on. I wondered what I was doing with my life, and if there was any point to my existence.

After longing to return to the past with Legitimate One for far too long, I set my mind to moving forward. In the process, I collected countless tales in the next instalment of my still-unsuccessful search for my one true love. The men I encountered through online dating didn't see me so much a person, but rather one of a few products with similar specifications; a price-versus-feature comparison was required prior to purchase. I didn't know where I stood with these men until they'd received itemised quotes on all products.

Particular Guy stood out amongst the crowd. I first saw him from across the road at the place and time we'd agreed upon via the dating site; a pizzeria at 5pm. For most people, 5pm is too early for a dinner date, but that was around the time Legitimate One and I would eat, so the time suited me well. Particular Guy was nice to look at, clean-shaven with clear skin and dusty blonde hair, though his face was devoid of expression.

Particular Guy's first words to me were, "You're just on time. That's good."

Although from his perspective things had begun satisfactorily, I held an opposing view. I immediately felt uncomfortable with how obvious it was that my every move on this date would be assessed. Speaking with a stranger was difficult enough, without confirmation that I was being harshly judged by the other person. An understandably awkward introduction followed, and we took a seat and looked over the menu.

"There's a special starting at 5:30. Let's do that."

Those were his next words. Before I'd had the chance to agree, Particular Guy had called over a waiter. He asked if they would be okay with starting the special early for us. The waiter seemed confused, and told us that we would need to wait until the specified time if we wanted to take advantage of the special.

After Particular Guy briefly muttered under his breath that the waiter was awful for not changing the time for us, we spent most of the next half hour on chitchat, waiting for the special to kick in. It became slightly less painful with each minute, and I actually began to enjoy myself. A pleasant surprise! More time passed, we ordered food, and we began conversing between bites of pizza. Out of the blue, Particular Guy decided that the time for shallow talk was over. He pushed the conversation into serious territory.

"I know what you're thinking," Particular Guy told me. "You're thinking I like younger girls."

The thought hadn't crossed my mind, but now that he mentioned it, I realised he was a little older than I was. Surely that wasn't something girls would usually take issue with though.

"It's not like that," Particular Guy said as he waved his hand from side to side, a gesture I associated with declining an offer, though one had not been made. I remained silent.

"It's like this. Girls my age are ready to have kids. When you get to my age, you'll be ready. That's when I will be ready. See? It's not actually about me liking younger girls at all!"

Two major trains of thought dominated my mind. The first was that this guy assumed far too much about me, and the other was that he was completely off base with regard to what I wanted or thought about him. And then there was the whole kids thing. I couldn't have kids, so I was briefly reminded that I wasn't a typical, fertile young woman. It occurred to me that I had gone through this whole dating procedure, from setting up my profile, to sitting here with one of the candidates, without giving any thought at all to my past. I had forgotten that I was different.

Conversation improved as the night went on, but I mostly answered questions and asked a few stock standards, distracted by his behaviour and rigid plan for both our lives that I would inevitably be unable to fit into.

We walked from the pizzeria to a dessert café, chosen because Particular Guy had a discount voucher that he realised at the last minute wasn't valid, so I was thrust into another awkward scenario that this time ended with a discount we weren't actually entitled to. By the end of the evening my feet were sore from walking, so Particular Guy, in all his gallant splendour, offered to drive me home. He gave me some parting words before letting me leave the car, and for a fleeting moment, I thought of Original Companion, whose ghost, it seemed, had spent this whole time following me, just out of sight.

"Well, you were a bit quiet to start with, but you got better toward the end of the date. Now, I need to be completely honest with you. I've got a few more dates lined up, but once they're out of the way I'll let you know if you've made the next round. It was nice meeting you, Paige."

Closing the door behind me, I didn't look back, deciding that it was time to focus on friendships instead of dating.

Only a day later, I was sitting opposite a female Friendly Entity who had studied film with me. After years apart, we had reconnected following the breakup with Legitimate One.

"I think you could get a good following," Friendly Entity told me.

"What do you mean?"

Friendly Entity explained to me that on the recently developed site Twitter, you could follow anyone with a public account and anyone could follow you (if you had a public account). Unlike the Facebook friend concept, you didn't have to follow people who followed you. You would only see posts by people you followed, a feed that became a faster flowing stream as the number of people you followed increased. It seemed a fun concept, easy to use, and I was excited to be a part of something that was not yet mainstream.

I picked up a following quickly, just as Friendly Entity had predicted. This was in part because I had a foot in the door (being introduced by an accomplished user), and I started to attend meet-ups with the Brisbane Twitter Underground Brigade, or #BTUB. This was back in the days when every Twitter user from Brisbane meeting in person didn't make for a particularly large group. I fell in love with Twitter, and for a while I ignored most other forms of social media.

Discovering social media as an adult is a somewhat dangerous affair if you've spent most of your life avoiding social interaction. My social skills had improved greatly, mostly thanks to studying film, television and theatre in my youth, but there was still a lot I had yet to learn, and I was about to learn those lessons in public; two of them presented below. I can't imagine how much more stressful it must be going through puberty this way, and count myself lucky for reaching it prior to the existence of MySpace, Facebook, Twitter, Instagram and everything that has boomed and crashed since.

o

Social Media Lesson 1 – Assertiveness:
When I entered this phase of life, I had two settings:
1. Passive
2. Aggressive
I allowed people to treat me in a way that I disliked without speaking up, hoping that it would just stop (see: Passive Behaviour), and I would let everything bottle up until, quite suddenly, I would reach peak pressure and explode (see: Aggressive Behaviour). Exploding involved me muttering things in the heat of the moment that I didn't mean, that often didn't make much sense, and that would in some cases irreversibly damage relationships. This is not something you want to do in a public space that is recorded on the internet forever, but that's what I did. Many of us did; some still do. After quite a few outbursts, I completed the following short training courses and amongst other things, I learnt to be assertive:
How to Deal with Difficult People (Phone & Face)
Advanced Customer Service Skills
Building Emotional Resiliency
Managing Emotions at Home and Work

o

Training like this really should be a part of our primary school curriculum.

o

Social Media Lesson 2 - Dirty Laundry:
The Brisbane Twitter community was once described to me as an island (at the same time as being a stream; how non-binary of it) and, as with any island, people inevitably start to date each other. I started out with harmless flirting, and this progressed to overt sexual comments because I soon forgot (or ceased to care) that I was in a public space that could be viewed and later revisited by people without context. This is similar to the circumstances of fly on the wall reality television, where behaviour of participants evolves as they start to forget (or cease to care) that they have an audience. Continuing to live as if my years before gender transition had not occurred, I dated around the community, at times having stupid public arguments and lashing out on Twitter rather than privately dealing with issues. A few people got quite hurt, directly and indirectly, and it was the cause of much regret.

Mistakes aside, Twitter had a profoundly positive impact on my life. I developed a decent sized social network that only knew me as I was, and not for what I had been through. Almost nobody in my life had been around to see me awkwardly moving about in a pre-treatment stage of Outer Shell, or been around to watch the slow, confusing stage of transition. My self-esteem started to recover, the Ghost of Original Companion finally moved on, and my social skills improved. I was finally in a stage of my life where I didn't want to spend the majority of my time alone. I was happy, and although I didn't have a man by my side, I felt complete, unaware of what was waiting for me right around the corner.

• EMANCIPATION, PART ONE

THE LAST MESSAGE MY MENTOR EVER SENDS me is an update on how well she's coping with her latest treatment for oesophageal cancer. This is after several failed attempts to catch up over coffee or a meal, and it is only upon receipt of this final message that I realise it's not something I've said; she hasn't been well enough to see me.

Phew!

My feeling of relief is quickly succeeded by guilt, and again I try to schedule a coffee date. Several unanswered messages later, and My Mentor's daughter uses social media to capture a wider audience when announcing her passing. This is the last of a string of closely timed deaths of people I care about, and the one that affects me the most.

My grief peaks at the beautiful riverside memorial service her daughter organises, and, free of romantic distraction, I am naively compelled to make every future moment of my life worthwhile. I become more active as a Diversity Ally, attending every related networking event I hear about, and I devote the majority of my waking hours to writing about my own lived experience. As I dedicate more of my home life to the cause of improving the social standing of people in the Queer community, I become more ashamed than ever that I spend most of my work life hiding, pretending that Outer Shell never existed.

"What brings you here?"

The Host of the Workplace Diversity Network event I am attending is a first generation Australian gay man of Indian descent. Which of the two of us holds the most diversity cards is debatable, but considering his, I feel safe enough to present him with the diversity card that is most relevant to the present moment. I open my mouth to tell The Host a condensed version of my situation, but before I get the chance...

"Thank goodness, somebody I know!"

The owner of the voice is a short, curvaceous blonde woman, immediately recognisable to me as someone I've seen at a few work-related events. Feeling of safety shattered.

"Hi, my name is Test of Conviction," she tells me. "You're Paige, right? I remember you from that training we did together."

"Paige was just about to tell us about why she's here," The Host says.

"Yes, uh, actually," I falter. I'm already memorable to Test of Conviction, so anything I say here could easily make it back to my colleagues if she's the type of woman to spread gossip. But surely the type of person to attend an event like this would be more sensitive than that.

A well-dressed Random Guy walks over to us.

"Mind if I join the conversation?"

Although it's just three people, my irrational anxiety treats it like the strangers in this conversation are multiplying rapidly. I decide that making this step to telling strangers, in person, is more important than feeling safe. I convince myself that I just have to come out with it as fast as I can. Sometimes you just have to rip the plaster off in one go!

I take a deep breath.

"My name is Paige, and I'm here because although I consider myself a Queer Ally, I'm the T in LGBTIQ. I am a woman who has been through a gender transition."

Blank stares for a moment. I fill the pockets of awkward silence with more speaking.

"I've written a blog about it. Life has been arduous as a direct result of my gender transition, and I'd like to help reduce that for other girls in my situation if I can."

Raised eyebrows, a gaping mouth.

"Wow, I honestly had no idea," Test of Conviction admits, looking me up and down. I ignore the scanning eyes, focussing on the happy fact that I've pushed past my fear to enlighten these people.

"Do your colleagues know you were a guy?"

Unhappy; I bite my tongue. I've already taken a huge leap forward today and I'm not strong enough to call her out without getting upset and muddling my words. This is definitely something I will learn to do fluently one day, but today is not that day.

"I've been thinking about how to go about it. It's none of their business, but I don't like hiding it, and it means I have to lie and be evasive sometimes."

All eyes are on me, and in my peripheral vision I notice a young man approaching as Test of Conviction asks her next question.

"How so?"

"Well, say someone asks about my period, or pregnancy. That comes up a bit when you're in a workplace with a lot of women."

"Oh, that never occurred to me."

"And also, I want to work on removing the stigma associated with my past, so it can be spoken about as if you're being told someone's had their wisdom teeth removed. I can't really tell everyone it's not shameful or an issue if I'm hiding and behaving as if it is. I feel like my specific workplace is one of the safer places to do this."

"Where do you work?" Random Guy asks.

"I work at The Medical College. We have a great Diversity Ally program there."

"What a coincidence! My boyfriend is a medical student. He's just… here."

Random Guy points to Medical Student; the young man I'd noticed earlier. Close up, I recognise him as not just any, but a student that attends at the Southern Teaching Hospital. I see him in the hospital hallway frequently. Without thinking, for the first time, I tell one of my medical students face to face about my gender history.

Later that night I stand tall, arm resting on the shovel that has been used to create the large hole in the ground before me. I look down at the old grave with fresh eyes. I rip the shovel from its steady position, and in a quick manoeuvre, thrust a small portion of dirt away from Outer Shell's face. Within a few repeated motions, I reveal the face completely. I uncover the traumatic childhood memories that have been repressed since my successful gender affirming surgery. I bring back the shame of my failed suicide attempts, and the awkward social interactions of my young adult self. Following one final thrust, I jump into the grave, scoop Outer Shell into my arms, and head to work.

Hours after waking from the prophetic dream, I approach work, listening to words from the past. I smile fondly as I hear Professor John K Young speak about the beauty of human anatomy and physiology; part of my unofficial medical studies. Gazing upon my work building feels different today, because I am going to speak with Academic Consociate about a special request. The day has other plans, however, and before I have a chance to summon up the nerve to speak with Academic Consociate, they have left for a holiday. Deciding that this cannot wait until their return, I write an email. Not long after, I receive a reply, and with endorsement from Academic Consociate, I email the entire team just before I leave for my own holiday.

•

Dear Academic Consociate and Professional Associate,
Some of you will by now have heard that I've written a book that may end up being published later this year. Life outside of here is odd and exciting right now!
The reason I mention this is because although the book is written in a fictional style, it's heavily based on true events from my life. Due to the sensitive nature of some of the content and the overall themes, there is potential for workplace gossip. You may or may not have heard some of it already. This is something I would like to minimise, or ideally, eliminate.
For the following reasons, I would like to provide you all with the first 6 chapters of my

book for reading over the holidays:
The chapters are crafted to bring the subject matter up in a gentle way;
I'd like you to be able to digest the subject matter slowly and in private;
It provides answers to FAQs that wouldn't be appropriate to ask;
It's important to me that everyone I work with here be aware;
I don't want to stress about "Who knows and who doesn't?"

•

Before long, I receive a few email and verbal responses from my colleagues, and I distribute the draft chapters to everyone I work with.

•

"I am sure that I speak for all of your colleagues here when I say that we would feel privileged to read your book. Thank you for sending us this email too…so eloquently written."
"I trust everyone here and I think we are a kind and trustworthy bunch and I am sure we will respect you and any sensitive issues. If not, I would be surprised, disappointed and angry!"
"Appreciate you trusting me to share something based on true events in your life. Will talk later."

•

I spend the holidays with Parental Being, and My Sibling drops in for short visits with their new child. Although it is far from the environment I desire, it is a vast improvement from every visit before it. I catch glimpses of Outer Shell in photos scattered about the place, but I keep my mental sunglasses off, reminding myself that I have come out of darkness.

When I return to work, I have several emails waiting for me.

•

"I read your 6 chapters and was so impressed with your honesty and courage. You are an amazing writer. Thank you for sharing your story with me."
"I finally read your bio on Friday. Far out! So much to go through. We all go through stuff but we usually don't know what others are going through. I hope things are going well for you now. Well done for writing. Not that you need my kudos and not that I know much about the technical side of writing….but wanted to say … I hardly ever…I mean ever! Do anything for myself. Sitting down and reading your bio…for a few minutes I drifted off and didn't think about anything but what I was reading and that was sheer joy I can tell you. It has inspired me to make sure I read more. I especially enjoyed the first section. I like that your sense of humour comes through your writing. Look forward to reading more."

•

With tears in my eyes, I pick up my phone to send Bosom Buddy the good news, and am confronted with a short video that solidifies something I have been deliberating over. Before I get a chance to follow through, however, I am interrupted.

Chapter Eight

○○ **BEACON**

"You need to do something," Parental Being insisted, face contorted to convey frustration.

Reluctantly, I shoved the skeletal Outer Shell into the car and we went to the local community college. Our mission was to look through the study options to find something that might appeal to me. It could have been weeks or months that I had spent lying around the house, but I didn't feel any better. I was too sheltered to realise what a burden I was being on Parental Being, so I didn't understand why I had to do anything at all. Ever. I'd always been fed and clothed, so why would it be any different now? It turned out we needed government payments that wouldn't come in if I wasn't enrolled in school. That's how it was different. We actually needed money to survive. My situation was causing inconvenience to others.

Inner Monologue: Great. Just great! This is the last thing I need.
Body Language: Hunching.

Outer Shell probably had a bit of a stench because I hadn't bothered to wash it regularly. I didn't care. What was the point in caring for it? What was the point of anything? A quick search of the internet and a few surveys confirmed to me that I was clinically depressed, and I felt justified in doing nothing for the rest of my life. With any luck, Outer Shell would passively waste away to nothing, and was surely already well on the way. I had good reason to be depressed; I just couldn't tell anyone what that reason was. Everywhere I went I heard comments that confirmed my suspicions. There was still not a soul in the world that I could trust.

Choosing a course was difficult when I had no desire to do anything with my life. I didn't see a future with me in it, because I could never actually be myself. In the end, after much deliberation, I chose Business Administration, because it involved a lot of computer work. I knew how to add and remove hardware, and I knew they used computers in offices. I was also familiar with installing and use of software, and from fiddling around at school and at home after we purchased our first personal computer, I had taught myself Hypertext Markup Language (see: HTML). I hated the thought of having to use the phone, but hey, there was nothing on the list that I was more than 25% interested in. That figure is generous by the way.

On the first day of class, where we learned to use some ancient version of Microsoft Word on the most 90s thing ever, Windows 95, I met Best Friend.

A wife and mother of two, Best Friend sounded traditional on paper, but she was as far from traditional as I had experience with. She was slightly shorter than me and possessed an unfamiliar cheeky sense of humour that I really liked. We clicked very quickly. There was this new feeling I felt around her. I felt... comfortable, like I didn't have to manipulate Outer Shell so much in order to be understood or accepted. She could sense that I was different, though I could tell she was mistaking it for something else because she couldn't quite see who I was inside yet.

Yet.

I started to feel hope again. Perhaps we would get to a point where I could tell this woman who I was.

Perhaps.

As our friendship developed, Best Friend mentioned that she was a member of the local amateur theatrical society. As it happened, they had an upcoming play with a part that Outer Shell would be suitable for. Acting. Of course! How had I not thought of that? I spent every single moment of my life acting! I considered myself to be more of a puppeteer, but I would essentially be doing the same thing. I would be manipulating Outer Shell to play yet another character that was not me, but it would be my choice to do so. I would be reclaiming it. I would be empowering myself!

Brilliant!

I joined the amateur theatrical society and threw myself in headfirst. I went to meetings, did secretarial work, worked on plays, performed and participated in workshops. I was particularly fond of helping to create posters for events, and I would scour the internet for images to use (remember, this was the 1990s, and there wasn't all that much on the internet yet). Best Friend and I spent more and more time together. I was around her so much that Parental Being even wrote her a letter, concerned that she may become a bad influence on me. An influence definitely, but surely the only person to make me feel comfortable in life so far couldn't be a bad influence. If anything, she was keeping me alive.

Outside of the theatre group, things didn't go quite as well. At TAFE, as soon as we got to the Business Administration subjects that involved speaking on the phone, I freaked out and dropped out. I just couldn't do it. Fortunately, as usual, Parental Being came to the rescue and I scored (or rather Parental Being scored for me) a traineeship in Information Technology Support at the school I had dropped out of the year before. While my former classmates completed their final year, I wandered around the campus fixing computers. At first it went really well and I was very popular with my boss because I picked up everything very quickly, reducing training time to next to nothing.

My social skills started to develop because I had to regularly interact with teachers, administration staff and students. For each of the units for the educational side of the traineeship, I was required to travel north to

Townsville (see: the closest city). This meant turning up to unfamiliar buildings, meeting and studying with strangers that I was unlikely to ever see again. During the training sessions, I would chat online with the other participants, because the time allowed for each exercise was excessive. Goodness knows why, but I competed against the guy in the class and went on a date with the other girl. It went well, but I didn't feel the need to see her again.

Because things seemed to be looking up, I decided to start taking care of Outer Shell's appearance. This involved going to a hairdresser for a cut and colour, rather than doing it myself, or having Parental Being do it. I also started to develop a sense of style, purchasing new clothes instead of wearing hand-me-downs. And, because I felt that Outer Shell's crowded teeth were unsightly, I saw an orthodontist in Townsville and acquired braces. This meant I need to travel to Townsville more regularly.

It was while I stayed in Townsville that I was introduced to a side of Australia I had previously been unaware of. After attending a local church service, I helped take some soup to a community that lived out of sight, in a camp. There were shelters that people lived in, and it was very dusty. I felt incredibly uncomfortable, not knowing how to behave, and perceiving the situation as a threat because the surrounds were so different to the culture I had been raised in. I wondered why it had taken so long to be introduced to a community that had clearly been established long before any strands of my family had arrived on the continent.

To make the perceived threat worse, a young girl came up to me. She was visibly upset. I noted that there was a broken bottle sticking out of her leg, and, understandably, she was bleeding. With no understanding of the culture I was dealing with, we took the girl to the local hospital for treatment. Confused, and unsure of how to seek answers to the questions this situation raised, I made a conscious effort to suppress the uncomfortable memory, and vowed to never return.

Partway through the twelve months that the traineeship took, Parental Being and My Sibling travelled around Australia in a caravan. I was left to my own devices for a few months, using the traineeship as an excuse to stay behind. I didn't waste any time, taking advantage of the video store special that allowed me to hire out 7 films on VHS every week. Most of them were horror, and all of them had high level (see: graphic) sexual references and nudity. I wanted to know everything about the world that I had previously been unable to access. I was disappointed to find that almost all sexualised nudity was female, which just made me jealous because they had the body parts I wanted. I didn't give much thought to why it was almost exclusively women that were objectified in this way.

When Parental Being and My Sibling returned, I found that life was a lot more difficult than it had previously been, because I now knew what I was missing out on. I had a whole new level of pretending to keep up with, and was no longer able to watch the graphic sex and violence I had become accustomed to. This made me very irritable, and it flowed through into the workplace. My former classmates had all graduated, and I felt more isolated than ever. Depression hit harder, and my ability to successfully communicate with my colleagues decreased. It took one particularly bad experience to push me over the edge.

The teacher who had been responsible for me dropping out of school was now my (superior) colleague. Back when I was in school, her son had been my classmate. I was there when he was poking his tongue out during a soccer or football game. He tripped and fell, almost biting off the tongue that was poking out of his mouth. I use the word almost because after the bite it was dangling, hanging there by a tiny thread. It was one of two events that occurred in high school that had been especially upsetting to me, even though I wasn't directly involved. The other was the disappearance of The Abducted, prompting an investigation that led to the arrest of a man that her parents swore could not have committed the crime. I wondered how such a physically attractive man could possibly kidnap and murder somebody, because in films, kidnappers and murderers were usually unattractive. The police still hadn't found the body, and I recalled that I had seen The Parents of The Abducted in a nearby city on multiple occasions, watching people in the shopping mall, still looking for clues. Like perhaps The Abducted had amnesia and that's why she hadn't returned to them. There was no body, no closure, just hope and desperation that refused to die.

"█████," the teacher said. Crap, I had been daydreaming. "I need this space," she said, gesturing to the area I had covered with student report cards. Generating these had become my responsibility because back then, doing a mail merge was considered a task for Information Technology Support. Teachers were required to provide me with comments on each student through a Microsoft Access database, after which I generated a report based on that data. It was most enjoyable. This situation, however, was not.

I can't remember exactly what my reply was, but I was a little aggressive and held up my hand when she started to reply to me. I wasn't finished speaking my mind, and she shouldn't interrupt! The altercation landed me in the office of the Registrar and I was reprimanded for being disrespectful to a superior. To retaliate, I wrote a letter requesting that my traineeship be terminated. I was convinced to stay, but I had done irreparable damage to my reputation; I had to think of a new plan for my life, however long it might unfortunately turn out to be.

○ **SUDDENLY SUBMERGED**

AFTER IT HAD BECOME CLEAR that no career progression was open to me in the laboratory, I sent out a few job applications. The first interview I scored was at The Medical College where Legitimate One had studied at the beginning of our relationship. It was my first panel interview, so I was terrified. I was also somewhat distracted. See, the interview was in the afternoon and since I'd taken the whole day off work, I took the opportunity to sit in an empty cinema and watch the heart-warming third instalment of a film series about toys that come to life. You know the one. During the interview, I hoped it wasn't obvious that I had been crying.

Perhaps it was because the other applicants were terrible, or maybe because I had said something that indicated a strong work ethic—the Ethics Professor was on the interview panel—I was successful; they offered me the job. I gave my notice at the laboratory, and weeks later commenced work at The Medical College, carrying out an assortment of administrative duties all related to the assessment of students studying Medicine.

"I saw some lesbians holding hands in the street," Work Colleague told me on my first day, screwing up their face to show me how disgusted they were. I did my best to hide behind a non-reactive mask, astounded at what I was hearing.

The work itself was enjoyable. I liked the variety, and responded remarkably well to the need for every task to be completed in one specific way, with little to no margin for error. Here, perfectionists were praised for getting bogged down in the finer details.

"I'm not suggesting that I think you are, but if you are a lesbian, don't let anyone find out or you will never go anywhere in this place," a variation of Work Colleague warned me, just a few weeks in. "The reason that girl didn't get the temp admin position? It's because she's a lesbian."

Inner Monologue: Oh my God. Lesbians are far more accepted in our culture than my Undesirable Past. If anyone finds out, I'll surely lose my job. I'll never gain employment anywhere else because I won't be able to get a good reference. There's nobody I can talk to about this, because I'm so far in the closet and nobody could possibly understand how high the stakes are!
Body Language: Slow, steady breathing, minimal movement.

In no time at all I was immersed in a sea of gossipy, bitchy whispers. During the year that followed, I barely kept my head above water, always going above and beyond the call of duty, constantly terrified that if I made one wrong move, I would be out on the street indefinitely. I could see no solution other than to shrink back into the darkness and work my way up to a position away from these people.

After proving that my skills were of a higher level than the position by means of a brief stint stepping up to cover Work Colleague, I was tapped on the shoulder.

"Can I speak to you for a moment?"

It was the second regeneration of Our Manager, and I was suddenly perturbed.

Inner Monologue: Have I done something wrong? Has someone found out about my past and passed the information on? Am I about to be fired? Is this something I can fight?
Body Language: Slow, steady breathing, polite smile.

"The Medical Placement Officer is taking a secondment in another role, and I think you would be a good fit as a temporary replacement. It's only for three months."

"What does a Medical Placement Officer do?" I quizzed Our Manager, breathing a sigh of relief.

"You'll take care of students on clinical placements," I was told, as if I had already been offered and accepted the position. "Clinical placements are practical work experience for medical students in a location and hospital department of their choosing. The current person in the role has done an exceptional job of setting up templates and timelines to make it easier."

I accepted, and with barely anything more than that conversation, I was moved into the position of Medical Placement Officer. At first I found it difficult to adjust. I had come from a position where I was micromanaged, and fallen into a position where I had no leadership whatsoever. Similar to a young bird that has been pushed out of the nest by its mother to prompt its first flight, I was forced to become more independent, and soon thrived in the role.

"Paige," the third regeneration of Our Manager called a few months in. "I'm sending everyone home so they don't get stuck here if the roads get flooded."

Inner Monologue: Hah! Awesome! Free time off! Hells yeah! I know exactly what I'm going to do!
Body Language: Casual nod.

I was hardly drowning in work that afternoon, so I promptly closed what I was working on, shut down the computer and headed home via the liquor store. Within minutes of walking through the front door, I had my laptop open and had started writing a blog post about how glorious this day was, sipping on a cool fermented grape beverage, nibbling on cheese and crackers. Beads of moisture built up on the wine glass and dripped down my arm, tickling me in a delightfully refreshing manner. I took a break to sprinkle some water on the plants I'd been growing in ceramic pots on the balcony. This really was an unexpectedly beautiful day.

News broadcast on Twitter indicated that the roads to our apartment would probably be cut off within a few hours, so I was grateful to have this luxury food and drink to consume for however long we would be stranded for. Perhaps it would be just overnight, or maybe a few days. At worst, I figured we might lose power, so I prioritised the consumption of anything perishable (see: EAT ALL THE CHEESE IMMEDIATELY).

My mobile phone rang, and despite it being a number I didn't recognise, I picked up.

"PK!" It was Grandparent's Child (see: one of the many siblings of Parental Being), and I noted the way I was addressed; a refusal to refer to me as Paige. To give you some context, this was a decade after Paige had become my legal name, and all of my identification documents had been amended to correctly display my gender as female.

"Your Sibling asked me to come and get you," Grandparent's Child informed me. "I won't be long, so pack whatever you need for the next few days."

It seemed a bit melodramatic to me, but after inhaling the rest of the wine and cheese, I packed an overnight bag, ensuring I had my laptop, phone and appropriate chargers. *Priorities*. When Grandparent's Child arrived, I was asked if I wanted to grab anything else quickly.

"Is there anything else you want to save?"

I laughed and declined, because I didn't think it likely that the river would reach our apartment. We were partway up a hill! It would take a substantial amount of water to immerse any apartments this high up. I quickly emptied my bladder, flushed the toilet, and we headed out the door, the faint sound of water rising in the cistern behind us.

For the sake of wading down memory lane to the floods that had occurred shortly after our family had moved to Australia in the 1970s, we drove to Kayes Rocks, by the riverbank in Toowong, the suburb Parental Being had lived in as an adolescent. I remembered the stories from The Grandparent and watched the river with Grandparent's Child in horror as I finally realised what was happening. It wasn't just the low parts of the roads that were going to go under. Our homes would also be submerged by nightfall and it was now too late to go back to get anything.

Only hours later, My Cousin stood beside me asking, "Are you okay?"

My Cousin showed support by touching my shoulder gently as I watched the television. We were far away from the drama, and it felt surreal. I could be watching any natural disaster unfold on television but I wasn't, and I half-heartedly shook my head. Limp body and red face, a small stream trickled down from my eyes, wetting my face and shirt. I couldn't speak, so I just wept silently, watching the footage of my suburb that had been swallowed up by a seemingly endless sea of brown liquid.

My employer—The Medical College—handled the situation exceptionally. Understanding how difficult it was for those of us who had been displaced, we were granted special paid leave to allow us time to find new homes, without the stress of having to work around standard business hours. I was also given the option of applying for an interest-free loan. This did wonders for reducing the stress of an unexpected, traumatic experience.

"I'm surprised you're taking this so well," Legitimate One commented as he helped me carry my bags into his combined kitchen, dining and lounge room. This room was the area that would become my temporary home until I could find a new long-term residence.

Staying with family had been a nice escape from reality and I had enjoyed spending time with them, but as soon as the roads had opened and we'd helped volunteers clean the mud, destroyed furniture and God knows what else from the apartment, I felt the need to return to the city. It wasn't just because of pressure to go back to work that led me to stay with Legitimate One; I had to escape the constant, suffocating presence of my family's religion that reminded me of some of the most difficult parts of my childhood.

Legitimate One and I set up the couch as a bed. The few bags I had with me were now most of my belongings, and I placed them neatly in the corner. From then on, every morning I would tidy everything up, placing it all back in the corner. During the day I would alternate between shopping, looking for a home, and socialising. I started to cook meals with and for Legitimate One, and pain grew in my heart as we found ourselves in so many situations similar to the years when we were together. I missed him, and I still loved him.

Quantum Cheshire wasn't confident he'd find a new place on his own, and the need to distance myself from Legitimate One was becoming more urgent, so although I didn't want to live with Quantum Cheshire again, I signed a lease for the first place we agreed on. Conveniently, it was an apartment just a few doors up from the old one and the few items we were able to salvage didn't have to be carried far. Because Quantum Cheshire's work was casual and lower paid than mine, I agreed to pay a high percentage of the rent, which was a large portion of my wage.

Within a few months of living in our new apartment, I came to resent Quantum Cheshire. Between government payouts, insurance payouts, and donations from friends and family, the financial profit Quantum Cheshire made from the floods was in excess of $10,000.00. It took a lot of time and effort on my part to fight for a small payout from the government. Between that and donations, I still made a hefty financial loss. Each time Quantum Cheshire complained, my bitterness grew. I was struggling financially and emotionally, and I was annoyed that he could consider himself to also be struggling when I perceived him to be so much better off than I was. Instead of dealing with the issue, I chose to avoid him as much as possible.

- **INTERESTED BUT CONFLICTED**

WHEN I SEE L2 FROM THE PEDESTRIAN OVERPASS that safely connects the

Southern Teaching Hospital with the bus station, it is as if a favourite fictional character has materialised before me, or perhaps the ghost of a friend. My heart leaps. This leap is followed by a pang, as I recall the frustratingly drawn out emotional and sexual development that abruptly vanished before it had a chance to become physical. By the time I set foot on the same bus station platform as him, my mind is a storm of memories and emotions, so I choose not to interrupt what is clearly a supremely strong connection between him and his mobile device.

L2 looks up, spots his bus approaching, starts walking, and moments before reaching the bus glances in my direction, causing our eyes to briefly connect before he swiftly turns away and enters the bus. Feeling suddenly self-conscious and undesirable, I whip out my own mobile device and pretend to read.

Do not message him, I tell myself. Several hours later, I am repeating the four words as I near the end of a $4 bottle of Pinot Gris.

Do not message him.

I try to distract myself with a trashy comedy on one of the streaming services I subscribe to.

Do not message him.

Where did you disappear to? And I've sent the message before I realise I've finished typing it. *Darn it.*

I see ellipses within a bubble, indicating that a reply is being crafted.

So that was you… huh.

I remind him that he disappeared.

I know, he replies. *I am quite sorry. Also rural relieving became quite traumatic. And I lost contact in general.*

I wonder about the specific circumstances, and what he means by "lost contact in general" but try not to get drawn in.

I was worried about that but felt weird about checking in, I tell him. *I take it you eventually bounced back? I'm heading to bed, but if you need or want to talk through anything my ears and eyes are good for that.*

I add a smiley emoji.

Talk to you later, if you want to.

Throughout the night, he has left a stack of one-sentence messages for me. When I wake, however, I've forgotten the wine-fuelled conversation. I flick back through the conversation, then read his new messages.

It's okay.

Just lots of flying sick people out, palliating crumbly old people, trying to smash my head against a wall AKA treating a severely litigious gentleman with horrendous diabetes and a non-healing ulcer.

I'm sorry I stopped communicating.

And lost your number when I converted back.

We had a fun thing going on.

You'll be happy to know I don't have any of the stuff we sent to one another either.

Hahah.

Package deal with my phone changing over.

His final message is a single winking emoji.

What I really want to do, is to tell him he was awfully rude to disappear without a word. But I have a stronger desire to reconnect with him, and correct the unfulfilled desires. I know this is an unnaturally strong attachment to someone I haven't technically met, but I ignore those thoughts and continue the conversation.

That's a huge relief. It was well timed actually. A bunch of people died so I wasn't good company for a while. Have you started a new job yet?

L2 wastes no time with a reply.

Oh, goodness. I'm sorry to hear that. And no, that's next year, January. I'm still wandering about the medical wards.

I smile, and I think about the photos and video of him that are still on my phone.

All good. Has to happen to everyone eventually. *shrug* I suppose I should clear my phone of your evidence to even the score?

As I tensely await his reply, I wonder whether my code of ethics is strong enough to follow through if his request is that I cleanse my phone of his naked, aroused body.

No, you can keep it. Return the favour again if you're keen. Hahah. Perhaps we can find time to eventually make a little material together. :P

An involuntary full body blush tells me that this is definitely something I would like.

We should definitely get hammered and cross the physical boundary. It surely can't be that difficult to find the time.

I wink, then follow it up with more realistic thoughts.

Reality: it will probably be difficult to find the time.

Moments before I start to add another thought, L2 sends a response.

Hahaha. Well, I have to work tomorrow but Friday is typically great for getting loose. ;)

Already this is difficult. I really want to see him, but I've decided not to cancel on Bosom Buddy for other offers. I know all too well how bad it feels to be on the other end of that.

So a Friday soon then? Already have plans tonight until late and I'm running a clinical exam next weekend so it'll have to be after that.

More bubbled ellipses.

Oh, poo. Well, that's ok. Hope the clinical exams go well. A few of my friends were asked to do it.

A reminder that for him, this is a conflict of interest. A reminder that we are connected through work. This is a risk. A dirty, sexy risk.

Thanks! I'm pretty excited. I really thrive on the stress of being responsible for anything that goes wrong and having to zip about putting out fires all day. Not literal fires. Although…

Days pass, and I find myself with little to do late in the work day, so I flick off a message to L2.

I made the mistake of letting someone help with my work and now I'm stuck in the office by myself with nothing to do.

L2 is prompt with his response.

I haven't even had lunch. I wish I had someone to help with MY work.

Having little to do, my response is more prompt.

I'd help but I doubt that's anything I could realistically and anonymously help with.

He laughs.

You don't want to come over and practice a few patient histories or exams?

How much effort is it to transfer handwritten notes into the electronic medical records system? Because I could write you notes, but you'd have to enter them yourself, because I don't have access since I'm not a medical professional.

L2 snorts.

Laborious.

Feeling cheeky, I attempt flirting. Our messages start to feel like a conversation that's occurring in person.

"Ooh, well if it makes it more frustrating I'm in!"

"It's Friday," L2 points out. *"Why don't you go home early? You're not unlucky like me and have work tomorrow. Go, be free!"*

"Hahahahaha," I laugh. "It's a combination of me being the resident workaholic and drawing the short straw. Debating leaving in the next few minutes. I've been alone since three PM and not a thing has come up that's needed my attention. But I feel like if I did leave early, it would be two minutes after I left that something would go down."

"And here I was hoping we'd avoid an awkward bus stop meeting," L2 laughs.

"We will. I probably catch an afternoon bus about once a fortnight. The other day was it!"

I poke my tongue out at him.

"Aww. Poo. Here I was practicing my suave moves," he says regretfully.

I pause, contemplating additional ways I can tease him.

"Were those moves going to include avoiding eye contact?"

I wink for added effect.

"Yeah. It was. My single move," he jokes. "You caught me off guard! And I was hurrying for a bus. And barely concentrating on my surroundings."

"Bla bla bla," I laugh, rolling my eyes at him.

Each day, I find myself drawn deeper into conversation with L2, and for a while I lose sight of some of the goals I've set for the year. We spend many evenings in our separate beds, having conversations with each other as we drink alone and watch whatever it is that currently takes our fancy. Every now and then, I throw him a little medical trivia picked up during my informal studies.

"Why do you know so much random medical stuff?"

"I stay in the office for an hour or two after I clock off to read articles and watch lectures on random stuff like Popcorn Lung because it's more fulfilling than having a real life," I say, mixing a joke with reality.

L2 is clearly impressed.

"You probably know more than me at the moment. I have forgotten so much. I'm doing a coursework masters next year to force myself into a syllabus to bring it all back."

The thought of him returning to study pleases me for some reason.

"I don't know much," I clarify. "I started writing a fiction book about abuse of methylphenidate, and had to research a bit, but stopped for a while because of those deaths and stuff. Looking forward to getting back to it."

I sense a potential lull in the conversation.

"Anyway," I say. "I'm exhausted and too pissed for intelligent conversation, so I shall be polite, withdraw, and let you watch your show in peace."

I smile at him affectionately.

"Feel free to say," L2 urges. "I'm all alone. Everyone else is gone for the weekend. I need a friend."

I exaggerate a sigh.

"Okay. If I am staying awake I need to watch the same thing as you."

"What should we watch? *Blue is the Warmest Colour*?"

I scowl at him.

"I'm sure I read a scathing review of that. Something about the male gaze representation of lesbianism?"

I exaggerate a pensive expression.

"Beautiful women kissing and fondling one another? Plus something about love, innocence…whatevs. French people! Boobs!"

For some reason I feel agitated, annoyed.

"What other suggestions do you have?"

"Whatever you'd like," he offers.

"Have you seen *Bad Education* or *Fresh Meat*?"

L2 laughs at me before he answers.

"All of *Fresh Meat* and little of *Bad Education*. Love the British man-boys, huh?"

He shoots me a wink with a smirk.

"It's the awkward humour," I say defensively. "Does a lot for me."

"*Fresh Meat* is great. A little depressing, but fantastic."

My laugh is followed by a sigh.

"I wish Netflix had *Green Wing*," I moan. "I hecking love that show."

"Also great," L2 affirms. "Stephan Mangan is a genius."

I screw up my nose and blow a puff of air through my closed lips.

"We could just text back and forth about the greatness of shows we are not currently watching. That's not at all sad."

I attempt a flirty smirk before continuing.

"I feel like you've watched all of my favourite shows and I have no good suggestions to offer."

"Probably," he confirms. "I did go to med school and all. Great time to discover shows."

I feel resentful.

"Back in my day, med school was harder to stay in than to get into… That should have been in quotation marks or whatever," I add.

L2 is silent for a moment.

"I think I need more scotch. I'm not even a little tipsy. I feel like it might distract me a little."

"I have no alcohol here," I tell him, sad that I've not even been able to afford a $4 bottle.

"Ugh. Sounds horrendous," he states.

"Why do you need distraction?"

"I don't want to work tomorrow," L2 admits. "And today sucked. Started off sucking. It was one of those I need to forget days, or brazenly embrace life days."

"I've had too many of them recently," I empathise, pondering possible advice. "Should you not attempt to sleep so you're at least functioning well tomorrow?"

"I start at midday. So I should be fine, regardless."

"I suddenly feel less sorry for you," I joke.

L2 scrambles to bring pity back out of me.

"I work until eleven PM. So… let that sink in."

"I suddenly feel like a bad person. Has anyone told you that you're good at demanding sympathy?"

L2 laughs.

"Oh poop. I think sending that makes me seem even worse. In my defence…" I blush.

"Continue..?"

"Oh. Sure. Well. My friend told me he was having trouble writing eulogy stuff. I moaned, telling him he was such a writer. I then said redacted, to alert him to a terrible censored thought. He pressed, so I told him the reason I said he's such a writer, is that he's still wallowing in self-pity and his mother has been dead a whole week! So in my defence, I can't say anything that is worse than that."

I blush and join my hands above my head to form a halo.

"Oh, that is quite lacking in tact…"

"I realised that partway through. We're still friends so clearly I can just continue on like that with all people... Anyway…"

"Bedtime," he says.

"Good idea. I doubt we can agree on a show tonight so I've shut down my laptop and I'm going to take advantage of the ability to get a long sleep."

"Perfect. Me too. Much better idea than *wallowing*."

I smile fondly.

"Thank you for the random chat and I apologise for my lack of tact. I trust you will perform adequately or better at work tomorrow while most of us are relaxing."

My smirk has a flirty quality.

"Mhmm. Here's hoping."

"Good night!"

"Goodnight!"

I put away my phone and smile as I drift off to sleep, unhealthily happy that L2 has returned to my life.

Chapter Nine

○○ **CARCINOGENIC**

"HI, I'M ▮▮▮▮▮," I LIED to the classmates at my fifth school, in Brisbane's west, introducing Outer Shell to them.

Making the move to Brisbane and leaving my childhood behind was a huge deal for me. It was the first time that I had rebooted on my own terms, and I had given thought to what I wanted from the future that would play out as I served a life sentence imprisoned in Outer Shell. This would also be an opportunity to develop in an environment where I didn't feel stifled by the knowledge that my every public move was watched. Running The Church meant The Family had to set an example for the wider community. In Brisbane I would still be on a bit of a leash, monitored by My Sibling, but I would have some freedom and anonymity.

With a new lease on life, I headed back to high school. The choice was made by researching schools that were known for film and television subjects, then choosing the most desirably located out of those. I was very close to ending up in Sydney, however the thought of going from a tiny country town to one of the biggest cities in the country was just a little too intimidating. That is how I ended up in one of Brisbane's leafy western suburbs. To ensure I continued to attend church services regularly, Parental Being and My Sibling worked together to find me accommodation linked to the local Protestant Church.

At first I loved the experience of being back in school. Drama was my favourite subject, followed closely by Film and Television. I enjoyed being the older, wiser person in the class and it felt like someone had turned on a light. All of a sudden the future was full of possibilities that I could see. I made a few friends and started to socialise with people outside of The Church, though dutifully continued to attend church services regularly to keep Parental Being happy.

Before I reached the end of my second attempt at Year 11, however, I was reminded that it was not possible for someone with such a poor memory to succeed in the current curriculum. Around the same time, Parental Being was admitted to hospital with severe mental health issues. The few times we spoke on the phone terrified me, as they included false, paranoid thoughts that Parental Being had been responsible for the disappearance of The Abducted, perhaps willing it to happen because of the pain The Abducted and Her Lemmings had caused me. My grades fell sharply, and again I dropped out of high school.

Having become somewhat independent, this time I didn't wait for a push from Parental Being. I had to sort my future out on my own. Without completing high school, I was not eligible to enrol in the arts degree I wanted, however I found The Film School. Located in an old building in the Brisbane CBD, The Film School was a private college that offered a Certificate IV in Film and Television Acting. I attended an interview, observed some classes, and enrolled.

Between enrolment and my first day of class, The Film School moved from the Brisbane CBD to an old wooden building in a suburb on the southern side of the Brisbane River. I was a little disappointed that I wouldn't be attending in the city building that I found fascinating, but I came to love the new location, forming and then forgetting many memories there.

The two weekly classes were Technique class, where we would learn theory, and then Scene class, where we were required to demonstrate our understanding of the theory through practical application. It took me a little while to get comfortable performing in front of the class and camera, but once I did, I knew I was right where I wanted to be.

Something I learned quickly was that in the film industry there was much more importance placed in how you looked than how you performed. You needed to look fairly generic, while at the same time possessing traits that made you stand out from the crowd. I decided that in order to open myself up to a wider variety of roles, I would need to correct what I perceived to be one of Outer Shell's biggest flaws, pale skin. I did some research and invested in a tanning package at a solarium.

"Have you had that checked by a doctor?" a male Friendly Entity asked, barely two or three treatments into my tanning package.

We were sitting on the back deck of a gay Brisbane nightclub where Outer Shell—sporting tender, red skin from exposure to the ultraviolet rays of the solarium sunbed—was masquerading as a gay man. Although it was all still a lie, it was as close to the truth as I thought I would be able to achieve at the time. Outer Shell was welcomed in by a bunch of gay men I had befriended through a chat room, and I felt safe and comfortable in their company. There was much less acting involved when I was around these people. It didn't matter so much if the real me occasionally shone through.

I ran Outer Shell's finger over the discoloured patch of skin under its right ear. The lesion was rough to touch, and was currently about 19.41mm in diameter (see: specifically the diameter of the Australian five cent coin). Before it had started bleeding, the size had been growing quite slowly. Now, appetite increasing, it seemed to be consuming more skin each day. I wasn't as concerned as anyone else, but to shut Friendly Entity up, I made an appointment with a general practitioner.

"I'll cut it right out," the doctor told me, and after injecting a little local anaesthetic, that is what he did. "Come back next week. I'll remove the stitches and tell you what type of cancer it is."

Outer Shell looked quite conspicuous with a large white patch under its ear, so I received a lot of questions that week. People offered their sympathy and educated guesses, based on my description of the lesion. It was one of the longest weeks of my life at that point, and I began to grow more concerned by the day. I had finally reached a point of acceptance and could see a possible future, but now I might lose Outer Shell. That future I was aiming for might not exist.

"It's an SCC," the doctor told me at my follow-up appointment. "Squamous cell carcinoma. We got it all, so there's no need to worry. Stop going to that tanning salon immediately, and make sure you protect yourself from the sun. You really shouldn't have these at your age."

○ PROLIFERATION SITUATION

"YOU'VE BECOME SO EFFICIENT at growing these, Paige," Dermal Saviour (see: General Practitioner with a special interest in skin) marvelled as he ran his finger over another abnormal patch of my skin. I was casually sprawled out on the examination bed in a bra and knickers that had been specifically chosen to be flattering but not sexy. My hair was loosely tied up for easier examination of my neck and shoulders.

"What do you think this one is?" Dermal Saviour quizzed me, as he pinched the skin on my right shoulder.

"Pearly appearance, raised border, telangiectasia. It's a basal cell carcinoma," I said confidently.

"And what treatment would you like for it?"

I shot him a cheeky grin before I replied to his question with a question. "What's on the menu, doc?"

"Cryotherapy, curetting, photodynamic therapy or excision. You responded really well to the photodynamic therapy on your leg," he added, admiring his own handiwork, of which there was no evidence (at least to the naked human eye). Dermal Saviour ran his finger over the area of skin on my leg that held a secret cancerous past known only to people who were there or who we had told. He smiled as I considered my options.

"Hmmm. PDT is amazing, but at this point I'm not particularly worried about leaving a scar. Work's quite busy at the moment, so I think curetting and excision are a bit too inconvenient. I think I'd like to go with cryotherapy for this one, please!"

"Great choice, Paige! If it doesn't take first go, we can always try again."

Dermal Saviour's eyes continued to survey the landscape that was my skin. It was a landscape made more interesting by many scars, each one of those scars keeping the remnants of a rich history in the present. Dermal Saviour screwed up his nose. "What was this one again?"

As Dermal Saviour read the keloid scar on my left shoulder like braille, I travelled back in time to when I was with Original Companion and he had pushed me to get a doctor to examine a sore that had refused to heal. The biopsy revealed another squamous cell carcinoma, so I made an appointment to have it excised. Lying face down, blade slicing through the upper layers of my skin, it took a little too long for the doctor to stop and ask me to explain why I was shaking so much. Local anaesthetic is only useful when you use enough of it.

Back in the present, Dermal Saviour was shaking his head, amused but disappointed at the ineptitude of some of the people in his field. I reassured him with, "That's the only story I have like that. Everyone else has been really good with my skin since I stopped going to the bulk billing clinics. I have mostly you to thank for that."

"What about your *Harry Potter* scar?" Dermal Saviour prodded the thin scar on my forehead that looked like a lightning bolt. This scar was produced while removing what a punch biopsy confirmed was a basal cell carcinoma (BCC). I chose to get a plastic surgeon to do it while I was under general anaesthetic because the procedure, known as a skin flap, was fiddly and on my face. I'm so glad I wasn't awake for it. Amusingly, when the results for the skin came back, only solar keratosis was found; the entire BCC must have been removed during the initial biopsy.

"I think I only bled a lot because of the location," is all I told Dermal Saviour. "While it was healing I felt quite self-conscious," I added. "But I don't mind it now."

Dermal Saviour jotted down some notes, then pointed to the strangely coloured spot above my left breast. "That one is going to require an excision. It looks deep. Would you like me to refer you to a dermatologist? I'm confident I could do a good job, but you might want to go with someone who deals with skin full-time considering…"

Dermal Saviour stopped short and waved his hands about to gesture in the general direction of my chest.

He made a good point; I did like to proudly display my cleavage by wearing revealing blouses. Under the assumption that someone dealing with skin every day would diagnose, and if necessary, treat my skin in a more desirable way than the GP I had grown so fond of, I agreed to a referral to Doctor Clown (see: dermatologist).

I fidgeted nervously as I sat in the waiting room. It's not unusual for doctors to run late, but because I was worried, my mind started to wander. Eventually I heard a male voice call my name, and I became more worried. Doctor Clown, as you might have already guessed, bore a striking resemblance to my clown doll marionette from childhood. His humorous and mildly creepy physical appearance was not at all reassuring.

Doctor Clown got me to strip down to my underwear and he examined my whole body, just in case there was anything I might not have noticed. Not likely. I had caught five of the last six bastard skin lesions on my own, and Dermal Saviour had found the other.

"The freckle on your shoulder is fine, but I will biopsy it for your peace of mind. That mole above your left breast, though, that's definitely something."

Doctor Clown outlined two courses of action that I could take.

o

Course of Action 1:
Return the next week for a biopsy, the following week for the result, the week after that for an excision, and then two weeks later to get the stitches removed.
Course of Action 2:
Return the next week for an excision.

o

The first action plan was not only expensive, but would require a lot of extra travel and time off work, so I decided to just get the pesky thing out the following week.

I could be dramatic and tell you that this was one of the longest weeks of my life, but you've come along for enough of the ride to know that I've had plenty of experience with waiting for potentially bad news.

This time it seemed like I spent forever in the waiting room and Doctor Clown appeared to be out of breath when he called me. That made me more anxious. He told me he needed to take me into a different room, because his was currently out of action. Strange, but whatever. Clown's Apprentice (see: nurse) helped me into a gown, and I lay down on a bed. A while later, Doctor Clown came in and administered local anaesthetic to my boob through a needle. He then vanished again to grab equipment from his usual room.

The procedure began as you'd expect, with Clown's Apprentice looking on as I felt a slight tugging sensation while Doctor Clown sliced me with a scalpel. It wasn't long before the procedure took an undesirable turn though; a turn that would allow me to make people feel weak for years to come.

I felt the wet trickling down my chest before I saw the first squirt.

Pew, pew, pew.

A glorious red fountain erupted from my left breast. Oh my!

Blood on Clown's Apprentice.

Blood on Doctor Clown.

The wall, the floor. I started to feel woozy.

"I appear to have hit an artery. I'm just going to try to tie it up."

After some fiddling around, he announced rather comically, "That has not worked!"

The bleeding continued. My neck was soaking wet.

"I don't have equipment to deal with this in here. Excuse me a moment!" With that, Doctor Clown vanished, then returned with some equipment. He plugged it in, waited for it to start up, and then the unfortunately familiar scent of burning flesh found its way into my nostrils.

"I'm just cauterising it to stop the blood flow," Doctor Clown reassured me.

It worked, and as I was stitched up there was a gentle feeling of tugging, but it was barely unpleasant compared to the throbbing that was now occurring in my head.

"All done! Now, we'll just biopsy that freckle on your shoulder."

To do this, I had to be turned over, and there was a slight issue. My skin was glued to the bed with my own dried blood. The sound of me being peeled off the bed made me gag, but the rest of the procedure was fine, and after a little help from Clown's Apprentice I was clean and tidy.

During the week I stressed and stressed. It was a week or two later that I returned to have the stitches out. Both the excised and biopsied tissue were benign; nothing sinister whatsoever. I tell people this story time and time again, with the concluding words, in a tone denoting authority, "And that is why you *always* get a biopsy!"

• THE DIVERSITY CHAMPIONS

FOR ONCE I'M ONE OF THE LAST to arrive at the Workplace Diversity Network event, and The Host spots me immediately.

"Paige!"

He leaves the small group of people he's chatting with to greet me with a hug and a kiss on the cheek.

"I read your blog. You're courageous and amazing."

After applying my nametag, The Host takes me by the hand, and leads me to the group.

"Everyone, meet Paige!"

The Host disappears. I note a few people I've met once or twice before at similar events, and we chat generally about what's happened in our lives since our last meetings.

"I took the liberty of getting some Pinot Gris for you," The Host asserts, handing me the glass of wine he's returned with. "Your poison of choice!"

I gladly receive the wine, and start drinking as I'm subjected to the usual superficial chitchat that I despise. That is until a realisation pops into the front of my mind, allowing me to inject more substance into the conversation.

"Oh," I say. "I just realised something fairly big has happened since we saw each other last."

"Yes?"

"I came out to everyone at work."

The wine glass touches my lips as soon as the words are out of my mouth.

"Oh my God! That just slipped your mind? That's huge! How did it go?"

As my thoughts come tumbling out of my mouth, all eyes are intently fixed on me.

"It was really good! With Academic Consociate's permission, I gave my colleagues some of my writing, so at the same time as coming out, I was answering potential questions and outlining boundaries for future conversation on the subject. Really, there's not been a single negative aspect to the whole thing!"

"I'm so pleased," The Host says. "You're already changing the world."

"Well," I say. "It's just my workplace."

"Don't sell yourself short, there are big things in store for you. All of those people have lives outside of work, and your message is potentially spreading to their friends and family, in the positive way we need it to."

"Huh. I can be pretty oblivious."

Everyone in the group laughs, and I smile at my oversight of not considering the lives of the people I work with beyond their interaction with me. How silly to not realise that the people they care most about, that they would feel most compelled to discuss my story with, would be people I have never met.

The Host presents me with another glass of Pinot Gris and I realise that the contents of my current glass have been depleted.

"On me," he offers, and he takes the empty glass from me. "You deserve it."

"Oh, thank you," I say, pleased that I have a little more social lubricant to help me through without dipping into my frightfully limited funds.

"So what comes next?"

"Oh," I respond. "Well, nothing much for the moment. My first book is sitting with an agent. I don't really have any plans until I hear back."

"Are you free next week, on Wednesday?"

"Yeah, I think so. I'm trying to cut down on weekday events, so…"

"Excellent, so there's this Women's Leadership Panel that you need to attend."

The Host takes out his mobile device and his fingers work furiously on it until he puts it away again.

"I've just emailed you the details," The Host tells me.

The next thing I realise is my drink is empty again, but someone else offers to replace it. Time moves forward too quickly for me to understand anything and the world becomes progressively dimly lit. I seem to have a brief sexual encounter with a man in the street, before spending a few seconds in a taxi that flies me home where I pass out.

The following week, I turn up to the Women's Leadership Panel. I note that the event has been created by a not-for-profit organisation called Intersectionality Advocates.

My first thought is panic, because there's not a single person there that I know. Fortunately, there's complimentary wine. I decide to limit myself to one, and that serves well to give me the courage to introduce myself to a few people, jumping right into telling them about my past.

"Hi, I'm Paige, and I'm here because I am a woman who has been through a gender transition."

I'm met with a range of reactions, mostly positive, although some people make comments that indicate they view me as a guy in drag; not a woman, but a successful impersonator. Mildly intoxicated, and still somewhat shy about discussing the topic in person with strangers, I hold my tongue and welcome the news that the panel is to begin.

It's great listening to the keynote speaker, a favourite senator, followed by a panel of three women that include one lesbian, one bisexual and one of intersex status. I feel annoyed that transgender people are not represented at all. I wonder if there are any that would be open to speaking on such a panel. *I definitely would*, I think. *But I will have to learn to do it without drinking first.*

After the event, I stay around and chat to as many people as I can, practising coming out to people in person. I also introduce myself to the senator, but at the last moment fear grips me and I cannot out myself to her.

The majority of the attendees leave, and there is soon just one small group, with one woman in particular that I feel drawn to.

I introduce myself to her, and find out that she is both an intern, and a lesbian. Although we haven't met, she recognises my name, as she was a student at The Medical College until the previous year. We chat excitedly with each other until we're told that we need to move on to allow the event organisers to pack up.

Leaving with some of the organisers, we both fight to claim to be the one who has more passion for changing things for the community. We both want to make a difference, and we both feel that we are not currently doing enough. We're told that the organisation have some volunteer positions that need filling, and if we're really serious, we should both apply.

The following day I do some digging to find the Intersectionality Advocates job listings, and I apply to be their Coordinator of Gender Diversity. While I wait, I start to feel lonely again, so I reach out to L2 to fill the void.

"Several hours of work to go still? She says, sipping wine, relaxing…"

"Yeah, two more," L2 moans. "I cannot wait. This is the worst shift."

"Poorly timed trolling? Soz," I apologise, backpedalling. "Why's it been so bad?"

"So many reviews needed. Simultaneously. Chest pains, PR bleeds, rectal prolapsed, and now someone is in atrial fibrillation. All require me to sit and think and physically see. But I get like three pages every fifteen minutes."

Trying to mentally put myself in his shoes, I quickly become anxious.

"That sounds awful. Not long until your several days off…"

He disappears for a few hours, and I sit around twiddling my thumbs. I realise that between work and diversity events, it's been a while since I've caught up with Bosom Buddy, so I give them a call and ask them to visit for wine, cheese, and deep discussion on all the things that are wrong with the world that we would change if we had the power of influence. In female form, Bosom Buddy opts instead drive over to pick me up, and take me back to her place.

Several bottles of wine in, and I finally admit to Bosom Buddy that I am in an unfathomably deep hole of debt, and have decided that the best way to dig myself out is to embark on another round of couch surfing between house-sitting gigs. I tell her that I've heard loads of people need someone to look after their pets and plants for several months at a time, so they offer free rent in exchange for some light maintenance. I also tell her how I've realised that I end up unhappy with every housemate situation long term, so I need to find something out of the ordinary that works for me. I figure, maybe a nomadic lifestyle would be more my thing.

Partway into explaining upcoming moves, I finally hear back from L2.

"Leaving hospital now! WOOHOO!"

Something between a cry and laughter escapes his body. Well, an emoji. This isn't IRL communication, after all.

"You're probably in bed…"

Bosom Buddy looks over at me.

"Who are you texting? Is that the doctor you were telling me about?"

I nod as I craft a reply.

"I'm philosophising," I tell L2. "Not in bed. Telling my friend about all my ideas about cultural discovery."

"Oh? Anything particularly revolutionary?"

"Nothing is revolutionary," I casually say. "But we are talking about thinking outside of societal expectations to find lifestyles that suit individuals. From nine to five jobs, to house sitting long term."

"Ah, well, if you think of a new job for me after tonight… I'd be grateful."

"But don't you have a new one waiting in the new year? I have advice I could try to dish out, but it's difficult to know if it would be any good in your specific situation. You know, mindfulness, that sort of thing."

"I want to try being more mindfulness. Sorry, typo. I mean mindful. And performing a little meditation."

The typo is another reminder that this is not a real life conversation, like the one I've been having with Bosom Buddy. Still, it feels so real, as does the strengthening connection with L2.

"We've been running a mindfulness course in medicine this year," I tell him. "I'll find you some resources and am happy to talk through stuff. It's a thing I enjoy."

I dish him up a satisfied smile.

"Hmmm. I think it'd help me. I'm feeling a little scatter brained."

Bosom Buddy decides to weigh in, telling me that it's weird that I haven't managed to catch L2 in person yet. With that in mind, I take some time to consider my next words.

"Well I can definitely try," I say. "In between sexy times."

My signature radioactive blush heats my entire body at the thought of our connection becoming physical.

Before I receive a response, Bosom Buddy tells me that she's too tired to stay awake, and I should update her in the morning. I wish her a deep sleep and let her know that I'll crash on the couch and find my way home when the sun comes up.

L2 laughs, then sends his real response.

"So you're still up you say…"

I bite my lip, and contemplate a reply, but he beats me to it.

"Actually I just had two scotches so forget driving. I am light weight as they come. Currently getting my dose of hyper masculinity by watching Conan the barbarian at midnight."

I grin.

"I'm over at my friend's place anyway."

"Because my brain won't shut off," he adds.

"Oh dear."

We both laugh. Both in our separate locations. Me, alone on my friend's sofa, cuddling a cushion. Him, presumably alone in bed, maybe naked or in the boxer briefs I'd seen in photos way back before his disappearance.

"I've a satisfied blush happening," he tells me. "This movie is so dumb. I love it."

"Cute face," I tell him. "I'd like to see that expression for real some time."

"My neighbours are being so loud," he complains. "Over the brazen violence of the film too. At midnight! What has this world come to?"

Frustrated that he's ignored my advance, I put my phone away. We both fall asleep intoxicated and alone.

Chapter Ten

○○ **HOMECOMING**

I TOOK A QUICK MOMENT to revise the plan in my head, hastily pushed Outer Shell through the door of the Fortitude Valley liquor store, clasped the cheapest bottle of vintage port on the shelf, surrendered my last few dollars and swiftly escaped back through the door. A short, hurried scramble and I was back in the shoebox apartment I lived in by myself, pouring the first glass. The alcohol would calm my nerves so I could follow through.

The apartment—or flat—that I was living in, alone, was at the top of a very steep hill in a suburb that was conveniently located a short walk from Fortitude Valley, the nightclub district of Brisbane. For only $60 a week, I was able to live in a decrepit old space with uneven, rotting floorboards that in some places I didn't trust to keep me from plummeting to the ground below. The windows didn't lock properly, but I doubted anybody would try to break in and burgle such a neglected building.

I threw back the first glass, not wanting to waste a single moment. Cradling the glass, I slowed the pace to savour the unexpectedly pleasing experience my palate was having. Thoughts became less coherent. I drank another glass, and my feelings became more positive. The sensation of intoxication warmed me from deep inside. Abandoning the glass, I nursed the bottle between swigs. I felt comforted as I downed the rest of the liquid. There was no world outside this moment. Maybe I didn't want to throw myself off the Story Bridge tonight. I would do it tomorrow, or whenever it was that I would be able to scrape together enough cash for another bottle.

"Don't apologise to me, apologise to yourself," a female Friendly Entity from my film class told me, stroking Outer Shell as it hugged the bowl of the toilet it was draped over. Another exciting display of digestive pyrotechnics, and then it was done.

The world went black.

The night wasn't meant to end that way. Months into film school, a group of us decided to get together to watch a few episodes of Star Trek because our scene for the following week was from one of the episodes. Outer Shell was to play Lieutenant Commander Data; I found that particularly amusing. I was slowly improving in my dealings with people, but still felt panic at the thought of interacting with my classmates in a setting with no purpose other than to watch the episodes and engage in conversation. Alcohol had become my friend for this type of situation, because it silenced whatever part of my brain it was that actively sought to sabotage my social endeavours. Or so I thought.

On this particular night, I had chosen a bottle of bourbon whiskey, because it was cheap and potent. In hindsight, it would have been better to go with something weaker. From the very beginning I found the situation highly stressful. Because I didn't know what to say to anyone, I accelerated my alcohol intake. Far too quickly. Most of that night has vanished, but I do remember a very awkward walk down a hallway, feeling as though the world was sideways, and of course waves of vomit coating Friendly Entity's bathroom, followed by my profuse, drunken apology.

I remembered just enough to feel ashamed when I dragged Outer Shell into class the next day. And I felt fear. You see, when you drink heavily and parts of your night disappear, you put yourself in a very vulnerable position. Anything could have happened during those missing hours. I could have owned up to inappropriate crushes. Perhaps I disclosed things that I had never told anyone, like how Outer Shell was just a puppet and nobody knew about me, the Great Invisible Puppet Master who was pulling all the strings. As it turns out—if I am to trust everyone I spoke to—I just became spectacularly vulgar, letting out a stream of obscenities. This is not uncommon for anyone who spends most of the time holding back.

Life inside The Film School was fantastic. We got to break down thoughts and behaviour so that we could sketch out every moment of a character. This is something that felt as natural to me as day to day life, because I was already living in that way in order to present Outer Shell as a character that aligned with the way it looked. I loved acting. I got to explore different characters, and wasn't confined to the one I'd created for Outer Shell. Enrolling in film school was one of the best decisions I had ever made.

I embarked on my new journey with the aim of achieving a Certificate IV in Film and Television Acting, paid for by Parental Being. Parental Being was always so good with stuff like that. Throughout my early life they made many sacrifices to give My Sibling and me a chance at a better future. I survived on very little money, and chose to walk everywhere, even if it took me hours longer. It's not like I had anything else to do, as classes were just two nights during the week and I spent the rest of the time reading and completing homework. This one time, I decided to walk to the set of a television show that hired me as an extra, and it took more than 8 hours. My walk began in the early morning, and ended when some of the crew picked me up from the side of the road, hours after the call time. I didn't get paid for that job.

Partway through the study program, the Advanced Diploma of Film, Television and Theatre Acting was introduced. Financially I couldn't afford to take it on, and I didn't feel right taking more money from Parental Being, so I struck up a deal with the principal to do odd jobs about the place instead of paying the additional fees. I will forever be grateful for having that option.

A different group of students were enrolled in the Advanced Diploma, and, flitting between those and the Certificate IV classes, I started to become a social butterfly, aided by the social lubricant that was alcohol for any situation that wasn't task oriented. The coursework included a lot of self-exploration, and it was then that I noted the difference between how I felt around people when I had a clear objective, and how I felt around people when there was no clear objective. Love of film was unfortunately not enough to keep me happy, and as classes continued to urge us to look deep within, I became increasingly unhappy with my lot in life.

○ ADDICTIVE PERSONALITY

QUANTUM CHESHIRE ANNOUNCED THAT he had decided to use his small fortune from the floods to relocate across the ocean. Still deeply resentful and unwilling to have an adult discussion, I was all too pleased. This presented me with the opportunity to cut ties with him, and return to spending a reasonable amount of my salary to put a roof over my head. New housemate plans fell through, and I decided to embark on an adventure to save money and develop as a person. I called myself Couch Paige, and lived on couches and in the spare rooms of my friends and family.

As I rode the train north to briefly live with Best Friend—the 7th of 14 temporary homes in a 9-month period—I didn't have the usual level of excitement running through my body. With my earphones in, I watched an episode of *Bones* on my laptop to try to distract myself from the nausea and dizziness I was experiencing; the reason I'd left work and was on the train several hours earlier than planned. Backtrack a day and I had excused myself from the table of the restaurant to regurgitate everything I'd eaten. We were celebrating the birthday of a Friendly Entity, whose form in this story is irrelevant. Backtrack yet another day and I was getting a spray tan that I proceeded to leave on a good 10 hours too long, causing my body—which was already reacting to me reducing my coffee intake—to launch into an allergic reaction that lasted several days. Not the worst reaction caused by my effort to obtain darker skin though (see: skin cancer).

> *Inner Monologue: Since I have vouchers to use up, I'll try the 'one hour' spray tan next time and wash it off quickly, rather than waste the vouchers. It's worth the chance of reaction to look good.*
> *Body Language: Slouched, still.*

So there I was on the train, still feeling the effects of the allergic reaction and the anti-histamines, heading toward my short stay at Destination 7. This was the same train I'd taken every few months for years to visit Best

Friend since she had moved her family south. Thinking about it, I don't think there's a single other friendship that has remained so close, for so long. I was excited to be seeing her again, but I was more than a little upset that it had to be when I was unwell. She had just moved her family to a place with a pool, so we were going to swim and drink by the water. It was exactly the type of relaxation I needed before continuing on to my next temporary home!

I was overjoyed to hear that both Best Friend and her partner had gone several weeks now without cigarettes. Since the controlling relationship with Original Companion that had forced me to quit, I found it increasingly difficult to be around second-hand smoke. It felt painful. Though I tended to blame Original Companion for a lot of the personal baggage I now had, I did feel a little grateful that because of him I was no longer indulging in something that would increase my chances of dying early, slowly and painfully. After all, I was already in several categories that made me a high risk candidate for cancer.

Really, though, better incentive for me was to maintain the ability to taste fine foods and to smell subtle scents. Well, not all scents.

Before long I had a tumbler filled with vodka and lemonade, and was sitting in a bikini by Best Friend's pool. The water was freezing, so I didn't go in any further than my calves. I just sat there with Best Friend and her child, chatting, drinking, relaxing...

Wonderful. Glorious! I felt great. The water felt so nice and the drink didn't even taste alcoholic, so I drank fairly quickly. Fast forward a few hours and we were in the kitchen, cackling at crude jokes and painful memories we could now see the funny side of. Great times! I felt fantastic! At some point it occurred to me that we were going through the lemonade too quickly, so I started to pour more vodka and less lemonade into each glass.

o

Journal Entry, 2012:
Everything becomes fuzzy from here, but then suddenly it's morning and my head is over the toilet and I'm violently vomiting. My head is hurting terribly and I just want to die. It's somehow hours later and the sound of a baby screaming wakes me. I open my eyes slightly but it hurts. My head is pounding and as I move... I jump off the sofa and run to the toilet to vomit again. I'm shaking. I fall to the floor, unsure of whether I should leave the toilet. In the background I can still hear the upset baby. Shortly after I stumble to the bathroom, rinse my mouth, splash my face with water, then head back to the lounge room and collapse on the sofa.

o

When I awoke there was silence. Thank goodness. I smiled, checked my phone, possibly tweeted or wrote something on Facebook. The movement was too much and I again had to run to reach the toilet before I threw up again. I was in absolute agony and considered asking Best Friend to call the hospital but I couldn't quite find the words, and then she was gone to clean the house she'd just moved out of. After hours of running to throw up it was no longer food or drink, but fluorescent goo (most likely bile). This torturous feeling went on until the late afternoon, when I was finally able to sip some water and not bring it back up involuntarily.

Despite the fact that I had been sick and was taking medication I should have known better because I had already lived that day over so many times. The word addiction played over in my mind. The cigarettes I had successfully conquered, the coffee I had reduced, but they were not my only addictions, and that was becoming so clear to me. There were two addictions still hurting me and those around me. I needed to deal with them.

The success of quitting smoking and progress made with caffeine reduction convinced me that I could do it. I wasn't confident that I could do it privately though, so I wrote about my struggle with addition in a blog. I figured, if people knew about it, I was likely to try harder to succeed. I cared more about letting other people down than myself. I just didn't think that highly of myself.

It should be quite obvious at this point that I had developed an addiction to alcohol, so I won't spend much time exploring it here. Since previous attempts to curtail alcohol consumption had failed, I set up some ground rules for myself. Unfortunately, I found ways to bend the rules, then to break them, and eventually to abandon them completely.

Perhaps a less obvious addiction involved spending money. Money that I didn't have. It started after the floods, as I repeatedly made purchases in an attempt to make myself feel better. Amusing to some, especially since the Shopaholic book series and film, but not amusing to me. Over a period of 12 months, with a feeling of helplessness, I watched myself fall further and further into debt. There were brief moments where I tried really, really hard to stop spending and save money and I started climbing back toward the black, but my efforts would always be sabotaged by the compulsion to spend.

Both additions were kicking my butt.

Each time I walked near my favourite clothing store, I couldn't resist going in. I struggled to go in without leaving with a new item, spending in excess of $100 each time. I found myself validating purchases here and there: coffee, wine, dinner, cider, clothing, whiskey, music, beer, movies, phones, coupons for anything that might possibly be useful at some stage in the future... Maxing out all of my credit cards was dealt with in the only way I knew how. I begged Legitimate One for a loan.

• A SLIPPERY SLOPE

THERE'S BARELY ANY TIME FOR ME to stress about my application to

Intersectionality Advocates, as I am soon called and emailed with details of my new position as the joint Coordinator of Gender Diversity. After a brief handover, I become the sole Coordinator, and throw myself in immediately by submitting a detailed plan for a series of training sessions aimed at creating better workplace allies for transgender and intersex people. It feels wonderful using the experience gained from my late mentor, keeping her memory alive through my actions.

As the time nears for me to move from my apartment, I host a games day with Bosom Buddy and Friendly Entity. Wine and conversation flow, and by the time L2 messages me, I realise I am already quite merry.

"Having a lovely Sunday?"

I ignore my friends momentarily to answer his message and leave the balcony to get water.

"Quite. Scrabble, friends, wine… Enjoying not being at work?"

"Mhmm. Cleaning, reading, relaxing. It's perfect."

"Sounds lovely," I quickly tell him while I wait for my Scrabble turn, downing an entire glass of water so I can return to the wine. "What're you reading? This is the worst game of Scrabble ever."

Somehow the game of Scrabble has finished and I don't recall my last few turns.

"Thinking, Fast and Slow," he answers. "And why is that?"

"I lost Scrabble. I am now having mournful face."

"Drink more," L2 encourages. "Heightened creativity."

"I drank more," I tell him not long after.

L2 laughs.

"I'm at the gym. Punishing my thin, academically oriented body."

I bite my lip and try to flirt. Surely I can get this thing into the physical realm!

"From what I've seen I find your body sexually attractive."

I hang my head at my ineptitude, wondering how my pissed self so often manages to pick up men in bars. I resolve to drink more quickly again.

"Eh. Also, podcasts! Yay for passive learning. My body has flab now. And when you're my shape you can't have flab. It becomes ridiculously obvious. Especially with business shirts."

"I've seen you," I tease, poking my tongue out. After all, I have recently seen him in person, in a business shirt.

"You sayin' I'm fat?"

I realise that the world around me is starting to move at a different pace. Bosom Buddy vanishes, as does Friendly Entity. My feet leave the floor of my apartment, and I land in a bar across town, confused.

"I would never say that!"

I blush for the umpteenth time, and poke at my disproportionately large beer belly causing L2 to chuckle.

"You're doing a lot of blushing. How much have you consumed EtOH wise?"

I giggle at his medical reference to alcohol, and he decodes it for me, just in case I don't get it as I realise I'm now in the company of a woman that I find unusually attractive.

"That is, how suggestable are you at this point?"

"Up. Um. I am passionately making out with a woman who is leaving Australia. Might be blotto."

There's a delay in his response.

"Aww. Can I come? That sounds fun."

Suddenly I'm scared that I'm at a point of intoxication that will prevent me from remembering the moment. I also realise that I'm finding it difficult to articulate my thoughts in person, let alone text, and I might need to vomit.

"Too many people," is all I manage.

L2 half-heartedly laughs.

"Fair enough. Well, have fun making out without me. Just don't do anything more fun. Otherwise I'll be really regretful."

Suddenly confronted with the following day, head pounding and tummy turning, I scroll through the conversation I don't recall. Squinting with my brain brings back flashes of indecent sexual behaviour with my female friend, and being thrown out of the bar for taking it too far in public. I weep as I respond L2.

"Aw," I type regretfully. "We really need to bump into each other, over and over, soon."

There's no answer, and after exactly three days, I decide to send a follow-up message.

"Sorry about all that," I apologise. "I was wasted."

Another three days pass, and L2 remains silent. Life around me begins to crumble, as my drinking increases, and there's not a day free of a hangover. I'm also hit with a threatening call from debt collectors, instantly pushing my debt into an even higher figure. A figure I can't conceivably deal with. But that's not all.

"I do not like this week at all," I tell him, refusing to let go. "This week is the worst. What's a light, funny show that's good for people who are experiencing all of the life problems?"

"*Brooklyn Nine-Nine*," L2 suggests. "Andy Samberg is adorable. Why so bad?"

"Clinical exams are approaching, and I can't stop obsessing over every detail. And there's all this info that I'm relying on other people to provide and of course they're not pulling their weight. I've got a stack of volunteer work to catch up on. There are suddenly all these important social obligations all this week and month. And the tax office sent me letters to an old address and now are all, *Paige, legal action now… explain yourself!* And after six months with a manuscript of mine an agent has decided not to represent me after all. It's just… all at once. Everything would be fine if it was just one or two things. But all at once I'm too overwhelmed to solve anything. Rant over."

Suddenly anxious about everything that has fallen out of my mouth, I poke out my tongue in the hope that it will diffuse any tension.

"Oh, and I'm moving but have almost no time for packing. I shall watch *Brooklyn Nine-Nine.*"

"Dang," L2 reacts. "That's a lot to deal with. I'm sorry. Not cool that the storm arrived."

Still anxious that I've made myself less appealing, I try to claw my way back into his good graces.

"Thanks. I'm sure in November I'll look back and laugh. Nudes could help."

I force a flirty smirk, and by the following day, there's still no response, so I decide to try a little harder.

"Many thanks for listening last night. I'm now all ready for the clinical exams and as of an hour ago have replaced the doctors who pulled out. Hooray!"

I force a smile to try to be cute. It works, as L2 responds with a bigger, genuine toothy smile.

"Phew! Well if you ever need a spare, I'm happy to help. I have done volunteer stuff for Academic Consociate before! I hope you do too! I'm working, so mine will be filled with frustration and anger."

As I continue to allow escalation of my fantasies with Imbibidy Bob and L2, I progressively lose sight of the bigger picture. They quickly become the only two constants in every day, Imbibidy Bob causing me to sink further into debt as both my mental and physical health deteriorate. Despite our increasing conversational intimacy, L2 and I continue to avoid anything more physical than accidental glances in the workplace.

Chapter Eleven

∞ **REVELATION**

"What's gender dysphoria?" I asked via Outer Shell, curious about this unfamiliar phrase.

Quantum Cheshire, feeling especially brave after a few beers, explained the mental and physical situation he was in. He confessed that the female body I could see didn't match up with what was inside. What I could see wasn't who he was as an actual person. Sure, he looked like a woman, but on the inside, he was as male as any guy I knew. Perhaps it was too foreign a concept for me to understand, but there, he'd said it, that's how it was.

He was male.
His body was female.
My curse was not unique!

Inner Monologue: OH MY GOD! BE COOL!! HOLY F■■■*!!!*
Body Language: Frozen.

My heart began to pound, my eyes started to get moist, and I felt myself quickly sobering up as I continued to listen. Quantum Cheshire was seeing doctors to talk about his issues, and it was likely that a gender transition would take place. His female body would undergo a series of treatments, and at the end, he would be male inside and out. All he had to do was pass all the psychological testing first. His family didn't know yet, but that wasn't something he needed to deal with immediately.

Inner Monologue: There's a cure! It's not even a magical transformation. This is a real situation that people know about, and there is a real solution!
Body Language: Frozen.

Eyes widening as Quantum Cheshire continued to talk, I played the supportive, accepting friend, privately wishing the time away so that I could be alone and think. How had I been so sheltered that I didn't know there were others like me? How had I missed out on hearing about a cure? Did I already sense that he was male, even though everything I could see indicated otherwise? Is this why we connected with such ease, even though we had almost nothing in common? I was overwhelmed by all of the unanswered questions I couldn't yet voice.

I allowed some time to pass before bringing the topic up again. When I did, ensuring that he immediately knew that I thought no less of him and wasn't freaked out, I confessed that I was the same, but the opposite. I told him how I was trapped inside this male body where nobody could see the girl that I was. Before he had told me, I didn't know that there was anybody else like me, or that there was some form of cure. Quantum Cheshire was the first person to ever know me, and from then on, we talked about very little else.

Every step along the way, I would listen intently as Quantum Cheshire went into graphic detail about his thoughts on what he was experiencing. I was an ear for him as he agonised over upsetting dealings with his conservative, resistant family. I did my best to be understanding as his moods fluctuated; a reaction to the hormone injections. We grew close and supported each other through the confusing times, and for the first time in my life, I was no longer alone.

For me to commence my own treatment journey, I first had to conquer a lifelong fear. I had to make a phone call. When the time finally came, my eyes shifted from the piece of paper in Outer Shell's left hand, to the phone handset in Outer Shell's right hand, and then back again. I took a deep breath. I took another deep breath. This wasn't like calling Parental Being or My Sibling. I was calling a stranger to make an appointment with a stranger, to talk about something that only one other person on the planet knew about. There was moisture building up in my eyes. My heart was aching from the strain of tachycardia. Even without this phobia of speaking on the phone I would have been terrified. I forced Outer Shell to punch in the numbers.

> Sex Change Diary Excerpt, 2001:
> *I guess in my present state you could consider me to be awkwardly handsome. I'm 19 years old and live in my roughed up denim jeans and unironed t-shirts. Today I was facing something I have literally been avoiding for a lifetime. Had I accidentally stumbled across the building before seeing the sign, it wouldn't be a surprise that it was a community health centre. It had that derelict industrial feel of something the government put as little money into as possible.*
> *I stood there for ages. If it wasn't for someone leaving and looking directly at me, my feet would have stayed glued to the pavement outside, disallowing the final steps into the building. Once I had crossed the threshold and was inside, I cautiously looked around. It felt like every set of eyes knew why I was there and it made my heart beat sickeningly fast. It's stupid how afraid I was of taking this single step. I know that everything to come after this will be so much more difficult. Maybe it was that playing in my mind that made this seem like such a big deal.*
> *I had to pull the crumpled piece of paper out of my jeans pocket and flatten it out enough to read the address I had scrawled down. I was on the wrong floor so I had to find an elevator to go up to the next level. It took some wandering around before I found it, and once I was confronted with it, I became anxious again. As I pushed the button, I felt like I was crossing another threshold.*
> *The elevator opened up right into a surgery waiting room that was littered with*

posters and flyers about HIV and unwanted pregnancy. There was a lot of focus on homosexual health. Looking in my direction, waiting for me to approach was a receptionist who could best be described as a very masculine man dressed as a very feminine woman. I hope I don't look like that.

"Yes?" Transgender Receptionist said in a deep, gender-ambiguous voice.

"Hi," I said as I walked over, unsure of how much eye contact was appropriate. "I'm, uh, here to see Doctor..." Shit, what was the name? "Nurture Essence."

Transgender Receptionist smiled and handed me a clipboard and pen. "Complete this form, please."

I had almost nothing to write down on the medical questionnaire, so completed the form quickly and handed it back.

"All done," I told Transgender Receptionist.

"Take a seat," Transgender Receptionist told me.

I sat down and flicked through a pile of pamphlets. None of it was of any interest to me, so I just sat there, twiddling my thumbs.

"███████?"

I looked up at Nurture Essence. She looked so kind, so friendly. I felt welcome. There was a motherly warmth to her.

"That's me," I whispered.

"My office is this way," she directed after a brief introduction. She started to move in the direction she had pointed. I pushed Outer Shell out of the chair and followed Nurture Essence down the hallway and into the office. She closed the door behind us.

"Please," she gestured to the chair by her desk and I sat down.

I couldn't push a single word out. My mouth was dry. How did I manage to find the courage to be here? What if this was all some big joke that was being played on me? Oh, God. Maybe someone had read my journal.

"What brings you here today?" I could barely hear her over my intensifying heartbeat. Ever the percussionist.

After a little coaching, I started to tell Nurture Essence about Quantum Cheshire, and then how that related to me and my situation. She listened, smiling. I couldn't believe how comfortable she made me feel talking about things that I had kept buried deep down inside my whole life. Every now and then she would pose a question, prompting clarification or further information. It didn't ever feel pushy, so I obliged. By the end of the appointment, I had the next few years of my life mapped out in my head. This was actually happening. Outer Shell and I were going to become one. The first thing I needed to do was to leave the closet I'd been hiding in.

○ COMPULSIVELY OBSESSIVE

"I DON'T KNOW IF I CAN DO THIS," I admitted to Pivot Point.

Sitting in his stationary truck, staring ahead, my face was a tapestry of black streams created with mascara and teardrops.

Inner Monologue: How did I let it get this far? Fear.
Body Language: Shaking.

Things had developed far more quickly than I wanted them to. I needed things to be slow, so that I could develop trust over time and then reveal my past, but things hadn't gone slow. One month in and I was already in love. He was also in love, and he didn't know this important thing about me. I still didn't know him well enough to know if he would be okay with it, but I had to tell him now or forever hold my peace.

"I wasn't always like this," I started. My entire body was shaking. "I wasn't born right. I had surgery to correct it."

At first Pivot Point was okay with my past, and we promptly started to discuss marriage, but days later, there was silence. A few days after that, messages started. He demanded to know if everyone had known, and if he was the only one left in the dark. Was he being made fun of? Each message cut through my heart, as he made it clear that his feelings about me had changed with this one piece of information. He did not love me anymore. I was now the worst person on the planet, and it was important that I know that. Eventually the messages became too much for me to cope with, so I changed my phone number.

Pivot Point soon noticed that his messages were going unread, so he took to twitter, publicly humiliating me by broadcasting his version of my past for all to see. No, this would not do. My past was not something to make fun of. It was not something that should be humiliating if I was outed against my will. The world needed to change, and I was going to do it!

Meanwhile, still couch surfing, I woke up on a couch in a suburb to the north of the city.

Click. Click. Click. Click. Click.

Sitting alone in the dark in front of my laptop, I followed a bunch of Twitter users who had an interest in right-wing politics.

○

Nine Months of Couch Surfing Discovery #42:
I can only sleep in a shared space if I am passed out, drunk.

○

Weeks passed and I woke up in a bed in one of Brisbane's western suburbs.

Tap. Tap. Tap. Tap. Tap.

I continued to work on a secret manuscript.

o

<u>Nine Months of Couch Surfing Discovery #13</u>:
I like people, but I need to be alone to recharge. I do not fit into the introvert-extrovert personality model.

o

Some time later, I fell asleep on a mattress on the floor in a family room.
Click, click, click, click, click.
I unfollowed a bunch of Twitter users who didn't follow me back.

o

<u>Nine Months of Couch Surfing Discovery #69</u>:
I can be brave and face my fears.

o

I stared at the ceiling unable to sleep, somewhere, in some suburb.
Tap, tap, tap, tap, tap.
I rewrote the manuscript.

o

<u>Nine Months of Couch Surfing Discovery #1</u>:
I don't want live in a way that feels like hiding. I shouldn't have to live in a way that feels like hiding.

o

I stared at the screen of my laptop in a dark room.
Tap tap tap tap tap.
Obsessive.
Click click click click click.
Compulsive.
Click click click click click.
I was going to change the world.
Tap tap tap tap tap.
I needed as many people to be watching as possible.
Click tap click tap click tap click tap click tap.
DONE!
I checked into a hotel.
I took my clothes off.
And I hit record.

• ROMANCE, WORKAHOLIC STYLE

IT'S A SHOCKER OF A START to the day. The ride-sharing app fails because my credit card is declined. I then have to sign up for a new account with the app in order to add a new credit card, because it's associated with a deactivated social media account. I miraculously arrive at work early to set up for the clinical medicine exams I'm coordinating, and I work so quickly in my panicked, manic state, that before anyone else has even arrived, there's nothing left for me to do but make myself an instant coffee and twiddle my thumbs.

It's probably too early to message L2.

"Good luck today!!!"

A whole face smile erupts. L2 has such great timing.

"Thanks! It's been so exciting already! Hope there's not too much frustration and anger for you."

By the time his next message comes through, administration and clinical staff have arrived, and for a while, it's non-stop action.

"Where are the clinical exams this year?"

I read the notification, but pocket my phone, deciding that a reply can wait. A few hours later, I manage to slip away for a few minutes to send a reply.

"I'm running one at the Southern Teaching Hospital, but it's also at the Northern Teaching Hospital simultaneously. We're competing in terms of timeliness. Also, people are dumb. And slow. Oh my God."

My face is strained as I add, "My site is running five minutes behind!"

L2 clearly has nothing happening today, and before I have time to get up, he laughs and clarifies, "The students or the helpers?"

"Helpers," I confirm.

L2 laughs again.

"I was going to say – those aren't the words of an enthused educator!"

I chuckle to myself.

"Don't get me started on the students…" I wink, and then laugh pathetically.

L2 laughs at my response, and I put away my phone so I can concentrate on redeeming myself at work.

"WE MADE UP THE TIME!!! We are now ahead of time because I'm loud and pushy."

I smile and blush at L2.

"Totes gonna beat the Northern Teaching Hospital," I tell him.

"How are you going to party?"

"As it happens, it's my friend's 30th so I'll pretend it's an exam celebration!"

"Hahaha, good work!"

I ask him how his day has been.

"Ok actually. Just walking out now. Just consistent. Also, it's Saturday so by default a little bit shittier than usual."

"Well that's mostly good," I say, smiling.

Bosom Buddy arrives, and after stopping to pick up beer, wine, and Friendly Entity, I sit in the back of the car as my friends chat non-stop for the duration of our drive to Friendly Entity's birthday celebration. We spend the night drinking, laughing, eating and playing games. Partway through the night, time speeds up exponentially until I'm transported to the accommodation lounge room the following morning.

"Would you like some coffee now?"

Bosom Buddy is nearby in the kitchen, and has noticed me stirring. I grimace, and try to make sense of how I am where and when I am.

"Yes, please."

I look at the clock. It's early in the morning.

"We agreed last night that you would have the last pod," Bosom Buddy tells me.

"Oh," I murmur.

I force myself to finish a few glasses of water and the coffee, then change into my bathers and sit by the pool with my phone. If it is possible for a body to feel severely depressed, that is what my body is currently feeling.

"Good night celebrating?"

My smile is gentle as I read the words from L2. I take a photo of the view and send it with my reply message.

"It was!"

I force a big, toothy smile. My head hurts so much.

"We are down in the Gold Coast Hinterland and Joking Hazard was played last night. Always fun. How good is that view?"

"I'm rather jealous. That's incredible."

"I needed this so much," I say, smiling more genuinely now. "Are you off to work again today?"

"Yeah," he grumbles unenthusiastically. "It sucks. Actually it's okay, sort of slowly doing the job of three residents."

After I spend my single day weekend hungover in the countryside, I plunge right into another especially busy day at work, this time organising suturing workshops for several groups of students. As soon as I have time to catch a breath, my mind wanders to L2, so I decide to send him a message.

"Suturing workshops done, excellent feedback about the clinical exam from the weekend, CV updated… How's your day been?"

"Very, very busy. Ridiculously so. Suturing workshop? What's that? Are you going to be a surgeon?"

A bittersweet smile sweeps over my face, as I'm once again reminded of my desire for a different role within the field of Medicine.

To L2, I laugh as if I regard his comment nothing but amusing.

"If I was to go down that path I would definitely veer off into the surgical direction," then as a side note add, "maybe I still will, I'm unpredictable that way. However, in this case, it was around 62 students that I organised suturing workshops for. It was stupid of me to organise them for the Monday after clinical exams. I wasn't able to give the class the attention it deserves. Skimming the evaluations, and beaming med student faces thanking me this afternoon, at least gives me the impression it was good enough. I've lost the ability to articulate clearly in a few words, it seems. Why so ridiculously busy on your end?"

L2 takes a few minutes to respond.

"This department. Monday. Unexpected deaths, messy patients."

"Need to vent through it?"

"Hmm. Yeah. It's okay. Just raging. I'd prefer to forget about it. I'm off tomorrow as well. So party tonight… That is, loneliness and drinking."

The message reaches me as I'm walking home via a bottle shop. My thumbs hover over the keypad as I contemplate the subtext of his message. I decide to put the phone away, and respond when I've reached home.

"Well before that last message I would have written enjoy but now I can't! What will you be drinking? I'm finally home, sipping on wine, but I don't plan to have much since tomorrow is work, plus birthday shenanigans."

Following a laugh, his message comes through more quickly this time.

"Good call. Can't be messy for work. After beating the Northern! South*ern*! South*ern*! South*ern*! And I'll be drinking whiskey. Scotch whiskey."

I grin.

"Saturday, amazing reputation! Tuesday, fired for hangover. What's the whiskey of the evening?"

"Glenfidditch. I'm poor."

When I wake, I'm thirty-four years old, and that is the first thing I think about. As I prepare for and travel to work, messages and social media comments flood in, congratulating me on the achievement of doing no more than surviving another year of life. Although hitting thirty-three felt momentous, today I don't feel particularly special for having survived yet another year. I think about L2, and wonder if he noticed my subtle birthday reference in yesterday's message. The context was ambiguous; it could have been the birthday of anyone. As if reading my mind, a message from him enters the mix.

"Having fun at work? I'm about to do PT. Gettin' my beach bod ready."

"I am! I turned up for a meeting that was my birthday morning tea in disguise. Professional Associate knows me too well. Is *enjoy PT* an appropriate thing to say?"

"Is your birthday today? Why don't you share these things? I didn't even know."

I read over his message a few times, and I examine our situation. Two people with a developing friendship, who flirt, keep each other from feeling lonely, but who never speak in person. At most, our interactions in the real world are no more than glances. Should I have told him it was my birthday? Are we even really friends? Lovers? If all this was as real as it felt in my head, it would make sense to label it as a romantic relationship. Boyfriend and girlfriend. Partners. I feel slightly sour at this realisation.

To L2, I force some laughter with my reply.

"I also just got in trouble from Academic Consociate for keeping it a secret," I tell him. "Just didn't feel like a big song and dance this year."

I spend the majority of the work day checking messages and sorting through equipment and paperwork from the recent clinical exams. A reply from L2 is noticeably absent between all the other messages, so I decide to initiate contact again.

"I've spent hours sorting through clinical exam paperwork and there's still shit everywhere. If only it didn't have to be confidentially disposed of."

He ignores the message, clearly more interested in the fact that it's my birthday.

"How many years have you graced this Earth if you don't mind me asking?"

"Thirty-four. I feel so immature for that number."

There's silence again for a while, and again I give thought to an impatient initiation of contact. I feel increasingly frustrated that this hasn't entered the real world, and our dynamic feels awkward at best. He breaks my conversation with an unexpected message.

"Well very happy birthday!"

I can't tell if it's enthusiastic or snide.

"Thanks! I'm celebrating by going to trivia. Apparently that makes me weird," I add, making reference to something one of my acquaintances has said.

"Nope, something you seem to love. Sounds like a brilliant way to spend a night."

I smile, and head off to the pub for Birthday trivia.

"Oh my," I tell L2 shortly after my arrival. "The trivia man gave me a birthday cheek kiss. Awkward."

"Aw."

I put my phone away, and spend the next few hours with the friends who have made the effort to be with me in person.

"We came second last," I tell L2 resentfully when I've made it home to bed. "Oh hey, any chance you're free Friday night?"

"No, sorry. What were you planning?"

I throw my hands up in the air and growl, then breathe out the frustration before I reply.

"Just trying to see if we could catch up."

"Ah, that would be good. But unfortunately not available Friday! Combined family dinner. Can't miss it."

He sends me a kissy emoji. An emoji. This isn't real.

"Ah, well, can't drag you away from that," I say, deflated.

Several days pass, and I receive an email with feedback from one of the doctors who teach our students.

•

Dear Paige, even though I have never actually met you face-to-face, I have had nothing but positive contact with you. You have always been prompt and accommodating. Your commitment to the medical student's teaching is absolutely evident. I wish you the best in your next role.

•

Beaming, I send it to L2.

"Honestly, it's emails like this that really keep me here through the stressful times. I have the most ridiculous grin on my face."

"Aw, that's lovely. When are you moving down to Melbourne again? I've completely forgotten these life affirming decisions you've made."

The blood drains from my face, and I recall the mindset I had been in when I had originally connected with L2. The first time, before he had vanished. Back when we had filled each other's phones with sexually explicit content. Friends with benefits didn't seem appealing at all now. Especially not with him. I was far too fond of him, and disliked the thought of one day receiving the news that we would have to stop because he'd met someone he wanted to be in a relationship with. Goodness knows there was little chance he would end up feeling that way about me.

"Hah! I've realised almost everything about my life has changed since then."

His reply is so fast it's as if we're exchanging words in person.

"Oh? What's the new plan?"

I try to think of a way to cut my whole situation down to a reasonable size for a single message.

"Well I move in less than a week. Have cut my belongings down to five to ten bags. Will be couch surfing and house sitting for at least the next year or so and will be staying within Medicine for that time... but probably moving to the Northern Teaching Hospital. I think that was one of the reasons I didn't chase you up initially when you disappeared. But then I just forgot."

I add laughter to try to make it feel lighter. There's no response from L2 and days pass.

"Dilemma... I've found a perfect job at the Northern Teaching Hospital, but the Head here wants me to say and I love it here and wouldn't have even looked if I had certainty of contract renewal but there may not be another job like this in years... I realise I could have articulated my thoughts more clearly the other day. I enjoy our banter but understand that the safety of me leaving in December changes the dynamic somewhat."

"What do you mean, the dynamic?"

I reject the opportunity to be more honest about how my ideals have changed.

"I guess for me it makes it more risky, in a less sexy way. My brain is a bit too preoccupied with stuff to articulate much better than that today."

"Yeah of course. I get it. It had a timer on it. More adventure for much less risk. Now it's, oh crap, we might bump into each other in more ways than one, some very awkward."

"Pretty much gags. I mean, haha. I did not gag. Awkward typos are awkward."

"Hahaha. Still, general naked fun is fun."

I disappear to join Bosom Buddy on a road trip.

"Yeah. It's a dilemma. I need to embrace the interconnectedness of things, I think. I'm on the Sunshine Coast and of course one of our students from a few years ago is here."

"Oh yeah? Sounds like fun. Doing anything in particular, or just relaxing?"

"My friend's brother hosted a screening of The Room. If you haven't heard of it, it's hailed as the worst film ever made, and a group screening makes for an amazing experience."

A few days pass, and again I find myself initiating contact to express frustration I'm facing in the real world.

"Ugh! Why do people make moving more stressful than it has to be?"

"How so? I had a killer day as well. I'm so drained. People dying, impossible cannulations, dickwad families. The works."

Despite the negative tone, I feel happy that I have any words at all from him.

"Oh mine wasn't that bad. Just people pulling out of stuff at the last minute and pressuring me to go against legal advice. Think it's all sorted now, and as far as I know, nobody has died."

"Huh. Legal advice?"

"Not a huge deal, just was getting pressure to sign stuff I shouldn't sign."

Chapter Twelve

○○ **EMERGENCE**

EYES CLOSED, OUTER SHELL'S FEET GLUED to the floor outside the threshold that was the front door of The Film School, I focused on breathing. I counted slowly to 10 as I inhaled through its nose. I counted slowly to 10 as I exhaled through its mouth. These actions repeated were a technique I had been taught to alleviate performance anxiety. The first breath separated me from the situation I was instinctively reacting to with a Fight or Flight response. The counting gave me something else to focus on. The continued, slow, deep breathing provided the added oxygen my brain needed to function properly in a situation with perceived heightened stakes. Moments ago I had considered the option of packing up and moving to somewhere new, just to avoid what I was required to do.

It's okay, I will only have to do this a few times, I convinced myself naively, eyes still closed. I opened them, pushed Outer Shell forward, and we crossed the first threshold.

To begin with, I sat opposite the principal in her office, avoiding eye contact and fidgeting as I collected my thoughts. Jump forward and I'm running Outer Shell's fingers over the cartoon I'd drawn in my journal for the theatre teacher, considering final changes. Take another jump and now I'm holding the hand of two classmates, a part of a big group circle, mentally preparing myself to speak. And then, just another little dash into the future and I'm hugging Parental Being tightly, willing my heartbeat to be felt to indicate how extreme my fear is.

Falling back, back, back and back, from behind her desk, the principal listened as I explained my situation in as few words as possible. At the end, I was abruptly silent.

"Okay," she said, in a manner that seemed to be the very opposite of a reaction. "I always thought it was a shame for a man to have legs like yours. When I lived in Sydney I was just down the street from where girls would go to get surgery. They checked in as men, and checked out as women. Would Thursday night in Technique class be a good time to talk to your classmates?"

Maybe I laughed in response. It seemed that until recently, everybody knew about this situation but me. I must have been one of the most sheltered people in existence.

Traveling forward a day and I am handing the journal with the drawings to my theatre teacher and giving her a heads up that I was disclosing some big stuff in my journal this week. Life-changing big. It was important that she read it. *Really important.*

Traveling forward again and it's now Thursday night, Technique Class, and I'm in a circle consisting of my classmates, with principal looking on. I'm telling them about the journey ahead.

One last forward motion through time, and I'm letting go of Parental Being, reconsidering as I gaze upon the facial expression that indicates concern. In a state of panic, I make one of the biggest mistakes of my life. *Parental Being couldn't possibly understand the situation. Parental Being hasn't been out of hospital for all that long yet.* So I lie and tell a story that I think will soften the blow. I tell Parental Being that ▮▮▮▮/Outer Shell is a gay man.

In all points of time my eyes widen as a wall of reactive comments come at me from all directions.

"You're so lucky, you get to be a woman but you won't have to deal with periods," one of the girls in my class is telling me. "Your life will be so much easier!"

Inner Monologue: Life will be so easy on the other side. Sure. I can totally see how this will make my life easier.
Body Language: Non-reactive. Tight smile.

"Make sure you don't become too hot, or I might have to date you," one of the boys in my acting class is teasing.

Inner Monologue: Dating will be so different on the other side. I might actually want to do it.
Body Language: Blushing. Slight grimace.

"I'm not referring to you as anything but ▮▮▮▮ until I know you've had the snip," another girl is stating defiantly.

Inner Monologue: I wonder what your genital situation is. Am I allowed to ask? Do I get to treat you the same way as you're treating me?
Body Language: Non-reactive. Tight smile.

"You're so lucky," a female classmate is saying. "Men don't get cellulite."

Inner Monologue: I'm not a man, though.
Body Language: Slight frown. Uncomfortable smile.

"That makes sense."

Inner Monologue: You COULD see me!
Body Language: Blushing. Awkward smile.

"To be honest, when I first met you I thought you were a woman already. I had to do a double take."

Inner Monologue: Cool.
Body Language: Tiny, genuine smile.

"I thought there was something weird about you."

Inner Monologue: Get f█ked.
Body Language: Non-reactive. Tight smile.

"Does this mean you like boys or girls?"

Inner Monologue: How is that even relevant? Gender and sexuality are two different things.
Body Language: Non-reactive. Tight smile.

"Are you going to be wearing dresses all the time now?"

Inner Monologue: This is not about the clothes I wear.
Body Language: Non-reactive. Tight smile.

"I won't accept you unless you tell me that you prayed to God about it before making a decision."

Inner Monologue: That's your religion, not mine.
Body Language: Non-reactive. Tight smile.

"But you would make such a great father!"

Inner Monologue: Stop.
Body Language: Non-reactive. Tight smile.

"You're just a silly, confused boy!"

Inner Monologue: Please.
Body Language: Non-reactive. Tight smile.

"You're an abomination!"

Inner Monologue: No more.
Body Language: NON-REACTIVE. TIGHT SMILE.

"There is no such thing."

Inner Monologue: I do exist. I do. I am real. I am.
Body Language: Slouched posture, defeated. Wet eyes.

With only disclosure out of the way, I was already exhausted, and hadn't even commenced the real journey. This was going to be the most difficult challenge of my life.

○ BIG TEASE

<u>BLOG POST, 2012</u>:
If you had the status and influence to do it, what would you change about the world?
It's no secret that I am working toward something that I feel will help make the world a better place for some. The information that is undisclosed is the how, what and why. I know within myself that it is what I have to do in order to feel as though my life is worthwhile. I know that it is going to be difficult, and I will make a lot of personal sacrifices to make it happen. But even if I make life better for just one person, then I will consider Paige Uncensored a success. To me, each and every human being is as special and important as any other.
Is there anything you can do now to change the world for the better?
You don't need to do anything grandiose to affect someone's life in a positive way. It can be something small that causes a butterfly effect. A smile, or a hug or a thank-you can travel far beyond that one person. Being kind to someone who is gruff with you may reduce the anger they're feeling. Any one of these things could be just what someone needs to keep going, or to prompt them to get out of a bad situation, or give them the strength to jump headfirst into a great opportunity. A single smile to someone can lead to them smiling to someone else, who may smile to someone else...
Can you see where I am going with this?
If you want to make a positive difference in the world, and you don't think you have the power to make a huge change, start with something small. Whether it's buying The Big Issue as you walk to work, thanking a customer service officer for helping you out, or letting someone know that you care about them, just go for it. Smile at a stranger, write someone a card, ask someone how they're feeling. What do you actually have to lose? You can read about my small start, The Thank-You Challenge, *here.*
My next attempt, Paige Uncensored, is coming in just over two weeks...

○

Blog Post, 2012:
If we could just have a few more hours each day, I wonder how much closer we could get to achieving all of our goals.
It's the hectic weekend just gone that has me wondering about this. I spent most of it stressed to the max, certain that there was no way I could complete everything in time, and concerned that I was going to snap and not get through any of it. It all started on Thursday morning, when I realised that I wasn't able to get my spray tan as

scheduled on Friday because I was presenting at an information session. Fortunately I was able to shuffle a few things, leave work early, and get the spray tan on Thursday afternoon instead.

Friday was less kind.

After a leisurely workday, I rushed into the CBD for some last-minute shopping. Shopping, stressful? YOU BET! See, at the beginning of the week my agent had put up a link to a photographer on Facebook. Since my headshots are all black-haired and I have since returned to blonde, I figured I should take the opportunity to get my headshots by the recommended photographer. According to my calendar Sunday was a good day, so we booked that in.

This is where couch surfing is starting to become quite inconvenient.

Since I have limited space, I have a very limited wardrobe at present. For headshots, you need to be really picky. The clothing can't be a colour that draws attention away from your face. The clothing can't be a design that draws more attention than your face, and can't draw attention to your breasts. As it happens, none of the clothes I have been carrying around meet these requirements, so I had to do a last minute shop to find a few different options.

Have you ever tried to quickly look for clothes that don't draw attention?

It's close to impossible. I flurried around from shop to shop, scanning for pastel colours. If any pastel colours managed to catch my eye, I would rush to them and check out the design. Most of them had decorative buttons, plunging necklines or logos on them. All unacceptable. At the same time I was also looking for a wardrobe for my Paige Uncensored shoot, which required clothing that was eye catching – basically the opposite.

The time came to take a bus out to see my brother, and I was almost in tears.

I sat, waiting for the bus, trying to work out if I would be able to find enough time between appointments on Saturday to complete my failed shopping mission. I waited, and I waited. No bus came. After quite some time I decided to check what time the bus was supposed to arrive. With horror I saw that I had missed the final bus. I scrambled to find a new bus but the more I thought about it, the more I realised that I had to cancel on my brother or I wouldn't get enough sleep for Saturday. In tears, I cancelled on my brother at the last minute, and how glad I am that I got a full night's sleep.

Saturday came along and I was up and out of bed before you could say, "Good morning, Sunshine!"

Washed my hair, showered, rushed back to the CBD. Burst through the shop doors as soon as they opened, grabbed anything and everything that might remotely be appropriate and swiped my card. And repeat. And repeat, and repeat. Got to my hair appointment just in time, got stressed about it being styled differently to how I wanted, upset a hair stylist, swiped my card, rushed back home. Ate. Met a new makeup artist, got my makeup done, rushed back to the CBD to check into a hotel. Rushed back to the shops to grab some last-minute items. Rushed back to the hotel to meet the Paige Uncensored photographer. Spent two hours on the photo shoot. Ran to a 21st birthday celebration. Broke a heel. Guy I'd just met fixed broken heel.

Caught a taxi to a birthday dinner. Broke the heel again. Caught a train back to the hotel. Deleted a heap of photos from the shoot that didn't work. Went to sleep. On Sunday I rose after having less than 6 hours sleep, which is considerable less than I need to function well.

I quickly tidied up the hotel room, which had clothes all over it, pulled off the false eyelashes from Saturday, rinsed my face, got changed and checked out. I made time to have a coffee and a croissant, then walked for an hour to get to the headshot photographer. I made it in time, but my hair and skin was sweaty. She was quite obviously not impressed. The wardrobe options I presented also didn't thrill her. This was quickly turning out to be the worst day of the weekend and I felt terrible that I was paying a large sum of money for this.

Things started to look up when we chose the three outfits.

The first style made me look young and fresh. You could, in fact, have mistaken me for a teenager – until I spoke in my husky voice, of course. My self-esteem started to rise. The second style made me look confident, powerful, but also approachable. The third style made me look stunningly beautiful. Seriously, if those shots don't get me a lot of modelling work, I'd be very surprised. We spent most of the time between photos speaking of philosophy, and it was really quite enjoyable. By the time I left I had a huge, genuine smile on my face and felt like I could take on the world.

Right now I feel an awesome sense of satisfaction for achieving every goal of the weekend.

Let's just hope I don't have to repeat it any time soon...

o

<u>Blog Post, 2012</u>:
Several weeks ago, there were only four people who knew any details of what Paige Uncensored was to be. Since my first ideas last year, it has evolved several times, to become something almost completely different to what was originally intended. It's not just the general idea that has changed, but the form of delivery. Originally, I was going to keep everything top secret from almost everyone, even my closest friends, until the last minute. It was going to be a sudden, bold statement. My video blog was going to be visually stunning.

But who I was six months ago is not who I am now.

Through my couch surfing adventure, I would like to think that I have matured as a person. Where my original plans for Paige Uncensored came from a negative place, almost wanting to lash out, I adapted my goal to be more positive. Before it was more about reprimanding, anger, bitterness... Now it is about creating a better future, and in order to do this, I don't need some expensive, edited video like Kony 2012. What I have to say comes from the deepest part of inside of me, so why not present it as just myself, speaking to you.

This crazy week for me has been a sign of what's to come.

Yesterday I spent an hour in my manager's office in tears. The stress of the build-up was getting to me, and I basically told her all about it. To my surprise she was completely supportive, and was more concerned about how to approach my workplace situation. Today, after further consultation with my manager, I spoke with my team.

The response I received from them was overwhelmingly positive. I have also, over the last two days, disclosed partial plans to several friends who I felt I was close enough to trust with the information.
It's been emotionally draining, but 100% positive.
I will never be able to gauge exactly what will come after May 11th. There is no way for me to accurately predict the aftermath of that first Paige Uncensored Video and Blog. The thing with people, is that each and every one of us is beautifully unique. None of us see life through exactly the same eyes, and none of us can predict with 100% certainty how someone else will react to anything. But no matter what the reaction of each of you, I am happy with the knowledge that I have an exceptional support network around me.
And I know I'm going to need it.

• PSYCHOSIS, PART ONE

TODAY I BEGIN TRAINING to become a Mental Health First Aider, and I'm as close as I can get to the future without it becoming the present.

Thinking about it though, really, isn't that every moment I'm ever experiencing?

A thought for another day, perhaps, but by then I'll have had so many more. My thoughts these days are so many and strange.

The trainer seems gentle, with grey hair scooped up in a loose bun, and a flowing dress of earthy tones. Her eyes are kind and knowing, as if she has seen all pains and is no longer capable of viewing anyone as inherently bad. Something that comes to mind is the quote about how our enemies wouldn't be such if we got to know them, but I can't remember the exact quote or even who said it.

My memory these days is as bad as it's ever been, I think.

As the rest of the participants enter the room, the trainer silently observes, quietly watched by myself intermittently. In my hand is the fairly small *Mental Health First Aid Manual*, the cover of which is a clinical mix of blue and green. I quickly flick through the crisp pages to give myself an idea of the content I will be covering and through the blur, the words depression, anxiety and bipolar jump out at me. Seen also, substance, suicide, abuse, and trauma.

I should check in with Bosom Buddy, I think.
Me: *Mental Health First Aid today!*
Bosom Buddy: *Yours or someone else's? Need to chat?*
Me: *It's a course.*
Bosom Buddy: *Ah.*
Me: *To help me be a more useful human.*
Bosom Buddy: *I'm glad you're doing this.*
Me: *Me too.*
Bosom Buddy: *Check in when you're done?*
Me: *Okay! It's two non-consecutive days.*

Bosom Buddy: *Check in when you're done!*
Me: *Starting. Bye for now.*

One of the first things we do as participants, is each of us tell the class who we are, and why we are here. I'm one of the last, so by the time I get to speak, I feel I have enough of a gauge of the people I'm sharing the room with that I can be fairly open and honest.

"Paige?" The trainer knows my name because we've each been required to self-identify by writing our names on a place sitting at our desk.

Deep breath.

"Hi, my name is Paige Wilcox, and I coordinate hospital teaching and workshops for medical students."

Pausing, I look around the room and take note of Academic Consociate and Professional Associate, who are also present. I would prefer to be in a room with people I might not see again, with what I am about to say. But also, it is important to me that I reduce stigma, and that is not something I can do by silently behaving as though what I've endured is shameful.

"I am here because when I was young I became deeply depressed. By accident, Parental Being prevented me from ending my life. The whole situation could have been managed better, especially if there'd been earlier intervention. I am here because I want to be the person I needed back then, before it got so bad that I could only see one way out."

My skin is red and bubbling, hairs all standing on end, and I can tell that the trainer is concerned, though she is remaining silent. She thanks me for speaking, and the next participant tells of their reason for attending the course. For a while, I don't hear anything else, because a battle rages inside my head. My chest feels tight. I'm silently suffocating. I breathe deeply, force a smile, and lean in to the person next to me.

"I've got to use the restroom."

Because the course is littered with potential triggers, we've been told that if we need to leave the room, we should let someone near us know why. Just in case there's a crisis occurring. It makes sense that in a course preparing us for assisting in mental health duress, something like this is highlighted.

In the bathroom, I think deeply about the second of three reasons I am here. To calm myself, I take myself back in time and wander through my friendship with Simmering Spectacle.

•

Just moments before the landmark age of 30, I have many fleeting love interests, seemingly catching the eye of every single man I cross paths with. With one of them, I join a group of fit, intelligent people on a day-long bushwalk through a rainforest. We have enough in common that conversation flows reasonably well, which is fortunate because technically, this is the second date and only the third time I've met him. Meeting such a large number of his friends in a situation I can't escape from is more than a little daunting.
The hike itself is lovely, and includes several small waterfalls, one of which we walk

under. *Viewing the world from behind flowing water feels magical, and I have fleeting thoughts back to a childhood full of dreams unhindered by reality. My introspection is interrupted by a man who will become another fleeting love interest, and I also connect with Simmering Spectacle. My crush on her is immediate, and our mutual love of food and travel experiences allow us to easily connect.*

On the next date with Fleeting Interest, he subtly attempts to move things into physical territory. Instead of excitement, I feel panic and spiral into an unproductive thought process. I curse my complicated existence that disallows me to lose myself in the moment.

After some deep thinking, I come to the conclusion that Fleeting Interest and I have the potential for good rapport, and I really like his friends. I decide that I am interested in pursuing something. For this to occur, however, I need to tell him about my past gender transition, and because I don't know him well enough to tell him in person, I write it out in a text message, asking that he take his time to digest the information before replying, as his initial thoughts caused by shock may change after he has some time to think.

When his respectful rejection comes through several days later, I'm hurt by the pain of every other rejection due to my past because so many men are happy with everything about me except that one thing. I decide to keep in touch with him as friends, because I am curious about Simmering Spectacle and would like to see where the friendship might lead.

It's not long before I'm able to catch up with Simmering Spectacle, and she asks me, "Why, when you seem so well suited, did it not work out with Fleeting Interest?"

After some consideration (five seconds, at least), I decide that it's fine to tell this woman that I cannot have children. Because I don't expect it, when she stares me in the face and asks me to tell her exactly why I can't have children, I tell her that I'm not comfortable talking about it. I might tell her at some point, but not today.

The conversation doesn't get much further, because we are interrupted by a male friend of Simmering Spectacle who just happens to be single. He's secretly been invited to join us, in the hope that he and I might connect well. We do, but I soon have to leave for another event.

Several weeks and many legless nights later, a friend of Simmering Spectacle sends me a message that indicates that she now knows about my past. I work hard to conceal that I feel confused and hurt, firstly because I don't recall passing this information on, but also because my enjoyable day has been interrupted by a sudden reminder of my traumatic past. Before long, the news of my transition spreads throughout Simmering Spectacle's social circles, and although I never remember having told her, she tells everyone proudly of it, boasting that she's never considered it an issue like others do.

Simmering Spectacle introduces me to man after man, with the hope that romance will develop, but it never does. Sometimes the men have been told of my past before I meet them. Sometimes they're in the dark.

"Don't worry," Simmering Spectacle tells me when my expression is of concern. "I only tell people I think will be fine with it."

Over the years Simmering Spectacle and I become closer friends, and on many occasions I contemplate asking how she found out about my past, but can never bring myself to say it aloud. Perhaps I do it grogged up, but it's never mentioned sober, so I assume I haven't. We get slaughtered together, support each other through each breakup, occasionally kiss passionately while wasted, and attend social events together. My social network seemingly grows exponentially, I drink more, socialise more, bushwalk more, and then Simmering Spectacle lands in hospital.

It takes some time before I become aware of the full story of her personal experience with psychosis. We take a walk together by her grandparent's home, and she chooses to describe a psychotic episode in great detail. Following physical manifestation of symptoms, a drawn out series of investigations eventually lead to a psychiatric and medical solution. As my social circle continues to grow, hers begins to dwindle, and stories of my past are replaced with conversation of her own struggles. She starts to tell me that she now knows what it's like to have this one thing that causes men to turn in an instant. This one terrible, shameful thing.

Except, our lived experience is not shameful, but rather a reminder of the diversity of humanity, what can go wrong, and how little we understand about ourselves as a species. As she inadvertently insults me over and over by struggling with her mental health issues, it becomes clearer to me that she doesn't really understand my situation. Each time I remain silent, but sift through ideas in my head, waiting for The Instigator to push me over the edge, cause me to write an Open Letter about my past, and then a much more detailed blog, after which Simmering Spectacle at first fawns over me but then continues to express her displeasure at being absent from the stories.

•

Back in the present, as I re-enter the *Mental Health First Aid* training room, the trainer looks at me with an expression that indicates concern. I smile and shake my head to communicate that there's no need for such concern. *The worst*, I think, *is behind me.*

No.

It most certainly is not.

Chapter Thirteen

○○ **VOICELESS**

"You fucking freak!"
I jumped, startled and disoriented.

Inner Monologue: It's okay. I'm back in my bedroom now. Alone, safe, hidden. No, I'm not okay. How am I going to go through with this?
Body Language: Quivering heap.

I stumbled out of bed, dragged myself to the bathroom and stared into the mirror at myself. Halfway between genders, make-up smeared, there was no contesting that I was ugly. How the hell was I going to go through with this? I watched my image distort as tears obscured my vision, prompted by an overwhelming flash flood of memories from the preceding evening; my first night out presenting as female.

"I have to admit, I still don't really understand it, but I'm your friend and I support you," Friendly Entity told me. Friendly Entity, my high school friend, the second person in the world to know me.

"Thanks," I said. "I'm really scared and I needed to hear that."

"Do you think people can tell?"

"I think so," I shrugged. "I don't look very good yet."

"You don't look that bad. Let's dance!"

Friendly Entity grabbed my hand and pulled me onto the dancefloor of the pub. I felt incredibly fortunate to have his unconditional support. Here was a guy who couldn't wrap his head around what I was and the journey I was beginning, but he was supportive anyway. Our friendship was too deep for something like this to get in the way.

Awkwardly at first, I bounced around to the rhythm of the music. This dancing thing was new to me, and I didn't really understand it. How did people look so good; so natural? I felt like a marionette with twisted strings, operated by a puppeteer that didn't know what they were doing. I tried to imagine my body as a percussion instrument, and it became a little easier to move in time with the song. I decided that dancing wasn't my thing though. I would do it that night, but this wasn't something I would ever find enjoyable.

Friendly Entity shot me a grin. He was having fun, and this knowledge made me feel even more at ease.

"Hey!"

An aggressive male voice from behind me jolted me from my pleasant emotional state. I tried to keep dancing as I turned my head to see who the voice belonged to. We locked eyes.

"Yeah, you!"

The owner of the voice was tall and muscular, wearing a blue singlet. He had an especially thick Australian accent.

"You make me fucking sick!"

I shrank back and stopped dancing.

"Fucking faggot. You fucking freak!"

Friendly Entity dove in front of me, shielding me from the advancing stranger.

"Leave him, her, sorry, leave her alone," Friendly Entity commanded.

"I..." I stammered.

"You think you can take me?"

I grabbed Friendly Entity by the arm.

"Please, let's just go. I don't want any trouble. I don't want you to get hurt."

"There's nothing wrong with who you are," Friendly Entity affirmed to me, and then he turned to the stranger. "There's nothing wrong with who she is."

"You don't belong here! This is a pub for normal people!"

"Please, let's just go," I begged. "I've had enough anyway."

Friendly Entity nodded, and we retreated. He was seething, and he punched the wall outside the pub.

"It's not fair! I care about you. It's not fucking fair!"

Similar to preparing to create a new puppet as a child, I laid out the items that would be used to present Outer Shell as a woman for the second time, one week after the traumatic first. The list of items was put together from a combination of articles I'd found on the internet about How to Pass as a Woman and magazines for teenage girls that were very thinly disguised advertisements for cosmetics. At this stage, everything was smoke and mirrors, and the purpose of each item was either concealing or misdirecting. Nothing was truthful.

Only one or two IPL (see: Intense Pulsed Light) hair removal treatments in, before commencing, I had to give my face an especially close shave. Once the mottled black, brown, red and blonde facial hair was removed, I applied concealer under my eyes and around Outer Shell's mouth. Using black eyeliner, I drew around my eyes to bring attention to them, and away from Outer Shell's other—possibly too masculine—facial features. With a sponge, I painted on thick foundation, a little darker than my own skin tone so that there was less contrast if I had missed any facial hair when shaving. I then applied thick, black mascara.

"I like that you're using your own hair, and not a wig," an effeminate gay Friendly Entity with impossible David Bowie cheekbones told me a few hours later. He took a break from speaking to suck his cocktail up through a straw. Up until this point, he had been one of my favourites, mostly because he was so nice to look at, and he would occasionally buy me drinks or throw me a little bit of cash after I allowed some physical activity to occur between us. I also enjoyed how witty he could be when he insulted everybody around him, but had not yet been on the receiving side.

Inner Monologue: Well of course I am using my own hair. I am a woman, not a drag queen! I wish people wouldn't think of me this way! At least it will be different after I have all the surgeries.
Body Language: Rigid.

"Thanks," I said.
"I wouldn't go with that hair colour though, if I was you. It brings out the unfortunate red tones in your skin," he explained as he stroked my freckled arm.

Inner Monologue: F██k you! Can't I look how I want to look? I like this colour and I don't mind what it does to my complexion!
Body Language: Withdrawn, flinching.

"Oh," I said.
"Although, you do look a bit like that redhead on Sex and the City," he mused.
"She's like twice my age!"
"And hella ugly," the gay man graciously added.
"I have to pee," I lied, excusing myself.
"Men's or women's toilet, darling?" I heard him snigger as I walked away.

I was confused. The Queer community had been a place in which I had felt safe enough to behave as myself, but I realised that the acceptance had been based on assumptions that were not true. I was no longer a part of the close-knit group. I had to be reclassified as a Fag Hag, a position usually occupied by chronically [sad] single women who hung around gay men. As a Fag Hag, I was not entitled to be as close to the gay men as I had previously been, because that closeness was reserved exclusively for men.

In college, I faced an invisible form of ostracism. Male classmates remained friendly, but shared a little less with me, most considering me to be a male cross dresser or transvestite; it wasn't until I was kicked out that I was even aware that I had been a member of exclusive Boys Clubs. Female classmates generally took one of two approaches when [negatively] reclassifying me.

Female Reclassifications:
1. The *You Can't Sit With Us* club. Women in this club would often subtly (and sometimes overtly) make comments to ensure that I was

aware that I wasn't a genuine woman. The more gracious members of this club would tell me that I would be welcome in the club after having the necessary medical procedures on my genitals. These gracious women would be waiting with open arms, but until then, I should keep the fk out.
2. The *I've Always Wanted a Live Doll* club. Women in this club were obsessed with helping me to present myself to the world in a way that they wanted me to be presented. At times, this would assertively come through in gifts of clothing or cosmetics that I would be required to wear, accompanied by comments similar to, "You're like the little sister I never had. It's different to what you would have chosen, but you'll love it."

The beginning of a gender transition as an adult is a wonderful opportunity to re-evaluate how you would like to be perceived by the world, beyond gender. This is when you get to be playful with colours, styles and themes. Perhaps the sight of you conjures up preconceptions that you're a hippy, or someone who is especially conservative. Maybe you look particularly strong-willed, or like maybe you allow people to walk all over you. More specific for a transition from male to female, are harsh, superficial judgements concerning who you are as a person.

What Your Female Presentation Says About You:
1. If the top part of your outfit is low-cut, displaying a fair amount of cleavage, you are promiscuous; a slut. *Or, perhaps you just like how that clothing looks on your body?*
2. If you're wearing anything frilly, flowing, or floral, you're trying too hard to be a woman and should tone it down. *Or, maybe these designs just make you feel happy?*
3. If the lower part of your outfit is high-cut, allowing your upper thighs to be seen, you are a tramp, easy, ready for spreading your legs and engaging in casual sex; the way you're dressed could be interpreted as consent. *Or, perhaps you just like the particular style of that piece of clothing, and you can still decline sexual advances?*
4. If you're wearing pants, tees, or military styles, shouldn't you just remain as a man? Why are you even bothering with a transition at all? *Or, maybe these designs just feel comfortable?*

Very early on in my transition, I found myself torn between a desire to be accepted, and a desire for freedom to express myself honestly. Considering my personality was passive-avoidant, and I had spent my entire life leading up to that point in hiding, it made sense that I chose to be accepted. I allowed people to tell me how I should dress and behave, telling myself that it would only be for a short time. After I had finished the transition, when all treatments and surgeries had been endured, I could truly be myself, rather than the person everyone else wanted me to be.

The trick to pushing past the disempowerment I was experiencing with regard to visual presentation, was focusing on and taking control of something else. I chose to take control of changing my voice. I had two options for adjusting my voice to match my new gender identity; I could undergo expensive, risky surgery that could leave me without a voice, or I could dedicate time and effort to using vocal exercises to change the range and quality of sound produced. As an acting student who was struggling financially, the decision was a no brainer.

Fortunately the curriculum at The Film School included vocal exercises, so used them to my advantage. Prior to each practical lesson, we were required to do a vocal warm up that exercised every body part responsible for sound articulation. The lips are used in different positions to articulate the sounds of b, f, p, and a few others. The tongue is manipulated to articulate d, l, s, and many others. Letters like g and k require use of the soft palate. The Film School had a vocal exercise that warmed up all of these articulators, and we used additional exercises to help with speaking words fluently. This is particularly useful for cold reads and improvisation.

How I Got My Voice:
1. *Articulators Exercise*. I started by voicing, "Abababa, ebebebe, ibibibi, obobobo, ubububuh." Using the same vowel sounds, I worked through every consonant (the next was adadada, ededede, and so on). After "uzuzuzu" I went through consonant sounds created with two letters (ch, ng, sh, zh, th). Each time I did the exercise, I did so in as high a pitch as possible.
2. *Vocal Range Exercise*. I sang numbers, rising and falling, then rising, rising, falling, falling, rising, rising, rising... This allowed me to sound more natural when speaking at a higher pitch, rather than resorting to the unnatural sounds of falsetto.
3. *Pronunciation Exercise*. I chose pieces of text in books, telling myself that I was Reading as a Woman. This helped me to be more fluent when speaking, as I had spent a whole life speaking every word in a male voice. During the transitional period, I was required to alternate between speaking in a male voice, and speaking in a female voice. Sometimes I had to flip back and forth multiple times in one day.

With my vocal challenge conquered, I was ready to move on and tackle my next hurdle!

○ **FALSE BRAVADO**

A DECADE AFTER EMERGING AS PAIGE, I stood in the hallway of Parental

Being's new home, closed my eyes, and focused on breathing for a few minutes. I opened my eyes and concentrated on everything in my field of vision that was not a photograph. Gradually, as I rehearsed, the photographs disappeared. This is how I existed for the duration of each stay with Parental Being; creating darkness around me to save myself the pain of seeing images of an outer shell I couldn't identify with. It was just one of the ways I actively sought to deny my past.

In Parental Being's home there were no photos of me; only Outer Shell. *But that's okay,* I convinced myself. *Because I will soon return to Brisbane where I can open my eyes again.* It was only a matter of time before I could leave this unsettling augmented reality. I suffered through it, because I was not yet strong enough to stand up for myself.

"This is our Paige," Parental Being introduced, when someone from The Church dropped by unexpectedly.

"Hi," I said, awkwardly.

"Paige lives in Brisbane, and works at a medical college," Parental Being told the stranger, careful to avoid any words that would confirm or deny my gender. "Paige is staying with us over the holidays."

I saw a look in the stranger's eye that indicated an internal process. The stranger looked me up and down, and then looked around the room, presumably at the family photos I was absent from. The stranger then attempted to inconspicuously look me over again, eyes scanning a different area each time they returned to me. This made me especially uncomfortable, but I reminded myself that the moment would soon be over, and the holiday would soon be over, and I could soon return to a world that didn't make me feel quite so unwelcome. My *Paige Uncensored* project was as important as ever.

As soon as I returned home, I set everything in place. I uploaded the video, and from the Final Destination of my couch surfing adventure, I scheduled the final #PaigeUncensored tweet, closed my laptop, and headed to work.

"Truth" Transcript, 2012

```
If you are watching this, you're about to hear me be
more honest than I've ever been.
Before I speak my mind and reveal what this is all
about, I want to make it clear that I firmly believe
that I don't have to tell you any of this. Nobody
should have to tell anyone what I am about to tell
you, but we should feel comfortable to do so if we
want to. What I'm going to tell you is not in my best
interests, but will hopefully help others.
This is not an issue of religion.
This is not an issue of sexual orientation.
```

This is not an issue of race.
Some of you will be confused. Some of you will think I am a freak. Some of you will be angry. Some of you will cry. Some may empathise, some may sympathise. Some of you won't care. Some may never speak to me again. Some will verbally abuse, speak out against me, and treat me like I'm not even a person. These are the reactions I've experienced.
For years I have censored myself to avoid offending others.
What started as a defence mechanism, you know, stopping me from being ridiculed, killed, whatevs, has ended up causing a lot of trips to the bathroom to privately cry. For years people have offended me because I have censored myself and they haven't known any better. Well the censoring ends now.
I identify as a heterosexual woman, but in order to feel comfortable within my own skin, and to match the inside with the outside, I had gender reassignment surgery.
We'll deal with the associated physical and emotional pain in another blog. For now there are a few things we need to be clear on, and again, I'll elaborate in later videos. I do not identify as transgender. I do not identify as a transsexual. I do not identify as queer. I do not identify as homosexual. And for the record, I don't have anything against anyone who identifies with any of those labels. I am a woman. I am human. I think, I feel, I dream and I make mistakes.
I can't speak for everyone in my situation, but here's the deal with me.
I am not a man. Don't ever refer to me as a man. I am not gender neutral. Don't ever refer to me as 'it.'
If you refuse to call me Paige, you are offending me. If you refuse to refer to me as female, you are offending me. This is NOT a lifestyle choice, this is a medical history, and one that generally has little impact on the present.
To reiterate, this has nothing to do with religion or sexual orientation; I am just a woman, and it's time to work on changing the warped way society views us. You have only two options here. Option 1, you can be supportive. To show your support and take away the stigma associated with my past, you can like this video and share it around. Option 2, you can be against who and what I am. To do this, either dislike the video or doing nothing.

Support, like and share. Against, dislike or do nothing.
See you soon.

While I attended a full day workshop to become a Medical College LGBT Supporter (Supporting the diversity of sexuality and gender of students and staff), the first *Paige Uncensored* video was automatically released. During the day, while I was away from my phone, the scheduled tweets ensured that no matter what time people checked Twitter, they heard about my video. Mentions and retweets came in thick and fast, without me around to notice them, and I started to trend on Twitter. My IMDb profile shot up in popularity as curious people looked into the girl behind the video, and in my absence, a discussion on transgender issues began. Without wasting any time, I uploaded a second video.

"Shadows" Transcript, 2012

Let me paint you a picture.
You are born. You interact with your first people, your family. You form bonds with these people. You learn to trust them. You age and engage with them. You learn to talk about your feelings with them. When you feel confident, you open up completely to them. You tell them everything that's been bottling up inside you your whole life that you've never really understood because it doesn't seem like anyone else is going through the same thing. You are called an abomination. You're told you're sick. You're told you'll go to hell. You're labelled a freak.
Most people with my medical history will go through this.
The first people we learn to trust inevitably destroy our ability to trust new people as adults. Our family, our childhood friends, most of them, out of ignorance will drive us into the shadows. We can't change what we feel, who we are. Those of us who aren't successful at suicide, we will still go after our dreams, but we will abandon those who we once held dear. Those who we'd trusted enough to reveal our deepest, darkest secret. We'll stop at nothing to blend into the background, to hide our past.
Disclosure is not as easy as you think.
When I meet someone new, I have an automatic assumption that if I tell them I've had gender reassignment surgery, they will verbally abuse me, rape me, try to burn me at the stake. When I start a new job, I have an automatic assumption that if my

employer finds out about my medical history, they'll let me go immediately. When I find myself in a relationship, I have an automatic assumption that if I allow them to find out that I previously had another name, they will hate me and leave me like those I first trusted.
So please, don't judge me, this is not like telling someone you've had a tooth removed.

For six months I was flooded with messages from friends and strangers. I was bombarded with questions, commendations, threats, and requests to mentor or counsel women in similar situations. At six months, I didn't want to talk about the subject at all. I became annoyed whenever someone brought up the word transgender, mentioned my videos, or asked me how things were going with my family. I started snapping at people and asked them to leave me alone, desperately trying to escape my past again. I attempted to find love, and failed miserably. At six months, majorly pissed off, I decided to return to the limelight with another video.

"Christmas Special" Transcript, 2012

Do you ever blink and realise you've just done something?
This has been a long-standing issue with me, mostly with compulsive shopping. It's no secret that on occasion I will suddenly realise that I am outside a store with bags full of purchases, wondering how it all happened. Gosh credit cards are evil, not just for the fact that you can spend money you don't have, but also because you can do it with such ease. For years this was the case with a particular fashion boutique, though I have managed to somehow overcome that, probably mostly because I avoid walking into the store in the first place, but also because I so rarely have an occasion that suits the type of attire they sell.
Why am I bringing this up?
Well, around January 2010, when I was fairly freshly single and feeling lonely late at night, I signed up for internet dating. The ad was so enticing that I had to at least fill out the survey that's supposed to help with matching you with potential partners on deep levels of compatibility. Or whatever. By the time I got to the end of the survey I was exhausted. Seriously, there were so many questions about so many different things! After spending so much time on the survey it seemed a waste to not sign up and give

myself a chance at finding love!

I'm not sure what I expected, but whatever it was that I expected, it wasn't.

For starters, I was sent in excess of 300 matches in my city. Seriously, there were 300 single men in my city that were deeply compatible with me that were also on the site at that particular time? Unlikely. I quickly became overly picky, deleting any match that seemed less than ideal. I'm not sure how many dates I went on, but they were many and varied. Coffee, dinner, cocktails, bowling, bike riding, walks along the river... With each date I felt my energy fading, my hope of finding someone special steadily decreasing. After a while, I gave up and deleted my account.

Skip to this year.

I was lying in bed, cuddled up to my pillow, under my fleece blanket and doona watching Bones. Watching the developing love stories between different characters, I started to feel really lonely. My thoughts went back to a dating site, and before I knew it, my credit card had a new charge and I was browsing through matches that had been deemed compatible with me. I was quite excited at first, reading through the profiles, checking out what different men thought of life and love and whatever else they decided to share on their profile. I have a much clearer sense of who I am now, and that was pretty evident in the specific matches sent to me.

I don't regret signing up, but I wish I'd given myself a day or two to think about it.

Though I tried not to, I let myself get caught up in it all, and became obsessively picky about who I'd take a chance with. Sure, it's great to be able to choose not to meet someone who smokes or takes recreational drugs, rather than meeting at a club, developing chemistry, then realising that you're not compatible. It's great to be able to consider their age before meeting them, rather than realising that they're "too young" after a few dates. But you kinda need to set a boundary before you start looking for some Mr Perfect, because whether or not my Mr Perfect exists, I'm not perfect and therefore he'd have no interest in me!

"She always does things in halves," said nobody ever about me.

I'm not ashamed of my reputation for a full throttle approach to everything, except when it comes to internet dating. After signing up, I planned out my whole approach to maximise opportunity of meeting the best guy for me and minimise risk of ending up with nobody at the end of it all. I was determined to have as many first dates as possible, not miss an opportunity and keep my options open for as long as possible. Unfortunately, things didn't exactly go according to plan. I started hot and heavy, responding to almost every guy who contacted me, but several weeks later, my pace all but ground to a halt.

Are any of you Buffy: The Vampire Slayer fans? I bring this up because there were girls in Buffy called Potentials. These were girls who were all set to become Slayers, just in case the currently active Slayer was killed. Just because I am a bit of a geek, I adopted this term for internet dating guys I communicated with. So anyway, this time I had a heap of Potentials lined up. They were all guys who seemed worthy on paper, and I planned to eliminate a few after the first date, a few after the second date, until I was left with a guy who could shed the name of Potential and become whatever the dating equivalent of the Slayer would be.

At first I had just three first dates, and only one second date.

Three is my favourite number, and coincidentally, where this story takes place is after three dates with a Potential who seemed very promising. I found myself in a very weird situation, where I guess I was in a position to be really picky and keep my options open, but I started to feel like I didn't want to. It wasn't like I wanted to quickly rush into a relationship with this guy, but I didn't feel like continuing the search. At that stage he'd ticked all the boxes that are possible to tick within 3 dates, and he crossed a few off the list that I realised I didn't actually need.

There was still one very important box that needed ticking.

This is THE box, the most important thing to me. A box that you can't really see, but it's there, and I can't completely open myself up without a tick being placed firmly in the middle. It's a box that most of my friends and family tick. The box, basically, is being aware of stuff I've been through, which has very little impact on the present, and still wanting to stick around either because I'm worth it, or it

just... doesn't matter. Either way I knew I wasn't quite ready yet, but I was hopeful and decided that it wouldn't be long before I would say to him, "This is how it is, are you cool or aren't you?"
Here's how it went down.
After two amazing dates, date number 3 was fairly spontaneously organised. I don't think a single day went by that we weren't sending each other text messages. The frequency increased, and it was like we were constantly in a flowing conversation for days on end. I love text communication, so it was no surprise to me when this made me fonder of him. I didn't really want to wait until our next scheduled date before seeing him again, so I hinted at being available earlier.
Fortunately, so was he.
Both of us were fairly tired, so we met at his place, wandered down the road, and had a bite to eat. A few times he touched my leg with his hand as we ate. It was nice. At the bus stop is where it got more exciting. We turned to face each other, and just like in a film, if you were looking on, you knew that a first kiss was about to take place. The glance at each other's lips, then back into each other's eyes, the closeness and silence. For brief moments the world around grew dim to me and we locked lips ever so softly. We parted, paused, and then dove back in with more passion.
The intensity of it all increased very quickly after that.
I started thinking a lot about baggage disclosure and I knew I had to do it quickly, because things were progressing faster than expected. I decided to hint at it so he knew something was coming. You know, kind of preparing him for potentially bad news. With his permission, I wrote a blog about how things were going. I ended with a hint about disclosure being on its way, but noted that I was not ready. Curiosity got the better of him and he didn't have to look very far to find out exactly what I was disclosing. The first Paige Uncensored video is a tad confronting, I've been told, and is really not the most appropriate way for a potential partner to find the information.
We were thrown into a storm of confusion.
Work and health were not the best at the time, so when the text came through telling me he'd seen it and didn't know what to do, I left work upset and

smashed out my emotions in the gym. I assumed I would just not hear from him for a while and then he'd let me know he wasn't interested, or I would just never hear from him again. But we kept texting each other through our thoughts. Though I have faced the disclosure and rejection over and over in many different ways, this situation seemed really different. See, prior to having this information about me, he thought I ticked all of his boxes. It was obvious that he really liked me, but I no longer ticked an assumed box.

Being up front about infertility is a tough gig. It's one of those things you can work through if you're in a committed relationship, and love each other. You can consider adoption, surrogacy... But if you know in advance and want children that are the product of yourself and your partner, why would you sign up for this? You wouldn't, and so far nobody I've wanted has. If that isn't enough of a flaw to turn a potential partner away, there's reputation. Most people care about how their friends, family and society view them. It's no secret if you watch my fourth Paige Uncensored video that there are a lot of people who view girls with my past very negatively. But you know what, over the last few months, as I've disclosed over and over again, I've been surprised at the support I've received.

Put yourself in my shoes for a moment.

To me, I am completely normal. I don't remember another life, I don't feel like the things I do from day to day differ from other girls, and I've never identified as anything different. So for me this situation, no matter how many times and in how many ways I've faced it, it's weird. It is weird that people have to "get their head around" who I am and what I've been through. It's weird that people "need space" to "figure out if I'm worth it." It's weird that people need counselling to cope with the fact that I exist, and that they're attracted to me. It's weird that people aren't sure if they can cope with the social aspects, such as friends and family finding out about my past.

It didn't work out with that guy.

Or the next, or the next, or the one after that. Maybe things will never work out for me, but that seems less important. What seems most important right now is that I keep getting out there, spreading awareness, helping the uneducated see that people like me are no different to any other person.

• A FALSE ENDING

NOW THAT THE FUTURE HAS BECOME THE PRESENT, and I'm crossing what I thought was the final threshold, I realise that really, I'm only partway there. What I thought was my end goal, that's not it at all. Not to cheapen it, but this event is merely changing me in a way that is preparing me for the rest of the journey; one that I can plan for, but not plan out. This event, is just the first of many big things Intersectionality Advocates will help me achieve.

The high stakes of this situation—my pushing through despite the overwhelming anxiety causing me to want to back out—is causing my brain to evolve more rapidly than it ever has before and I now feel that I'm operating on an entirely different level. Time no longer feels linear as it once did. I am now aware of every moment I have ever experienced all at once. As if it were a surge of electricity, this knowledge provides me with the power to complete my current mission.

I get lost when I try to find my way through the high school, and when I introduce myself to the event organiser, there's the typical full body scan. This is done subtly, but to me it is obvious that they are doing calculations in their head. People do this quite frequently, and in most cases I have forced myself to become blind for the sake of my sanity because everyone is much more obvious than they realise. What they're doing is looking for any physical attribute that communicates male.

I tell the organiser that unfortunately I will be presenting on my own. I will need to speak for the full amount of time that had been allocated to us, and will flick through the other person's slides, but mostly, I will be going rogue, speaking off the cuff about my lived experience as a woman who has gone through a gender transition.

"We're trying to make this day positive," I'm told. "Try to make it positive?"

"I can do that," I oblige. This is not to be a sob story, but one of success. I remind myself of the letter Academic Consociate has written for me, endorsing my skills in the hope that it land me a job at the Northern Teaching Hospital.

•

Over the past year in my role I have had the valuable and enriching experience of working alongside Paige Wilcox.
Paige has consistently contributed to the team working environment at the Southern Teaching Hospital. In her role as teaching coordinator she has developed very strong working relationships with students. She has been proactive in promoting an environment in which students feel at ease to approach clinical unit staff and to also give feedback while simultaneously maintaining her professionality.

In her role she has also had significant interaction with both senior academic staff and hospital clinicians. From an academic's point of view it has been very reassuring having Paige in this role knowing that her interactions with clinicians have always been very professional and clearly there is mutual respect.

Her extensive organisational skills have been demonstrated repeatedly throughout the year in arranging student orientations, master classes, workshops, and regular ward teaching. She excelled at managing the delivery of the clinical examinations which was attested to by the comments of many clinical examiners on the day.

Throughout the past 10 months I have also valued Paige's creative ideas particularly in terms of timetabling, liaising with students and gathering student feedback and ideas for teaching recognition. In fact over the past ten months I have often found myself expressing thanks to her for very effective ideas and suggestions.

Overall Paige's dynamic, personable and creative nature have made her an inspiring individual to work alongside. Although she will be greatly missed at this site I would certainly recommend her for any position that would further utilise and enhance her strengths.

•

It works, helping me feel more confident, and ready to sell my story as one of success.

I'm given a tour of the auditorium, introduced to a few people, and then told how the event will play out. There will mostly be students of all year levels, and also some teachers.

The way I am introduced, it takes a few minutes. Adapting my own words, the Master of Ceremonies talks through the major plot points of my life. It occurs to me that this is the first time I have been in an auditorium full of people where my summarised life story is being told in a way that I approve of. Also, all of a sudden I am one of those public figures that is announced with a grand biography. Huh.

I relax my hand and look at the crumpled piece of notepaper with my scrawled topic list on it.

•

Part One – Child
5 years old
Outer shell / disconnect
Fantasy world
Hiding for safety

Part Two – Teen / YA
Puberty / emerging adult
Attempted suicide
Met opposite friend
Sought help and treatment

Part Three – Work
Ally, Volunteer
Medicine

Writing and mentoring

•

Most of these plot points have been covered now, so I decide to rework my plan of attack. I'm still partway through this thought process when the MC has finished announcing me, and has asked me to the podium to speak.

There is applause, and this is nothing like high school was for me. I look out at the teenage strangers, and over at the faculty staff members, and although I don't feel safe, I feel welcome.

"Thank you for that thorough introduction," I say. "I'm not sure I have anything to say now!"

There are a few laughs from the audience. I hold up the piece of note paper.

"I wrote some notes, but I think I'll try something different."

I unlock my phone and open a copy of my first book.

"I'm a bit nervous, so I'm going to start with a reading."

I begin to read.

"*Within these initial memories, I already knew that I was very different to those around me. There was a distinct disconnect between Outer Shell and me.*"

I pause, look up from reading, and say, "Outer Shell is the name I gave my body. *I could see that other people were one connected being, but Outer Shell was a completely separate entity to me. I had to concentrate to move Outer Shell, and was convinced that together we did not make a whole person. I watched the children around me and tried to work out why I was different to them.*"

"*I used the puppets as context to understand the unique situation I was in. Although I could seek refuge in Outer Shell and control it like a puppet in order to communicate with the outside world, I didn't feel powerful. It didn't evoke the same feelings as the puppets that could be taken off and put away. I felt trapped; the seed of feelings that later developed to become claustrophobia. I had to find a way out, but I knew that I had to keep this knowledge secret. From this point forward in life, I considered myself to be completely alone.*"

I put my phone away.

"I promise this story has a positive end, but back then, I didn't know how to seek help. Parental Being ran a church, and there were a lot of comments that made me think it was unsafe to talk about these issues. I clung to the idea that one day a magical transformation would occur, and I would begin to look like all the other girls. Unfortunately, puberty hit and I realised that my body was instead turning into an adult male. I became depressed, and tried to end my life. Fortunately…"

Tears well up in my eyes. I gulp. Auditorium of adolescent strangers aside, this is a level of detail I'm almost only accustomed to telling in writing.

"Parental Being interrupted me."

A single tear tries to grow large enough to drop, but I fight hard to keep it too small to do so.

"I'm incredibly lucky, and I feel so sorry for Parental Being. It wasn't until years later that I realised the pain they must have felt."

I take a break to reset, preventing myself from sobbing at the thought of Parental Being finding me mid-suicide. Looking around the auditorium, I see that I have a captive audience. Nobody appears to be bored, or physicalizing some desire for me to conclude, so I continue at the same pace.

"Because I felt that my home situation made things worse, I decided to move to Brisbane to finish high school. It was during that time that I met Quantum Cheshire, who confided in me that he was male, even though his body was female. I cannot adequately describe how amazing I felt, that as a young adult, for the first time in my life, I realised that I was not the only person like me."

I notice a teenage girl holding her hand to her chest, tears in her eyes.

"From there, I sought treatment, successfully adapted my body to match the woman I was, and I began my career."

The audience are a mottled mix of amazed and upset. All unflinching.

"Because it seemed better to appear to have no qualifications, than to explain my situation, all I could get were cleaning jobs. After a while I did a few courses that allowed me to start work as a typist in a pathology lab, and eventually I gained the skills required to administrate part of a college medical degree."

The event coordinator gestures at me to finish up.

"I promised that this was a success story. Earlier this year, I gave my colleagues a draft of the first few chapters of my book as a way of disclosing my past gender transition, and I am now out of the closet at work. I am well respected, have a bright career ahead of me, and have even been nominated for two Excellence Awards since. Outside of that, I am doing volunteer work in the gender diversity sector, which is how I have come to be here today, speaking to you."

There are less sad faces, and more smiles, but with tears.

"My take-home message is this. No matter who, how, why or where you are born, there is support available, and you can be open about who you are, and be respected and successful. I stand here today, as living proof."

Following the event, I am approached by several students who are dying to meet me. Most of them thank me for my bravery, and apologise for what I've been through. A single student waits until all others are gone, then tells me their story. They are in a similar position to me, but slightly different.

"Usually I wouldn't come forward like this," they tell me. "But because of what you have said, I finally see that I can have the life I aspire to. You've given me permission to both be myself, and succeed."

Listening to them speak, it's difficult to keep from getting emotional. I contemplate how different my life could have been, how much trauma would never have occurred, if someone like myself had visited my high school. This thought strengthens my conviction, and reminds me that even if I don't witness the results, I am making a positive difference.

A small lunch with some faculty members is organised for me, and representatives from the student body join us. For an hour or two, as we nibble on cake and sandwiches, I answer questions about myself, and Intersectionality Advocates. It feels incredibly surreal answering so many questions in real time, looked to as an expert on the subject.

When I finally finish, I see that as well as a lot of messages, I have been sent a video. When I open the file, it automatically plays.

"I love you, Paige."

The image returns to a freeze frame with the Play triangle over the top. I tap on it, and the video plays again. Tears well up in my eyes as I watch the three year old girl's declaration. This is no longer about being the role model I needed as a child and adolescent, I realise. There are current children in my life. I return to my accommodation with a heavy heart, and the realisation that I'm not yet the role model I need to be for the offspring of my friends and family.

Chapter Fourteen

○○ **ROSE**

"It's time to think about whether you want some semen frozen," Nurture Essence told me during my next appointment, tackling the confronting truth head on. "It is likely that sperm will be irreversibly unviable after you've been on hormone replacement therapy for a few months, so if you'd like to have children of your own someday, you've limited time to make arrangements."

"I don't want to keep any," I told Nurture Essence. "I would like to be a mother, and since I will be having children with a man, the specimen wouldn't be useful."

"There are options," Nurture Essence started, but I cut her off.

"If my sperm is used in the process of the creation of life, that would make me technically a father, and I do not wish to ever have that title."

"I understand," she replied. "I will check in with you at the next appointment though. It's important to think everything through each step of the way. There's no going back, so I want you to be certain about each choice before you commit to a decision."

"Yes, I understand," I confirmed, nodding.

"Have you given any thought to what you will use as a name going forward?"

"I'm stuck on that, but I am going to work it out when I go home."

"I look forward to hearing your new name in our next appointment," Nurture Essence said, smiling kindly at me.

I went home, happy with the two homework assignments of choosing a name and considering saving reproductive material for possible future use.

"I can't be Sarah," I announced to Quantum Cheshire, disappointed as I thought about the name I had carried inside throughout my childhood. "There are two girls in my class called Sarah and I think it would freak them out." I let a loud sigh escape from Outer Shell, dropping the shoulders to a position that displayed defeat. "I wish Parental Being could rename me."

"What about ███████ette?"

"No. I have a friend by that name, and I don't think it fits my personality anyway."

"What else is on your list?" Quantum Cheshire asked, distracting me from my negative train of thought. "Not Madonna or Kylie," he joked, a reference to the CD that was playing pop music in the background. He looked over Outer Shell's shoulder to see what I had been writing.

"Mary, Marie, Crystal, Jasmine and Claire at the moment. I'm not really sold on any of them. I want to avoid anything overly feminine. I want a solid name, but one that will look pretty as an autograph. I also want to be free from Parental Being's religion, so don't want another Biblical name. And I don't want to share a name with someone that's really famous."

"You should be able to narrow it down fairly easily with that criteria," Quantum Cheshire remarked snidely.

As Sophie B. Hawkins' *Damn I Wish I Was Your Lover* started to play, I wandered over to the TV cabinet and started to look at DVDs while running my finger along the edge of each case, enjoying the tactile sensation. I came to a stop at a film called *Heartbreakers* that starred Jennifer Love Hewitt and Sigourney Weaver. It was a silly movie, but for some reason I really enjoyed it. Probably because I fantasised about being Jennifer Love Hewitt's character, so adored by men that I could give them suggestive looks to lure them in. *Hah! As if I will ever become attractive enough for that.* I pulled the case out and read the back cover. Quantum Cheshire watched me curiously, silent.

"Jennifer Love Hewitt's character in this... Hmmm... I wonder what it means."

I fired up the computer, and sang along to *Cherry Lips* with Shirley Manson in the few minutes it took to fully load. By the time the Garbage song had finished, I had my answer. I smiled, nodding to myself.

"Young child. I have my first name. I'm going to be Paige."

Quantum Cheshire grinned, and nodded to show his approval.

For my next appointment with Nurture Essence, I presented Outer Shell as female for the first time. This was terrifying for me, because prior to that day, I had only done this at night-time. Why? Night-time was more forgiving. During the day, it was less socially appropriate to be wearing thick makeup, and any cosmetic error was clearly visible. I met society in the middle, achieving a look that covered all perceived tell-tale signs of the process that I was going through. It went well, and I was referred to a psychologist for the second opinion that was required to approve me for hormone replacement therapy.

"What did you decide on for a middle name?"

I was in the office of The First Auditor (see: psychologist), who was hiding behind a notepad. I amused myself by visualising the notepad as a security blanket like the one I had carried around as a young child. He was bald like a baby, which assisted my imagination.

"Krystal, with a K." I explained that it was a manifesto, or symbolic or... something. I could now be seen, and I wanted to be *crystal clear* about who I was. This was a truthful version of myself, and I wanted to celebrate that, pushing the point that I was a woman, and had always been female on the inside. I was definitely not a cross dresser. I also thought it was a nice compliment to my first name, a promise to hold on to some playful childishness throughout adulthood.

The First Auditor wrote down a few more notes, furrowing his brow as he did so. I wondered if the expression was genuine, or if he just did that to feign consideration.

"Alright, I'm happy to recommend you for hormone therapy." My eyes lit up. He continued, "I'll write up a letter and send it to Nurture Essence so we can get this ball rolling."

My first approval! This was so exciting.

I went straight from my appointment with Nurture Essence to a pharmacy to obtain my first pack of hormone replacement therapy, which, at this stage in the transition, was simply an oral contraceptive pill (predominantly the "female" hormone oestrogen), to be taken with an anti-androgen (a testosterone blocker). The pharmacist's gaze shifted from the drug script to Outer Shell and then back again. She pursed her middle-aged, wrinkling lips disapprovingly.

"First time with this?" she asked through clenched teeth.

"Yes," I said sheepishly, upset that I could so clearly see that she thought negatively of me.

"Take a seat. We'll call you when it's ready."

Inner Monologue: Oh my God, this is so humiliating! How did it not occur to me that I would be in these situations where complete strangers, who have nothing to do with the process, would be aware of the journey I was beginning? This is not like seeing a doctor who specialises in the area! F██k!
Body Language: Shrinking as far back into the chair as possible.

I thought back to the uncomfortable experience of shopping for women's clothing for the first time, when I was still presenting Outer Shell as male. The shop assistants would look Outer Shell up and down, smirk, and ask what size my very lucky girlfriend was. How interesting that she was exactly the same size as Outer Shell. *What a coincidence!* They jokingly asked if I ever tried her clothes on, enjoying the feelings of shame they elicited. I did not get any enjoyment from this, but I kept my feelings to myself, bottling them up for a dramatic eruption at some later stage.

At the beginning of the transition, everything felt a bit like a lie. I felt like I was putting a mask on top of a mask. I had to dress in ways that made my body look more feminine than it was, and achieve the same for my face with cosmetics. My voice had to be manipulated in a way that felt unnatural. None of these deceptions were for my benefit, but rather everybody else's. I needed to do this so that people weren't confused by what they could see and hear. It was during this period of my life that I realised that other people were far more preoccupied with thoughts about the genitals of strangers than I was.

Only because I was so desperate to become myself was I able to push through feelings of anxiety to present the Deed Poll documents that were required for my name to be legally changed. The woman who served me made me feel just as uncomfortable as the pharmacist and shop assistant had. Without the use of words, she made sure I was aware that she was disgusted by what I was doing, and who I was. I was not welcome in her world. I shouldn't exist, and although she wasn't allowed to tell me that, she could behave in a way that ensured that I knew.

Hours later I loudly burst through the front door of our little flat, clutching a piece of paper in my hand. Quantum Cheshire came out of his room to see what the commotion was.

"It's official," I beamed. "I'm now Paige Krystal Wilcox! So long, ▮▮▮▮! It was shit while it lasted!"

We celebrated in the usual way, with cheap snacks and alcohol. As I puffed on cigarettes I had rolled, I constructed a letter to my family, announcing my new legal name. To demonstrate my understanding that it would take time for my family to accept me, I offered the gender-neutral nickname of PK; an initialisation of *Pastor's Kid*. The Family could call me this during the adjustment period. Also during this period, they could avoid words denoting gender. In time they would embrace me, but for now, for a brief period of time, this would be okay.

I regret being so graceful.

○ THE AFTERMATH

YET AGAIN, I ATTEMPTED TO SLIP as far back into the closet as was possible, unsure of what I despised more; my actual past, or people's awareness of it. Expanding my social network, I started to spend the majority of my free time with people who were not aware of my gender transition, nor the brief social media campaigns. I gave up on dating, actively declining every romantic and sexual advance, no matter how appealing I perceived the person to be. I drank to forget, and as staff turnover was so high with a restructure on the horizon, I was able to be partially in the closet there too.

Work at The Medical College became increasingly stressful, and on one particular day I arrived to 698 emails that all required me to take some kind of action. Stomping down hard on the rising feeling of panic, I focused on slow, deep breaths, and crafted a reply to the first email. After quickly proofreading my work, I hit the send button, and then gasped. There were now 699 emails awaiting my response. Before I could reply to the second email, I noticed the number of emails had increased to 700, and I was then interrupted by a phone call from a student demanding to know when they would receive a response to the email they had sent.

703 emails.

The light on my phone was flashing, indicating a new voicemail had been left. Moments before I lifted the handset, the phone rang again. The receptionist informed me that there were students waiting to see me in person with urgent queries.

Our Manager had vanished during the fourth regeneration, leaving us leaderless, so I took advantage of the Employee Assistance Program that allowed us a few free counselling sessions each year. Between sobs I told a counsellor of the stress I was under, and I begged for a solution. Although it was highlighted that I was exacerbating my stress by leading an unhealthy lifestyle, it became apparent that to bring my stress down to a healthy level, I needed to reduce my workload, or find another job.

After several weeks of increased exercise, decreased alcohol intake, and a better quality of sleep due to improved sleep hygiene, I was feeling happier and less stressed. I'd also managed to delegate some of my work, but I couldn't silence the voice in my head that was telling me that without any specific career goals, I would be unhappy in this occupation long before it was time for me to retire. Perhaps a new career would be the answer.

o

"Introduction" Blog Post, 2013:
Let me introduce myself.
My name is Paige. Confident, 30 years old, know where I'm going. It wasn't always this way. Skip back to my childhood and I was either the one you didn't notice was there, or the one you picked on. Socially awkward comes to mind. My friendships, they were set up by my mother. A fair portion of my life was spent on tank water, goat's milk, in hand-me-down clothes, with no television. The bruised fruit and vegetables from the bargain bins. My best friend was my imagination and in each of the places our family moved to I'd quickly find a space I could escape to, a place to be away from people.
Life experience changed all that.
Not knowing if I could afford to eat every day until my bank account was topped up. Fine dining, hiking. Travel over oceans, over land. Shopping alone for food and medication in a country where the people didn't speak my language. Getting drunk with colleagues leading to such bad things I swore I'd never do it again. Standing up for my rights in the workplace. Bearing my soul to strangers. Gaining friends, losing friends. Being fired, employed. Studying acting. Couch surfing. And after it all, good and bad, I feel that these unique set of experiences that have been my life have led me to be here, exactly where I am meant to be.
This blog is as much for me as anybody reading it.
Last year I went through some pretty tough stuff, and at one point, all areas of my life (work, health, home) seemed so horrid that I knew I had to put on my thinking cap and find a new direction. Paying a personal trainer to help me get fit and moving to a place that better suited me don't seem all that relevant to this blog. Chatting with one of my close friends does, as it is how I started to see vague direction. She trains people. I realised that I wanted to train people, so I completed the Certificate IV in Training in Assessment.
That wasn't quite enough though.
Over breakfast with another friend (who is applying to go into the Navy), I got

asked, "What do you want to train people in?" I didn't know. My answer was, "Things." That was a direction too vague to head toward, so it was back to thinking. I was looking out at the sky, as I often do, watching a Qantas Boeing pass. Possibly a 737, but to my untrained eye it could have even been an Airbus. The relevance of the passing plane was that I was in a holding pattern. Until I had clear direction all I could do was fly around in circles. It was a good few days later that I realized the Air Force might be a good direction.

So I started to research.

The more I read about the Air Force, the more I knew I wanted to be there. I could train people in Air Force things! Of course with no relevant training and experience, the specific job I have my eye on is out of reach. So I am left with two options. The first is to apply (and hopefully get in) as an Administration Officer, a position I have the right training and experience for, then find a way to work towards my goal. Or I could keep my current job and work hard to get the relevant training and experience needed to apply directly for my desired job. On Wednesday I had thought I'd made up my mind.

But that was before Thursday happened.

After a hectic day in College Administration (the day job), struggling with flu for the second week of working overtime instead of taking sick days, I spent the night doing work experience. It involved facilitating a training session I designed for international students about Australian Workplace Culture. I'd facilitated it once before as an assignment, and they'd asked me to come back to deliver it to a new lot of students. The experience, while equally as awesome as the first, was completely different. I can't wait to try it on a third group!

Sorry, I get carried away when I am bursting with excitement.

I told the other trainer of my plans to apply for the Air Force. We discussed my passions and then the possibility of getting more experience with other training sessions. Everything seems to be coming together, but I still have to make a decision about which of the two paths I'll take. Guess it's time to converse extensively with my friends again. I'll be back soon to share the next part of my journey to the career I want. For the moment I am going to go to bed and get some much needed sleep.

○

"Direction" Blog Post, 2013:
The bullet has been bit.

Where I am is on a train to another town to see a friend for the weekend. I'm listening to Savage Garden. In my luggage is a Calculus text book, Air Force brochures, an envelope of papers from the Defence Force and the results of a survey that were instrumental in my bag not being full of things that are more suited to a relaxing weekend away with friends. I feel satisfied that at this present moment I am doing all I can to prepare for the direction I have chosen. Just in case you didn't pick out that important bit of information, I decided on the Air Force.

How did I decide?

The trainer who has been helping me find direction sent me two things. First was a pack of resources to design and facilitate a Customer Service training session. We *both thought I might do it well. Second was a survey that required me to choose a 'best' and 'worst' of four options for a broad range of scenarios. As I went through the Customer Service resources I realized that although I was passionate about providing good customer service, it was something that I would find exhausting to teach. Interacting well with people is not something that comes naturally. I have to constantly work at it.*

Okay, so that blocked off an avenue.

It was the survey that opened up my eyes to what I hadn't given much consideration. I grew up in a creative household. I'm left handed. My whole life I've been told that I am supposed to be creative. People have called me creative, but what could be perceived as creative (in my opinion) is the product of my naturally analytical, structured way of thinking. The way I write isn't creative. I've chosen parameters for myself to guide me. After I've written the basic structure that delivers the point I want to make, I go through and add details that I think will make it personal. I'm tired, so please forgive my poor written English.

Where I flourish is in the details.

I am most comfortable dealing with black and white situations. I don't like wishy-washy. Sloppy, vague, non-specific, these things drive me crazy. Soon. I like to know what causes things work. Mathematics was something I excelled in until the end of Year 8. Graphics (technical drawing) was enjoyable. Between trouble coping with physical changes and going from an amazing teacher to a terrible teacher, my grades took a complete nose dive until halfway through Year 11 I finally left school altogether. I wonder, had circumstances at that time been different, where would I have gone? What would I have pursued after school?

I don't think it's too late to start.

Dropping out of school after failing most subjects closed most career doors. The first thing I studied out of school was Business Administration, followed by Information Technology Support. Going in a completely different direction I spent years immersed in Film, Television and Theatre. It was writing the page of homework on each line of dialogue that I did best, but anyway, I know I want to train people in how to do things. And now I have figured out I want those things to be technical. I want to teach things that more often than not have a right and wrong answer.

Entry into the Air Force isn't guaranteed.

And even if I get in, I may not be offered the opportunities I need to get where I want. I really hope it works out, and that I not only get into the Air Force, but I get into ADFA, so I can be paid to do a degree in something I would be happy to train people in. That's why I have the Calculus textbook. I have just a few weeks before my aptitude test that will decide what options are open and closed to me. Of course I have a Plan B all worked out, but I don't really want to spend years at university only to have to pay it all back.

o

<u>"Obsession" Blog Post, 2013</u>:
All or nothing, that's me.
In most things, I either feel very strongly, or just don't feel. If I like a boy, I really

like a boy. When I choose to focus on something, I will dedicate a lot of time to thinking about it. What I hear from others is that it's not like that for most people. Where most will find an interest, I will almost always go that little bit further. In my case, the word interest is an inadequate label, because it is so soft. My supercharged version of interest is the reason we have the word obsession.

It doesn't have to be a negative thing.

When I get given a special project at work, being obsessively focused is quite useful. I will plan everything out. Once the big picture is there, I'll fill in the dots with detail. And then, I will strain my brain to think of as many worst-case scenarios as possible to make sure that the finished product is as close to perfect as humanly possible. The less time I am given to complete this product, the less perfect the end result. There is another element however. Give me too long on a single product with no new challenges, and I'll quickly lose interest.

There isn't always time to obsess over the details.

This has been highlighted for me recently in my office. I've been given the responsibility of managing a few new processes that were devised by an external party. Prior to having to use these new processes, I was given no time to go over them with a red pen, to correct or add detail. 'Hit the ground running' is a term you might use. How many times I've tripped over obstacles I wasn't aware of, I don't even know. It's been stressful, annoying. The problems would be smaller if I'd been given more time and control.

In case you can't see the problem, I'll tell you.

The need for time and control create performance limitations. Having had the luxury of time and control consistently for so long, my ability to perform well is hindered when I don't have them. Now that I have identified these specific issues, I need to work toward a solution. Should I get into the *Air Force* as hoped, time and control will be in very short supply. The problems I've had at work over the last few weeks have been good. They've shown me where I have a weakness, and additionally, have required me to immediately start work on strengthening that area.

Don't expect to hear too much from me in the coming weeks.

Early August is when I face the first of many hurdles required for entry into the Air Force. I don't have a lot of time, and I sure as hell don't have control. But what I do have is my specific brain. If I can use this obsessive nature to continue immersing myself in planes, defence force news, fitness and aptitude tests, I might just have a shot at getting somewhere with this. The thought of being able to stand up and fight against my weaker parts and succeed; that makes me feel awesome. I will do this, and if I fail, it won't be because I didn't try my best.

• PSYCHOSIS, PART TWO

THROUGHOUT THE FINAL DAY of the *Mental Health First Aid* course there is a lot of discussion, and I have the luxury of hearing opinions from a wide range of people. Many of them are slightly ignorant, which makes me happy that they've made an effort to correct it. One of the male participants annoys me, however, because his questions and comments make it clear that he has ulterior motives for attending. He is here for no other reason than to learn more about mental health in order to use it against his former partner in a custody battle. What a prick.

I learn a lot about language on that final day. I learn about labels and phrases that have been phased out, and why they have been replaced. What was once commonplace, is now acknowledged as problematic. As I learn, I think about language around my gender transition. I examine words and phrases that I deem problematic, and I make a mental note to do a little digging online, so I can put together some written material to help educate people in my social circles who don't understand why their words are offensive.

It is the discussions that take place as we delve into substance use, psychosis and bipolar disorder that shift my attitude from a place of wanting to help others, to urgency of needing to fix myself. As we wade through the coursework, I feel heavier and sicker. Every warning sign provided as an example has already occurred in my own life, and it becomes impossible for me to deny the truth I've been trying desperately to ignore. If I continue my relationship with Imbibidy Bob, I will eventually slip into a state I cannot return from.

Even without the fear of irreparable mental damage, there are many reasons it's easy to make the choice to completely cut ties with Imbibidy Bob. The enormous debt will be easier to pay off without the high cost of refilling my glass. I've had my last painful hangover, and can use that time to be more productive and increase my potential. There won't be any more of those conversations where I apologise for something I don't remember doing, and I won't have to trust the word of those who were around with regard to what, where, and how events played out. Perhaps most importantly, I won't wake up with vulvar discomfort and no memory of who may have caused it, and how I could have possibly consented in my intoxicated state.

L2 is on my mind as I leave the workshop. I think about the times I could have met him, if only alcohol hadn't been in our way. For a moment I am distracted by the thought that alcohol has played a big part in a lot of our interactions. On so many nights we've kept each other electronic company as we have both sat alone, drinking. I also think about the decrease in initiation on his end, but the fairly consistent response rate. There's still a part of me that hopes that this could become something real.

"How's things? I did a two day *Mental Health First Aid* course. Was really good!"

"Oh yeah?"

I see the little bubble telling me he's writing more.

"What kind of material did you cover?"

All of my thoughts spill out.

"Anxiety, depression, suicide, psychosis… mostly those. Oh, and a lot on substance abuse. Drugs and alcohol, that is. It was good, but pretty heavy for the last intensive day. A great thing to come out of it was realising I'd responded well in some recent situations. I think Medicine needs some quick catching up in that area. I've been having some conversations with a recent graduate that really confirm that for me, so I want to work out how to help that."

I sit on a park bench by the river and look out over the water as I wait for his next message.

"How do you think you'd do it? I can say personally I don't have enough patience for mental health conditions, which is exactly what they need."

I briefly think about broaching the mental health of myself and L2. From my limited perspective, he's clearly troubled, and I can't see enough of his reality to know if he's receiving the help he needs. Instead, I keep my message distant.

"I think it should be fairly easy to highlight the mental health gap in the curriculum with the help of the student union who have deemed it necessary to curate a mental health social media page aimed at medical students. I get students coming to me anyway though, and it's not too difficult for me to be patient if I realise it's a mental health issue. I'm living with children at the moment so it's been a nice test of that. Patience, that is."

L2 laughs.

"I feel bad about it. For example in emergency medicine I tend to avoid mental health patients because it just frustrates me. I really need to improve that. I don't think I'm valuing organic disease above mental health. It's more I don't feel I'm treating mental health well."

My first sober week is great, and a complete success! To ensure I don't have time to focus on the absence of alcohol from my life, I create an especially busy schedule, seeing as many people in person as possible. So that nobody accidentally tempts me in the early stages of sobriety, prior to every social engagement I ensure everyone's aware that I've had my last alcoholic beverage. Surprisingly, rather than the feeling of missing out on a sensation I've enjoyed for so long, it's dealing with people's comments that I find most difficult.

Some friends express that they're disappointed that they'll no longer be able to drink alongside me, and I feel hurt that they seem to care less about my health and safety than their entertainment. Others take it upon themselves to tell me that I'll be able to learn to drink in moderation, ignoring that I've told them that for me, it's important that this be a lifetime commitment. Everywhere I look, I see an unhealthy focus on alcohol as a requirement for social gatherings. It's clear why it's so easy for those of us with issues to ignore it as a problem for such a long time.

With my calendar fuller than it's ever been, L2 slips my mind until I see him on a busy workday as I rush between two rooms that are either side of the hospital café. I'm instantly annoyed by the reminder of the overall unfulfilling nature of our dynamic, and decide not to reach out. It's hard to imagine our first real interaction being anything but extremely awkward now that I won't have alcohol to loosen me up. I also don't want to tell him that I've gone sober, and talk through all the reasons why. I pretend to not have noticed him sitting with his colleagues.

My phone buzzes. Unusual, since I typically have the vibrate function switched off because I receive so many notifications throughout the day. Now in a lecture theatre, assisting with watching students sitting a multiple-choice exam, I quickly slip into the settings and return them to normal. I note that it is L2 who has caused the distraction.

"How is the exam going?"

"Snore fest," I tell him stealthily, poking my tongue out. I slowly add more as I continue to watch the studious exam-takers, letting him know that I also noticed him.

"Odd time for lunch."

"Such is life in my current department," he promptly replies. "You had the watchful mothering look to you. Also, I told my med students not to study for your exam. Hope that was the right thing to do."

He also pokes his tongue out. I realise that some of these students—who are completing Professional Associate's part of the degree—have had more physical interactions with L2 than I have.

I shoot him a few emoji's, then notice a student raise their hand, so assist with the student query before typing another reply.

"I've been running between the exam and another suturing workshop. And oops I missed a student query because I was texting."

L2 laughs as he responds.

"Ooh, suturing too? I might wander over and have a go. Get you properly distracted."

I slowly craft a response, only glancing at my phone intermittently, as I scan the exam room. These two tasks are difficult to do together successfully.

"Cruel. Invigilating boring. Could do with sexing it up."

L2 is amused.

"Basically anything is a little more fun sexed up I guess. Being an invigilator probably more so."

I laugh.

"I'll sexy invigilate you," I say, poking out my tongue. I instantly regret the message, and put my phone away for the rest of the day, disappointed with myself for not doing that in the first place.

Professional Associate relieves me from my invigilation post, and I spend the rest of the day on duties relating to the suturing workshop. I buzz around resetting equipment for each new group, taking note of attendance, distributing and collecting feedback forms, and, eventually, removing all equipment from the room and returning the room to its natural state, ready for whatever class has it next.

Because it's already after my work day officially ends, I stash everything in my office in piles. I take a photo and send it to L2.

"My office is disgusting right now. I can't even think around this mess."

"Huh," he responds. A word I'm starting to find irritating. "Doesn't even have that organised mess to it, huh?"

My thumbs hover over the keypad as I ponder a follow-up to my earlier attempt at flirting.

"Sometimes I read back my texts and think, do you even have a brain?"

L2 erupts with laughter.

"I was curious as to sexy invigilating."

I smile.

"I've no idea what sexy invigilating would involve. Probably role playing? The mind boggles."

L2 laughs a little less enthusiastically.

"Golly I'm tired. Just before I finished my rotation in this department for good, a patient arrested and I had to run the resus. Literally as I was contemplating leaving."

He's doing well at un-selling the profession I've spent a lifetime dreaming of joining.

"Nothing like a good send-off… What's your next rotation in?"

"It's going to suck. It's basically the same again, just in a different ward."

I bet he's going to spend the evening drinking.

"Really just not in your element right now, are you?"

"Hmmm, I just don't like ward rounds I think. And paperwork. The medicine is mostly interesting. And running resus is a real kick. But it's just not me."

I wonder if there's any area at all that would be suitable to him.

Chapter Fifteen

○○ **SEVERED**

NEXT TO QUANTUM CHESHIRE, I shifted uncomfortably. Quantum Cheshire was in a body that still looked female, and my body still looked male. We were seated together on a couch in our flat, opposite Quantum Cheshire's mother and father. I was there for moral support, because Quantum Cheshire's conservative religious family turned out to be not at all supportive of the changes he was going through. We had decided to tell Quantum Cheshire's parents that I was his equal and opposite. We figured, maybe that would make things better somehow. Quantum Cheshire wouldn't be the only person they knew with the condition. It didn't work out so well.

"We have a better solution for you," Quantum Cheshire's mother announced, after spending a considerable amount of time silent. His father looked down at his feet, and then over at the window. And then back at his feet. Anywhere but at his child and his child's equally confused friend.

"You two should be together. That would solve everything."

"I'm sorry, but how would that solve anything?"

"You could be together and it wouldn't go against anything in the Bible."

Should I comment? I looked at Quantum Cheshire but couldn't read anything but awkwardness in his face and body. *I should say something.*

Unfortunately, I couldn't find the right words, so I sat in silence, providing no more support than a body in the room that was on Quantum Cheshire's literal and figurative side.

News of my gender transition was communicated to my greater family through emails that updated them on my progress. In return, I was sent a lot of religious propaganda, with the purpose of reprimanding and attempting to reform me. Parental Being, My Sibling, and a large portion of the religious side of the extended family made it their mission to gently remind me that I did not exist as the being I claimed to be. I politely accepted the religious material and comments, at times voicing my displeasure, but usually keeping my opinion to myself.

Unfortunate family situation aside, the journey I had embarked on was going really well. Although I was continually confronted with embarrassing situations, I was facing them head on, becoming stronger each time I rose above my fears. On the days when life felt particularly difficult, I reminded myself that this was just a temporary phase. Soon I would be able to settle into a normal life as a woman. I would one day get married and adopt some children. My husband and I would enjoy a very traditional lifestyle, but raise our children not to judge others. I would never have to look back.

Each time I pushed past the anxious feelings to be open and honest with someone about the journey I was on, I felt myself become a little stronger. Each time I spoke about what I was going through, I became a little better at articulating my thoughts. Step by step, I was letting go of the terrified little girl that had spent her life in hiding. Very slowly, I was shifting away from the passive-avoidance that had held me captive for so long.

Several months into the process, I paced back and forth on the front balcony of the flat—bulky dinosaur of a mobile phone in hand—as I spoke with Parental Being. Aching nipples briefly distracted me, and I gently massaged my blooming breasts to alleviate the discomfort. I let out an audible sigh. The phone call was more taxing than I had anticipated. I didn't know what it was, but something was making each phone call with Parental Being more difficult than the last. My energy was fading, as was my desire to speak with them.

Stopping to stand still, I leaned on the metal railing of the flat but soon felt uncomfortable, agitated; I was having trouble adjusting to the hormonal changes. I returned to pacing, playing with a strand of my lengthening hair. The red long gone, it was now a bleached blonde with a previously undiscovered natural wave through it.

After a quick recap, again telling the truth about myself, I pleaded with Parental Being to accept me as Paige.

"It's just a phase," Parental Being argued. "We're praying for your healing. You're just a silly, confused boy!"

I couldn't handle it any longer. Things would never change. The whole thing was pointless.

"This conversation is over," I spat angrily into the phone. "Don't ever fucking contact me again!"

I promptly hung up, and just like that, I no longer had a family. Although not all of them were to blame for my anger, after that phone call, I refused to speak to any person who was related to me.

○ A FATALITY

MOMENTS AFTER DECLINING YET ANOTHER call from My Sibling, a text message came through.

My Sibling: *I need to talk to you about how difficult it has been for me having you as a brother.*

I lost my shit.

Inner Monologue: BROTHER?! Are you fucking kidding me? After thirteen years you are still referring to me with male pronouns?! After watching my Paige Uncensored videos, you still don't understand how wrong that is? WHAT THE

ACTUAL FUCK? ARGH!
Body Language: Red all over, shaking. Inflamed.

I exploded, furiously mashing the keypad with my fingers, spewing forth a string of loosely related angry curse words, barely able to see what I was typing through the salty spring that had erupted from my eyes. I suppose I should tell you how this became so heated.

Around 13 years after emerging as Paige, I sat with The Family in front of the television. It was November. We weren't at Parental Being's house, but because it was still the house of a family member, I had my mental sunglasses on, blocking out the photographs that lined the walls. It was one half of Parental Being's birthday and a group of us had come together to celebrate. This included a presentation of digitised photographs that had been put together by the other half of Parental Being. It was amusing to see young versions of both halves of Parental Being. We laughed and said aww as appropriate.

By then almost everyone called me Paige, but My Sibling and most of the older generation (see: Grandparent's Children, inclusive of Parental Being) still avoided any pronouns denoting gender.

<begin sarcasm> *Thanks Past Paige for offering them that option. F██ker.* </end sarcasm>

I had to actively take my mind to different places to reduce the pain of being dehumanised. If I suspected that someone was going to mention me, I steered the conversation in another direction. This reduced the occurrences, but didn't eliminate them. Here, in the room with the television, I was able to let my guard down. Similar to the school library in childhood where we would sit to watch educational programs, I was safe while all eyes were fixed on the television.

"Who's that?"

The sudden question came from a young family member. The family member was younger than 13, not coincidentally the number of years since I had emerged as Paige.

My jaw dropped. In front of me, taking up the entire screen, was an image of Outer Shell. The being I had buried over a decade ago and escaped seeing an image of since. I froze. Heat flushed through my body. Salty water built up in my eyes, causing them to sting. I could feel reddening of the sclera.

Someone scrambled in a panic to skip quickly to the next slide and I was confronted with another photo. And then another. The name ██████ flashed up on the screen. Parental Being glanced in my direction, grimacing.

"Excuse me," I choked. "I need the loo."

I slipped out of the chair, hastily walked down the hallway, and hid in the bathroom.

"Breathe," I told myself.

My breaths were too fast and too shallow. My chest felt tight, my throat like it was closing up. I fled from the bathroom, down the hallway, out onto the back deck. I was shaking violently as the world around me grew dark. I blocked everything out and then teardrops started to flow. I sat down, rocking back and forth, hoping that the oscillation would comfort me, and I slipped away from reality. A figure approached me and I defensively shooed the watery shadow away. It was My Sibling.

I'm not sure how I got back to Brisbane, but after I did I spent some time alone to think. When I felt ready, I constructed a letter to The Family. I typed, edited, and then read the letter aloud before committing to it. To me, it was clear, polite, assertive, and 13 years too late.

○

<u>Letter to The Family</u>:
To The Family,
I have been wanting to write for a while, but I didn't want to write while I was feeling strong, negative emotion.
For me to continue to be around you, there need to be some minor changes. I've held back from saying anything sooner, as I didn't want to offend, but that has continued to be to my detriment, souring every family event for me, and I see that my silence was a contributor to the recent traumatic evening.
It is painfully obvious when you word your sentences specifically to avoid referring to me as a woman. It's not okay. Either refer to me as a woman, or do not refer to me at all. For a transitional period more than a decade in the past, it was a compromise. I cannot tolerate it any more. It's dehumanising. It hurts so much that when you do it, and you all do, I am too upset and angry to say anything because I know it won't come out right.
I want to be clear, black and white, no ambiguity.
I'm female, a woman.
I can be referred to as she, her, miss.
I'm a daughter and sister. One day I'll be a wife. Hopefully I can adopt and be a mother.
How I looked, what I was previously referred to as, that is a very long time in the past. It was not a happy time for me for the majority of those years. My happy memories, they have no connection to the identity you saw. The images etcetera are purely a reminder of the parts of my childhood that hurt most. I understand that you may not see it that way, but this is about me and who I am. It is not about anyone else. My previous identity should not be mentioned in front of me, and images should never be presented in front of me.
The woman I am today, I was always this person inside, just younger and less educated. This is who I will always be. I shouldn't be treated as though I am anything or anyone else.
A reply is not required. Please just read and let everything sink it. It's all very important and I feel stupid for not saying it all sooner.
Regards,

Paige

○

It wasn't long before I received a reply from My Sibling.

○

Hi Paige,
After reflecting on your e-mail I'd love to be able to share my thoughts with you. I would prefer to have this discussion face to face, but I understand if you would prefer to have this discussion via e-mail.
Love,
Your Sibling

○

A discussion? I felt pain in the pit of my stomach, scared of what My Sibling might want to discuss. This didn't require a discussion. Was My Sibling still expecting to be able to reform me after 13 years? Surely not! Defensively, I wrote what I thought was an assertive reply.

○

Hi Sibling,
Along what lines are your thoughts? I'm not interested in hearing justifications, and won't be told who I am or how I should let people treat me. Just in case that's what you had in mind.
Cheers,
Paige

○

Fortunately, very little time passed before I received a reply, because I was compulsively checking my email for one. I was anxious to find out what My Sibling's intentions were.

○

Hi Paige,
I just wanted to share my heart and journey in being your sibling... Trying to understand this whole process hasn't been easy for me either.
Your Sibling

○

Suddenly all of my feelings of rejection, everybody making me feel like I was unwelcome on the planet, came to a head. This time I didn't bother spending much effort on the reply. Being polite and assertive wasn't getting me anywhere, so I just needed to be clear.

○

I have had enough people tell me how hard it is for them that I exist. I've well and truly had enough.

○

I read My Sibling's deaf reply in bewilderment. Brat!

○

Paige,
This is very confusing. Two weeks ago I was very upset about those photos being

shown. I wanted to comfort you. I also wanted to ask your permission to speak to Parental Being about why they would do this. Instead of being able to comfort and defend you, I feel shut out and attacked. It is not hard for me that you exist. It is hard for me not to be able to share with you that I have vulnerabilities and insecurities, and I wish I could share this with you. I had hoped that the last six years was evidence that I desire to love, accept and appreciate you. I'm not going to always get this right, but I'm always trying. I don't understand how it is okay for you to tell me what you want and think and you won't allow me to share my thoughts and feelings. I know you must be feeling a lot of pain. And I want you to know that I love you.
Love,
Your Sibling

o

With tears saturating my face and clouding my vision, I shot off a reply, again not bothering with greetings or pleasantries.

o

My defensiveness was because you wrote 'trying to understand this whole process hasn't been easy for me either' which sounds exactly like the 'it's hard for me to cope with you existing' that I've had from so many people for so many years. Obviously I misunderstood your meaning and what you want to discuss. I'll read your email again tomorrow as I'm a bit upset this evening and I don't think I'm reading properly.

o

I took a breather before I formulated a reply. It was important to me that I was coherent, and the hurt and confusion was impairing my ability to articulate my thoughts.

o

Hi Sibling,
Thanks for your email. I'm not really sure what to say. I understand if you want to talk about things. When I hurt, I need to be alone. I've always been that way, I always will. I'm not like you. Time with people drains me, and if I'm recovering from trauma, I can't handle people on top of that. You've shared lots of your vulnerabilities and insecurities with me. I don't understand why you're saying you haven't. That has me baffled and I don't know what it is that you want from me. I have no idea what I'm supposed to do in this situation.

o

Very little time passed before My Sibling's reply came through.

o

Morning Paige,
Thanks for your e-mail. I understand that you need to be alone and I appreciate the effort that you have gone to in giving yourself this space to remain in this conversation, which must be extremely painful. Yes I have shared vulnerably with you. However, when you're in a place to talk, I'd like to share my vulnerabilities specifically in relation to your transition from living as my brother, to wanting to relate to me as my sister. I want to share my feelings and confusion, but each time it feels like I'm met

with an ultimatum. I'd like to be able to have intimacy with you where I can see you and you can see me and if that is different, it's ok, we can find a way to make it work. Would appreciate knowing your reflections on this.
Love Sibling

o

I felt a surge in gravity's force and whimpered. So many words exchanged, only to find out that everything was as bad as I had originally thought. Why had I even bothered at all? I wept for days, and as I write this—in a public space, years later—I am crying again. I don't know if I can express how painful it is to have your family tell you how bad it has been for them that you have had to endure what you have endured, and to blame you for their pain over your existence. Heart aching, I did my best to reply to My Sibling's email. Though I saw no real solution, I at least needed this behind me.

o

So I was correct and right to be defensive. You DO want to tell me about how hard it has been for you that I exist. I'm surprised and disappointed that you could possibly think that's appropriate. I spent a lot of years helping people through coping and coming to terms with my existence and nobody should have to endure what I have. What you're asking me to go through, yet again, with another person, is horrid. How can you not see how damaging it is to even mention that? It's the kind of thing you talk through with someone else. I shouldn't be put through this over and over.

o

Oh my FUCKING GOD! There was another reply. Fuck my life hard in the arse. Shit! Without reading the email, I forwarded it to an emotionally intelligent male version of Friendly Entity, asking him to read the email and let me know if it was okay for me to read it. I was at the end. I could not cope with any more. Friendly Entity assured me that it was fine to read the email, so I reluctantly did so.

o

Morning Paige,
I've taken some time to think over what you've said. Thank you for taking the time to share your heart. I'd like to move toward what you asked in your initial e-mail. This will be slow and I'd like to do it collaboratively. I'd like to find a way forward together. Love to know your thoughts.
Love Sibling.

o

I began to sob. I hated that I was in this situation. I was envious of everyone who was able to live a straightforward life. I was jealous of everyone who didn't have to endure this. I can barely see the screen through the salty water obscuring my vision as I revisit these intense, painful memories.

o

Hi Sibling,

I'll need some time to recover. While I do that I can only be around people who see me as I am and know me. Your email unfortunately made it clear that you're not one of those people. Will be in touch in the New Year.
Regards,
Paige

○

It was many months later that I sent a follow-up email.

○

Hi Sibling,
I've been doing a lot of thinking since your emails in November. My polite email laid everything out clearly and simply. It was not an ultimatum; it outlined the minimum requirements to not be a horrible person to me.
Maybe you don't understand because of your white Australian middle-class cisgender privilege. Nobody has fought to take away your rights. They've fought to take away mine. People insist that I am not who I say I am, that their opinions and feelings about me are more important. They discuss whether or not I exist, and if maybe I should just be put to death. Maybe you can't understand because you've never experienced that.
After so clearly stating this is who I am and begging you to stop treating me otherwise, you told me I am not that. You indicated that your opinions and feelings about who I am are more important than who I actually am.
I AM a woman, I WAS a girl. I was ALWAYS a sister. I've always been who I am now. What you perceived, what you perceive, it is NOT RELEVANT. I've already made that clear, but obviously I have to state it again.
Who I am is not open to debate. I am not just some hunk of flesh. I am a human being, and a bloody good one at that. I always accepted who you were, and listened without judgement as you told me of your struggles, and the thoughts you were ashamed of. I trusted you to do the same with me. You've broken my heart and I don't think I can trust you again.
I'm sorry, but for now I cannot have you in my life.
Regards,
Paige

○

I didn't expect a reply, but of course I received one. My Sibling always had to have the last word.

○

Hi Paige,
My apologies for the delay in reply. I was devastated and unsure of how to respond. It grieves me to see you in such pain. Just wanted to know that I love you deeply and my arms are open longing to hold you again when you feel we're able to share this journey of life together again.
Much love,
Sibling

○

It wasn't the worst reply, but I decided that after everything that I'd been through, I was much better off without The Family.

Again.

• EMANCIPATION, PART TWO

HAD IT BEEN TWELVE HOURS EARLIER, I would have been curled up, arms hugging my flexed legs as I wept. What I mourned were the days I lost to alcohol. Tears soaked my pillow as I confronted the painful reality of an unknown number of sexual encounters that I could barely remember. I cried over the many that wouldn't have occurred had I been sober. I had spent hours on the bed, using all the strength I had, just to stop myself from reaching for the bottle to soothe the painful residue it had left behind.

Right now, however, I feel stable as I reach a state of mental clarity with regard to my next step. Now that I've passed the last step of my meticulously planned year, and have become someone my younger self could aspire to be, I'm going rogue, making it up and re-evaluating everything as I go.

In addition to my full-time role at the teaching hospital, and my voluntary gender diversity role with Intersectionality Advocates, I also put my hand up and become the Acting State Director of Intersectionality Advocates. This is to get a feel for the role before potentially taking it on long term. Although a huge cross to bear, each of these responsibilities are important, not only for being a role model, but for assisting me to prompt the change in the world I want to see.

The next thing I need to do, I decide, is to re-write my Open Letter with 18 months of experience, for a fresh audience of friends and family. It's time to look at my boundaries, and adjust them as appropriate, so that I can achieve all I need to without burning out. I write, I re-write, and I post.

•

Dear You,

Before I begin, I ask that you read this letter in its entirety before commenting or messaging me about it. Please be respectful if you do choose to respond. Over the past 16 years I've discussed the content of this letter with thousands of people, and I've been greatly hurt by many of the resultant ignorant, intolerant and hateful comments and behaviours. Some of this letter may seem unnecessary to you, but I assure you, every word has been prompted by interactions that I have had with people in the past, making every word necessary.

Really, this letter is all about the following statement: "I'm Paige, and I'm a woman who has been through a gender transition that included psychological therapy, several medications, and surgical procedures."

<u>*Purpose and Background*</u>
Back in 2015, I wrote an Open Letter that provided some information about what the above statement means, and I outlined some personal boundaries. This was followed up

with a narrative blog of my associated life experience, and I've since fleshed that out and edited it into a series of three novellas. I mention this only because that process caused me to grow to the point of feeling the need to write this letter. One that is more detailed, better articulating my current thoughts.

Although I knew from an early age that I was female, it wasn't until I was in my late teens that I met a man who introduced me to the terms gender dysphoria and transgender. This meeting was life-changing in the best possible way. That man was a transman who at the time had a female body. Because of his own diagnosis and treatment, he was able to put me in touch with medical professionals who provided me with the counselling, medication and surgical procedures required for me to feel comfortable in my own skin.

<u>Privilege and Lifestyle</u>

It is important to me that I acknowledge my own privilege within the space of gender diversity. This doesn't mean that I haven't struggled (I most certainly have), just that there are certain struggles I've been able to avoid. I was born in Australia, to a family who always had enough money to provide adequate food, clothing and shelter. Although the cumulative time and financial cost of transitioning from male to female was equivalent to some bachelor degrees, I've had relatively easy access to healthcare, education, and am now employed by an organisation that actively promotes staff diversity and inclusiveness. Most importantly, because of the way I look and sound, I'm not forced to be "out" about my gender history.

In my day-to-day life, I'm not required to think about the fact that I have been through a gender transition. That truth shocks some people. From brushing my teeth, to ordering coffee, chatting with people, preparing lunch, having sex and responding to work emails, I usually don't give it any thought. Simply because it doesn't get in the way of any of these routine tasks. There are two situations that cause me to think about it, however. Firstly, when someone specifically asks me about it or "outs" me in public. Secondly, when I'm asked about something that is affected by it. An example is that of pregnancy. Because of my gender affirming surgeries, I have no ability to procreate.

<u>Public and Private Disclosure</u>

Never, under any circumstances, should you disclose my past in a space that I am physically in. NOT EVEN ONCE. No matter how comfortable you may feel about my past, outing me in this way has the potential to put me in immediate physical danger. Trust me, I don't have enough fingers to count the times I've been approached and threatened by demanding strangers and acquaintances as a direct result of what another person has said about me. I do not owe those strangers an explanation of my lived experience, and I do not deserve to be attacked because of it.

If you ever do disclose my past to someone, you should lead them to the literature on the subject that has been written by me: this letter, my blog, or my books. The story to tell is mine, and mine alone. It is incredibly frustrating trying to educate someone who has been misinformed of my situation by an ally who doesn't quite get it.

<u>Identity vs Behaviour</u>

Generally, I just think of myself as a straight woman and that's how I prefer to be perceived and referred to socially. I'm more complex than that, though. For starters, sometimes my romantic and sexual experiences are with women. Perhaps because same-sex attraction is rare for me, and I don't seek out long-term partners of the same sex, I don't identify with bisexual as a label. The recently popularised label heteroflexible is probably most accurate.

Healthcare

In some medical situations, it's important to categorise me as a post-op transgender woman (a transgender woman who has had a vaginoplasty). This is so medical professionals can have a better understanding of the anatomy and physiology they're working with. There's no need to refer to me that way socially.

Making Allies Great Again

So you're supportive of the fact that I exist, and that's just great! All you need do to show me that you are supportive of me, is to remain in my life. That alone is a powerful statement. Yes, many people abandon friends when they are told that the person has a different gender or sex to what they had assumed.

Telling me you saw something trans-related or sending me articles about trans issues is not an appropriate way to display support. What this does, is points out and reminds me that you see me as different to other women. That's not a nice feeling. Between my writing and volunteer work in the gender diversity space, I see as much related literature as I care to.

In my leisure time, I'd just like to relax and focus on things I enjoy like playing board games, reading fiction, going hiking, watching films, and eating cheese. In my down time, I don't want to be reminded of the most traumatic times in my life. Shocking, I know. When I was younger, it was a huge deal to just be aware that there were cisgender people who thought it was okay that I existed, and in fact I had to wait until age 19 until I was aware of any such people. In 2016 however, we've gone beyond the point of needing allies purely for visibility and social media likes. If you'd like to be an active ally and really make a difference, there are options.

One option is to fill out surveys that will help contribute to resources I plan to develop to educate allies about issues experienced by people who are oppressed and/or discriminated against as a direct result of their sex or gender. Or why not join an organisation and volunteer your time and expertise? I have provided a list below in case you don't know of any.

Leave It In The Past

It's never appropriate to refer to me as the name or gender I was assigned at birth, make reference to how feminine or masculine I am, or mention physical attributes of the past (you know, like sex organs). The act of doing the first has recently been defined as deadnaming. Also, you definitely shouldn't point out how you've examined my photos and noticed my continued gender transformation over time. Hearing that from a friend really shocked me, as I have never thought to use photos to scrutinise someone's change in appearance from less to more passable as a particular gender, let alone tell them about it.

Questions and Support

Please be aware that my active involvement in providing support to the LGBTIQA+ community already takes up a lot of time and energy.

So, if you feel traumatised by what I have had to go through to become the woman I am today, please seek professional assistance and do not tell me about it. If you know a young person who is in need of support, check out the links below and provide the appropriate resources to that person.

If you or someone you know has questions about the lived experiences directly related to my own gender history, you can read my novella Outer Shell. If you have questions about how you can help support people in the LGBTIQA+ community, please check out the links I have provided below.

●

After reading through the letter a few times, I add links to organisations and resources that can help readers without them needing to contact me. The last thing I need is to become burnt out by yet another flurry of curious activity. I feel pleased with myself, but realise that I'm no longer completely open and honest about my history in the workplace. Assuming that Academic Consociate has not taken back their blessing, I send another bulk email with the dual purpose of updating existing colleagues, and outing myself to the newest to join our team. Again, I do this before taking some time off, to allow any awkwardness to dissipate before they have to interact with me in the workplace.

●

Hi Everyone!
I realised possibly only half of you may be aware that I finished writing my first autobiographical book this year (semi-fictionalised).
For most of this year I was unable to do anything with it, as it was sitting with an industry person, however they released it to me a while back with some great feedback.
Anyway, because of a combination of my volunteer work, the professional feedback, and ideas from an online master class, I've split the book into three novellas.
I'm excited to say that I've now released the first edition of Book One quite cheaply as an eBook.
Hope you're able to have a bit of a read. :)
Kind regards,
Paige

●

On my first day back at work, I notice Professional Associate walk up to my office, see that I'm not alone, and then walk away. This happens several times, until Professional Associate invites me to assist them with setting up one of the teaching spaces. I oblige, always keen to help and also step away from my desk, and it doesn't take long for me to realise that there have been ulterior motives.

"I read Outer Shell," they blurt out, referring to my first book. "I don't want to make a big song and dance about it, but it broke my heart."

I smile gently at Professional Associate.

"Life is really good now, though," I reassure them.

"Reading about that poor little girl," Professional Associate continues, looking at me with painful eyes. "All alone."

We spend some time chatting, and it feels good to have disclosed those painful pre-transition years. Although I know not everyone at work will read the entire thing, they're all now aware of my past in a general sense, and I no longer have to concern myself with concealing it.

Feeling satisfied that I've moved forward enough for now, I decide to step back and rest for a bit by watching some streaming content I've not had time for. I watch a few episodes of *Black Mirror*, and feeling quite creeped out by the storyline of one of the episodes, my solitude becomes noticeable. Naturally, I send a message to L2.

"Got any suggestions for something to follow up the new Black Mirror*? I don't think I can sleep after the third episode."*

The reply isn't immediate, so I start looking through the list of available comedy series. I realise that because my year has been so intense, I've watched most of the light content available to me. My phone lights up with a response from L2.

I only just got started on Black Mirror*! And I think Netflix started me on season 3. I've only watched the one episode though, the social media likes one. So no, unless you want to get a subscription to HBO and watch* Westworld*. Or just download it.*

Having nothing else to do, I reply immediately.

I need to get my hands on that. People keep recommending it and I noticed it's not on the services I subscribe to.

Nothing in return. I start watching a few different films but feel agitated, and before long I log off and drift to sleep.

Chapter Sixteen

○○ **DESOLATION**

> *On the balcony of my flat, Outer Shell sat slumped, silent and alone, as I looked out at the sky, reflecting on life.*
>
> *Looked? I was staring blankly.*
>
> *No family, hardly any friends, stuck halfway through a gender transition I wasn't sure I could afford to complete, life was fucking awful, so I wept until it became physically impossible to continue.*

○ **NECROTIC ISSUE**

THERE WERE 124 INDIVIDUAL POSITIONS listed on the document entitled Paige's Job Opportunities. This was surprising to me, because the list was personalised, based on how I had performed in the Aptitude and Mathematics tests. As a high school dropout who had failed miserably at even the simplest maths problems in the final years of schooling, I had diligently used a website to learn what my teenage self could not. Apparently it had worked, and I barely touched the notepad during the test, opting instead to make most of the calculations in my head.

Unfortunately, this list did not take into account my issues with colour perception. A second list was presented, displaying jobs that were open to people who were colour-blind. I was disheartened to see that my most highly desired positions were all missing from this list. Still, entering into the Defence Force would be a great way to get the necessary education for a fulfilling career in training.

Despite my exceptional test scores, because I hadn't finished high school, I was required to undertake further study in order to proceed with the recruitment process. I was given the option of a Certificate IV in Tertiary Preparation, which would require me to achieve high marks in both Maths Pure and Physics, or I could complete a Diploma of Business. Because the qualification was more easily transferable and relevant to working in an office, I chose Business. The aim was to re-enter the recruitment process after completion, but life had other plans for me, and it's just as well considering the memories that later resurfaced when I read through my childhood journals. Memories that would inevitably have caused me to drop out (see: suicidal tendencies).

"Can we stop for a minute?"

I was with a fiercely brilliant female incarnation of Friendly Entity, and we were slowly sweating our way up a bush trail not far from Brisbane. Being typical Australian bushland, I didn't consider it to be the most beautiful trek—leeches aside I had a preference for rainforests—but I was happy just to be getting outdoors with Friendly Entity.

Friendly Entity paused to allow me to stop, catch my breath, and focus. I was confused by what I was feeling. The unfamiliar pain was sharp, deep inside my leg; it was in the bone. I chose to ignore the pain and deal with it later. Whatever it was.

"Thanks for the lift," I called over my shoulder a few hours later. "Drive safe!"

As I approached my new home—limping ever so slightly—I noticed light creeping through the crack under the front door, and I could hear voices. I would soon meet the people I was living with. I took a deep breath, turned the key, and opened the door to the tiny student apartment.

Before anything else, I noticed the intense, dark eyes of Volatile Force. We had an instant connection, and really, in that moment everything had already ended. His strong European features were incredibly enticing. I smiled, and he smiled back at me. The exchange was only a few seconds, and then the introductions came. With his mellifluous voice he spoke English reasonably well, but with a thick, European accent. Another hook pulling me toward danger.

At first Volatile Force and I were a little awkward around each other but with each interaction I came to like him more. We started to schedule time to sit together and watch things on television. He would accidentally touch me. We would cuddle. I would pull back. And then we kissed. And I pulled back again.

I freaked out. This couldn't happen. Not while I was living with him. He didn't know about my past and there was a strong possibility that he wouldn't be okay with it. Telling him my history would make my home life unsafe. I kept pushing him away, but he persisted. For two months he persevered, gently pushing toward his goal, gently attempting to reel me in.

"I will leave," he offered one day, or perhaps it was a threat. It felt more like a threat.

"I don't want you to leave," I whined, helplessly. "I like having you around."

"Well what, then?"

I didn't know.

For my 31st birthday—instead of organising the typical eating and drinking festival—I disappeared into a national park for a multiple-day hike with several sweaty male versions of Friendly Entity. Also in attendance was my dear male friend The Abandoned. This was to take advantage of being at my fittest, thanks to all the physical training I had endured in an attempt to enter the Air Force. As a bonus, it allowed me some time away from Volatile Force to think. The pain in my bone had become quite bad by then, so I took a cocktail of painkillers every few hours for the duration of the hike.

On the second day, I woke up in a campground with no memory of the night before. My head was throbbing, but I didn't feel too nauseous. I took a handful of pills that I was already going to take to dull the bone pain, and chatted to Friendly Entity to work out how the night had played out. They told me I'd been so drunk that I'd decided to try to sleep next to the tent and The Abandoned had awkwardly dragged me into it. Quite an achievement considering I was in a tiny hiking tent.

The Abandoned had also been drinking, but was much sicker than me. He told us that his partner was on the way to pick him up, and that Friendly Entity and I should continue with our planned hike. I figured since we were leaving The Abandoned in a campground, maybe this was okay. I cannot stress this enough, don't ever leave anyone behind.

Not even once.

On the third day, while scrambling over rocks, I fell and hit the part of my leg that had been hurting most. Lucky I already had painkillers! It wasn't until we were on the trip home that I had mobile phone coverage again and caught up with what had happened to The Abandoned after we had deserted him. He'd knocked his water container over, depleting the supply, and the tap water at the campsite could only be used for drinking if you had something to clean it. He didn't. The partner of The Abandoned had lost her way and took much longer to find him than anticipated. Severely dehydrated, he was taken to a hospital where the staff unknowingly gave him medication contraindicated by a drug he was already taking.

When I got home, Volatile Force was waiting for me. Distress clearly evident in my face, he pressed for information.

"I think I just lost a friend," I told him. As I recounted the story he hugged me.

"I can't believe that you would do that," he said, shaking his head, and I felt worse, consumed by feelings of guilt. "I thought you were a good person."

Volatile Force comforted me with gentle strokes against my arm. He wiped away my tears as he looked at me. We kissed, and I let it continue to escape the pain.

I decided that the following day it was time to visit Dermal Saviour to get another skin check and to find out what was going on with my bone.

"You're saying you were in pain, and then you hit your leg during your birthday hike?"

"Yes," I told Dermal Saviour, putting my blouse back on.

"Paige, are you sure you didn't hit your head? Suffer from dehydration? This isn't Wonderland. Here, the pain comes *after* the injury."

I rolled my eyes at Dermal Saviour and slipped back into my trousers.

"I'd really like to look into this," I pressed. "Something's not right."

"Alright, I'll send you for an ultrasound. I need to cut that out by the way," Dermal Saviour said, pointing to the spot on my arm he'd taken down notes about.

"Yeah, I know. There's no rush though, it's still small and it's only a BCC."

Back at home I decided to open myself up to Volatile Force.

"I need to tell you why I've been turning you away. I can't stand it anymore, but I'm so scared. I'm terrified."

I launched right into telling Volatile Force about my past, wailing as I did so. At first he didn't understand. His English wasn't good enough to understand the ambiguous way I chose to speak about it, refusing to use labels or mention the sex organs I had been born with. Unsure of how to clarify without using words I disliked, I directed him to a search engine. *Gender reassignment surgery.*

Volatile Force held me as I bawled some more, nodding as he read, but not verbalising anything.

"Let's take a walk," he said finally.

We wandered down the road and walked to a park by the river. We sat on a bench. He moved closer. The river, the silence, so much of this reminded me of disclosing to Legitimate One, but somehow it was even more intense, and this was after I had passed on the sensitive information. The build up to this moment had been more painful, and the stakes were higher this time because we lived together. It felt dangerous.

Volatile Force looked me in the eyes. He hugged me, pressed his cheek against mine, then adjusted his head so that our lips touched, and we began to kiss.

Everything happened quickly after that. We compared schedules to get as much time together as possible. I told him that I couldn't just go straight to bed with him. It had been a long time since I'd had sex, and that meant that I would have become tight, so to engage in the act would be uncomfortable. I needed to loosen up before we could have sex. In the meantime, we would have to settle for just exploring each other's bodies, and we wasted no time.

After work the next day, I went to get the ultrasound that Dermal Saviour had recommended.

"Where did you say the pain was?"

I pointed to the area of my tibia that seemed to be the source of my lower leg pain.

"I'm going to recommend that Dermal Saviour send you for a bone scan."

"Why?"

I tried and failed to read the expression on the radiologist's face. The radiologist showed me the image and pointed out a specific area that looked different.

"See how the appearance changes in this area? The change indicates necrotic tissue."

I went home and told Volatile Force about my appointment. He comforted me and we went to his bedroom.

Several days later I was back at the radiology clinic, lying on a bed, waiting for my bone scan to complete. A different radiologist poked her head out of the office and called out to me.

"You don't have a pain in your hip?"

"No," I said. "Is there a problem?"

"I think I've stumbled onto something. I'm going to scan your full body instead of just the legs. You might need an MRI. Check with your doctor when you go back."

Volatile Force and I ate together, went for walks together, and took selfies together. I put one on social media to let everyone know that I was now with someone. I felt proud and excited. Life was heading in the right direction.

"We need to talk," Volatile Force said out of the blue, and I could tell that something was wrong. The words he used felt cold and distant, he avoided making eye contact, and there was no kiss.

"Let us take a walk," he said. I went to take his hand but he shook his head.

Volatile Force admitted to me that he struggled with mental illness, and he told me how he was jealous of me. I was so strong, and he wasn't. He told me that because of this, we couldn't be together. Because of this, he had to end things between us. He wanted to explain in more detail, but was limited by his ability to speak English. I just had to accept that he had made up his mind, and we could never be together.

Our conversation ended by the river, where we had shared our first kiss, intensifying the pain I felt. As Volatile Force began to weep, I was torn. I cared, but he had just dumped me, so I left him alone to cry by the river, and I went directly to the bottle shop to purchase something I knew from experience would dull the pain.

Alone in the living room, bottle slowly emptying, I cried and cried. I had thought that he would be the one to give me the future I had spent my entire adult life longing for. I had spent so much time resisting him and had finally given in. I had told him everything, and he cared for me anyway. This was supposed to be my fairy tale ending but everything had gone to shit.

"I think I made a mistake," he interrupted, standing over me. He'd returned from the river to get me back.

"You didn't," I told him, inhaling the rest of the bottle of wine I'd purchased. "You've made the right decision. But it hurts."

After a sleepless night, and a difficult day at work, I went back to see Dermal Saviour to get more test results.

"Well?" I tapped my foot on the floor impatiently, and then smiled and tilted my head to the side to ease the tension. "Do I get some bionic legs now? Yeah? How good are bionic legs?"

"How good, Paige?"

"So good."

Dermal Saviour rolled his eyes.

"See all the bits that lit up?" Dermal Saviour pointed to several parts of the bone scan.

"Pretty," I said, nodding. "I look like I'm covered in fairy lights! Is that normal? I've never seen a bone scan before."

Dermal Saviour shook his head.

"The lighter parts show increased osteoblastic activity. They're all your fractures, Paige. What I'm more concerned about though, is that really bright area."

Dermal Saviour pointed to my left hip.

"It's a lesion of some kind on your left proximal femur. Come back and see me after your MRI."

My instinct was to tell Volatile Force, and seek refuge in his arms, but instead I avoided home. I started to sit in bars, sometimes with Friendly Entity, sometimes alone, and drink the hours away, mourning the loss of my family, my health, and my most recent relationship. Volatile Force begged me to forgive him, and sometimes I felt like I had, but at other times I decided that I hated him. Living there became more difficult by the day, and before it had even been 12 months, I packed up and moved out.

"Well?"

My whole body was tense as I looked at Dermal Saviour, some time later.

"What does it say? What does it mean? You can tell me the truth, I'm ready to go. I've lived a good life."

"Don't say that, Paige. Features favour benign," Dermal Saviour told me, smiling. "We'll keep an eye on it, but lesions like this rarely metastasise."

"No osteosarcoma?"

"No osteosarcoma."

"Yes!"

I punched the air, breathed a sigh of relief, and a few tears fell from my eyes.

"What should I do about the fractures?"

"My friend is a physiotherapist. I'll write you a referral. For the moment, stop walking everywhere. It's not as good for you as you think."

• DERMAL SAVIOUR RETURNS

WITHOUT THE PRESSURE OF RENT, or the expense of alcohol, I quickly dig myself out of debt enough to allow me the wiggle room to do something I've been putting off for far too long. Before I head to the medical centre to see Dermal Saviour, I stand completely naked in front of a full-length mirror in my temporary bedroom, scanning my skin. There are quite a few scars. These are predominantly due to complete and successful removal of a variety of atypical skin growths.

•

Skin Growths Removed To Date:
- *Dermatofibroma (see: ugly, harmless abnormal growths)*
- *Solar keratosis (see: growths that sometimes progress to become skin cancers)*
- *Basal Cell Carcinomas (see: easily treatable in early stages; see also: a type of skin tumour that rarely metastasize)*
- *Squamous Cell Carcinomas (see: easily treatable in early stages; see also: a type of tumour responsible for the disfigurement and death of many people)*

•

Less exciting, but more interesting, there's the scar on my pelvis that's partially obscured by pubic hair. This is not only a reminder of my first trip to hospital as a young child, but my first self-directed healthcare investigation.

On my right forearm, I can see where I accidentally stabbed myself with a chisel during Year 8 Woodwork Class, and nearby is the long, thin scar caused by a glass light-shade that I accidentally shattered while dancing on a table top. I recall that it occurred a week after I had just seen Pulp Fiction.

I'm the thinnest I've been since hitting 30, but I still have more padding than I did in the days of my psychic imitation of Serena van der Woodsen. For once there's no sunburn, but I have developed a light, healthy tan from the small amount of sun that has been allowed to creep through the protective layers of stockings and 50+ sunscreen to my legs, arms and shoulders. I'm still pale elsewhere, and I'm no longer repulsed by this as I once was.

What I'm doing is not at all sexy. It's my own, regular skin check. I examine every bit of my scarred body, looking for any sign of change. If I note anything out of the ordinary, I'm supposed to send myself off to the skin doctor for early diagnosis and treatment. As they say with flatulence, better out than in, and the earlier you get them out, the smaller the scar that's left behind and the less chance there is that you've grown something to the point of no return.

I mean imminent painful death.

To my knowledge that last part doesn't apply to farts. Although on the topic of farts and cancer, some research indicates that breathing the former in could prevent the latter... I doubt there's more than one study to back that up.

In the past, I've been incredibly fortunate, because I've left a lot of my abnormal patches of skin untreated for longer than I should have, but—and this thought dominates all others as I tally up the new suspicious lesions—there's a possibility that this time, I've left it too late. Something I wouldn't have done if I hadn't so recklessly and drunkenly pushed myself so far into debt.

In my head, I build a list of the reasons regular skin checks are crucial for me.

<u>Regular Self-Assessment Crucial For Me Because</u>:
- *I've got a family history of skin cancer*
- *I've got stacks of moles*
- *My skin burns easily*
- *I've been severely sunburnt*
- *I've spent loads of time outdoors*
- *I used a solarium until my first skin cancer*

As I watch Dermal Saviour reading through his notes, I find it impossible to push aside thoughts about the last time our eyes met in this building. I had been in tears, waiting to see a different doctor. In the appointment with the other doctor, I had revealed what was not on my medical record; lack of periods due to no uterus. Also, gender reassignment surgery and suicidal ideation. That moment is now an enormous elephant in the room, causing me to be especially chatty. Dermal Saviour, as always, is perfectly professional.

"It's been a little longer than I intended," I start to tell Dermal Saviour.

"Two years, it's been about two years," he tells me.

"I guess that's why I've got so many spots for you!"

Dermal Saviour swings to face me.

"What do you have for me today? I'll check those out first, and then we can do a full skin check."

"There are about five, I think," I tell him.

Shortly after, I'm half naked, stretched out on the examination bed twiddling my thumbs as Dermal Saviour photographs suspicious patches of skin, and compares them to photographs he's previously taken. His eyes stop at the site of my hormone implant.

"Is this just a scar?"

"Yes," I confirm, making a last-minute decision to withhold further information.

"I always wonder," he tells me. "When patients stop coming in, if it's something I've said."

I laugh.

"You didn't think maybe I had died?"

A flashback to him seeing me in the street.

"I know you didn't die. You missed one. There are six," he tells me.

"But I've never missed one before! Well, not in years, anyway."

Dermal Saviour starts typing up his notes as I put my clothes back on.

"The one you missed is on your back. There was nothing there at all during your skin check."

I feel sad. This is the kind of thing a romantic partner could pick up. My mind wanders back to my early days with Legitimate One, and then on to the weirdness of L2.

"Come back next week and we'll take some biopsies before we move forward with any treatments. Some of these are going to require large excisions."

"Sure thing," I say, adding in a salute to be silly. "I probably shouldn't have waited so long to come back."

"Indeed," Dermal Saviour confirms flatly. "See you next week."

At work I become preoccupied with thoughts of all the treatments I'll have to finance with money I'd intended to use to get me out of debt. I also worry about the time that has passed, possibly allowing some of the lesions to develop beyond the point of treatment. With my history, and with the weird physical symptoms I've had of late, it's possible that I'm already past the point of no return. *Oh God, I could be dying!*

Several days later, at the end of a work day, I reflect on an amusing situation, and decide to tell L2 about it. We haven't exchanged messages in a while, and I'd like to try my luck again before it's too late.

Apparently my social skills are lacking today, I text him.

An hour or so later, he responds with, *Why is that?*

I launch into my story.

Last week one of the guys who teaches my students was introduced to me. We hadn't met before. He apologised for all the emails he sends me with issues. I meant to tell him that it didn't bother me, but it came off as me telling him he's nothing more than a number to me. Today I ran into him and tried to apologise, saying I was just a bit off that day because of the mental health training, but somehow I messed that up too. I started by asking him if we had met the other day! So really, I just confirmed my rudeness from last week. And then I awkwardly bumped into him again this afternoon and grimaced! I don't do colds well, I add, hinting that I'm not feeling well.

L2: *Hahaha very smooth. Do you work in contact with him regularly?*

I shake my head, realising another element to the situation.

Me: *Yeah... I put him in contact with the head of school for some stuff and then forgot about it.*

Several boring days pass, and I receive bad news.

Me: *Poo. Didn't get shortlisted for the job I applied for.*

L2: *Which job?*

I remind him about the job I had applied for at the Northern Teaching Hospital, and add that I've at least been invited to meet with someone from Recruitment Services to get feedback on my application.

Me: *Quite bummed. But I might get to stay at the Southern Teaching Hospital for another year, which would be nice.*

Only a day or two pass before I receive word that my contract is available for extension. Without hesitation, I agree to stay on for another year, and quickly shoot off a message to L2.

Me: *Well, I've been offered another 12 months at the Southern Teaching Hospital. *holds up coffee mug* Here's to more awkward run-ins! *cry laugh**

L2, immediately: *Haha, perfect. I'm sure one day we will actually exchange words. Congratulations. Hope you're satisfied with the appointment, compared to what your ideal was.*

I smile. A lot.

Me: *Thank you! :D Hmmm. In a week I'm house sitting alone for two months. Perhaps a good opportunity to actually exchange words that are not written?*

Again, L2 wastes no time with a reply.

L2: *Yeah, potentially. Luxury apartments or multi room mansion? Or perhaps a small writers bungalow? In any case, I'm off Wednesday and Thursday next week. Working all other days.*

I groan. Of course he would be available when it's not convenient for me. Busy people are so difficult to catch up with when you're also a busy person.

Me: *I'm there from next Thursday. Know your availability for the following week? It's... a weird place. I checked it out the other night.*

It feels as though L2's response reaches me before I've had a chance to even hit send.

L2: *I'm free the other nights as well.*

Without a thought, I make an offer.

Me: *So games and stuff this time next week?*

Silence. A day passes.

L2: *Games and stuff?*

Annoyed at the slow response, I also allow a day to pass.

Me: *Well apart from exchanging words, what else would you like to happen?*

I wait a few hours, and don't hear back from him, so I send another message.

Me: *From my side, I'm feeling pretty relaxed and open minded.*

Another half a day passes before I receive a response, and it's not exactly what I want or expect.

L2: *Haha, me too. However to be honest I have been on dates recently. And I don't generally like to date multiple people. Play the field, I guess. So it'd be as friends.*

L2 sends the emoji with its tongue poked out, as if that somehow removes the seriousness of the message. Too annoyed to send a nice response, I put my phone away and hang out with Bosom Buddy for a while. After I feel my head is level again, I respond.

Me: *That's fair enough. Sad to have missed the boat, but definitely keen to be friends, and you're still welcome to visit and chat.*

Chapter Seventeen

○○ **LACERATION**

I YAWNED TO POP OUTER SHELL'S EARS and stretched its arms toward the overhead locker, and I suppose some onlookers may have likened Outer Shell to a cat. The announcement bell sounded, followed by the soothing voice of the Captain. I listened intently at first.

"Ladies and gentlemen, as we start our descent, please make sure your seat backs and tray tables are in their full upright position." I peered out of the tiny window, now only half paying attention to the Captain's message. I looked around the cabin, amused, as less organised passengers followed the directions. We were told to ensure that electronic devices remained switched off until we were inside the airport; airplane mode would not exist for quite some time.

For the twenty or thirty minutes of the descent, I pondered the meaning of this trip. Although I had spent a lot of time, money and effort getting here, I was nowhere near my end goal. This was just the first of several trips to Melbourne that would be required before approval for my final surgery, a procedure that was not available in Queensland due to the efforts of people like Parental Being and the greater family. It was upsetting to think that people were so against the idea of my existence that they would fight to make the source of my future happiness illegal. Should not all people be allowed to find peace?

The announcement bell pulled me out of my head and back into the plane.

"Cabin crew, prepare for landing," came the soothing voice of the Captain. Moments later, a female flight attendant took over. My heart began to race, as time slowed to a painful pace.

"Ladies and gentlemen, we have just been cleared to land at the Tullamarine airport. Please make sure one last time your seat belt is securely fastened. The flight attendants are currently passing around the cabin to make a final compliance check and pick up any remaining rubbish. Thank you."

I smiled a little too eagerly at the flight attendant as she moved past my seat, and her face reacted quizzically. She was young, with flawless presentation. One day I might look as good as her, and maybe even do her job. I enjoyed flying. I made a mental note to look into the possibility at a later date.

"Cabin crew, please take your seats for landing."

As we completed our turbulent descent, I closed my eyes. I tried to picture my future, where I was whole (see: the way everyone else was from birth).

"Ladies and gentlemen, welcome to Melbourne."

My heart leapt at those words, signifying the beginning of the end of this difficult journey. I could barely believe I had scraped together enough cash for the flights, let alone the upcoming appointments and surgical procedures. This was happening! It occurred to me that perhaps security staff at the airport would be able to tell that I had the opposite genitals to what they'd expect. I pushed the thought as far to the back of my mind as possible, shifting my focus back to the announcement.

"Local time is 9am and the temperature is a brisk 15 degrees."

When the Fasten Seat Belt signs went dark, there was a sudden flurry of activity throughout the plane. I peered out of the window at the tarmac, my excitement growing at the prospect of wandering alone through a big, new city.

Immediately upon leaving the airport building, I noticed the air. Unlike anything I had experienced before, it was icy, crisp, and dry. The only dry air I had encountered prior to this had been hot, and for the last ten years, I'd had an exclusive relationship with the humidity of the East Coast of Queensland. I took a deep breath in and the smell of jet fuel took over. I didn't dislike it, so I took another dose.

Once I was in the Melbourne CBD, I became a little overwhelmed by how busy it was. There were so many people, buildings, cars and trams. Everything but the buildings were moving, all having somewhere important to get to, yesterday if at all possible, and my goodness there was so much noise, a frantic soundtrack to the dance before me. I looked at the maps I had printed out and found a quiet park to sit in to collect my thoughts.

The first day of Melbourne appointments was tightly scheduled so that I could return to Brisbane in the evening, and I didn't perceive any of my new Auditors as people so much as hurdles I was required to jump over. Everything that came out of my mouth was somewhere between the truth and what I assumed they wanted or needed me to say. Whatever it was that I said, it worked, and I was finally faced with my second last gender-transition-related trip to Melbourne.

"I was considering asking about a breast augmentation at the same time, but I don't feel strongly enough to add that cost and risk." In nothing but knickers, I stood in front of The Final Auditor (see: the surgeon who was to slice, toss, manipulate and stich, refashioning my genitalia into something more comfortable).

"You have the breasts of a model," The Final Auditor told me, and I supposed that made sense, since my dimensions were in line with model requirements of the time, long before it was considered appropriate to hire models with an average or above average amount of body fat.

"Oh, I've always thought they were a bit too small," is how I responded, because I didn't really know what to say but felt uncomfortable with silence.

"They look good the way they are," The Final Auditor said flatly.

I considered the situation I was in, and travelled back into my head. I felt incredibly uncomfortable being there, almost naked in a halfway transitioned body, but it was a necessary evil. I thought back to my childhood, and my first hospital experience.

"I'm worried about this," I told The Final Auditor, pointing to a scar on my pelvis.

"What's that from?"

I felt embarrassed. "I had two operations when I was very young, at the same time; to treat an undescended testicle and hernia." I hadn't said that to anyone in a very long time, and certainly not during the time I had been presenting Outer Shell as female. "I'm worried that I might have scar tissue or insufficient skin for the operation."

"It won't be an issue, you've got plenty to work with. Don't worry about it. You should get some laser hair removal prior to surgery, though."

"I have to what?"

"That area will be inside after the operation. After that, it will be too late."

I considered this. In my dual-gender physical state, I couldn't imagine going somewhere to get it done. How would I even bring that up in a consultation with a beauty therapist? It would no doubt be far more embarrassing than the experience of buying hormones and clothes early on. No, this was definitely something I couldn't do. But I would have to, wouldn't I?

When I returned to Brisbane my finger hovered over the call button but I couldn't do it. I couldn't make the call. I couldn't explain how I needed laser hair removal on a part of my body that they would assume I didn't have because I was a woman and only men had that part in this world of people that either disapproved or didn't know of non-binary gender. Nope. I couldn't do it.

I took to the internet for research and found that you could get DIY Home Laser kits. Not exactly a cheap option, but worth the cost to avoid another humiliating experience. I found one and ordered it. When the kit arrived, I was quite disappointed. Not only was the machine less effective than those in cosmetic clinics, the procedure took a long time. Still, this was much better than facing another person. I didn't want anyone see what I had down there. It was bad enough that The Final Auditor had to. At least I would be asleep when the rest of his team saw it.

In the months prior to my final surgery, there was a lot more preparation required than hair removal. I had to sign and mail countless forms, pre-purchase medical equipment for post-operative care, and arrange for six weeks off work. *Wait, what? Six weeks?* That would require a medical certificate, and deplete my sick leave and recreation leave. I would also be unable to hide from my employer that I was traveling interstate to be operated on by a plastic surgeon!

Somehow, everything came together, and I checked into a small private hospital in Melbourne. The Final Auditor came to visit me to chat about the operation, and to ensure that I was psychologically ready. I also got to speak to my Anaesthetist, and a medical student seeking approval from me to view the operation. I didn't want the student to watch, but because I was potentially helping out future girls in my situation, I gave my consent.

The last person to visit the night before my operation was a nurse who gave me a glass of liquid to drink, along with a large jug of water. Before I went to sleep, it was important that I finish both. The liquid didn't taste very nice, and was a little salty. It wasn't the most disgusting thing I'd put in my mouth however, so I downed it, and then, one glass at a time, emptied the jug of water. Hours passed.

Leaping out of the bed, I flew to the bathroom and sat down on the toilet as quickly as I could. *Just in time.* Again. Thank goodness I had a hospital gown on or there'd be a bit of cleaning to do. It felt a little unreal that I was finally there, the night before the final surgery, prepping my digestive system so that if anything went wrong I at least had a good chance of being discharged without a nasty infection. The unfortunate tasting liquid was doing its job very well.

I checked the clock. Only a minute had passed.

I checked the clock. Another minute had passed.

I stared at the ceiling, counting the imperfections.

I looked over the medical equipment in the room.

A few more minutes passed.

OH COME ON!

I ran my finger over the sheets, feeling the texture of the weave.

Eventually, after a few more trips to the toilet, I fell asleep with Outer Shell for the second last time.

"Ten, nine, eight..."

On the operating table the next day, we slipped into our last deep sleep together as two separate entities.

○ LUSTFUL WANDER

THE MOMENT I LOCKED EYES with Stranger Danger, it was clear we had a strong, mutual attraction. Mid-birthday of a vegan Friendly Entity, by the time the handsome Stranger Danger and I began to interact I was quite well socially lubricated by means of wine. Conversation flowed easily and naturally. There was just enough flirting to communicate interest, but not enough to indicate desire for what later occurred.

Being one of several events back-to-back, the time came for me to move on to the final event of the evening. Though I was sad to leave Stranger Danger, I've never been one to bail on friends for a man. He offered to walk me out.

> *Inner Monologue: How sweet!*
> *Body Language: Loose, alluring.*

We walked out to the street where a female polyamorous Friendly Entity was to pull over and pick me up. Had I been less intoxicated, I may have grown suspicious by Stranger Danger's request that we duck into the dark alley by the building and kiss. But I was quite drunk and Friendly Entity was still a while away, so naively I followed. We shared a passionate kiss as he pressed me against the wall and himself against me. He grabbed my hand and guided it down to the erect dick that he had quickly pulled out of his trousers.

"I think I just heard my friend. It was so lovely to meet you," I called as I ran off.

Days later I was drunk at another birthday party, sitting next to the tall, dark and handsome Irresistible Man.

"Is this okay?"

"Yes," I assured Irresistible Man.

The excitement of what was secretly happening right under everyone's nose increased the enjoyment from the feeling of his hand up my dress. Irresistible Man stared at my lips. I felt the rush of blood to my cheeks as I returned the gaze. He had big, full lips, and I wanted them against my own. Our faces moved closer. His eyes were wide, a sign of adoration.

"My kisses heal anything," he told me. We both smiled, enamoured, but he had more words to add.

"So if you've got any STDs..."

I momentarily pulled back, laughed, and kissed him despite the massacred pick-up line.

"I'm having trouble breathing around this smoke. I'm just going to go take a walk," I announced, suddenly getting up from the table. I wanted to keep this interaction private. I looked directly at Irresistible Man and smiled, hoping he would understand what I was doing. He did.

"I'll come and keep you company," he offered.

As soon as we were out of sight, like rabid animals we grabbed each other. I threw myself back against a dumpster and pulled him in close, wrapping my arms and a leg around him. His hand found its way up my dress again, then beneath my underwear.

"You feel amazing," he said as he explored, causing me to moan.

My eyes were closed as I enjoyed the feeling, forgetting about the rest of the world. It felt so good. Violently we kissed, squeezing each other, unable to get close enough. And then, without warning, my brain started to catch up, and I could smell the dumpster. I became aware of my surrounds and that I was with a stranger. What was I doing?

"I've got to head off," I told him, panicking.

We exchanged contact details, and I made a hasty exit.

During the weeks that followed, I tried to slow down things with Irresistible Man, but every time we saw each other, within moments his hands would be all over me and I wouldn't object and then we would have sex. It became a bit of a comedy, the way it all played out, going from hot, to cold, and returning to hot again. When we were apart, I wanted to slow down and get to know him, but when we were together, I was unable to control myself. And then a condom broke inside me.

Irresistible Man didn't bother to put a new one on, and I screamed out for more but was then pulled out of the moment by the words, "I don't want to get you pregnant."

Inner Monologue: Oh my God, he doesn't know!
Body Language: Sudden reduced passion.

"It's okay, I'm on the pill," I told him. It was a dishonest way to tell part of the truth, but I couldn't tell him the whole truth while he was inside me. That was less safe than the sex we were having!

A combination of too much alcohol and fear caused a sickening feeling to rise up inside me. I started throwing my hands against him, calling out.

"Pull out, get off, I need to vomit!"

Irresistible Man quickly removed himself from me and I fled, barely making it to the bathroom in time for my scream hurl to mostly end up in the toilet bowl. Waves of spew erupted from me and I coated the bathroom with a thick, slimy layer of goo. Irresistible Man came into the bathroom and held my hair back for me.

"Please go," I begged him. "I feel disgusting. I don't want you to see me like this." I also needed time alone to think.

"I want to make sure you're alright," Irresistible Man told me.

o

Spending a few moments focusing on orientation after waking up, I stretched my body out and yawned in an especially feline fashion, then grabbed my phone, unlocked it, and checked my calendar. I was surprised to find that my schedule was especially clear, with just one date organised for the afternoon. My phone informed me that it was a clear, sunny day, but not too hot. Excellent! It was a rare weekend morning when I was without a hangover, so I decided to take a long walk by the river. Because I didn't want to waste a moment of this lovely day, I shot out of bed, showered, dressed, and skipped out the door. *Today is a Good Day.*

My leisurely stroll took me through the centre of Fortitude Valley, the setting for dancing and portrayal of Outer Shell as a gay man in my late teens, over the Story Bridge, the site I had planned to use for suicidal purposes as a young adult, and down along Southbank, beside the river, a location strongly attached to the memories of opening my heart to Legitimate One all those years ago. By the river, the cool breeze on my skin and in my hair felt wonderful. So refreshing. I thought back to the time when I had met Legitimate One there to tell him about my past. Although it hadn't worked out, I had fond memories of our time together, and was now able to reflect without feeling any pain or regret. I must have looked radiant as I reflected on the past. I felt at peace, looking out over the water, happy that I had finally let go of my quest to recreate what I'd had with Legitimate One.

I'm told that I look people in the eye and smile more often than most people, and perhaps that is why strangers approach me so frequently. On this good day, I walked past a tall, slender gentleman with reddish brown hair, and, as usual, I smiled at him as I passed. My heart leapt, registering his returned smile. I felt desirable, increasing my feelings of satisfaction with the day, so my smile widened as I continued to wander. A few minutes later, he was in front of me, using the familiar gesture that was a request for me to take out my earphones. He wanted to speak to me.

"Hi," I said, smiling, cheeks rosy.

"I'm sorry to interrupt you," he apologised. "I gave it some thought, and I would have been really annoyed at myself if I didn't tell you that I really like the way you look. I'm Master Whirlwind."

"Thank you, Paige," I gushed. I searched through my brain for open-ended questions that would allow conversation to flourish, but all I came up with was the very closed, "Where are you from?"

"I'm from Birmingham," Master Whirlwind told me. He added more detail to save me from my fatal conversational mistake. "Here on a working visa. Where are you from originally? Your accent isn't typically Australian."

"I've moved around a lot. Before Brisbane I was living in North Queensland."

"I've been there!" His eyes lit up with the recognition that we had something in common. "I did seasonal work up there before I came down here to Brisbane."

There was brief silence.

"I should..." I gestured to the path, in the direction I had been walking.

Master Whirlwind hesitated, looked down at his feet, and then softly requested my phone number so we could arrange to have a drink together. I handed him my phone.

"Put your details in here and I will text it to you," I directed, placing all power of contact in my control. Master Whirlwind obliged.

Not long after our farewell, a message came through from Unreliable Dude informing me that he was going to be late, so I sent a message to Master Whirlwind telling him that I would be at my friend's bar if he wanted to go for that drink. He would have to turn up almost immediately. He did.

We had a nice (albeit brief) chat, and then I got a message from Unreliable Dude telling me that he was on his way. I told Master Whirlwind he had to go. As Unreliable Dude and I messaged back and forth, I organised a date with Master Whirlwind. I gave him the task of choosing the location of date two, since I had chosen the first location.

Between Master Whirlwind taking off, and Unreliable Dude sitting down, the barman, who was more than an acquaintance but not yet a friend, laughed and shook his head.

"Does this happen to you a lot, Paige?"

"Yes," I confirmed. After everything I had been through, I felt okay revelling in smugness over being desired.

A few days later, I purposefully arrived earlier than required. I found a nearby perch where the lighting was good (see also: flattering) and where Master Whirlwind would be able to see me from a distance. I opened a book and started to read so that he would associate me with intelligence. It seems an appropriate time to deconstruct Master Whirlwind's deliberate look that would take several dates for him to admit to.

o

Master Whirlwind's Appearance, Deconstructed:
His hair was short and neat, to attract women who liked Neat Men
He had a beard, and it was thick but well maintained, to attract women who liked Rugged Men, but not be dismissed by women who liked Neat Men
He wore stylish glasses instead of contact lenses, to attract women who liked Geeky/Nerdy/Stylish/Hipster Men

o

"I find it amusing that I have lived here for fifteen years and somebody who is passing through is introducing me to somewhere new," I told Master Whirlwind when he interrupted my reading. I looked admiringly at his Neatly Rugged, Stylishly Nerdy appearance.

We had a fantastic date, looking over the river at the Story Bridge that I had crossed prior to meeting him for the first time. We took turns buying rounds of drinks. There were big smiles and blushing cheeks. It all felt delightfully romantic, but there was a very safe distance between us, and you'd be forgiven for thinking we were saving someone a seat. Hours after I'd told him I needed to go home, we had become so physically close that you could no longer fit a person between us. We were also at the point where our eyes were darting between the lips and the eyes of the other person. We both wanted to kiss.

"I've had a cold," I warned, leaning in, and you could no longer fit a coin between us. "I'm probably still contagious."

Master Whirlwind leaned in closer, and you could no longer fit anything between us.

"Worth it," he whispered, and we kissed.

Three fantastic dates later, Master Whirlwind announced to me, "I'm drunk enough that I'll let you do to me what I was going to let you do to me when I was sober."

"This has never happened to me before," he said, 20 seconds later. We cuddled for a while, and then tried again. I completely let go, liberated by the fact that we had a hard expiry date. The dates—and intimate moments—became more frequent and lasted longer, until it was his final week in Australia. I saw him every day, and he slept in my bed next to me.

Everything was equal. I introduced him to a place he hadn't been to before, and he paid for my drinks. He introduced me to a place I hadn't been to before, and I paid for his drinks. I started to feel a little sad that this wouldn't continue, but I reminded myself that the only reason this was so wonderful was that he was leaving and while we didn't have time for games, we also didn't have time to develop trust, so I hadn't told him anything about my past.

For what was to be our second last date, I cooked, we ate, we chilled and watched Netflix, we made love, and then he left, choosing not to stay over that night. Watching him walk down the hall away from the apartment following a parting kiss, I had this weird feeling, like that would be the last time I would see him, and it was. A message came through the next day informing me that he probably wouldn't be able to make the time to see me again before he left, and shortly after that came the confirmation that he definitely wouldn't be able to see me again. He thanked me for the amazing time, including some of the best sex he had ever had—we really did improve a lot each time—and promised to add me on Facebook. Although this was exactly what I had consented to, I felt incredibly sad that it was over so suddenly.

• A LEGITIMATE END

My time couch surfing comes to an end, and Bosom Buddy helps me move to the house I will be looking after for two months. I'm astounded by how quickly we move everything I own; several minutes to load the car, and less than sixty seconds to offload at the other end. It feels incredible to be travelling so lightly, though I do miss having a large selection of dresses to choose from for work. Realising that I am being photographed more frequently for medical and diversity events, I make the decision to occasionally buy a new one, and discard any dress that has been in several photographs.

The relocation comes at a good time, because biopsy results confirm that a previously treated skin cancer is growing back through the scar it left on my neck. Standard recommendation for this is prompt excision with fairly large margins. Dermal Saviour warns me of the possible dangers of cutting into me so close to a nerve, but despite him pretending it has all gone wrong while the scalpel is in my neck, the excision is successful and we laugh at his terrible joke.

Before he dresses the fresh wound, Dermal Saviour does me the favour of offering to show me his handiwork. Of course I gladly take the opportunity, and am confronted with a much larger scar than expected. I joke that he should have just gone all the way around the whole neck so I could save on Halloween costumes in future. He's not as amused as I am, and I return to the examination bed to be patched up.

During the first few nights following the excision, pain prevents me from sleeping through the night, so during the day I'm tired, irritable, and have limited ability to move about. By the time Friday afternoon arrives, I'm desperate to get out the work door, so I leave early to feed the house owner's cats, before heading over to Bosom Buddy for a scary movie viewing session. While I sit on the bus, scrolling aimlessly on social media, a message from L2 arrives.

L2: *Hey – day off. What's up?*

I tap away and send my response.

Me: *Hi! I thought you had yesterday off.*

L2: *I got my weeks mixed up. That's a week from now.*

I'm sceptical of his reply, but shrug and enter the conversation anyway.

Me: *I've left work early because I have way too much flex time apparently.*

L2: *What's flex time?*

Intuition tells me I shouldn't engage, but I can't help myself and launch into an essay.

Me: *But I'm heading back to feed cats then visiting a friend. Aw you wouldn't get flex time huh? When I work extra hours I can tally it up and take those hours later. It's a bit limited though. Anything past 9.5 hours in a day can't be claimed, so I get short changed a bit. How're you spending your day off?*

L2 sends through emoji that indicate he's been sleeping, studying, and masturbating.

L2: *I alternate. Breaks up the study aspect.*

I recall that his formal study doesn't start until the new year.

Me: *Started studying already? You're a glutton for punishment.*

L2: *You don't have a lot of time to sit around and think in emergency medicine. So I figured I'd try and cram it all in now. Perform well. Get good recommendations and a reputation. Ruin said reputation by jumping into anaesthetics. And then have a happy life.*

I laugh at what is clearly a dark stab at the notion that one's life can be happy.

Me: *Sounds like a fairy tale.*

L2: *Exactly.*

I laugh and the conversation starts to feel more organic again, and I feel happy that he's reached out to keep up the friendship I've become so fond of.

"I couldn't tell whether I should read some of that in a sarcastic voice,"

I say. "What topic are you studying today?"

"Electrolyte disorders. Mainly training to remember the variety of mechanisms of dehydration in DKA."

I grin.

"Maybe you need flash cards."

He smiles.

"Do you have any?"

He smiles with a bead of sweat on his forehead. Hopeful.

I type "ketoacidosis flash" into a search engine and it autocompletes for me. Amused, I take a screen capture and send it to L2.

"Did not think that would be a popular search," I tell him.

L2 laughs. For a while there are little bubbles indicating he's writing something. They disappear for a moment, then reappear. Shortly after, he hits send.

"And here I was hoping."

I screw up my face.

"My phone is clean," I tell him.

"Is it? Such a shame. We will just have to generate new smut."

I cannot believe it. I scroll back through and conversation to confirm that our last one ended with him rejecting my advances. Confirmed.

"If it weren't for that typo, I'd totally have obliged just now," I joke. I try not to let my frustration show, and add, "Says the mistress of typos."

"Pfft," is all he responds with.

As I grin I notice I've almost reached my destination, so I put my phone away as to not accidentally stay on the bus for too long. After feeding the cats, I head back to the bus stop, and get on a bus to Bosom Buddy's place. I realise there's an unread message from L2.

"Dinner with the parents tonight."

I stare at the message, trying to see something to respond to.

"Well, then," I state.

"Then afterwards. Who knows," L2 suggests.

I start to feel a little bit cheeky, and spend some time crafting an ambiguous reply.

"What time with parents? Asking for no reason. *You're definitely free to leave your phone on the table.*"

L2 laughs.

"Around five to seven. Anytime thereafter is a gateway to whatever we can think up."

I arrive at the bus stop closest to Bosom Buddy's home.

"My super long public transport trip to my friend's house is almost done so I shall leave you be for the moment. Enjoy study, procrastination and the parents. Talk to you later."

I put my phone away, and give Bosom Buddy a rundown of the situation with L2, expressing how frustrated I am, bewildered. Bosom

Buddy listens, nods, and we escape into a fictional world of blood and gore.

My phone lights up. L2 has sent through an upside down emoji.

I open my phone and quickly type a reply.

"Are you upside down? I'm watching a scary movie. *Lights Out*."

L2 asks if I'm cuddled up with someone.

"I have a comfortable distance between me and my friend. I'm curled up in the corner of the sofa like a scared little child. Must. Not. Turn. Out. The…" I add a lightbulb emoji.

"You should take a picture of your bum to calm down. Might work?" He adds the smiling emoji with forehead sweat. Hopeful again.

I steal a close up image of a peach and send it to him with a smirk.

The film finishes, and I feel sore, so I ask Bosom Buddy to drop me home. After I tuck myself in to bed, L2 sends another message.

"How goes the movie? I'm now twiddling my thumbs watching Layer Cake."

"The ending was terrible. How's the film? No big grand plans for the rest of your Friday night? My friend has dropped me home and because I'm a sad case I'm going promptly to bed so I can get up early and go for a wander. Enjoy the rest of your night."

I hope it doesn't sound too cold, but L2's response tells me it does.

"Oh. Ok. Goodnight!"

Several days pass and I find myself initiating contact again. Although I love the ability to go home alone and recharge my social batteries every day after work, I'm reminded that there's nobody in the world who holds me as a priority. I try to occupy my free time with writing and volunteer work, but crave a romantic partner. It frustrates me as I look around and everywhere see people in relationships who are unhappy or treating their partners poorly.

As lonely as I feel, I don't feel up to starting from scratch, so again I reach out to L2.

"Work day today?"

"Mhmm. Post take resident. I've discovered a new job that I dislike. Intensely."

I roll my eyes.

"Oh my God that's like your favourite hobby. Sorry. Couldn't resist."

"So true. Less horrendous than expected though."

I decide to probe.

"What makes you dislike it so intensely while also considering it as less horrendous than you expected?"

There's no answer for days, and, stuck at home alone, unable to move much, the hours feel like days and I'm unable to stop myself messaging L2 again.

"Have you seen *Crashing*? It's bloody weird, but so funny."

"No?"

I can't work out how to respond to his message, so I just leave it. For the first time in a while, he initiates contact again.

"Partying it up tonight? I'm home watching nineties action movies before going to the gym."

"I want to kick my cold as soon as possible so I took sick leave from social plans," I tell him. "What films are you watching? *True Lies*? *Robocop*? The Christmas one?"

"Actually now I've swapped over to early naughties. I was getting sick of the *Point Break* reruns. I wanted some nu-metal rap rock with my movie!"

My mind travels back to all the nights of the past months we've had these conversations. Now that I'm sober, it seems a little sad, but I'm lonely so I continue.

"What's your naughties pick? I've been watching *Chewing Gum*. It's... different."

"Hmmm. I've picked *SWAT*. Which apparently has Jeremy Renner in it. Who knew," L2 adds.

I laugh.

"I'll probably regret this, but I've switched to *Never Ending Story*. Pretty sure I knew JR was in *SWAT*."

A long day passes, made longer by the extra time it takes to travel to and from work. I find myself reaching out without even realising it.

Something unexpectedly enjoyable about this couch surfing and house sitting business is finding different ways to get to work on public transport. There are all these bus services I never knew existed.

He takes a while to send his short reply.

Oh yeah?

Yeah, I reply. *I've been going to the The Medical College and it's easy to get between here and work.*

What are you doing back at The Medical College?

I smile. Today is one of the days I'm becoming a better role model.

Discrimination Support Officer training, so I can better support LGBT students. Lots of policy and legislation stuff today. Next week apparently there'll be more hands-on type stuff.

Several weeks pass, and I manage to curb my compulsion. As I walk out of my office to meet Friendly Entity for lunch and a deep discussion, however, I am confronted with the image of L2. He is sitting at the café opposite a woman I don't know.

"Hey Paige!"

I turn and smile at The Bodyguard, and return his greeting, letting him know that I'm meeting someone for lunch and will catch up with him later.

"Sure thing," The Bodyguard tells me.

When I return my gaze to the direction of the café, L2 and his female friend are leaving. For the first time, our eyes do not meet; not even for a second. I reach out one last time with a message that will go unanswered forever.

Instead of sad, I feel freed. And I feel a little grateful. I think of all I've managed to achieve in the past year, because I've not had to consider a romantic partner. The times I've sacrificed my privacy for the greater good, and accepted invitations to speak without first having to run it by someone who might prefer I spend time with them. Someone who might prefer that their family not know they're with a woman with a past like mine. I smile as I contemplate the bright future this situation has allowed.

As I wander along the Brisbane River, deep in thought, I receive a call from Parental Being.

Chapter Eighteen

∞ OSSEOUS

When I remember waking up, I was back in the bed in my private room, my legs bound by compression stockings, those wrapped tightly in compression sleeves that inflated and deflated continuously, because the last thing you want is a blood clot to form from spending so much time in bed. It would have been impossible for me to get out of bed at this point, but there was no need because my digestive system was empty, and I was attached to a catheter that transferred my urine directly to a bag that the nurse had to replace frequently because I was drinking so much water. I did this not because I was thirsty, but because I had some idea that peeing a lot post-surgery would be good for my urinary tract.

In the beginning, I was protected from severe pain; hooked up to a machine that intravenously provided me with morphine whenever I pressed the button. Unfortunately, it turns out I don't respond well to morphine, which caused a scene far too similar to one in The Exorcist. After barfing while restrained to the bed, I decided that I would endure whatever pain oral painkillers could not shield me from. I was soon in an incredible amount of physical pain, but finally, in my 20s, I felt like one person. There was no Outer Shell and Inner Me, there was just Paige. Me.

When I first woke up, my vagina was packed to prevent it from fusing together. When I was sufficiently healed, this packing was removed and I was required to replace it daily with my own packing, created by rolling up foam and placing it inside a condom. There has been no occasion before or since that I have been in so much pain. Even just lying still in bed my fresh axe wound was agonising, but when I had to put fresh packing in, the pressure caused pain that was almost too much to handle.

I spent days in bed and had to do leg exercises, which caused the surgical site to hurt even more. Before long I started to return to walking, and with all that extra pressure on the area, I felt like my body was trying to tear itself apart. As I write this my legs are tightly crossed. I'm wincing as I remember the insane level of pain I was in. I hope I never have to endure such pain ever again.

The next challenge I faced after surgery was learning how to urinate again. One of the surgery risks I feared was incontinence, but I was pleased to find that although there was a lot of blood at first—from the surrounding area, not my urinary tract—I was still able to control my flow to a degree. At first I sprayed urine everywhere, but as I healed and the area was less inflamed, urinating became a much less messy ordeal. I returned to Brisbane shortly after the surgery, and after an excruciating plane flight, I was able to spend the rest of my six weeks at home, walking only when required.

One of the benefits I was looking forward to post-surgery was a shift from requiring expensive oral contraceptive pills, to commencing subsidised hormone replacement therapy. As usual, my body had other plans for me.

"What does it mean?" I asked Nurture Essence, concerned at the post-surgery hormone-related follow-up appointment. Couldn't anything go smoothly for me? Why did I always experience the rare or atypical stuff?

"If we do nothing, you'll end up with osteoporosis. This means that the bones will become brittle and fragile from loss of tissue."

"Annoying," I commented. "What are my options?"

"There are two courses of action we can take. I can put you on something to increase your levels of calcium and vitamin D, or we can permanently increase your hormone dose."

"What are the risks?"

"You'd need to be monitored taking a calcium supplement long term because it could lead to hypercalcemia," Nurture Essence informed me, handing me a pamphlet. "There are a list of possible symptoms here."

"And increased hormones?"

"It would mean keeping you on an oral contraceptive pill, which isn't subsidised like the hormone replacement therapy you've been on. It will be a lot more expensive long term, but much lower maintenance."

I pored over the documentation given to me by Nurture Essence.

"So the hormone option would be preventative, and the calcium supplement would be a treatment, right?"

"More or less," Nurture Essence confirmed.

"Let's go with the preventative option," I said. "I can always make sacrifices somewhere else in my budget."

Follow-up appointments aside, there were two main tasks to complete during the weeks I was stuck at home. Firstly, I had to bathe in salt water several times a day to stave off infection. Keeping a surgical site clean is one of the most important ways you can positively contribute to the healing process. Secondly, I had to progressively stretch the vaginal wall, in preparation for sexual intercourse. To begin with, this was achieved by increasing the amount of foam in the condom. After all bleeding stopped, however, firmer objects were required. As recommended, I was prepared for this with a set of four dilators of different sizes that are used to treat women with a condition called vaginismus. I was soon able to comfortably accommodate the largest dilator, which meant one thing.

I was ready to embark on my new journey as a whole woman, and my top priority was to lose my virginity.

○ **GOOD DAY!**

"I KNOW ABOUT YOUR HISTORY," Work Colleague whispered at the farewell for Our Manager. Maybe it was the seventh or eighth time Our Manager had regenerated, taking on a new form.

"You know what your problem is?"

Inner Monologue: Oh please, why don't you tell me about myself? Everyone else seems to have an opinion about me that somehow has more weight than my own.
Body Language: Relaxed, casual, and friendly.

"You're too concerned with being how you think a woman should be," she told me. "Paige the little, delicate flower that wants everyone to like her and accept her as a woman. You need to let go of that and grow up. Take charge and you will actually get another job."

I decided to keep my defensive thoughts inside. I had been complaining about how, after six years and several brief stints taking secondments in other roles, I was back in my low paid position but with a much higher level of responsibility. I loved the more complex work, but wanted appropriate remuneration. I was well and truly fed up with working purely for compliments.

"I should go chat to him," I abruptly stated, pointing to a random Work Colleague who was seated across the room. "I promised him we would hang out tonight, so I should go do that before he leaves."

"This is Blank," Work Colleague said, introducing me to the guy he was sitting with. "He's a really good guy."

There was a slight wink, and the introduction worked with the alcohol to make me feel safe with this new guy, but for the life of me, I couldn't seem to retain his name and asked for it multiple times. Every time I tried to recall it, my mind went ███████.

My feelings of attraction were increased because I felt sad about losing Master Whirlwind sooner than expected. Work Colleague started giving me extra free booze. Vodka shots, Sambuca shots. Someone else gave me more sparkling wine.

We started to discuss some of my passions, which included leadership. ███████ told me about a book, and I tried to make note of it in my phone to look up later, but my phone froze so ███████ took my number, found a link, and messaged it to me. I thanked ███████ and then we continued with our conversation, smiling and ███████ ███████.

People were leaving, and although I didn't remember getting there, I was hugging them goodbye. It was just me, the café staff and ███████ now. We went back inside to have more drinks and ███████ ███████.

It was just me and ███████, and the café owner. The other staff had finished and left. I looked around.

Inner Monologue: How did I get here?
Body Language: Loose.

I went to the toilet and ███ █ ███.
"I'll see her home safely," ███ announced, and we began the walk back to my place. He ███ █ ███.
We were in an abandoned building, in the dark, and I was pushing ███ to explore it with me. But how did we get here? Eventually, he conceded and he got out his keys and ███ █ ███.
I was up on the windowsill, legs spread, ███ between them. I was expressing my pleasure by calling out, occasionally spasming and ███ ███ ███ was kissing me at my front door, and I was saying "███, ███."
███ ███ ███.

I was naked in bed by myself, unsure of how much of the previous night was reality, and how much was a bizarre sex dream. My tights were in my handbag, placed there while I was in the abandoned building with ███. The rest of my clothes were on the floor, taken off after I had arrived home. At least some of the sexcapades must have occurred. A few days later, I received a curious text from a number that wasn't associated with a name. I knew it was ███, because the only other message in there was a link to a book on leadership.

o

<u>Text Message From</u> ███:
Today's exam is a multiple choice and short answer and will comprise 50% of your semester grading:
1) You are very busy at work and a person only barely known to you offers to buy you coffee at a venue close to your work. Do you - A) accept the offer of a free coffee and a nice distraction; or B) tell them you are too busy and take a rain check.
2) If you answered A) to Q1. Using the twenty four hour clock and rounding to the nearest half an hour, what is the best time in your work schedule to take a coffee break? __:__ If you answered B) to Q1. then choose i) will let you know; or ii) thanks but I don't think so for now.

o

It horrified me that someone I didn't have a name for, who I probably wouldn't recognise in the street, knew me well enough to make contact with such a message. Meeting ███ for a coffee, I drew enough information out of him to confirm that we'd had a sexual experience in the abandoned building, but I didn't press for details. The meeting was fairly brief and exceptionally awkward. ███ seemed nice, but, concerned about how this would affect my career, I decided not to pursue anything. I loved being a part of medical education, and I didn't feel like any risk associated with sex or dating was worth it.

Less than a month later—far too soon—I woke up naked in my own bed, with no memory of getting there. This didn't scare me so much anymore, but perhaps it should have. Hundreds of similar situations had led me to work out to handle it like a pro. At least this time there wasn't a stranger next to me, and I knew I hadn't been with colleagues. I flicked through my phone and checked messages and social media for clues. I had been at a house party. A stupidly hot, brainy Friendly Entity I not-so-secretly pined for had driven me home.

As had become custom, I sent Friendly Entity a message thanking him for getting me home safely, and apologising for anything I might have said or done. I used language that was just vague enough that it wouldn't be obvious that I had no memory of the evening. I put my phone away and stared up at the ceiling.

Ding!

I grabbed the phone again. The response from Friendly Entity was different to what I had come to expect, and at the time I didn't quite understand it. He reprimanded me, and sounded annoyed; angry even. I decided not to seek clarification.

The following Friday afternoon while I was at work, I received a message from Revelator Woman (see: a highly intelligent and perceptive female friend). Revelator Woman had been at the same party.

"Hey dude," I read on the notification that came up on my phone. I stopped what I was working on, flicked my phone open and continued to read. "I know you were drunk on Saturday but you were specifically saying details about suicide and ideation."

I blinked. The pit of my stomach began to hurt and my cheeks became hot. I didn't understand what I was reading.

"I'm sorry I was serious about it but I have to make sure you're okay, by law and because you're my friend. You're obviously going through some fairly major depression at the moment. Are you seeing someone, taking medication? Do you need me to help you access services or recommend anything?"

I panicked. What had I said? What had I done? Was this the first time? I didn't feel depressed. Did I? Well, there was...

I took a breath and replied, "I can't remember Saturday past my first Flirtini. Sorry if I've stressed you out. I'm working on stuff, more or less on top of it."

I sat, staring at my phone, waiting for the reply, unable to think of anything else but this conversation and what it might mean in the greater context of my life. After what seemed like an eternity, I received a reply.

"Okay. But I do have to inform you that if you specifically speak of suicidal ideation and methods of execution in my presence like you did and I deem that you are a risk to yourself – I am bound by oath and law to take you to hospital. I nearly redirected Friendly Entity on Saturday but you were mad because you didn't want me to admit you. Which I didn't either but I couldn't work out if you were serious or not."

Now the strange message from Friendly Entity made sense. This hadn't just been my usual drunken night out where I was flirty and silly. Revelator Woman continued.

"That was far more serious than I've encountered in a while. I totally understand the difference between jokes or drunk ramble but you did not sound like you were joking at all."

At this point, tears were streaming down my face and I had completely forgotten that I was at work. My eyes stung, my lips felt dry, I wanted to puke.

"So I'm just following up. Just letting you know I care and also that I was concerned on Saturday. It wasn't a stress so much as you were serious enough to warrant admission. We care for you dude. No need to be embarrassed. I know you might be anyway but you know us."

She was right, I was embarrassed. No, mortified would have been a more accurate descriptor. I didn't know how to take any of this. I didn't want to be a part of this conversation. I needed to abort.

"Thank you for caring and following up. Sorry to have caused a stir."

I snapped out of it and immediately called Dermal Saviour's practice. He wouldn't be available today. I would have to wait until after the weekend.

I quickly shot Revelator Woman another message. "I've got an appointment on Monday morning. I hope that reduces your worry."

I was so terrified of the situation that I was in that I slipped back into my old ways of being unable to communicate in a natural way like other people. I was forever haunted by the formerly disconnected Outer Shell.

Sitting at my desk, staring at my screen, unable to move, I decided that this could not wait. I couldn't have this weighing on my shoulders for the entire weekend. I called the practice again and then updated Revelator Woman.

"Actually I am going in an hour. I really appreciate you bringing this up."

At the front counter of the medical practice, the receptionist handed me a box of tissues, prompted me to sit down in the waiting room, and brought me some water. Somehow her concern made me feel worse. How many people knew about this? Of all the times I had blacked out, how many people kept secrets about me that I had no knowledge of?

It felt weird to be in the waiting room I'd been in so many times before, there to see a different doctor. Actually everything felt weird. How had I come so undone? I wondered what my plans for suicide had been. Those plans that were locked in some part of my brain that I didn't currently have access to. I wasn't curious enough to ask Revelator Woman or Friendly Entity.

As if I didn't feel humiliated enough, Dermal Saviour walked by. He looked strange through my wet eyes. Usually I was happy to see him, but not today. This was not a version of being undressed that I was comfortable with.

"Hey Paige," he said, smiling at me as he walked by. I grimaced and smiled quickly, then turned away before I could see his reaction to my state.

"Paige," the new doctor called.

I pushed myself up off the seat and followed the doctor down the corridor to his office. The world around me felt dark, like nothing existed more than a few feet away from the two of us. My head was throbbing, my nose and eyes leaking. There was silence. He had asked me why I was here. I couldn't voice it. I was so scared. I didn't know this man.

"I got drunk," I announced suddenly. "And I don't remember anything, but my friend sent me messages telling me that I was threatening to kill myself."

I started hysterically sobbing. I couldn't see the doctor at all through the tears. I could have been talking to a wall.

"I don't think I want to kill myself. I'm a remarkably happy person," I blubbered, my words distorted by tears and mucous. "I have a good life, job, lots of great friends."

The doctor guided me through my thoughts, and made sure there was no immediate threat of suicide.

"When was your last period?" he quizzed as a part of some standard list of questions.

"I haven't had a period," I told him.

"Why haven't you had a period?"

"I don't have a uterus," I clarified. He looked through my record, screwing up his face.

"Why don't you have a uterus?"

"I have had sex reassignment surgery," I blurted out. Again he looked at my record.

"There's nothing on file."

"There's been no reason to ever mention it," I offered. There was brief silence, and I became increasingly uncomfortable.

"Something is extremely wrong with me," I finally admitted, pushing past the awkwardness that had stunk up the room. "I've been feeling sick for months. I wake up and my heart is pounding and it won't stop and it hurts and I can't study and concentrating on anything is so difficult. It hurts so much. I'm hurting so much," I sobbed. "I don't know what is wrong but I need to find out and I need to fix it. I want to get better. I really want to live."

o

Why I ended up at Outer Shell's grave several weeks later was clear to me. I stood at the foot of Outer Shell's grave, shovel in hand, thinking deeply about why I had unravelled. Although I had taken on too much responsibility, too quickly at work, and pushed myself to attend too many social events, that was only a fraction of the problem. I'd also been eating too few nutritious and too many unhealthy foods. And perhaps I had been indulging in a little too much alcohol, a little too often. The most important realisation, however, was that I was hiding from everyone, being dishonest with myself, and striving for a life that I could never have; the life of a cisgender woman.

The increase in exercise at first caused my bones to ache again, but I persevered and through diligence I learnt my limits and began to hover a safe distance from them. I became assertive at work, taking on only as much as I could comfortably handle. I let a few friends know about my issues, and for a while I was in control of my alcohol intake. I started to say no to social events, and scheduled time for myself. I also came out all over again, through the open letter and a blog about my life experiences, holding Outer Shell up to the world for all to see. I then received a letter from My Parent.

o

Letter from My Parent:
Dear Paige,
In respect to what happened at the birthday party, I would like to explain what happened with regard to the slides that I presented for that occasion.
It was my intention to bless The Family by showing some photos of their life. In the time leading up to the party I was unable to set aside time to compile a new group of photos. In my haste I selected a slide presentation which had been prepared for a celebration back when we lived in North Queensland. I did not know what was on the CD. I had not pre-viewed it and I was very uncomfortable when it was shown, which is why I looked in your direction a number of times. I was feeling very uncomfortable for you and was hoping the childhood photos would soon finish.
There was no malice or intention to hurt you in any way. Over the last 10 years or so I have sought to support you the best way I know how.
I offer my most humble apology – if I could turn back time I would rewind and do things differently. If only life were so simple.
I simply ask that one day you will find it in your heart to forgive me all the hurt I have caused you in your life and particularly this last incident.
I love you very much and am very proud of you and your achievements.
Your Parent

o

Having gained strength through the acceptance of my family, I resolved to learn to carry Outer Shell with me wherever I went, without shame. I knew it would be a lengthy, perilous journey, but it was high time I learned to push past the safety of videos, open letters, and blog posts. Within a relatively short period of time, I had everything planned out. Head held high, armed with the first six chapters of a book about the topic, I approached my work supervisor and entered an entirely new world I could never have imagined.

• PARENTAL BEING'S DAUGHTER

THE YEAR OPENS AS I SIT with Parental Being on the back porch of the house I'm minding. We are looking out over the leafy suburb, both smiling as we sip on the sparkling water I've come to enjoy more than alcohol. The atmosphere is relaxed, peaceful. There is a gentle breeze cooling us. Although I can feel several recent surgical sites that are at various stages of healing, the mild discomfort doesn't bother me much. So far the histology reports have all confirmed clear margins; all atypical tissue has been completely removed.

I take a slow, deep breath, and exhale quickly.

"I love it here," I tell Parental Being, beaming. "I think, when I finish with house sitting and get out of debt, I should save up for a deposit to buy a place like this. Maybe without the snakes, though."

"Snakes?"

Parental Being looks suddenly skittish.

"I didn't tell you! Can I tell you a story? Please let me tell you!"

Parental Being laughs nervously, then smiles as they reminisce about my childhood.

"Do you remember that you once found it so difficult to talk to people that I deliberately put you in situations that forced you to do it?"

"Yes," I smile. "And now look at me!"

Parental Being takes on a pensive facial expression.

"You were always able to talk to me, though. I remember you wouldn't let me go, following me around the house and yard until you got to the end of one of your stories. Okay, Paige, you can tell your tale."

I beam at Parental Being, who is smiling fondly. I realise that this is the first time we've been together and reminisced about the past, in a way that has been mutually positive.

"See that narrow door at the end of the balcony? Through there is a rickety spiral staircase down into the dark. When I first came to visit this place, I was taken down there, to what feels like the back passageways of an old theatre. Think *Phantom of the Opera*."

Parental Being shudders, and I continue.

"At one end was a door, padlocked and covered with spider webs and their creators. All along one wall were four doors leading out of this creepy, narrow, decrepit hallway with an especially high ceiling. I looked through the first, and saw that it was a big room without a floor. That is, if you walked through the door you'd have to jump down onto piles of dirt. Each of the four doors led to a similar room, and I pondered how these chthonic spaces would be big enough to make two spacious apartments. Or a wine cellar. Or dungeon. I figured they'd currently be home to many spiders and snakes."

"Ooh," Parental Being exclaims.

"The story behind this unusual space? It was once squash courts. To make the house, they elevated the floor to sit on top of where the ceiling to the courts had once been, leaving a hidden wasteland beneath."

I pause and give thought to how I would like to tell the next part of the story.

"Responsibility-wise, there are many plants here, some of which have died in the heat. There are also two cats to look after. Neither dead, but... there's another story here if you want to hear it."

"I couldn't stop you," Parental Being laughs.

I poke out my tongue at Parental Being, and we both grin.

"One of the goals I've had while house-sitting at this place has been to write a book, so early on I set myself up in the study and tapped away at my laptop for hours, until I realised I was out of sparkling water. When I got up and headed into the main living area, I was confused and then shocked. Just casually, a long snake was hanging out there, and probably had been for most of the time I was lost in my writing."

Parental Being squirms.

"Upon seeing me, or perhaps feeling, the snake started to slither to the side of the room. I had no idea what to do, so I took a photo and posted a social media shout out that the owner saw. Friends warned me that based on appearance, it could be a whip snake, and I received a message from the owner concerned, requesting that I not let the snake bite the cats! When I looked up from that specific message, of course one of the cats was swiping at the snake. Fleeting terror at the thought of pets dying under my care, I dove to the sofa, scooped up the cat, then locked it in the bathroom."

"You're a bona fide super hero, Paige!"

"When I returned to the living area, I was frustrated to note that the snake had found a successful hiding spot. I checked under the sofa. Not there. I checked under the fridge. Nope. Nowhere to be seen. It could have been anywhere!"

Parental Being's eyes are wide, terrified.

"There's a snake loose in the house?"

I shake my head to alleviate Parental Being's distress.

"A friend came over and we turned the house upside down. Not a sign of the snake, and only a suspicion of its entry point; a cat-flap to the garage where the kitty litter was located, but with the flap removed. The cat-sized hole was potentially free entry for anything possessing the dexterity required for garage access."

Parental Being glances around the balcony nervously.

"That night, and for several after, I slept with the cats on my bed. Well, I didn't really sleep so much. In the same week I arrived home to an enormous carpet python blocking my entry to the house. It was dark so I didn't get a good photo, but my attempt was enough to send it slithering into the nearby bushes. Would you like to see?"

Parental Being shakes their head forcefully.

"Some time later, after a particularly hectic week, I was lazing on the couch for way longer than I usually would, binge watching some stupid show, and eventually I had to get up because my bladder said so. As I walked up the corridor I noticed the stupid cat was staring at the cat hole. I thought that odd. Then the cat swiped its paw at the hole, and the now-visible snake assumed an attack position. I stood, frozen, bladder full, frustrated, scared and overwhelmed. No way was I grabbing the cat by lunging in front of a snake that had been worked up into a state of aggression! I just stood there, until the cat grabbed the f▮king snake by its teeth and pulled it into the hallway! Oh, sorry for the language, Parental Being," I apologise, then I pick up the pace, racing through the rest of my story.

"Anyway, the cat carried the snake toward me, but I started yelling at it, telling it to drop the snake and would you believe, it didn't listen to me at all? So I threw an object at the cat, who flinched, allowing the snake to slither into the spare bedroom. I quickly called a snake catcher. Now, I'm not sure if you know this, but one thing you're supposed to do when a snake is in your house, is contain it. Being in the spare room, I had the perfect opportunity to close the door on it while I waited for the snake catcher. As I bolted to the door, the cat darted in before me and the snake came flying out, roughly thrown from the room by the stupid, idiot cat. I swiftly swivelled and bolted back in the other direction. The snake decided that offensive moves wouldn't work, and tried passively defensiveness, pulling itself into a tight little package to look like a rock. This gave the cat the opportunity to trot over to it, pick it up, wander to me, and drop it as a neat, little package on the floor between me and the front door. The cat then draped itself around the compacted snake, as if it were the discarded wrapping paper from the wonderful gift it had just left me. Paralysed, I waited for the snake catcher to arrive, at which point I immediately excused myself so I could use the restroom. Miraculously the cat and snake were both uninjured, and that's why the kitty litter is now in the hallway and the cat door is boarded up."

"Bravo," Parental Being congratulates me, radiating. "We're so proud of you, Paige."

The words—being less about the story and more about how I'm thriving as my authentic self in life—bring tears to my eyes.

Sitting in silence with Parental Being, I allow myself to travel back to the beginning. I reflect on the negativity I received in my early adulthood that I had to push past in order to be open and honest about who I was. I think about the sacrifices I made to tell my story, to come out at home and work, to outline boundaries, and to advocate for social change in the gender diversity sector. I recall the opposition I faced head on until I was strong enough to rise above it, and be a role model for those who were afraid to be themselves.

Am I scarred? For sure. Was it worth it? Most definitely. The proof of success is not in my own words, however. Success is evident in the most unlikely of places. Following my Open Letter, proof of success can be found in the comments section.

•

"Just continue being true to yourself, that alone takes more courage than some people have."

"I have always respected and been inspired by your ability to rise above the confines of those minds who cannot see you for who you are: a courageous, thoughtful, considerate, passionate, highly intelligent, successful, sassy and beautiful woman who is the truest and most loyal of friends. Those that know you, love and adore you for all these reasons and your ability to accept and welcome people of all sorts from all walks of life. You are open, honest and respectful of others thoughts and opinions even when they conflict with your own. You hold your tongue when others are quick to condemn. Anyone who judges you for your past, needs to take a minute to stop and think about how it's made you who you are. I for one love your past because in the years I've known you I have had the privilege of those fleeting insights that help me understand how you've become so remarkable. I love you from the tips of my toes to the top of my head. I will always support you. x"

"You f‌‌‌‌‌‌king rock. For a myriad of reasons, apparent from this post."

"You'll always have my support. Sorry for any time I've made you uncomfortable - it was unintentional!"

"Your great strength & heart never cease to amaze, thank you for being my friend."

"I just think of you as my Twitter/FB friend on the other side of the globe, whom I've never met physically, but she's pretty damn awesome and I am proud to call her friend."

"This post is courageous, honest and just awesome all around - which is you in a nutshell. It therefore changes exactly zero in how I see you or relate to you as a friend."

"I'm sorry to hear you had to hide this from some people. And I can't wait to eat cheese!"

"You are an amazing woman, love you Paige."

"Paige = Paige. That's all I've known, all I care about and honestly, all that's my business. Labels and history don't make a person. You are you, and that's why we like you."

"I didn't know any of this before, Paige, and it makes precisely zero difference that I know it now. Well, except that I think you're even more awesome than I thought you were before, because see above; but apart from that, zero difference. You are awesome, you are Paige, and people who take exception to any part of the process that got you to being awesome and Paige are people you're likely better off without, because who wants friends who feel threatened by one's humanity?"

"Before you posted this, I simply thought you were an awesome person. But now that I know you don't have the same teeth you had when you were born, I need some time to process this..."

"Though I haven't known you long, I haves always seen you as an endlessly understanding and vibrant person. You deserve everything. Thank you so much for sharing x"

"I met Paige as this vivacious women, I still think you're a vivacious women with a heck of a lot of courage <3 xx"

"Paige, I don't care if you had all four wisdom teeth out at once! I'm still your friend! ;) Seriously though, you're an AMAZING woman. You're strong, intelligent, beautiful, and very funny. I'm proud to call myself your friend xxxx"

"Good on your for laying down the law on what isn't approriate or anyone else's business. You're wonderful and I love you x"

"Paige, I'm so grateful to have you as a friend. Thank you for allowing myself and the other supportive people here know and appreciate you a little more. <3 <3 <3"

"All that matters to me is who you are and you're one funny, intelligent and very capable individual. I am very curious, but I would never ask you anything about this highly personal topic - that would be insensitive and rude of me. You rock Paige."

"You're such a brave woman Paige! Thank you for sharing, I think you're even more amazing! X"

"I don't understand how anyone could even think it was acceptable or appropriate to even ask or comment! Your history is yours and is no ones business! I applaud you for your honesty in this post but am somewhat saddened that you felt it necessary in the first place. You are who you are and we love you :) <3"

"Phew, for a minute there I thought you were going to tell us your real name was Krystal! I don't think any differently toward you, other than admiration regarding how much strength it must have taken to get to here. Thank you for sharing with us. *hugs*"

"You are too too awesome!! People should learn from you because you have the greatest ability to be completely proudly you without offending others!! I hope in person you are just like Facebook Paige because I love cyber you!!"

"I've only ever known you as you. Nothing's changed."

"Love you even more than I did yesterday, if that is even possible?"

"It takes a strong will to do what you have done, it takes a stronger one to put it out there for people to see. Whilst I may not see you or talk to you as often, you are always in my thoughts and I support you wholeheartedly. xxx"

"Thanks for being such an excellent educator, and just generally fascinating, funny, and kind."

"You're just Paige. Paige is beautiful, & funny, & quirky, & smart. Paige has lived & experienced things, just like every other human being on the planet. You're you. I love you, Paige. xx"

"I had absolutely no idea. And this doesn't change a thing. Keep being wonderfully, hilariously, and unashamedly you!"

"Thanks for being so open and honest, by helping us to understand how you feel you are spreading awareness, compassion and acceptance and making our world a better place. Xo"

"Thank you for posting that beautiful message. You should be so proud of your strength! Sending love :)"

"Paige is the best Paige. That's all anyone needs to know"

"Love you Paige. I think everything else I wanted to say has already been said. Glad to have you in my life. Xx"

"Oh Paige you are such a gorgeous girl. I am humbled by the beautiful way you write. It's a gift and I am deeply honoured to have been included. I hope to see you soon in Melbourne. x"

Volume II
2017

**Isolated Moving Human Target
(Memoirable Book 4)**

— o —

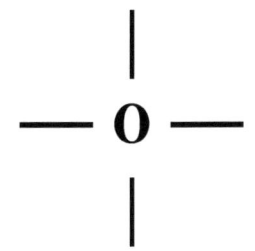

*In both matters of love, and of war,
all is most definitely not fair.*

ROSA LOUISE MCCAULEY PARKS wished to be known as *a person who is concerned about freedom and equality and justice and prosperity for all people.* I've drawn immeasurable strength both from her words, and knowledge of her actions, and would like to be known as having similar concerns. That is, on a much smaller scale of course, for both my efforts and barriers have paled in comparison. Having achieved a great deal before she passed away in 2005, Rosa is one of those people everyone should know of. Me, not so much.

During the time she generously gave to the Civil Rights Movement, Rosa Parks also gave us many inspirational quotes. It is one in particular that I would love to have had the opportunity to ask her about. See, there's something about it that drives me quite mad.

THE QUOTE THAT DRIVES ME MAD

"I have learned over the years that when one's mind is made up, this diminishes fear; knowing what must be done does away with fear."

As someone who became a leader, I want to know the truth behind that statement, because for me it is not true. For all the training, for all the experience overcoming hurdles of steadily increasing difficulty, and for all my determination, fear never left me. In my case, at most, I learned to temporarily manage my reaction to an immortal fear that resides at my very core. I learned to do no more than to ignore that fear during the moments in which it felt absolutely necessary to spend my limited energy doing so.

So, this book. As it's the fourth novella in a series (*Memoirable*), I find myself in something of a predicament. There's a chance you've already read a great deal about how I ended up here, as this especially fearful leader. Also possible, is that your eyes have landed on this page without that context, and I dare not turn either of you away. With that in mind, I'll be dancing a fine line in an attempt to provide relevant, necessary details about the past for the sake of the new audience, without so much that it becomes boring to those who already know it all. Or so they—or you—think…

As in all previous written works based on the true events that have occurred in and around my person, I'm inclined to warn readers of potentially triggering content. There is a Potentially Triggering Cast who play recurring roles in my life. I'd now like to introduce you to them.

The Potentially Triggering Cast
(In No Particular Order)

Mental Illness
Sexuality
Addiction
Cancer
Suicide

Special Guest Appearances by
(In Various Disguises)

ASSAULT!

Because of this cast of varying palatability, and also the varied digestive skills of the readership, I tread associated trails with tender footsteps, without going so far as to ignore what needs to be discussed. In the business of World Changing, there are times when the bitter aftertaste is necessary. If it's any consolation, the taste of the retelling never nears the pain of the original experience. But enough of this fanciful talk, for there are things I must explicitly state before we travel together any further.

Explicit Statement One

The thoughts and ideas expressed in any book that I write are my own, and have absolutely nothing to do with any of my employers, past or present.

Explicit Statement Two

No character descriptions should ever be considered as accurate representations of real people.

There are three deliberate actions I have taken to protect the privacy of all players in my life. I will point out though, that it's not feasible to write about thousands of individuals in detail anyway. And yes, my life is such that I do interact with thousands of story-worthy individuals every year.

Protective Action Taken

I've written collectively about people, information has been divulged in a way that is not linear, and at times I have explored emotion associated with an experience, rather than providing details that could be used to identify a real place or person.

With the above in mind, I would like to tell you plainly that none of the content explored in this book should lead you to feel negatively about any specific person, with one exception; *me*.

Something that sets this book apart from the trilogy that was my earlier life, is that each chapter includes a section from *before*, and a section taking place *now*. The *before* component of each chapter is an eighteen-part side story that has occurred somewhere between birth, and now. For reasons that will become apparent as you read, I've gone to greater lengths to ensure there are no details that connect this story to a specific time, place, or person. What is of utmost importance, is the psychological impact that the ordeal had on me.

Next, I need your agreeance on something.

Your Agreement

By reading beyond this page, you acknowledge that you have read and understood the words above.

Do we have an agreement?

Only then can we begin.

— 1 —

Sometimes a symbol of rebirth, transformation, immortality, and healing; sometimes just a snake.

Once upon a time…

MY SAFE SPACE HAS BEEN UNWELCOMELY PENETRATED yet again. This isn't like those times that went unreported; there was no sexual element on this occasion. Although I ranked the altercation as relatively low intensity, this time it felt more important that I fight against my fear, to ensure that there were consequences for the assailant, however menial those consequences might be. That is why, once upon a time, the following, jarring words travelled through the phone line into my ear.

"You've described assault," Investigator Man told me matter-of-factly through the phone.

Well obviously, and technically. I purposefully hadn't used that word though. You know, for fear of being told I was being a melodramatic woman, and that I just needed to toughen up because the world was a cruel place at times. All I wanted was to ensure Vulpine Foe didn't do something similar again; to me, or to someone else. The reporting was more about his potential victims. I didn't want to be indirectly complicit in his future bad behavior through my own silence.

"Oh, ah," I stammered.

Anyone who knows me well—and I guess also a bunch of strangers who've read my previous books—would be aware that I hate speaking on the phone at the best of times. The call from Investigator Man was so much worse because of the entire situation surrounding it. I was *almost* physically alone, in my *almost* Safe Space, so my body decided that it was okay to whip me with a vibrant red rash around the neck, that then travelled down my chest, as if to seek comfort between my modest mammary mounds.

I turned to my left, where Male Ally was sitting, leaning back in his chair, completely relaxed because the nature of the situation wasn't new to him. My body movement was subtle enough to protect my rash from visibility, and as Male Ally glanced at me, I casually averted my gaze, hoping he couldn't see the level of distress I was in. Credentials aside, as someone I didn't know very well, I felt uncomfortable being so vulnerable, and in need of his support. Investigator Man, who I didn't know at all, demanded more attention.

"Can you talk me through exactly what happened? Tell me everything from the beginning, until the end of the interaction with Vulpine Foe."

An involuntary shudder spread from my core, outwards, as the sound of the name Vulpine Foe reached ear. I closed my eyes, took a deep breath in, and let it out slowly. I opened my eyes, and because I had been commanded to do so by a man in a position of power over me, I did something that I had become very good at. I travelled back in time, to a place I had no desire to revisit.

No desire at all.

Meanwhile, right now…

WHAT YOU DON'T WANT from your first house sitting gig is an experience that makes you worry that this big life change you've made could end up being an *out of the frying pan and into the fire* situation. Considering the rollercoaster otherwise known as my life that led me to be here, I really shouldn't be surprised that things have turned out the way they have. Life can change dramatically in an instant, and mine often has, sometimes with a resolution that is… surprising.

When you're meeting me, what's left of my personal life fits neatly into 13 bags that are stashed near the front door of the house I'm looking after. *Where* I am, is on the large balcony out the back. It looks out over a leafy suburb in the west of Brisbane. The atmosphere is relaxed, peaceful. Although summer is just around the corner, a gentle breeze is snaking its way through the trees to cool me. I take a slow, deep breath, and exhale quickly.

I love it here, I think to myself. *Getting rid of my debt this way is going to be so easy. I definitely made the right decision.*

Turning to my right, past a long line of large, potted plants that I'll be required to nurture for two months, I see a narrow door at the end of the balcony. Curiosity leads me over to, and through the door, where I face a rickety, spiral staircase down into the dark. I flick a switch that provides adequate—albeit flickering—light, and make my way down to what feels like the back passageways of an old theatre. Think *Phantom of the Opera*, if you know it.

At the passageway end that is nearest to me there is a door that is padlocked. It is covered with spider webs and their creators. I swing my eyes to scan all the way to the other end of the passageway, noting four doors leading to... well, I don't yet know where. I walk to the first doorway, and gaze into a big room without a floor. That is, if I walk through the door, I'd have to jump down onto piles of dirt. It's easy to imagine the dirt as a sea of brown serpents staring up at me. I shudder.

Moving on, I find that each of the four doors leads to a similar room. I ponder how these chthonic spaces are big enough to make two spacious apartments. Perhaps a wine cellar. Or a kinky sex dungeon. But those would all take a lot of time and money, and in the present moment, although unseen, I figure they're no more than a home to many spiders and snakes. We are, after all, in Queensland, Australia.

What the owner has told me, is that this space underneath the house was once squash courts. In order to create the house above—that is, the house I'll be looking after—the floor of the courts was elevated, so that it now sits on top of where the ceiling to the courts had once been. This has left a hidden wasteland beneath the house, divided neatly into four. My preference is to imagine a more exciting past for the space, but enough of my fanciful rambling for now. Reality is exciting enough.

Responsibility-wise, there are many plants in this home. The back balcony has large plants in pots that need to be watered weekly, so I'll see to them only eight times before I move on. Inside the house are a few small plants that also demand very little effort. It is the area out front that is my main concern while I stay here, at least, in terms of plant life. It is an area of dense vegetation, some potted, some in a garden, some edible, some not, but all requiring a good deal of attention every single day. Before I leave, I'll have watered this area around 60 times.

There are also two cats that I am to look after. One of these cats—a black and white Himalayan Cat— is a bit of a loose cannon. I've been given strict instructions not to let Loose Cannon Cat out of the house. The other, I'm told, may be let out whenever, and has often been known to disappear for overnight adventures. It's not a worry if she's gone a long time, as she's likely developed adequate survival skills. Loose Cannon Cat, has not.

There is a separate, personal goal that I have set myself to reach in the two months I'll live alone in this house. That is to write the full first draft of my third autobiographical book, *Synthesis*. It is because of this that early on I set myself up in the study, and tap away at my laptop for hours on end. It is not until I realize I am out of sparkling water that I get up from the desk. The sparkling water, by the way, is an important detail.

At the time of this story, I'm freshly sober, following many years of frequent, heavy drinking. The years of surrender to alcoholism had been a toxic combination of temporary relief from traumatic memories, while leading me down several paths that ended in new trauma. In some cases, I was unable to remember specific details, and this memory loss felt like fortune smiling upon me.

The temporary switch to sparkling water is one of several techniques I use to reduce the jarring effect of immediate loss of frequent, excessive amounts of alcohol from my life. The technique is effective; it allows the continuation of physical motion in a healthier way, and is relatively cheap, so works well with house sitting toward my goal of debt elimination.

When I head into the main living area, I am confused and then shocked. Just casually, quite a lengthy snake is chilling out on the floorboards in the middle of the room. The snake could well have been there for most of the time I was lost in my writing. The thought of it existing unseen in my past temporarily causes me more distress than it being visible at my feet in the present. The human brain is odd in the way it functions sometimes, mine especially and progressively.

In this moment—instead of being useful—my mind is travelling back in time, as it often does. I start to worry that I've made a terrible mistake. I consider how everything I once owned that didn't make it into one of the 13 bags I have with me, fits into one of 3 categories. Instead of focusing on the snake before me, I think about the items I put in the first category during The Great Cull.

Back when I last lived in a place where my name was on the lease, there were only a few material possessions in my home that had any sentimental value. By that, I mostly mean that I'd received them as gifts, and the giver would be offended by my choosing to permanently part with them. This might seem a brutal statement if you don't understand how it is I came to reject the idea of gifts that take up physical space.

The way my mind works since losing the majority of my favorite items in a flood in 2011, is that I no longer form an attachment to new objects in the way that I once did. This is purposeful, though I don't entirely feel I have a choice in the matter. Always in the back of my mind is that little voice telling me, *there's a chance that you'll lose this, so best keep emotional distance from the beginning.*

Of course, none of us can live a life with friends and family in it if we completely disregard the wishes of those dear to us. That is why, when doing The Great Cull prior to abandoning permanent residency, I chose to leave the sentimental objects with a few different friends. Whether or not I will ever take ownership of them again seems less relevant than the fact that they can be used or cared for by people who are in my life. Those sentimental things have not been discarded, and are still connected to me in some way.

When my mind returns to the present, I notice that upon seeing me—or perhaps feeling the vibrations of my steps, breath, or whatever details snakes can pick up—the snake has slithered to the side of the room. I have no idea what to do, so I take a photo and post it to social media like a good little *Xennial*, the supposed label for someone my age who doesn't quite identify as either *Gen X* or *Millennial*. I figure, someone in my social network will know what to do.

Two things happen. Firstly, friends send me electronic warnings that based on appearance, it could be a whip snake, and secondly, I receive a message from Home Owner, who is concerned. The assertive message tells me, *do not let the snake bite the cats!* When I look up from that specific message, of course Loose Cannon Cat is swiping at the snake. This is the kind of coincidence that has followed me throughout my entire life, and I'd forgive you for not being a believer.

I experience fleeting terror at the thought of the pets of my first gig dying under my care. There are several layers to this, as I have come to genuinely care about the pets, their owner, and also my future ability to secure similar situations. Rather than working to find a solution, my brain reminds me that time travel of the backward direction is something it can execute expertly at the most inappropriate time.

Again I've ended up during The Great Cull. Much simpler to deal with, were the bits and pieces of my life that had no emotional value to me, that I definitely didn't want to carry around from house to house, but that could be useful to someone else. These were easy to identify, and I was able to either give them to a friend, or donate them to charity. In both cases, I was able to recycle the items, and I never gave them another thought.

Upon returning to the present again, and also without giving it much thought, I dive to the sofa, scoop up Loose Cannon Cat, spend no more than a few seconds soothing it as I run to the bathroom, which is where I lock it in, before returning to the main area that the snake has under siege. I'm frustrated to note that the snake has found a successful hiding spot. I check under the sofa. Not there. I check under the fridge. Nope. Nowhere to be seen. It could be anywhere!

My briefest mental trip into the past considers the third category of culled item. Somehow, I'd accumulated a lot of sh█t that felt deserving of immediate disposal in the trash. Before I have the chance to feel too bad about my part in the planet's decay, the owner of the house summons me to the present with a message to say that they've called Important Human to help me deal with the snake.

A friend that I share with Home Owner, Important Human is a tall, lean person who has a fully functional female reproductive system, but who socially embraces a non-binary gender identity. The pronouns I use for Important Human are *they*, *them*, and *theirs*. Although I found it difficult to transition to referring to them this way after years of *she*, *her* and *herself*, it now feels so natural that the current pronouns slip off my tongue as if there were never any others.

Important Human arrives, and we turn the house upside down. In the case of the furniture, use of the phrase *upside down* is literal. To our dismay, there is not a sign of the snake, and only a suspicion of its entry point; a cat-flap to the garage where the kitty litter is located. The flap has been removed, meaning it is just a cat-sized hole in the door that is potentially free entry for anything possessing the dexterity required for garage access. The reason the cat flap has been removed, is that Loose Cannon Cat never could quite get the hang of pushing through it.

That night, and for several after, I sleep with the cats on my bed. Well, I don't really sleep so much. What I actually do is lie in bed, wide awake, worrying about where the snake is. What if it slithers into the bed, and strangles me in my sleep? What if I get up to go to the toilet in the middle of the night, step on it, and it bites me? Fortunately, I'm not stuck in the unproductive mindset for long, as my body demands that I return to achieving adequate sleep.

PUBLIC TRANSPORT ROULETTE IS A GAME I start to play as a way of reframing the disruption caused by a much longer work commute than I'm accustomed to. In order to talk you through the game, I first need to draw you something of a map. The house is located a short walk up a winding road that leads from the main road, further into bushier areas of the suburb, where the snake density is likely higher. There's a bus stop on this road on the opposite side to the house, just before the intersection with the main road. Past the intersection, there's a long walk down a hill to the left to get to the next bus stop.

Each morning, I walk down the street in the direction of the main road. If I see a bus approaching the first bus stop, I dash across the road and jump on that bus. It takes me on a scenic route to a nearby shopping center, where I'm able to catch a connecting bus the rest of the way to The Southern Teaching Hospital.

If that first bus doesn't come, I walk down the main road and catch whichever bus first arrives at the second bus stop. Some buses will take me a different way to the same shopping center, where I catch the same connecting bus. Other buses take me express on the highway to The Medical College, where I can catch yet another bus that travels efficiently along a busway to The Southern Teaching Hospital and beyond.

I'm pleased to say that the game gives me great pleasure in the mornings, however I'm unable to achieve similar in the afternoons. After what seems like an especially long work day because of the commute, I'm always very tired. I do get excitement one evening however, when I arrive home from work in the early evening to an enormous carpet python blocking my entry to the house. Daylight having already faded, I don't get a good photo this time, but my attempt to do so is enough to send the snake slithering into the nearby bushes. Once there, it is completely invisible. No doubt, so are its family members.

Some time later, after a particularly hectic week, I am lazing on the couch for way longer than I usually would, binge watching some stupid show as I recover from several skin lesion excisions, and eventually I have to get up because my bladder says so. As I walk up the corridor toward the toilet, I notice that Loose Cannon Cat is staring at the cat hole.

That's odd, I think. *What's Loose Cannon Cat staring at?*

Loose Cannon Cat swipes its paw at the hole, and the now-visible snake assumes an attack position. I stand, frozen, bladder full, frustrated, scared and overwhelmed. There's no way I am grabbing Loose Cannon Cat by lunging in front of a snake that has already been worked up into a state of aggression! I just stand there, stunned, until Loose Cannon Cat grabs the f█cking snake by its teeth and pulls it into the hallway!

Loose Cannon Cat then carries the snake toward me, but I start yelling at it, telling it to drop the snake and would you believe, Loose Cannon Cat doesn't listen to me at all? I throw an object at Loose Cannon Cat, who flinches, allowing the snake to slither into the spare bedroom. I quickly call a snake catcher.

Now, I'm not sure if you know this, but one thing you're supposed to do when a snake is in your house, is contain it. Being in the spare room, I have the perfect opportunity to close the door on it while I wait for the snake catcher. As I bolt to the door, Loose Cannon Cat darts in before me, and the snake comes flying out, roughly thrown from the room by the stupid, idiot cat that I love dearly.

Swiftly, I swivel and dash back in the other direction. The snake decides that offensive moves won't work, and tries passive defensiveness. How it achieves this, is by pulling itself into a tight little package to look like a rock. This gives Loose Cannon Cat the opportunity to trot over to the snake, pick it up, wander to me, and drop the snake as a neat, little package on the floor between me and the front door.

Loose Cannon Cat drapes itself around the compacted snake, as if it were the discarded wrapping paper from the wonderful gift it has just left me. Paralyzed, I wait for the snake catcher to arrive, at which point I immediately excuse myself so I can use the restroom. Miraculously, both Loose Cannon Cat and the snake are uninjured. I bring the kitty litter into the house, and block up the cat hole for the rest of my uneventful stay.

— 2 —

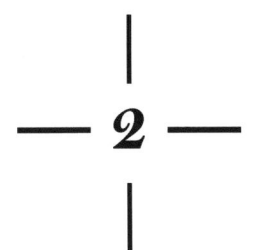

*A source of eternal torment is
my strong desire for authenticity,
teamed with the frequent need to lie.*

Previously, in my life…

IMMEDIATE ALARM IS WHAT I FELT when I saw Vulpine Foe, but for what reason, I couldn't determine; it was instinctual. How you could imagine the situation in the wild, is if I was a small animal who has encountered a predator that hasn't yet exhibited any predatory signs.

Moments earlier, the elevator doors had opened, I'd walked in, and it was upon swiveling to face the open doors that I was confronted with the image of Vulpine Foe in the distance. The moment before our eyes met, he'd been headed somewhere else. After our eyes locked, he headed toward me, and shortly after that I was no longer alone in the elevator.

As the metal doors entombed us, Vulpine Foe was standing far too close, causing my heartrate to rise. There was no reason for us to be so close in this space we shared with nobody else. Attempting to correct the personal space issue casually, I moved to lean on the railing of the opposing wall of the elevator.

There was a violent clunk as the elevator commenced its descent.

Vulpine Foe moved toward me, and then he began to speak. He told me I needed to learn my place. He said that I would need to follow his demands, if I was to survive in this place where we both were. This place was his world, and I was an unwelcome visitor. Unwelcome yes, but also potentially useful for the success of his dubious plan.

My heart had somehow travelled up into my throat, so I cautiously swallowed, allowing it to travel back down to its rightful place behind my ribcage.

There was another harsh clunk as the elevator came to a halt.

More was said, and little of it made sense other than to be a clear threat against my safety.

The elevator doors opened.

Dazed, I left the elevator.

He followed me out.

In the present…

IMPORTANT HUMAN IS LEANING on the balcony railing out the back of the snake house, their thoughts privately traveling some vast distance from our immediate environment. Their dark hair is cut short on the top, graduating to near inexistent down toward the lowest parts of the sides and back. The style is known as a crew cut.

Important Human spins 180 degrees to lean back against the railing, and face in toward the house. They turn their head to the left to face me, and raise their eyebrows as they open their mouth to speak.

"Didn't you have 13 bags?"

I smile.

"Technically I still do," I say.

"But there are only 10 by the door," Important Human points out.

"Home Owner said there was space to leave a few things here that I haven't used in the past two months."

"Are you getting nervous about where you'll be next?"

"Yes," I tell them. "Obviously we both know Home Owner, so this gig was easy to find, and I know a few other people who might need me at some stage."

"Nobody so soon though?"

"No," I confirm. "I've found a site though, so I won't be on your couch for too long."

"Oh, yeah?"

"It connects people like me, who need places to look after, with people who need someone to look after their place."

"But no luck just yet?"

I shake my head.

"I've not published my profile yet."

"Your usual little ball of anxiety inside?"

"Yeah."

"Need someone to proofread your profile?"

I nod.

"Ha ha, I love reading your profiles!"

I vanish into the house, and return with my phone that I hand to Important Human, who takes it, and winks, then grins.

I roll my eyes at them.

"Hi! I'm Paige, like in a book, but with an 'i' in the middle. So not really like in a book at all. Oh, Paige..."

"Shut up," I say, grimacing.

Important Human stops leaning on the railing, stands up straight, and turns toward me. They suddenly have the presence of a stage performer, so I sit down to watch the show.

Important Human clears their throat in preparation for continuing to read my words aloud.

"*For work I combine my two greatest passions of Medicine and Education by coordinating hospital-based teaching for medical students. This is a full-time position. I'm also acting as the Queensland Director of a volunteer organization that assists marginalized young professionals navigate the early stages of their careers through a mentoring program.*"

Important Human drops the phone to their side momentarily.

"You're not going to specify who these *marginalized* people are?"

"No," I say.

"I'm disappointed."

Fair call.

"I'm scared," I say.

"Of what?"

"Of discrimination."

Important Human looks displeased.

"After everything you've been through, things like that still scare you enough that you alter your behavior?"

"Yeah," I say glumly. "What if I can't find enough places to live, because the people who want someone don't approve of our community? You know, My Sibling wouldn't take anyone in without trying to convert them."

Important Human presses their lips together tightly, then nods somberly. They've seen enough in recent times to know that my concerns are valid. There's been talk of a survey to see if enough Australians approve of same sex marriages to justify updating the law. Comments from those opposing have been particularly unkind.

Important Human picks up my phone again to read.

"*Lifetime of Experience with Animals*," Important Human reads in a manner describable as lackluster. "*I was raised with the chooks and goats that provided us with eggs and milk. We also had cats and dogs at different times when I was a child. In my teens I looked after an albino rat. As an adult I've looked after a goat, fish, dogs and cats.*"

Placing my elbows on the table, I lean in and cradle my jaw with my hands.

"*Treatment of Animals and Property*," they announce regally. "*Over the years I've had the pleasure of looking after many homes and pets for friends and family. The feedback I receive is always very positive with regard to keeping things clean and tidy, and* ensuring plants thrive. I treat people's pets respectfully, taking on both the requests of the owners, and paying careful attention to the behavior of each pet as I interact with them."

I smile up at my friend as they continue to read.

"*Why Am I House Sitting? The first time I got a taste for house-sitting was after the 2011 floods displaced me and forced me out of my comfort zone. This time I'm doing it because I've chosen to, in an effort to level my debts and save for a home.*"

Important Human pauses and locks eyes with me, as they silently read over the section again. I anticipate their thoughts.

"I don't think strangers need to know the whole truth," I justify. "It's doubtful that mention of alcoholism, frequent medical intervention, and two big tax mistakes would lead me to success. There's potentially a nod to the alcoholism or health issues in the next bit anyway."

Important Human nods without determinable expression.

"*You might also like to know, I don't drink or smoke, and I try to minimize my negative impact on the environment. Reading and wandering along the river are two things I do a lot of in my free time. It's not a lifestyle for everyone my age, but it works well for me!*"

Important Human laughs.

"*Should you need it, I've plenty of people who would happily verify the above.* Great profile. I mostly approve."

"Thanks," I say. "I know you're disappointed, but sometimes you need to compromise."

"I know," Important Human agrees.

They hand my phone back.

"You know," Important Human says. "I might use you, or this, to help explain what intersectionality means."

"How so?"

"Well, there are certain ways in which you are disadvantaged by being a person without a fixed address, and also by being a person within our community. In addition to that, you're disadvantaged in other ways by being someone from our community who is living without a fixed address."

"I don't think that makes it any easier to understand," I tell Important Human. "But it blows my mind that people don't understand it anyway, so feel free to use me."

"I will. Alright, let's get your bags in the car, and you down to the river to shoot this video for Intersectionality Advocates!"

I'M WEARING A GREEN, FLORAL DRESS that's been chosen to make my eyes pop, and to highlight my feminine figure. Similarly, I've attempted an especially feminine hair style by scrunching my red locks of hair. Usually this leads to bouncy curls, but cleaning and packing took longer than anticipated, so I skipped washing my hair to save time. Consequently, the look I've actually ended up with is something that looks more like I wasn't expecting to be in front of a camera. Or that I didn't sleep at home, which is true, because I technically don't have one.

Camera Man has set us up in a shady spot outside the Brisbane Powerhouse, which is one of my favorite venues for concerts, comedy acts, and exhibitions. It's in a trendy suburb, beside the Brisbane River. In the early morning there aren't too many people around, but there are a few curious passersby that make me feel awkward about what I'm here to do.

"Alright," Camera Man says. "So I'll prompt you, but I want you to talk to the camera."

I nod, leaning casually against a sturdy wooden stool.

"Tell me a bit about why you've become involved with Intersectionality Advocates," Camera Man directs.

"Well, I..."

The air is hot, and there are people walking by. Strangers.

"Let's try it with you sitting on the stool. You look very uncomfortable."

I slide onto the stool, and pull my shoulders back. Camera Man scrunches up his face in disapproval, and silently considers something. He looks me up and down, and I think decides not to voice what's he's actually thinking. Perhaps that I look like a wooden puppet, so at least I compliment the stool.

"Try relaxing your posture a bit. You want to seem friendly, and approachable."

Humans are so weird. It's not enough that I actually am friendly and approachable. I have to fake body language to provide a visual signal as well. I drop my shoulders, focus on the words *peace*, *calm*, and *welcoming*, and lean slightly.

"Just straighten up a bit."

I hate this so much.

"That's good. Okay, so tell me why you're here."

I take a deep breath in, let it out slowly, smile, and try to think of the camera being Important Human. Rigidly staring doe eyed at the camera, not a word comes out.

"What is Intersectionality Advocates?"

Again, I take a deep breath in, let it out slowly, and smile.

"Intersectionality Advocates is a not-for-profit organization that seeks to assist young LGBTIQ professionals navigating the early stages of their careers through a free mentoring program."

"Why did you get involved?"

"I got involved with Intersectionality Advocates because I had lots of difficulty in my early professional life as a direct result of my place in the community."

I seamlessly come out on camera, as if I'm casually mentioning having had my wisdom teeth removed.

"I'd like to change that for others," I add.

Camera Man raises his eyes, indicating that my words are not something he was expecting.

"Why do you think people should volunteer?"

Time starts to warp, and I say something about how having the weight of an organization behind you can help you achieve more. I think. I'm unsure, and feel as though I'm not really here. As has occasionally been the case in moments I've felt extreme stress, my reality has become fractured in a way that prevents a solid memory forming. The next thing I remember, is that we've finished recording, and I head straight to Important Human's house. When I arrive, the first action I take is to post my house sitting profile.

"What I wanted more than anything else, was for the recording to be over," I tell Important Human, after the profile has gone live. "I don't feel like mine is a face that is worth watching. It doesn't seem like I am the best person to be the face of a call to arms."

I do feel a little weird about the profile, in particular, the parts that are not entirely accurate, or evasive at best. Those parts that have been highlighted by Important Human. It's not that I think strangers don't need to know that a large part of sinking into debt was through the excessive consumption of alcohol and medical procedures. And it's not that I'm not proud of the community I help through volunteering. I'm just so afraid of those things being held against me.

Unexpectedly, it is something else entirely that causes me to be unsuccessful on the site for the first few months. I make contact with a few owners through the site, and it quickly becomes apparent that I've got a lot of competition. Unfortunately, some of my competitors are retired couples who can offer something I cannot; vast amounts of free time to spend with needy pets. It's even explicitly pointed out to me that I seem to have too many responsibilities to be at home very much.

It is in this time of need, that some of my closest friends reveal just how much they care, by offering up their spare rooms for as long as I need. As is always the case, I've a complex mix of associated emotion. A journey that was meant to be empowering, has had an opposing effect due to what seems like failure early on, and I begin to worry that I'm racking up new social debt that's perhaps worse than if I'd asked for financial handouts. In an attempt to stop my hosts from seeing me as an inconvenience, I try to be out as often as possible, and limit the number of weeks I stay at any one place.

What I really need right now, is something big and new to distract me from my unproductive worrying. As has often been the case throughout my life, a timely romance presents itself to rid me of the free time that allows such worry to occupy so much of my mind. It also provides a temporary solution to another problem.

— 3 —

*Of this I am most sure,
my love lives are nearly up.*

In another time…

ALTHOUGH WE WERE IN AN OPEN CORRIDOR, no longer confined to the small space inside the elevator, I felt that I was unable to leave Vulpine Foe's presence until he gave permission for me to do so. Having finished with all overt threatening language in the privacy of the elevator, out in public Vulpine Foe opted to end the exchange with words that would have seemed innocuous to anyone in ear shot.

The way it played out was seamless. Not necessarily pre-meditated or rehearsed for me. It seemed more opportunistic. It was seamless in a way that screamed

REPEAT OFFENDER!

"That is my only advice to you," Vulpine Foe said smoothly, a sick attempt at a smile plastered over his villainous face. I was stunned. As if in silent, slow motion, I watched as Vulpine Foe raised his right arm. He was still smiling. I was confused. I wanted to dodge, but I was scared to make a scene. The palm of his hand collided with my upper left arm, or maybe it was more shoulder than arm. A very firm tap.

He left.
I fled.

Right now…

REFRESHINGLY FAMILIAR; REQUIRING LITTLE to no effort. That's how I might describe the next love of my life. Because he also spent a fair portion of his childhood and adolescence in regional Queensland, we have many shared experiences. These have shaped our core values and general perception, and the similitude does not end there.

Like me, Refreshingly Familiar has chosen to reside in the city of Brisbane as an adult. We've both visited other cities, some overseas, but neither of us have managed to move on from Brisbane, despite initial intentions to do so. Additionally, neither of us would consider what would seem like a backward move to a regional area similar to the communities we were raised in.

Sorry!

I realize I've accidentally leapt into the future in all my excitement to introduce you to him! Okay, focusing... and... we're going back to the place it began...

WHATEVER DATING SITE IT IS that I've decided on this time is not really relevant. It's a site that has taken the typical approach. Tick boxes are offered to allow easier matching, there's an option to upload several photos for physical assessment, and a free text comment box enables your personality to shine through by means of a short bio. What *is* relevant, is that I have all intention of being honest, I really do, but it just... doesn't happen that way.

With respect to honest intentions, I should state that I'm definitely not referring to romantic ideals, an area in which I've been purposefully dishonest. In my old age of 34, there are now several different types of relationship that I feel I could be content with. For fear of alienating anyone who is less open to alternative relationship goals, I'm deliberately evasive; I don't specify what it is I'm looking for.

My greatest fear, is that I'll scare off a great potential partner with my openness to non-monogamy. For someone unfamiliar with the concept, it can easily be confused with an inability to be committed, or to be monogamous. Goodness knows knowledge of said openness has attracted an unfortunately large number of people behaving unethically in their relationships. That is, they've pursued me while allowing their spouse to falsely believe that the situation they are in is one of monogamy.

The dishonesty that I *am* referring to, is with regard to certain other parts of my life history. One part in particular that has many times been held against me. The truth that so many suitors have deemed undesirable enough to justify an immediate emotional swing from adoration, to disgust. Just from that one, little piece of information about the past. Is my bitterness showing through? I blood well hope so.

How everything plays out is different entirely. Before I've done much more than tick a few boxes, and upload some photos, my profile has gone live. With a boatload of experience behind me, I've become very good at selecting the best combination of photos to sell myself, so it doesn't take long for several messages to land in my inbox. I'm now faced with a choice between doing what feels more *right*, and what I feel is more *safe*.

I sift through the messages I have received. A few are from men who seem like they could be a good match. I've a strong desire to communicate with them to see if we click. I consider the information I've left off my profile. Perhaps if that information had been there, some of these messages would not be. The senders might not take kindly to it being added as a surprise for whenever they return to remind themselves of my stats. Or to show their friends who it is on the site that has piqued their interest.

I choose the option that is safer, but safer only in the more immediate sense. What I don't want, is for any of these potential dates to see I've added information that causes them to regret their decision to make contact with me. That could lead them to confront me about it. Maybe they will be aggressive, respectfully tell me I'm not some*thing* they're open to, or they could even block me from making further contact. Each and every one of those will hurt, and because I know this from experience, I decide to withhold.

It's still on my mind when I start to gravitate toward Refreshingly Familiar, and progressively ignore the others. We seem to have online chemistry, and I feel the urge to be honest with him. I chose not to, however, because it doesn't seem right to suddenly disclose something so big during the phase of light banter in the lead-up to meeting for the first time. In any case, I figure I might not even care to see him again, or he, I. For the moment, I will just pretend like I don't have this big secret that he needs to know about before he can truly know if he likes me.

Something that I do have on my profile, that I feel will aid me with disclosure if the need arises, is my volunteer work. I note that I lead the state of an organization with a focus on emerging LGBTIQ professionals. The weight of the role I hold with the organization will definitely lead suitors to the assumption that I'm somehow closely connected to one or more of the letters LGBTIQ.

To my dismay, Refreshingly Familiar and I have an amazing first date. He's intelligent, polite, and we somehow seem physically complimentary to each other, in the way that an old couple might be. What I'm trying to describe, is that seamless dance between two people who've spent enough time together to instinctively anticipate each other's moves. It's the kind of connection you can't ignore, because it's visible to observers. It's the kind of connection that will be disrupted by dishonesty.

"Can you tell me a story?" he asks, as we sit at our first café. "You mentioned on your profile about spilling coffee on the ceiling at work. How on Earth did you manage that?"

"I'm so glad you asked," I say, grinning. "Well, it all started when my colleague asked me to get her a takeaway coffee one cold winter's day."

"Nice set up," Refreshingly Familiar says.

The compliment makes me glow, and I excitedly continue.

"Thanks! So, when receiving the order of both our coffees, against my better judgement I declined a tray to carry them, choosing instead to hold my purse snugly under my arm, and a cup full of coffee in each hand."

Refreshingly Familiar shakes his head. He can already see where I had gone wrong.

"Where I work is something of a modern, beautiful fortress, so it's a peculiar door that leads into our office," I continue. "There's first a prox card required, and then you have to turn a heavy handle down and thrust it forward. At the door I realized this was going to be difficult to achieve but I was feeling like taking a risk that morning!"

"Rookie mistake," Refreshingly Familiar comments, as he edges closer to me.

"Balancing the coffees, squeezing my arm against myself so as not to drop my purse, I used two of my small fingers to grab my prox card and swipe."

Refreshingly Familiar grimaces, as if he's watching the scenario play out before him, while he's powerless to prevent guaranteed disaster. I start to use my arms and hands to demonstrate the actions occurring in my story.

"I then pushed down on the handle with my elbow, at which time I lost balance, and forcefully threw the coffee that was mine, into the air," I tell him.

In the present, at the café, I throw my body back against the back of the chair, and my hands up in the air. A few strangers who are passing by glance in our direction.

"My colleague's coffee was uninjured. There was a little bit of a mess, and nobody has asked me to get coffee for them since."

I give Refreshingly Familiar a toothy grin, and he laughs, then shakes his head in a bewildered manner.

"What am I getting myself into here?" he asks.

"This is me," I say, shrugging.

How the rest of the date plays out, is as a Café Crawl that lasts for hours, where we're wandering along, and over the river between each venue, wrapped up in constant conversation. Several times his body language is a clear attempt to lead us to kiss, and each time I casually prevent it from happening.

Throughout the multi-venue date we cover a good deal of topics, including a little about my volunteer work. This is of course without me disclosing why it is I found my way there, and why it's an issue that's so close to my heart. Refreshingly Familiar reassures me when he mentions that his sister is a lesbian, and he has some understanding for why the organization is needed. Eventually, it is my volunteer work that calls me away, and ends the date.

Before we part ways, my published books naturally come up in conversation. Although Refreshingly Familiar confesses that he's not much of a reader, he is keen to know what I've written. I promise to send a link when I'm done with my volunteer work for the day. I do so, and in doing so, emotionally disengage, as a way of preparing myself for the rejection I feel is inevitable.

The messages I receive from Refreshingly Familiar later in the day, indicate that the date was as good for him, as it was for me. In fact, he labels it as the best first date he's ever had! Not knowing whether he's done any digging just yet, I try not to let this excite me too much. I fear it will only make the impending rejection all the more painful.

Not long after, his face and name pop up as a friend request on Facebook. What this tells me, is that he has followed the link to the book, and now knows my full name. Whether or not he's stumbled on the bit of information I'm nervous about is still open to debate. I'm hesitant to be the one to bring it up, so do nothing more than accept his friend request, and reply directly to messages received.

TEXT MESSAGE RECEIVED

I'd like to call you.

AND ALSO

When can you chat with me on the phone?

— 4 —

*You can never go back to be
the person you were before the trauma.*

Before today...

"He saw me as I turned, just after I'd entered the elevator," I told Investigator Man into the phone, several weeks after I'd reported the incident. That is how long it had taken for my report to make it through some complicated chain of command and into his relevant hands. That is how long it had taken for any kind of forward motion to commence. At every stage prior, I'd been asked if I really wanted to continue.

In my Safe Space, Male Ally was burning holes in the back of my neck. I couldn't decide if I felt fortunate that Male Ally just happened to be there when I'd received the call, or if I wanted to be alone. It seemed that my lot in life was to always be around men who were strangers when I was most vulnerable.

What I didn't want, was for Male Ally to see me as a victim. Nor did I really want anyone else to view me that way. I wanted people to see me as a strong, independent woman. Especially now. I didn't want to be caught out as being emotionally affected by something that was so benign compared to... things I'd endured when I'd been too drunk to protect myself.

This was *nothing*.

By comparison.

"Vulpine Foe had been walking elsewhere, but he changed direction to enter the elevator with me."

That detail seemed of importance.

I glanced at Male Ally, who nodded gently.

Male Ally smiled kindly at me as I heard Investigator Man begin a line of questioning at me through the phone. I cut him short, because I wasn't quite finished.

Today...

TWO DARK GREY BAMBOO SHEETS and two matching pillow cases are resting in a crumpled heap on the bed in Important Human's spare room. Refreshingly Familiar watches on intently from the doorway as I take a pillowcase, smooth it flat, and fold it neatly. I do the same for the second pillowcase, enjoying the tactile experience as my fingers connect with and glide across the soft, smooth fabric. I then yank the flat sheet from the pile, and in a swift, violent whipping movement, I flatten it out, then fold it in halves until it's the same size as the pillow cases.

"These sheets are a bit of a grounding thing," I tell Refreshingly Familiar as I grab the fitted sheet.

"Oh yeah?"

I roll the fitted sheet up into a ball and shove it on the pile.

"I knew that it was going to be a bit disruptive, moving about from place to place, so I thought about what I could do to give myself some consistency."

"And you chose sheets?"

"Yes," I tell him, as I place the sheets in my suitcase. "No matter what bed, in what room, in what suburb, I will be going to sleep on the same sheets each night. I figure it will help me feel more like I still have a home."

"Did you read books on minimalism before you started all this?"

"No, I just thought about it, and then did it."

I fold my seven or eight work dresses, and in something like a game of Tetris, I place them precisely in the most space effective positions within my suitcase.

"Need my help with any of this?"

"No," I tell Refreshingly Familiar. "This won't take long."

I gather my socks and tights, and place them in my white washbag, then zip it closed, and add the washbag to my suitcase. I take the washbag that is covered with drawings of bras, fill it with bras, seal it, and pop it in the suitcase. Finally, I grab the washbag that is covered with pink hearts. My knickers all end up in that bag, before I close it up and pack it away in the perfect spot in my suitcase.

Next, I flip out the base of my laundry box, then fold it into a flat square, and place it neatly on top of everything that's already in the suitcase. I give it a pat, flip the suitcase closed, push down, and in a swift movement, pull the zipper around to lock everything inside. Refreshingly Familiar lets out a breathy sound to indicate something between surprise and awe.

I grab a tote bag and fill it with the assorted laundry and bathroom items that are all scattered nearby. There's a spare toilet roll, some stain remover, laundry liquid, body wash, shampoo, and a small bag of cosmetics. I then add hiking boots, and a pair of quick-dry trousers to my hiking pack.

"Right, all done!" I announce.

Refreshingly Familiar's jaw drops, and he laughs and throws his hands in the air.

"You literally packed your entire life up in under 10 minutes," Refreshingly Familiar states. "I thought you were talking it up."

I grin.

"Well, this isn't actually all of my things," I confess. "I started out with 13 bags, but I realized pretty quickly that I didn't need a lot of it, so I left some things with a friend, and stashed a few bags at work."

"So cool," Refreshingly Familiar says. "Right, let's get these bags to my car and get you to your new home!"

All of this is a lot different to what I had been expecting, and as we sit in the car, silent, I allow my mind to take a stroll back through time to a conversation that occurred on the phone in the room I've just left. Even though we're hanging out right now, I've not yet had time to process the call.

REFRESHINGLY FAMILIAR DOESN'T GIVE anything away when he proposes a phone call. Knowing that my irrational phone phobia gets worse the longer I put a phone call off, I make myself available that same night to speak to him.

"You didn't have to tell me that," Refreshingly Familiar blurts out suddenly. This is after we've exchanged a bunch of words that have no meaning other than to stall for time. I'm relieved that he's decided to push the conversation where it needs to go. I haven't been able to find the courage. I'd happily spend hours talking about nothing rather than prompt the required discussion.

Because I still don't know what this means for him, I don't respond with anything. I'm just awkwardly silent. I do however think about how amusing it is that I'm being told that disclosure isn't something I needed to do, when I've a long history of aggressively being told the opposite. It feels like I'm stuck in some stupid game that I can never win. I'll be opposed no matter which action I take.

"I started reading your book already," Refreshingly Familiar continues. "So I know why you wanted me to read it, but I'm not going to continue reading."

I feel deflated. The rejection is coming.

Wait, I think. *Was that... was it just then?*

I guess Refreshingly Familiar felt it would have been impolite to let me down in a text after confirming what a great time he'd had with me on our first date. This sucks. Sometimes I really hate my life. It's so unfair.

"Oh," I murmur halfheartedly.

"I just felt like it was too intimate, and it was one-sided. I'm really looking forward to getting to know you as a person, as you get to know me.

I don't want to do it through a book, and have you know nothing about me in return."

I'm stunned.

"I don't really know… I might have questions. At the moment I don't have any, except, when can I see you again?"

I couldn't be more pleased.

"I am babysitting tomorrow," I tell him. "But we could do something after their parents come home if you like."

"Oh, maybe I can come over and get with the hot babysitter when the kids have gone to bed!"

I laugh.

"No, I think I would find it weird inviting you to someone else's house. We could drive somewhere and go for a walk?"

Refreshingly Familiar continues to surprise me exclusively in good ways. Setting him apart from all who have come before, he arranges my favorite date of all time; to the state museum to see an exhibition on the Large Hadron Collider. This includes a short documentary on the discovery of the Higgs boson, and I squeal with delight when Professor Brian Cox appears on screen disguised as a guy bringing coffee to laboratory staff. My squeal draws attention, and Refreshingly Familiar reacts with what has already become signature; a laugh, as he shakes his head, and buries his head in his hands.

The Large Hadron Collider is a particle accelerator that, at the time of the exhibition, is the largest and most powerful in the world. Aside from validating the enormous expense of the Large Hadron Collider, the discovery of the Higgs boson has had some pretty cool implications for the field of physics. And Professor Brian Cox? He's just one of my favorite physicists, who was also once a rock star. In my eyes, he still is.

Refreshingly Familiar is going to be the first person I have sex with since going sober. That thought terrifies me so much that I feel fortunate when I realize I've something I can use as an excuse to hold off; several healing skin excisions. Eventually though, I decide that I just need to get the first time over and done with. It's delightfully awkward, and we fall asleep in each other's arms. Beautiful; natural.

Because I've been couch surfing rather than house sitting, I'm able to spend a few nights sleeping beside Refreshingly Familiar. Within a few weeks, he makes a point of telling me that there have been no days since meeting that we haven't spent time together. That is, if you count the phone call, which he does.

What if I fall for him, and he decides I'm not worth it all?

I keep these insecure thoughts to myself, and try to project a carefree vibe to Refreshingly Familiar.

"This must be something really special," he tells me.

Instead of taking the comment at face value, I start to worry that he's trying to convince himself that I'm worth my baggage.

Refreshingly Familiar moves to a new apartment that is close to The Southern Teaching Hospital where I work. It makes sense to sleep there most nights, then get a lift to work with him and his flatmate in the morning. For a while, I stop trying to find house sitting gigs, because it will get in the way of my sleepovers, and the developing relationship. Life, at least for a little while, can be described as *sweet*.

— 5 —

*In everything I now do,
I prepare for what I will do.*

Back then…

"He followed up the threat with a firm tap on my shoulder," I told Investigator Man into the phone, wrapping up my story.

Then the questions began again.

"Was it your left or right shoulder?"

Didn't I already say that?

"Right."

"Was it his left or right hand?"

I'm sure I mentioned that already.

"Left."

"Was it before or after you left the elevator?"

Oh.

"Left, I think," I stumbled. "I…"

Male Ally bit his lip, and I forced a weak smile.

"Were there people around?"

"I don't think so."

It was one of those conversations.

"Were you alone in the elevator?"

"Yes."

"Did you feel threatened?"

"Yes."

They were assuming I'd made it up.

"Where on your shoulder did he tap you?"

"Near the bicep."

"Were there any witnesses?"

"No."

My role in the conversation was to prove that I wasn't lying.

"Does the elevator have a security camera?"

"No."

They wanted to know my story wouldn't change.

"Why didn't you report it right away?"

And, I guess, whether I had an ulterior motive.

Now...

UPON RAISING MY HAND, there is an immediate, noticeable drop in the indecipherable chatter from the audience of 250-300 medical students sitting before me in the auditorium at The Southern Teaching Hospital. It is the space used for medical grand rounds, that I occasionally sneak into when I have time, despite having abandoned medical studies. The noise gradually diminishes, and within half a minute, there is silence. Total, and complete.

It's always difficult for those of us who are allocated to run an orientation event at the end of a full week of similar, but I've a plan to keep the audience engaged, at least in the parts where I'm the main point of focus. This is a skill that draws upon past experience in stage acting, as well as facilitation of corporate training. Both careers long behind me, it is a skill I deliberately continue to develop because of its future worth in my volunteer work.

"Thank-you, and good morning," I say into the lectern microphone. I'm using my radio voice, that is smoother and a little more sultry than my everyday voice.

I look down at a sheet of paper in front of me. It is positioned under a camera. The camera is a component of the audiovisual equipment. This allows a projected image of the paper to appear on two large displays, visible to all audience members (eyesight allowing). The sheet of paper is a printed hard copy of the first slide of my presentation, and says little more than *Welcome to The Southern Teaching Hospital.*

With my hand, I carry out a swiping motion. On the large displays, my giant hand swings from one side of the screens to the other, and back again. I then tap the paper with my index finger. Inquisitive faces watch intently.

"Sorry," I say. "I seem to be having some technical difficulties."

There are a few snorts, giggles, and sniggers from the audience. I tap my finger on the piece of paper, screw up my face, then flip it over so that the second slide is displayed.

"Welcome to The Southern Teaching Hospital," I say, grinning. "My name is Paige, and I'll be your MC this morning. Our first speaker is Esteemed Researcher, who is an esteemed researcher."

I pretend to fumble through pronunciation of some of their clinical research achievements, then move to the control panel, tap a few times, and the projection of my paper slide is replaced by Esteemed Researcher's electronic presentation slide. They say their piece, and following several other presenters, we approach the end of the event.

"There's just one more speaker today, and it is..."

I screw up my face, tap the keyboard, then displayed much larger than life, is a photo of...

"Me."

The audience laugh at the image of me standing in a crowd, hugging a clipboard, wearing a hard hat. The photo has been taken as I've been giving someone verbal direction.

"Like today, this year I'll wear a few different hats for you. As you might have guessed from this photo of me in a hard hat, one of those is to be your fire warden, and I'm pleased to be able to tell you that there were no reported injuries when I was required to evacuate our floor last year. As your coordinator, I will be your first point of call for all general queries during your studies here. As a Discrimination Support Officer, I can advise you of your options for related support. I'm also an accredited Mental Health First Aider, and part of The Medical College Diversity Ally Program."

At the end of my talk, there is applause.

"Now, are there any questions that don't relate to the issues with the online timetables that have come to light this morning?"

More laughter.

That night, Refreshingly Familiar's condom comes off during sex, and, caught up in passion, he doesn't replace it with another. We both want to have a conversation about what's occurred, but neither of us are brave enough to say anything in person. Rather than causing disharmony, we'd both prefer to remain silent about our concerns. It's one of several shared traits that don't work well in a relationship.

From my side, I'm worried about how the conversation will play out because of a combination of past experience, and knowledge of widely accepted sexual health perceptions. What worries me the most, is that I've become attached to someone who hasn't. I know we should be able to have the conversation in person, but I opt instead for text.

When I decide that I can't go on without dealing with the issue, I just blurt everything out, all at once. I mention that some men think they don't need to wear protection with women like me, because we can't get pregnant. I stress that outside of a monogamous relationship, safe sex is important. Refreshingly Familiar doesn't take long to reply.

"I'll get tested," Refreshingly Familiar offers. "But I'm not seeing anyone else anymore. Are you?"

"No," I tell him.

"Maybe... maybe we should save on condoms and be exclusive."

The following morning I'm sitting on his couch, putting my boots on, but because I hadn't anticipated spending the night I don't have a change of socks. I choose not to wear any, rather than using the same socks two days in a row.

"Oh no, I'm wearing my boots without protection," I say to Refreshingly Familiar. "Guess I'll have to wear them exclusively now."

Refreshingly Familiar blushes, instead of laughing and shaking his head.

"It's okay," I say. "I've been wearing the one pair for ages now anyway."

Refreshingly Familiar smiles.

"Your Intersectionality Advocates event tonight, can you tell me a bit about how it went? What did you talk about?"

Refreshingly Familiar has arrived after the event to pick me up and take me back to his place where I'll spend the night.

"It was LGBTIQ medical issues," I tell him. "I'm tired and just want to relax now."

"Okay," he accepts.

Several weeks later, Refreshingly Familiar again attempts to initiate conversation about my volunteer work.

"What was the panel you spoke on today?"

"Intersectionality in feminism," I tell him as I get into his car, so he can drive us home. "It wasn't a very big audience, but hopefully they got something out of it."

"Do you think it would be okay for me to come to these events sometimes?"

"Oh, I like to keep it separate from my personal life," I tell Refreshingly Familiar.

"Okay," he accepts.

Months pass, and although we never utter the words *I Love You*, that strong emotion is there. The majority of my free time is spent with him, and I notice a dynamic develop where my role is the opposite to what I had with The One Who Got Away, my favorite ex-partner formerly known affectionately as Legitimate One.

Back when he had been Legitimate One, he was a medical student. He liked to have me physically nearby when he spent nights and weekends studying. To keep him happy, I would potter about the apartment doing whatever I could, until such time as he was done with his study, and was again able to be with me both in mind and body. It was a small way I could be supportive of his studies.

This time, I excuse myself for state and national phone calls for my volunteer work, make notes about different things I need to achieve, and Refreshingly Familiar moves about nearby, quietly keeping himself busy until I'm able to return to his arms. Although I had done it with Legitimate One all those years ago, it is not until now that I realize how important it is for a partner to be supportive in this way.

"I'm a bit jealous of the freedom you've found through minimalism, even if that's not what you're calling it or why you did it," Refreshingly Familiar tells me one day when I've returned to him after a conference call with the national team of Intersectionality Advocates.

"Oh?"

"I've started listing some of my stuff for sale."

"Cool," is all I can think of to reply.

Refreshingly Familiar kisses me, steps back, and gazes upon me.

"You're very beautiful," he says. "And you somehow understand all my obscure jokes."

"Thank you," I say, bashfully.

"But do you know what I really like about you?"

"No," I say.

"You have a greater purpose. That's why I like you."

It seems strange to still be using the word *like* after so long, and the longer I think about it, the more insecure I start to feel. Simultaneously, several volunteers on my team resign, others stop responding to my emails and messages, and I worry that I just don't have the skills required to be a leader. I also find myself more frequently in situations where I'm required to assertively tell curious people to back off following sudden, invasive questions.

Everything on the surface with Refreshingly Familiar is wonderful. We love each other's company, spend a lot of time in it, and I immerse myself in his immediate social circle, which includes a few family members. It becomes exciting watching his material possessions diminish, and finding ways to treat ourselves with the money strangers have paid to add them to their own collections.

Something that doesn't develop, is our ability to openly discuss things that concern us about the other. Things do occasionally bother us, and sometimes we start to bring issues up, but then back down. It's a type of dishonesty that seems to be more widely accepted of couples than it should be, and the way this affects us sexually, is that things begin to plateau.

Then something unexpected happens. Because Refreshingly Familiar hasn't read my book, I've refused frank discussions about my past, and strangers take frequent stabs at my identity, I start to misinterpret some of Refreshingly Familiar's jokes. I interpret them as tone deaf, at my expense. Because we haven't developed an ability to discuss concerns with each other, I let my negative emotion bottle up, and up, and up. And of course, what bottles up, must eventually explode.

— 6 —

*For an audience of strangers,
I willingly open my heart and bleed.*

In the past…

"WE'LL BE IN TOUCH," Investigator Man told me at the end of the somewhat lengthy interrogation that left me feeling like I'd been the one to misbehave. It was demoralizing, but I was sure I had done the right thing. Both in reporting the incident, as well as pressing on to confirm the truth to someone who could have some influence on the future. And surely because the truth was on my side, everything would be fine.

So that was that.
No more questions, for now.
I could breathe easy.
Well, for a while at least.
"Thanks," I said.
I placed the receiver down to end the call.
I turned to face Male Ally, who was watching me.
He had kind eyes, and that was important.
It was still disconcerting to be so vulnerable in front of him, but at least I could see that he was kind.
Male Ally uttered the words I needed to hear above all others at that time.
"I believe you," Male Ally assured me.
I hit the *Save* button of my mind for later reference.
What I didn't realize, was how much I would need to recall them.

In the present…

AN ARCHITECTURALLY SIGNIFICANT CENTERPIECE of Brisbane's

Riverside, I'm located on one of the highest floors in the conference room of one of the most prestigious law firms in the city. Let's call it Prestigious Law Firm, because it's easy to remember, and we'll only visit this location once.

Between two other people, I'm positioned behind a long table with three desktop microphones, before an audience of well-dressed professionals that fill the room. Behind me, the entire wall is tinted glass, allowing the audience a spectacular view of the Story Bridge, the river below, and buildings that are nearby and on the other bank of the river. On this particular night, the bridge is lit up with three different colors, in support of a sporting team who will be playing a game on the weekend.

The two people sitting either side of me are both men who are gay. One of the men is some kind of professional consultant whose job I don't really understand. The other is a senior partner of Prestigious Law Firm. Sitting between these distinguished men, I realize that although we've done well to improve our representation of gender diversity, we're now faced with a new area to address.

There are likely people in the audience within a wide cultural and linguistic range. What they'll see on this panel, is people who have achieved professional success with relative ease. None of us have had to navigate barriers associated with being raised in a culture that differs from what is currently dominant in Australia. We've also all spoken English from a young age, so we've not faced any workplace barriers associated with language.

That we've nobody on the panel who can give adequate advice to these people is a problem I'll need to address another day. Right now, what I need to focus on, is moderating and participating on this panel. I'm going to build on my experience from speaking to the medical students earlier in the year.

"My apologies," I start, leaning into the mic.

Someone at the back of the room gesticulates that leaning in to the mic is unnecessary. It's state of the art audiovisual equipment, of course. Why would I expect anything less in such a building? I nod, smile, and sit up straight.

"I'm not accustomed to moderating a panel that I'm also a part of, so I've written myself some notes."

I reach into my left bra cup and pull out a piece of folded A4 size copy paper. I slowly unfold it, and this takes some time, because it has been folded in half six times. When the paper is again full A4 size, I place it on the table between me and the mic, and flatten it out loudly with the palms of my hands.

"Oh no," I exclaim. "Oh dear."

For a confused audience, I hold up the piece of paper, then flip it around so they've seen both sides.

"It's blank," I tell them. "Thanks Past Paige, this blank piece of paper has been most helpful."

Jovial murmurs from the audience help put me at ease. My hand dives into my right bra cup, retrieves my real notes, and we commence. There's laughter, subtle tears, and following a round of public questions, the formal part of the evening ends.

Several people seek me out as I mingle. This includes a trans woman who is near the beginning of her gender transition journey. After quizzing me about how I achieved my voice, she does something that serves as proof that great change has occurred since the beginning of my professional life, and since my own journey in the distant past.

"This is my boss," she tells me. "I asked him to come because I heard you were speaking, and I thought it might help avoid some unnecessary hurdles."

Her boss is a burly Australian bloke, that at one time I would have found intimidating. I confidently throw my hand into his.

"Thank you so much for coming," I tell him. "You're welcome to contact me with any queries that would be inappropriate to direct at your colleague."

"Might take you up on that," he says. "All this stuff is pretty new to me, and I'm scared of stuffing up."

After several intense conversations, I begin to feel fatigued. Questions start to feel more unnecessarily intrusive. Conversations feel like a chore. I excuse myself to send Refreshingly Familiar a message, telling him I'll soon be leaving. He responds immediately with an offer to pick me up, and I gladly accept, as it gives me a suitable reason to leave earlier.

Avid Reader appears as if from thin air. She's associated with Prestigious Law Firm, and I've enjoyed several event evenings with her.

"Want me to show you the way out, without having to go through the crowd?"

"Yes, that would be great," I say. "I've had a bit much of questions for one day."

"I thought so," Avid Reader says. "I've read all your books now, so I know what you're really like. Follow me."

I follow Avid Reader to the corner of the room, where there is an exit I hadn't noticed earlier.

"Thank you," I tell them, and I flee the event to escape into the arms of my lover.

"HOW WAS IT?" Refreshingly Familiar asks, when he arrives to pick me up from the event.

"Fine," I say. "It was nice to get out of there though."

He withholds his discontent with my response, and separately, I realize that something else is wrong. Rather than joining forces, which is what I have decided I want from a long term relationship, Refreshingly Familiar wants to set his own goals independently. After he's figured out the direction he wants to head in, he wants to run his ideas by me, to see if I can join him on his journey. Again, I'm unable to voice my discontent.

To make matters worse, a situation arises with one of my best friends, Simmering Spectacle. Her mental health issues are exacerbated, and she ends up back in hospital in the mental health ward, so unwell that she hesitantly agrees to let me visit, but then refuses to see me by the time I arrive.

What I should do, is reach out to Refreshingly Familiar for support, but I feel angry with him. It frustrates me that he wants to plan his life without my input, and it infuriates me that I am unable to tell him of my frustration. This doesn't seem to be reasonable behavior for an adult, but I just can't seem to behave in any other way.

On a particularly emotional day, I decide quite suddenly that I will just stop seeing Refreshingly Familiar. It is an incredibly immature way to not deal with a situation that desperately needs addressing. He respectfully allows me what he thinks is my need for temporary space to work through something I will eventually talk him through.

I go a week without seeing Refreshingly Familiar, at which point we join each other on a triple-date. It is exceptionally awkward, and I know that the others can tell that we are having issues, because one of the men makes specific reference to it. I can't wait to be alone with Refreshingly Familiar, so we can have the private conversation we are in dire need of.

"You need to be open, and vulnerable with me," Refreshingly Familiar tells me when we are finally alone. He is holding me as we sit in the dark on a park bench.

Without warning, I begin to weep. I tell Refreshingly Familiar about Simmering Spectacle. I open up to him about how helpless I feel. I confide in him about how insecure I felt when she refused to see me, and how upset I am that my friendship with her may never be the same again. How worried I am that she will never recover.

That night, following our most beautiful making of love, I fall asleep feeling safe and adored. In the morning, I am triggered by an unwelcome transphobic comment, and I flee. It is only when I am on the bus home, that tell him via text the specifics of what he said that caused me to run. I also tell him, that before I am able to see him again, he will need to finish reading my book *Outer Shell*. That is what I need to feel safe being vulnerable with him.

That week, it is Refreshingly Familiar who takes a step back, to objectively look at what we have become. I respectfully allow him the space he needs. When he arrives at the home where I am now house sitting a week later, it is as if a stranger is greeting me at the front door. And although it will take all night and include the most spectacular sex I've ever experienced, I already know in that moment that we are done.

— 7 —

Never underestimate your ability
to create as a form of escapism.

Some time ago…

FOR THE FIRST WEEK OF WAITING for some kind of outcome, the assault was on my mind a lot. I wondered about the closed-door discussions that were occurring about me and Vulpine Foe. Like, how many people were present? Did a group of men just sit around a large stained wood table to discuss the validity of my claims? Were any of these men groaning about the paperwork associated with behavior they felt I should have let slide?

Sometimes, I was able to chat about it with Male Ally.

Mostly, I pretended not to care.

Male Ally seemed to believe me, when I told him that I didn't care, because I had navigated more complex situations. Perhaps he didn't believe me. At the very least, he could tell I was purposefully lying to him, even if he didn't know that it was because I didn't want to seem weak in front of him.

Which of the two didn't really matter to me.

The important thing was that he respected my choice.

Right now…

THE BREAKUP COULDN'T HAVE BEEN TIMED more perfectly. As with pretty much all break-ups, I use my workaholic nature to get through. Fortunately, since signing on as a volunteer, there's work for me whether it's a weekday, night, or the weekend. Several hours after Refreshingly Familiar has left the apartment, I'm already conveniently locked in to deliver national training over a conference call. It is training that I hope will assist our national team of volunteers to deal more sensitively with people who are not cisgender. That is, people with a gender other than what was assigned to them at birth.

What the break-up has done—aside from the obvious—is it has served as an excellent distraction. It has prevented me from obsessively freaking out about the upcoming training session, that could be rewritten a dozen times, and still not feel like it is of adequate quality. What the current close proximity to the training session now does, is to serve as a distraction from the fresh pain of the break-up. I could not have planned these two events to work so well together.

Nobody actually knows about the break-up when I deliver my training, which I do alone, from the bedroom of a stranger's home. It isn't until the final question has been answered at the end, that emotion catches up with me. I howl, and howl, mourning until I feel I've no more tears to shed. I then use information I've gathered for the training session, and write openly and honestly for an audience of strangers. It is an intimate blog post that leaves me vulnerable to an unknown audience, in a way that I had been incapable of being with Refreshingly Familiar.

Now that I have purposefully returned to a closet for my house sitting profile, I feel ashamed. I decide that a bold new action is required that will both empower me, and prove my dedication to changing the world. Rather than distributing a link only to those who follow my social media accounts, I choose to include my professional network. Fortunately, this is achievable through two appropriate avenues; as an article on *LinkedIn*, and a post with a link on *Yammer*.

THE SOCIAL MEDIA POST

Because Wednesday 17th of May is 'international day against homophobia, biphobia, and transphobia' I figured it timely to inform/remind you that you all know of at least one person who has suffered greatly due to transphobia (me). I've been fortunate enough to survive everything listed below as a direct result of the trans label, but many haven't, and many won't (survive, that is).

In the past I have:
- *had thousands of individual negative interactions and reactions regarding my identity;*
- *struggled to access adequate support services, including medical;*
- *had my identity revealed without consent, shoving me into immediate danger;*
- *struggled to finance treatments essential to my wellbeing;*

- had difficulty gaining employment;
- been injured by false assumptions and gossip;
- endured physical pain;
- sustained violent language and behavior; and
- been dehumanized, both directly and via the media.

This post is definitely not to prompt you to contact me about the content. I've written concise letters and detailed books that you can read for education/entertainment without me having to relive the trauma. This post is to urge you to have a conversation about the linked article with just one new person. Through education we can reduce future occurrences of trauma.

THE BLOG POST, ENTITLED:
"ARE YOU THE ALLY I'M LOOKING FOR?"

Hi, I'm Paige, the chick in the below photos!

Are you the ally I've been looking for? Please read on, because I really need you. In fact, my whole community needs you!

If you've been following my public story recently, you probably know about the open letter I wrote in 2015 or the one from 2016, and the dramatic tell-all Memoirable trilogy about my emergence from a socially anxious girl trapped in a male body, into a strong, self-assured, successful woman and social butterfly. You might also know of my Paige Uncensored campaign from 2012, or current work with Intersectionality Advocates. If you've been following my public story, maybe you've noticed the steady escalation that has led to this article.

The original goal, point, whatever, was set way back in 2011, following someone broadcasting my gender history on social media.

Me, in 2011:
"I need to reduce trans stigma to a level where I can feel as confident disclosing my past gender transition in a room, as I would if I were disclosing the fact that I have had my four wisdom teeth out."

Not exactly a SMART goal, but it has been reasonably effective for keeping me on track these last six years, with the exception of 2013-2014, when I felt it necessary to hide myself away.

Me, right now:
"It took thousands of individual conversations to get me here."

That is, to a place where I now feel comfortable enough to start this article with information I once — for the purpose of damage control — felt the need to delicately and carefully expose. A place where I've personally provided this information to most people I work with in writing, sporadically outed myself during many social conversations, and on panels before a variety of audiences. A place where it's an accidental oversight if I don't tell a romantic or sexual partner, rather than a deliberate evasion.

As a current or potential ally, I just want to make sure you're on the right track, because sometimes good intentions are not actually enough. Sometimes inaction is as detrimental as fighting on the other side that's working tirelessly against our human rights, making the world a less safe place for us to exist in.

Please.

Help.

1. #NotAllTrans

It seems appropriate to start with this fundamental piece of advice.

Also me:
"Never assume an automatic understanding of everyone's trans experience because of information you've gained from one or two sources. Even if you yourself are trans."

Thanks to Kimberlé Williams Crenshaw, there's this word intersectionality. It acknowledges the basic truth that multiple social categorizations apply to an individual (e.g. race, class, gender). This overlap can cause interdependent systems of discrimination or disadvantage. So on one end, you have the very visible, wealthy, successful Caitlyn Jenner, and on the other, you have unknown transgender women of color living in poverty. People along this spectrum of privilege experience life differently, so their challenges and what they require from allies is not the same.

2. What's Your Childhood Trauma?!

The following truth is something that doesn't seem to occur to most cisgender people.

> *Me, earlier this year:*
> *"It's likely that a trans person has endured one or more traumas as a direct result of being trans."*

This could include:
- being outed without consent;
- negative interactions or reactions regarding their identity;
- difficulty accessing support services;
- financial cost of treatments;
- loss of or inability to gain employment;
- physical pain;
- false assumptions;
- violence of all types; and/or
- dehumanization both directly and via the media.

Some, like me, have experienced all of these. Some, repeatedly. I consider myself lucky to not have experienced employment issues in quite some time. Yay for me. As with all trauma, how a person is on the other side can vary a lot. A trans person who has been through the above could be feeling angry (often toward cisgender people), depressed, anxious, panicked, or even proud.

> *Me, quite recently:*
> *"What many self-proclaimed allies have not understood about me, is that because of the substantial trauma I've sustained, when they suddenly bring up my transness for whatever reason, they trigger memories of the strong negative emotions I felt during thousands of related traumatic experiences. It is a horrible experience for me 100% of the time."*

Be mindful of that.

3. Coming Out, and Being Outed

There are two main ways you will find out that someone is trans:
- *from the trans person; or*
- *from someone else.*

If you hear it from someone else, you should not pass this information on. It is a legitimate risk to the trans person's safety. The best thing you can do, is to reply with an assertive caution about how you should never, ever out a trans person. Also, definitely don't approach the trans person with your newfound information about them. That is likely to cause them stress, for no benefit whatsoever.

If you hear it from the trans person's own mouth/pen/keyboard, listen, acknowledge, and ask if it's something they actually want to discuss. Something cisgender people often don't think about, is that a trans person can become quite stressed with keeping their identity a secret. Telling you might be no more than removing some stress from their interaction with you.

Me again:
"When it comes to me, if I tell someone about my past gender transition, I am doing it for no other reason than to improve the situation for other people. I never do it to prompt intrusive questions. If you're curious, instead of asking me to relive the trauma, you can read my books on the subject."

4. I've Made a HUUUUUUGE Mistake

At some point or another, we're all likely to accidentally say or do something offensive to a trans person, because this is an area where we're all still learning. Even in the last year, I have had to change problematic language I was using in ignorance.

My advice is to offer a prompt, genuine apology. You may also wish to ask them if there's a way you can make up for your lapse in judgement. Some things to avoid however, are validating or excusing your mistake, invalidating their reaction, or making a huge deal about it. Listen more than you speak, and if it seems like they'd rather put the situation behind them, find a way to move the conversation in a different direction. If a reaction seems over the top to you, it's probably less about this isolated incident, and more about a lifetime of related situations.

> Me, right now:
> "Just realized that you've made a mistake while communicating with me? Please let it go, and resolve to never make that mistake again. Bringing it up will just cause me to experience feelings associated with the trauma all over again."

5. Actions Speak Louder Than Ally Badges

Based on my own experience, and chatting to a range of trans people, below are some ways that will clearly demonstrate to a trans person you are NOT an ally:

- *Bringing up the subject of their being trans. It should always be their decision to bring it up if they want to.*
- *Disclosing to them that someone else is trans. They might think you're likely to out them too, and would they be wrong?*
- *Asking questions about what's under their clothes. They're a person deserving of respect and some privacy, not a gallery exhibit.*
- *Likening their trans experience to something else. Chances are the simile will be offensively wrong.*
- *Discrediting their trans experience by quoting something you read in an article.*
- *Telling or sharing a joke where a trans person's identity is the punch line.*

Some ways to clearly demonstrate to a trans person you ARE an ally:

- *Always allow a trans person to be the one to bring up the topic.*
- *Call out someone when they disclose a trans person's identity.*
- *If a trans person brings up the topic, ask them if they want to discuss it.*
- *Respect a trans person's choice not to tell you all about their experience.*

- Announce your gender pronouns – not just to people you think are trans.
- Be hasty and genuine with an apology when you make a mistake.
- Allow trans people to speak, rather than quoting facts you've read.

Do you want to help more?

A great way to help right now, is to share or discuss this article with someone you know. This sentence is your permission from me for you to do so (and yes, this sentence is very important).

You can (and should) also broaden your knowledge, and see if there's a not-for-profit organization that could use your skills. The following links and quotes have been collated to make this easier for you.

THE ONLY WORKPLACE RESPONSES I get this time around are positive. There are no intrusive questions, no indication of malicious gossip, and nobody seems to feel less comfortable around me than they were previously. A few people mention they've read what I wrote, and they express appreciation for my bravery. Some ask if they can hug me, and I always oblige.

Several people in my professional network tell me that before the post they had been unaware of my past. They serve as the validation I need to keep active. These people have been in the dark despite the fact that I have now come out at work several times. Even though an internet search engine presents several wordings of my truth on the first page alone. It's also alluded to on my social media profiles. I decide that I must find a way to keep myself out of the closet, but it needs to be low maintenance.

— 8 —

The most aesthetically pleasing, can also be the most dangerous.

Previously…

SEVERAL MORE WEEKS OF WAITING, and I allowed my thoughts to be preoccupied with other things.
    Allowed is the wrong word.
    I tried.
    God, I tried so hard.
    But the assault was still in the back of my mind.
    Tormenting me.
    What would the consequences be?
    Of standing up for myself?
    How would I be punished?
    Not *if*, but *how*.
    I knew Vulpine Foe would find a way to fight me.

Now…

RIDING THE WAVE from my recent workplace outing, I see another opportunity for professional escalation, and I take it. Although my position at The Southern Teaching Hospital is a fixed term contract, I've established a good reputation. There's a solid chance that I'll soon have the opportunity to extend my contact. But I'm not sure I want to stick it out for another year in a job that already feels repetitive.
    Within a day of having the idea, I've updated my standard curriculum vitae, and it is a revision like never before. For the first time, I've deliberately included mention of the LGBTIQ community, and my place in it. I do this in part for my campaign to reduce stigma, but also because this

information can now be used as a selling point, rather than something to be counted against me.

Not just because diversity has become fashionable for business—which feels a tad offensive by the way—but because my writing and leadership position are professional achievements. It's not possible to mention the writing without making note of the topic. Nor would it make sense to leave out details about the organization that has put me in the position of Queensland Director, and why it is I've climbed the ladder so quickly.

Social Advocacy and Team Leadership
(August 2016 – present)

I hold the volunteer position of Queensland Director with Intersectionality Advocates, an organization that seeks to support young LGBTIQ professionals as they navigate the early stages of their careers. Within this portfolio, I lead a team of 16 volunteers, and work with the National team to deliver content, events and thought leadership, in the areas of gender, sex diversity and intersectionality. In April I provided in-house training (Being a Trans Ally) to a national team of more than 60 volunteers. Previously I was also the Queensland Gender and Sex Diversity Coordinator.

Autobiographical Writing for Social Advocacy
(October 2015 – present)

In 2015 I wrote a public blog (Version Thirty-Three) about 33 defining life experiences related to being a woman assigned male at birth. Due to how well it was received, the stories were then expanded to become a series of three novellas (Memoirable Series). Paperback and eBook editions of the novellas were published in late 2016, and early 2017. A full-length remix of the three novellas (Completely Memoirable) was published in both formats in March 2017.

JARRING AT BEST is the stark contrast between my current workplace environment at Satellite Hospital, and my former at The Southern Teaching Hospital. It's difficult to believe that a measly fortnight ago, I was staring at my computer monitor, bored, surrounded by people and noise in an open plan office. It was an office that shared airspace with the staff kitchen, as well as a thoroughfare to other offices, the occupants of which were lucky enough to have doors to hide behind.

I remember that as I sat there, bored, I felt annoyance that I was no longer ever alone at work. I remember the feeling of discontent as I worked through a list of tasks that were unchallenging because they were exclusively repetitions. What I craved was solitude, and new problems to solve. What I'm now reminded of, is the phrase that begins with *be careful what you wish for...*

Wide-eyed, I'm now sitting alone in my office at the Satellite Hospital. The office is tucked away in a corner of the hospital that nobody passes on the way to anywhere else, and the site is too small to justify me having any colleagues. It's just me, all alone, in a big, sterile office.

As far as the workload, in a vague sense I'm aware of what I need to achieve by the end of the week. Less clear than that is my knowledge of how to complete any of these vague goals. If I can't figure it out on my own, there is someone I can call for help, but it doesn't seem appropriate.

Two reasons that are tied closely together, are why I'm here in this job, and why I'm determined not to reach out to the one person most able to help. As an innovative, forward-thinking business move, there's been a three-way temporary job swap. The goal of this swap is to build a workforce that is more adaptable. Staff who are able to cover each other during periods of leave, with minimal disruption. It is a problem that has been in need of addressing for quite some time, and I'm pleased that my previous expression of professional discontent has gifted me the opportunity to be a part of the solution.

The three of us who are The Chosen Ones, we have all had a similar fortnight at work, split into three clearly defined parts. While ensuring regular workflow momentum, we've each trained a temporary replacement, and have been learning the basics of our new, temporary role. All three of us are now in those new roles, with all training behind us, with explicit instructions not to meddle with the jobs we have left behind.

It is my assumption that the three of us feel as though we're out of our depth. Also, that none of us want to be a burden by reaching out for assistance from someone who is learning a new job on the fly, though I'm fairly confident any of us would gladly be the recipient of such a call. This lack of support is the main element of the undertaking that I perceive as problematic.

By the close of the first day, I've successfully navigated several new scenarios, and I'm now able to seamlessly utter words that were at first somewhat excruciating.

The Words I Now Say With Ease

> "I don't know how to do that yet, but I will find out as soon as possible and get back to you."

I'm fortunate in that some of these students have previously been under my care. They know that I'm genuinely helpful whenever possible, and any failings are because of how rapidly I've been stationed here. Those students at least, have seen me at my professional best.

On my own external hard drive, I create a document entitled *Not Yet Successful*. The file houses a list of the day's failures, so that I can do some digging to close the required knowledge gaps as soon as I have capacity. I've also scoured the electronic files for anything that seems like a note on a process or procedure, and have added them all to a single procedural manual that I've decided to write.

The reason I've done all this is because I've been unable to determine any logical organization within the current system. I've no doubt that there is a system that was logical to the person who usually does the job, but I'm blind to it. My brain sees a complex mess in need of my specific brand of reworking into ordered structure.

Each day, I set myself a few easy tasks to complete in-between the many that are more difficult. This slowly helps me rebuild my professional confidence, that has taken quite a beating. I note that there's also something else that needs some work before I can feel more comfortable in this foreign work environment. Fortunately, it's easier to conquer.

At the end of each day, I spend a little time modifying the office to replace the overall impression of cold sterility, with one that is warm, and welcoming. This is achieved through the addition of some photos, a floral scent, and relaxing background music. Also, in the most visible position possible, I affix to the wall a watercolor rainbow skeleton that was painted for me by a former medical student.

Something that exacerbates the feeling of isolation is a new house sitting gig in the northern suburbs. When I'd accepted the gig, I was working at The Southern Teaching Hospital. It would have been a long commute then, and Satellite Hospital is even further south, so I spend more than four hours a day travelling to and from work. Additionally, there's a dog that needs to be walked daily, so I drop out of all social engagements.

By the end of my terrifying, sobering (ha ha) first week at Satellite Hospital, I meet Hospital Companion. You may imagine them as anyone, of any gender, who is reasonably tall, with a warm, friendly face. This is a near-flawless mask, which is something they have developed as a way to thrive in their world. We make eye contact, and it is quickly followed by a handshake, as seemingly less important things like words are exchanged.

My emotional attachment to Hospital Companion is forged in the same, drawn-out moment our eyes and hands connect. Of course, I silently consider why this is, while my body and another part of my brain carries out our first ephemeral conversation. This person is friendly, they are pleasing to look at, and there's a hint at something else just below the surface but I don't know what it is. Also a contributing factor, the sudden isolation and vulnerability caused by both relocations.

In any case, I decide that my workplace relationship with Hospital Companion is one that I will invest in. How it will play out, I've no idea, but we will become friends, and they will be the first person at Satellite Hospital to find out about my past from me. I figure, it is possible that there are people who have already found out by other means, but whether for good or bad reasons, nobody has made any indication of knowing. I'm not treated in any way that feels *different*.

Hospital Companion proves themselves to have a kind heart very quickly. They go out of their way several times to help me navigate the social politics of the hospital that are very different to what I am accustomed. It becomes a ritual on certain days to chat over coffee, and, just as intended, a friendship develops.

With each conversation, urgency of disclosure increases, but I also become more anxious about how Hospital Companion might respond. It feels as though I've gone back in time by years, and I am reminded that this is exactly why I had turned down a job offer earlier in the year. I'm now entirely in the closet at work again, and have absolutely no known allies.

As Hospital Companion and I get to know each other better, I'm able to tell them about my volunteer work. Their non-judgmental interest helps me feel as though they will be a safe person to disclose to, however I'm mindful that they're currently very useful in some areas of work I find most difficult. I also consider the worth of coming out in a workplace that is temporary. It might not be long before I'm swapped back into a role at The Southern Teaching Hospital.

I think about how I stand in front of strangers for Intersectionality Advocates, and bravely speak about my gender identity, and a variety of related experiences. Continuing to deny it in conversations with Hospital Companion, I start to feel as though I am a fraud. I'm not brave, and even less honest. This is an area in which I desperately want to grow.

One day, quite organically, my writing comes up in conversation. Naturally, so does the simple truth that I have published books. In a deliberate evasion, instead of telling Hospital Companion about my published works, I tell them about the speculative fiction novel I'm working on. Deliberately evasive, I don't mention that my published works are all autobiographical.

Hospital Companion is curious, of course, and I realize I've backed myself into a corner. What I've done through this conversation, is make myself worthy of an innocent internet search of my name. As if to confirm this, Hospital Companion asks how accessible my books are, because they would like to read one.

"I've been looking for something else to read," they tell me. "This is fate!"

Although I'm scared of the unknown potential of Hospital Companion to transform into a powerful adversary, I know that I don't want them to complete an internet search of my name. That is not the way I'd like them to find out about who I really am. So, for the most cowardly of reasons, I give Hospital Companion a paperback copy of *Outer Shell*.

"Wow, Paige I'm impressed," Hospital Companion tells me, scanning the cover of the book that is now in their hands. The sight makes it more difficult for me to maintain a calm façade.

"Start at the beginning," I urge them. "And don't flip through it in front of me."

When the name Hospital Companion is displayed in my list of phone notifications that weekend, I feel panic. They've definitely started the book, and probably already know that I started out life with a male body. What I desperately hope, is that their text message doesn't reiterate a multitude of negative reactions from the past. The dominant fear is that my truth has made them uncomfortable. The fact that it's had such a negative effect on many people is a frequent source of pain for me.

I consider the many potential words of the text message.

Potential Text Message

Oh, I could totally tell by the way.

Another Potential Text Message

I did actually wonder because of your voice.

Or Maybe This Text Message

It's inappropriate that you suggested I read this.

Or Even

I wish I could go back to not knowing.

After what seems an appropriate amount of preparing myself for bad news, I read the text message that Hospital Companion has taken the time to write and send before we see each other again at work. It confirms two things, one being something many other readers of *Outer Shell* also have.

Once Hospital Companion started to read, they found it difficult to stop reading, and at the time of the text message, they've already made it all the way to the end. Instead of any judgmental comments, what I've received is thanks for sharing, and confirmation that they're looking forward to our developing friendship. I feel proud, relieved, and excited.

Another text message arrives, this time from Important Human. My emotional reaction to Important Human's words is entirely different.

Text Message From Important Human

The nation is going to vote on whether same sex marriage is popular enough to justify updating the law. You'll need to get yourself an address so you can vote.

— 9 —

The life of a woman, is a salty one.

Once…

MALE ALLY'S HEAD popped into view unfathomably soon after I'd given the call.
 I could see the panic in his eyes.
 This was an educated physiological response.
 It was nothing on the panic that was my own.
 I held up the envelope to show him.
 It was the reason he'd been summoned.
 The envelope contained more papers than I'd expected.
 I left the room I was in to meet him.

Now…

EMOTIONAL BEYOND REASON, I leave the service counter of the Brisbane GPO. I've just been talked out of renting a small post box that would allow me to receive mail that I could collect at any convenient time I could find in my increasingly busy schedule.
 What a post office box would also allow me to do, is register to vote in favor of the law being changed to allow same sex couples to marry. What I've been told is that there's a nearby Post Office I should go to. There they will be able to offer me a post office box for a much cheaper price.
 As I leave the Brisbane GPO, I whip my phone out, punch in the address of the Other Post Office, and stick my earphones back in. Unreasonably tired, I drag my feet as directed by the voice from my phone. It takes me three blocks, and two corners before I've one person in line between me and my goal.
 The other person finishes their interaction, and I step forward, pleased that I will soon have a fixed—albeit postal only—address. I'll be allowed to

formally enter the debate on whether one group of Australians should have the same rights as everyone else. Although it doesn't feel right to have a say, I've a strong desire to vote in favor of a change in law.

Something I notice about Wishful Helper when she asks how she can help me, is that she has inviting, kind black eyes. Perhaps they're dark brown, but in this light, with my eyes, I perceive them as black. The way all visible parts of her come together, a welcoming, friendly vibe is created. I wish the person at the Brisbane GPO had been like that. Maybe then I wouldn't have felt so suddenly and severely deflated.

"I'd like a post office box, please," I tell Wishful Helper confidently.

"Of course! There's just a short form, and I'll need some ID, including something that confirms your residential address."

"I have my passport," I tell her. "But nothing with a residential address."

"Oh, that's okay, I can hold your application until you can bring something in."

"I can't do that," I say.

"There are a few parts on the form that can be left blank, but proof of residential address is mandatory."

I throw my hands up in the air, and tears start to flow from my eyes.

"But I can't prove that I have a residential address if I don't have one! I don't actually live anywhere in particular!"

Wishful Helper seems concerned.

"Where are you staying at the moment?"

"I'm house sitting, looking after someone's bird, but I'm moving out soon, and shortly after that I'll be somewhere else, and then I don't know where. Why does this, why is this so difficult?"

By now I'm sobbing. Over a post office box.

"I have an idea," Wishful Helper tells me. "Does your bank have a branch nearby? Could they print you a statement that has an old residential address on it? I assume you once had one."

"I could try that," I say.

Wishful Helper smiles kindly at me.

"I'll keep the form right here for you when you come back with your bank statement."

"Thank you," I say. "Sorry for getting so emotional. I don't know why I reacted like that."

"I've seen worse," she says. "I'll see you soon."

When I am eventually holding the bank statement in my hands, I just can't help myself.

"Motherf█cker!"

It proudly boasts my old post office box that is definitely not a residential address, and in any case, it will now be registered with the Wishful Helper under somebody else's name. I am furious, but I realize I have a date to get to, and I might be late if I don't get a move on.

HAND TREMBLING, I hit the dial button below the name Important Human. I hold the phone to my ear and listen to the digital audio effect that mimics a phone dialing. It rings a few times, then I hear Important Human's voice.

"Paige? What's wrong? Why are you calling?"

In the dark, under the bridge by the Brisbane River at South Bank, I lean back on a brick wall. The world around me seems to be wobbling a bit.

"I'm freaking out," I tell Important Human.

"You were on a date, right?"

"Yes," I confirm.

"Oh no, did they…"

"No, it wasn't like that. I mean, sort of, but no, just… everything."

"You aren't going to drink are you?"

I shake my head.

"Paige?"

"No. I'm tempted, but I won't."

"What's going on? I can't get to you right now."

"That's okay. I just need to talk. He… I've a lot on my mind now."

"I'm right here, and you can tell me anything. You know that, right?"

"Yes. Okay."

I focus to find the best point in the past to travel back to, then concentrate on the moment to prompt hasty backward movement of time.

"He was stockier than I was able to guess from photos," I tell Important Human, unable to avoid making it into a story. I slide down the wall into a sitting position, and also allow myself to slip back a few hours.

HE'S STOCKIER THAN I was able to guess from photos. His hair is a soft, golden blonde, and now that I come to think of it, soft is a good word to describe all parts of the picture that make up Pressure Point. He has soft facial features, a soft tan, soft grey eyes. Maybe they're green, but I perceive them as grey, and my perception that is hindered by a color vision defect is all you've got to go on.

Pressure Point looks up from his mobile device that has just tipped him off to my close proximity.

"You're tall," Pressure Point tells me.

"Oh, yeah, I guess," I say.

"Your voice is deep," he notes, like maybe I haven't realized this after three and a half decades of life. "I like that."

"Um, thanks," I stammer. Comments about my voice always cause me to lose my footing, even if they're meant as a compliment.

"I don't like small talk," Pressure Point announces. "But I can tell you don't either."

"Can confirm," I laugh. "Hate small talk. But it does have its purpose."

Pressure Point digs into his jacket pocket and produces two small pieces of paper. He hands one to me.

"I got us tickets to the later screening of *Get Out*, which is a perfect date movie, because we won't really be missing anything."

I gulp.

"So no small talk, but we've got almost… two hours to spend before the film you don't want to see."

"Let's walk. You're more intelligent than I expected, considering the volunteer work you do, and your gender of course."

"Lol, what?"

"And that is actually what I want to talk to you about."

"I'm all ears," I say, almost at a loss for words. I'm curious about what he has to say.

"Let's start with trans people," he says.

"Why not?"

"So, percentage-wise, how many trans people do you think take up the population?"

The way he's worded it, is as if our specific demographic are a drain on limited resources.

"I don't actually have any idea," I confess. "I'm not really concerned with how many of each type of person exist, more about which ones I can help, and how."

"Well it's a tiny percentage," Pressure Point tells me. "You know what's a bigger percentage than the number of trans people in the population?"

"Tell me," I urge him.

"The representation of trans people in film and television. People like you campaign for more trans characters, when they're actually already *over* represented in media. I'm not being rude or offensive. That's just a fact."

"I don't know the figures, so I can't fight you," I say.

"Couldn't if you did," he pokes, laughing.

I grimace, but I don't fight. Surviving this conversation without giving in to anger feels like necessary preparation for what's still to come. Today, and a little later than that.

"So what trans people should be doing is accepting that they're a minority. They're marginalized for a reason."

Pressure Point slips his hand into mine.

"Come, I know a nice place to sit by the river while we continue this excellent discussion."

"Okay," I oblige.

For a few minutes I walk hand-in-hand with the enemy along the river. Pressure Point has joy irradiating from his face. It's a far cry from what I'm feeling, and I'm only sticking around out of morbid curiosity, guilt over him already having purchased movie tickets for us, and the notion that maybe this will toughen me up.

Pressure Point and I arrive at a small deck over the river with a bench that we sit on. He slips his arm around me, and gazes out over the river.

"You people are also taking the wrong approach with gay marriage."

"We are?"

"Yes. I won't bore you with all the legal stuff, because you won't understand it anyway, but you're going about it the wrong way."

"I just think all people should be able to marry the person they love. I don't think it should only be an option for certain people. I'm not in the business of changing laws, just helping change problematic mindsets."

"Don't you feel bad?"

"About what?"

"People suffering in war-torn countries, starving, and you're spending your time, energy and other resources helping gay people who are already really privileged? I have less privilege than a lot of gay people. My life has been really hard."

Pressure Point goes on like this for ages, and I politely listen, fighting back minimally. What I want and what he wants is the same; for me to erupt in anger. But I won't. I tell myself that enduring this is character-building. There are tougher times ahead, and remaining cool, calm and collected in this situation is preparing me for what's to come.

I will not bite.

On the other side of eternity we're sitting in the dark, brutally critiquing the trailers before *Get Out*. Each sentence exchanged makes a simple truth increasingly obvious. We are as politically polar as is possible without either one of us being an extremist. Although he seems to be physically interested in me, I wonder whether his major motivation for this date has been to antagonize me.

Before the film starts, Pressure Point leans over to me, having finally stopped speaking out against my community, and he kisses me. I have not once felt the compulsion to kiss him since our meeting several hours earlier, nor do I feel compelled to kiss him back now. It comes with welcome silence however, and the act itself isn't entirely unpleasant, so I decide to just go with it.

When the film starts, I break away to start watching, but Pressure Point sees this as reason to progress intimacy in another way. In a single, swift movement, Pressure Point's hand is up and under my dress, feeling around atop my underwear. I realize it's been a while since anyone has been physically in the vicinity, and although I would prefer the touch not be from Pressure Point, I favor it over no touch at all. So as I watch the film unfold, I allow him to concentrate on finding a way beneath my final layer.

Around the mid-point of the film, Pressure Point's fingers have successfully navigated all layers of clothing, and as I stare at the escalating horror story unfolding on the screen, he diligently works me toward a climax of my own. As intensity builds, so does my anticipation of satisfaction both in terms of what will play out up on the screen, and also down below. It is not to be, however, at least in terms of my bodily reaction to Pressure Point's efforts.

In one wrong, awkward move, I slip off the theatre seat and land with a great thud on the floor, pulling my handbag with me, causing enough noise to draw the attention of those beside and behind us. After helping me back into my seat, Pressure Point tries to pick up where we left off, but I push his hand away, and the last time I touch it is as we shake to part ways forever.

"OH, THAT'S A LOT," Important Human says finally.

"Yeah," I say. "And now I wonder whether I'm doing the right thing at the helm of the state branch of Intersectionality Advocates."

"I've missed a connection somewhere," Important Human admits.

"He was right, I think. I'm not doing good work. Or enough good work. I think volunteers left because I wasn't a good enough leader. But I don't know how to do better, or more. I'm so tired, Important Human. I've barely socialized in half a year outside of work, you, and the people I've lived with."

"You don't have to do more, Paige," Important Human reassures me. "You help enough people now. I know you've told me about several who've contacted you recently about the impact you've had on their lives."

"But," I object. "What if me doing this work is getting in the way of help reaching other, less privileged people, and what if me being in this position is preventing someone more worthy?"

"I'm not sure I follow."

"Well, I'm not part of the community," I explain, and then it all just flows out of my mouth in a torrent. "The way my life played out, I've a predominantly heterosexual cisgender social circle, with just a sprinkling of queer friends. Almost everyone I have to connect with socially for this work is in addition to a social circle I've already been unable to adequately maintain! And being sober makes it so much harder. I didn't realize how much I relied on alcohol to get me through all these networking events before. They're so taxing now. It's too much for me, and I've been a sh██t friend, and I just keep being more sh██t to more people! I can't keep connecting with new people, when I don't have the time or energy for those I'm already connected to. I'm being such a bad friend to people who've put the most effort into our friendship, and really, I just think I need to resign from the Queensland Director role."

"No," Important Human asserts abruptly.

"I need to find a suitable replacement as soon as possible, give them a crash course in directorship, then go back to my former life. I'm not a role model, and I'm most definitely not a leader. I already fired off a bulk email about it to Intersectionality Advocates."

I'm panting.

"Paige, you can't go back. For starters, you spent a good deal of time drunk, with people you don't have all that much in common with. Your old life wasn't great for you, and that's not a version of yourself I'd want to go back to being friends with. You're actually a better friend now."

"Well maybe not back to the same life, but I can't go on like this, not while I'm still house sitting to get rid of debt. I'm so tired, all the time."

"I've another option that I don't think you've considered," Important Human offers. "My free time just increased, and I know a bit already. Let me carry some of your load. All I ask is that you remain at the helm."

"I don't know…"

"We can make it official. Call me a deputy or something. We'll get a position description drawn up."

"Really?"

"Please. You're helping more people than you realize by being a visible professional in this space. Sure, there are other people in the world who have different struggles, but these are people you are in a position to help. Don't vanish and take hope from those more vulnerable than you. They need it. Don't you remember how it felt to have nobody to look up to? Nobody visible to prove that a trans person can be professionally successful? Hasn't that been one of your major motivations? Surely that hasn't just vanished like you intend to."

I'm silent and hurt, which is often a side effect of being told the truth. Important Human is right. I'm sure there is someone better suited for the role, but until they make themselves known, I need to persevere. I'm in a position to do something, and I owe it to the community to take advantage of that.

"Okay," I agree. "I know what some of my biggest weaknesses are, and you can definitely help me there, and I'll keep being a visible leader."

"Good," Important Human says. "And people respond really well when you do your very raw public speaking."

It's just as well we have this conversation right now, because we're about to be on the front line of a war as we near the marriage equality vote. Not only that, but my heart will soon be broken by knowledge of specific people acting as leaders for the opposition. In these dark days ahead, I will need Important Human more than ever, and my community will need me.

— 10 —

The war with my family really began the day I drew my first breath.

Previously…

"He's made counter allegations," I told Male Ally, as I handed over the document.

Male Ally read it in its entirety in silence.

The several pages of the document served as both a factually incorrect retelling of the assault, and an attack on my character.

My very few words had been adjusted ever so slightly to give a different meaning, while his threatening words had all been removed.

The physical contact was denied, and although Vulpine Foe insisted the exchange was unremarkable, he also claimed that there had been witnesses.

People who could verify that nothing had happened.

They would all take his side.

A detail that made my blood run cold, was that he stated that nobody had ever *proven* him to behave in such a manner ever before.

Not in a very lengthy career.

He casually talked up his well-deserved position of power in the community.

Male Ally and I read his message loud and clear.

I'd chosen to stand up against a powerful adversary, against whom it was not possible to win.

Also impossible, was going back.

Now…

The handgun is purest black; a striking silhouette against a stark backdrop of soulless white, pressed against the side of a face expressing anguish. The handgun is obscured in parts by the hand gripping it, finger wrapped tightly around the trigger. The hand is brightly colored with stripes that are red, orange, yellow, green, blue, indigo, and violet. These are specifically the colors used on the flag that represents the LGBTIQ community. Beneath the hand and handgun, are nine bold, black, sans serif letters.

WHAT THE LETTERS SPELL

TOLERANCE

It is an image that has been designed to stop social media scrollers dead in their tracks, and in my case it has been effective. As I begin to read the image caption, I feel a dark cloud build, surround me, and close in. The writer fiercely appeals to an audience of people who feel oppressed in a world where they are forced to tolerate people who behave in *sick*, *unnatural* ways. They write about those *awful* behaviors that are associated with rainbow colors, and the letters LGBTIQ.

The image and caption are a *Call To Arms* that I'm familiar with from a childhood spent in a conservative Church in regional Queensland. The writer urges the reader to stand firm, to fight against the *abomination* that is gay marriage. They go on about how they're being discriminated against by being forced to tolerate those who identify in a way they disagree with. I can feel the hate as I read their words about these people who behave in ways they believe are *disgusting*.

I stop reading to take note of the person who has shared the post on social media, and my heart breaks.

BREAKER OF MY HEART

My Sibling.

In this moment I am bombarded with realizations. Even after all we have been through, I'm not really safe around my family. When it comes down to it, they will never truly accept me, because at their core, they still believe that I am not who I am. They believe that what I am is an abomination, and if forced to choose, they will sacrifice me for the sake of their religion, as read to me in Bible stories when I was a child. I realize in this moment, that if this is true, then what they call love is really nothing more than a superficial ideal.

In an attempt to distract myself, I jump back on the dating site. This time I don't even consider revising my profile to be more honest, and very quickly I connect with an engineer named Chivalrous Knight. He seems nice, though in the most unremarkable of ways. This feels exactly like what

I need. What I don't want, is someone seeping toxic masculinity, who will fiercely challenge my core beliefs, and force themselves upon me. What I want, is to escape from a reality I feel is too harsh for me to cope with.

Chivalrous Knight is persistent, and I almost ditch him due to his rapid fire message response rate alone. But I don't, because he seems so sweet. He is keen, and because he is on holiday, gearing up to go overseas, he has loads of time for messaging. Sometimes he replies so quickly to my messages, that I wonder if he anticipates my questions, and is ready with an answer before I've even finished typing. If things do progress with him, I figure he'll be much lower maintenance when he returns to work.

Because I'm very busy between full-time work, volunteer work, organizing future house sitting, carrying out tasks for current house sitting, and trying to occasionally spend time with friends, it takes some effort to make time for a first date before he leaves the country for a several week holiday where he will explore Japan alone.

The first date with Chivalrous Knight is far better than the first date with Refreshingly Familiar. He's incredibly funny, perceptive, and because his life experience has been so different from my own, everything that comes out of his mouth is interesting to me. Although I don't tell him about why I do it, we discuss my volunteer work at length.

"What does the 'I' in LGBTIQ mean?"

"Intersex," I tell him.

"I've not heard of that," Chivalrous Knight confesses. "What does it mean?"

"Some babies can't be easily assigned as male or female when they're born. I'm not sure what best practice is now, but in the past a sex or either male or female has been chosen for the baby, and they surgically remove or adapt anything ambiguous or opposing."

"Oh. I didn't know about that. Does it happen a lot?"

I feel embarrassed that I don't have a more in depth understanding of the condition, and its variations.

"I don't know. It's an area of controversy, as these babies were never given a choice, and when they find out as adults, some feel that they were mutilated."

"I would feel that way," Chivalrous Knight says.

It feels great not only that Chivalrous Knight has taken an interest in my volunteer work, but he has had no more than a healthy curiosity about what it means to be intersex. We both have such a good time that an entire day disappears together. So that we can have just that little bit more time together, he drives me to my volunteer commitment for the evening.

"Not on a first date," I smile affectionately as I decline a farewell kiss. "I'll see you when you return from Japan."

How I spend the evening is in a theatre, watching a play. This is a particularly satisfying watch, because what's on stage has been influenced in early stages by my own advice. Months earlier, with a volunteer from my Intersectionality Advocates team, I had met with the cast and crew. Together, we'd discussed the honest, respectful options for actors who are not LGBTIQ, playing characters who are. The final product is brilliantly executed, and brings tears to my eyes.

When the play finishes, I see I've already got messages from Chivalrous Knight. He's felt the need to tell me how great the date was from his perspective. He's also insistent that we find a way to connect while he's in Japan. He won't have text message access, but will have internet access. What he wants, is for us to exchange email addresses, or to connect on social media. I'm ashamed of the way I proceed.

My first thought, is that we can't exchange email addresses, because that will give him my full name. When he has my full name, a quick internet search will be very revealing. I can't imagine how confronting that would be for someone. There's a steadily increasing body of information that explains who I am, in a variety of different ways. No, I definitely can't email him.

What I do know, is that I want to see Chivalrous Knight again, and to do that I will need to keep in contact with him. I also know I'll eventually need to disclose my past, but I don't think that right after a first date, only moments before his overseas trip, is right the time to do it. Really, it's the timing of his trip that demands I be dishonest. Really, I feel that my hand has been forced.

Fortunately, there is a phone app that is easily accessible to both of us. This app requires no more than a phone number from both parties to open a line of communication that can continue as long as we've access to the internet. There is absolutely no need to provide any information that could be used to identify me. How fortunate that technology will allow me to be dishonest with such ease.

While Chivalrous Knight is overseas, without realizing it, I provide emotional support while he feels increasingly isolated in a land of strangers speaking a language he doesn't understand well. This causes an unnaturally strong bond to develop from his side, despite us having met only once. It's a huge relief when he finally returns several weeks later, and we're able to go on our second date.

Because we've spent weeks chatting, it feels like things are already more serious than they should be so soon. I don't know how to slow things down without a conversation I'm not ready for, so I allow things to become physical. It's the first time I've broken this moral code since going sober. Alcohol, evidently, has never been the sole reason I've misbehaved.

Our first kiss is very awkward; mechanical. Although we've a clear intellectual connection, physically, we've not had much time together to get in sync. We work through this by spending more time together, and spending more of that time kissing each other. This does wonders for our dynamic. Soon, he's the first person I think about when I wake up, and he's always the last person I've communicated with each night.

Oh, no.

I have developed genuine feelings, and I've not been honest. In fact, I've been purposefully very dishonest. This is going to be a difficult conversation to have, and the longer I leave it, the more difficult it will be. I start to think about how and when it will be most appropriate to bring it up. Fortunately, Chivalrous Knight sends me a message to let me know that he's off work, sick. I write to him, opening up, and not long after, I write another blog post that includes the letter I've sent to him.

THE BLOG POST, ENTITLED:
"Could You Date a Woman Like Me? Part One"

This three-part post is really all about the following statement that I was sure I just came up with, but it sounds really familiar, so perhaps someone else actually coined it first. ¯_(ツ)_/¯

"To date a trans woman, is merely to date a woman, and that is just to date another human being."

Not Quite Normal

Some humans are wrapped up in strict adherence to rigid gender roles and norms of the time and place in which they were raised. Others, not so much. There are many ways in which I operate quite comfortably within the societal norms of a 34-year-old single woman living in Australia. Simultaneously, in many ways, I don't. This doesn't make me more or less female than any other girl I know, rather it ensures that I'm a dynamic individual who is not boring to date. The way I stand out in a group of girls is by quirks that may cause any girl to stand out; it's not for trans-related reasons.

Similarly with dating, how normal I behave has very little to do with the label trans at all. I'll talk you through it…

The Big Reveal

Right now, I'm a single lady in my mid-30s, with quite a few long and short term ex-partners. The subtext here is that I'm experienced at coming out and the most important thing I've learned? There is no perfect time, nor a perfect way, to tell a potential partner that I've been through a gender transition.

Each time has been unique, as my motivation and constraints have differed with each romantic situation I've faced. I've been asked out at work, and in the street, connected with people at social gatherings, and through dating apps. Some partners felt I told them too soon, putting pressure on them to enter into a relationship for fear of being condemned as transphobic, while others felt I should have told them the moment they expressed interest in me. There were partners who wanted to digest the information and research privately, but others wanted to discuss everything with me in great detail, in person.

Recently I wrote this letter to a romantic interest.

> As you already know, I've faced significant challenges in life. I've shared a lot with you already, but there's something I've been through that hasn't come up yet. I'm nervously hopeful that this won't change how you feel about me, because although I think it's important to acknowledge the past exists, I don't define myself by it. Who I am now is exactly who you've come to know (and like).
>
> As an open and honest person, I feel it's important for you to be aware before we go any further. It's a conversation I didn't want to rush into, but late last night I started thinking about it. I feel a bit bad for not talking about it before we got so hot and heavy.
>
> Because this has a bit of stigma associated with it, it seemed appropriate to write about it to you when we know we've got a few days apart. I care about how you feel, so want to allow you to be able to digest the subject matter both slowly, and in private. This is partially for my benefit too, because I would be quite hurt if I saw a negative reaction in your face.
>
> So, here it is.
>
> Because of my rural-Church upbringing, I suffered with an unknown condition until age 19. I finally sought medical advice after moving to Brisbane, and was diagnosed with gender dysphoria. Essentially, this means I was raised as the

> opposite gender, and at 19 I went through a series of psychological, pharmaceutical and surgical treatments. There are labels out there, but I don't like or use any of them. I'm just a woman who had a slightly different journey to get here.
>
> Though I hope this doesn't change anything for you, I understand that you might want some time to think, and maybe you'll have some questions.

Unfortunately, that did change things for them.

It's an exhausting position to be in, having to open up early on about parts of my life associated with substantial trauma. And scary. With the types of reactions I've received, and the varied people who've dished out certain behaviors, it's impossible to assess who's safe to disclose to. Those who seemed respectable and good have taken some of the worst action following my disclosure. Others who seemed like larrikins or dickheads showed immediate compassion. I'm so grateful for the positive experiences they have provided me with.

This dating bio shows the current approach I'm taking.

> Apparently a bubbly, funny, eccentric storyteller, mine has been a life worthy of a book that begins with a page of content warnings.
>
> By day I am paid to coordinate medical student teaching, and by night I help young LGBTIQ professionals for free. Somewhere in there I find time to write, and am very excited about my current ambitious project.
>
> Also, when I was 19 I went through a gender transition which mostly just means I'm a woman who can't have kids.

Fortunately, there haven't been all that many trolls.

Sexual Orientation

Many people who have been attracted to me have questioned their sexual orientation upon hearing of my past gender transition. It's actually *really easy to work out. If you're attracted to me, depending on your own gender, you could be a straight man, a lesbian, or bisexual... There are a few other labels that may apply, but if you have a romantic or sexual interest in me, you're probably not a gay man or a heterosexual woman. They are attracted to men, and I am not one of those.*

Do Your Research First

The best dating experiences have been with those who found out about my history, hit up the internet for some advice and context, and then came back to me with minimal, respectful questions. These people just treated me as a human being they cared for, who just happened to have been through certain life challenges they hadn't. Rather than defining me by details surrounding my gender, their queries purely served the purpose of ensuring they wouldn't offend or trigger painful memories. Others have made assumptions, based on the misrepresentation of trans people in fiction.

Fiction's Part to Play

At this stage in my life, I don't necessarily need or want to view or read trans stories. It doesn't matter to me how characters were assigned at birth. Growing up, I saw myself in the stubborn, passionate, loyal, and intelligent Anne Shirley from Anne of Green Gables. I understood the isolation felt by Mary Lennox in The Secret Garden and Sarah Crewe in A Little Princess, and aspired to be strong and quick-witted like Elizabeth Bennet was in Pride and Prejudice. I don't identify with the trans character Nomi from Sense8, nor Sophia from Orange is the New Black, or Maura in Transparent, and at best feel traumatized watching them navigate similar experiences to my own.

But these stories are needed by pretty much everyone else in my life, to help them understand without dragging me through the mud.

As an adult, it's unfortunate how often I've been someone's first real trans experience. Before me, they've heard horror stories of men reacting with disgust after finding out they've had a sexual encounter with a woman who once had the appearance of a man. They've seen men dressed in drag, and see no difference between drag queens and a woman like me. Or maybe they've read a scandalous story about a celebrity who's been shamed for being caught with a trans woman. As an adult, I've dealt with far too many people with only that exposure. It's one of the reasons I've pushed past pain to write on the subject in such detail.

It's also why I want there to be more, varied trans characters, despite the fact that I don't actually want to see them.

DETERMINABLE FROM THE BLOG POST, things don't work out with Chivalrous Knight. Also evident, I haven't exactly stuck to my decision to make him the last in the round of dates. What I have done, is immediately correct my dishonest behavior by creating a new profile that includes the information I kept leaving out. It feels good to be putting myself out there in this open, and honest way. What it leads to, is not as good as what I expect.

— 11 —

You can reframe a lot of things as freedom as a way to get by.

Once…

MALE ALLY SCRUNCHED UP HIS FACE as he finished reading my proposed response to counter the allegations that had been a retaliation to my reporting of the assault.

"No," Male Ally told me. "I would advise against this."

"I don't really know how to deal with this situation," I whined.

I felt deflated.

I felt pathetic.

I felt terrified.

"It's okay, I have the experience to help you."

"Thank you," I said.

"There are two things I would like you to do before we go forward with anything."

"Okay," I accepted. "I do trust you."

"First, you should Google Vulpine Foe," Male Ally suggested. "I think it's important that you know who you're up against."

I frowned.

I hated it when people Googled me.

I didn't want to Google someone else.

"And also think about what it is you want to achieve. It might be worth your while to roll over on this."

Give up.

Let him win.

For my own safety.

Now...

THE FLAWLESS EXECUTIONER IS TALL, dark, and especially handsome. Although I feel it's too soon to move on from Chivalrous Knight, Flawless Executioner has lured me into meeting for the first time by way of lyrical flattery and promise. His poetic turn of phrase in all written communication causes me to wonder excitedly how he speaks and moves in person. It's difficult to imagine a person who is anything less than eloquent, who dances smoothly with his tongue, and I am not disappointed.

Flawless Executioner saunters up to me, reaches out elegantly, plants a hand on each of my shoulders, pulls me in close, then kisses me on the cheek. I can't be sure, but it sounds like he takes an especially deep breath in to capture my aroma.

"Hello," I say breathlessly.

"Hello, Paige," he says.

The way my name is uttered by Flawless Executioner feels like the most beautiful of all time. The sounds are deep and unbroken; his eyes are describable the same way. He is a magnificent creature that doesn't seem to fit the reality we inhabit. Yet here he is before me. We sit, and all I can utter is a single word.

"Coffee?"

"Please," he states, swiftly throwing a summoning spell into the air with his hand.

Flawless Executioner flashes his teeth by way of a cheeky, devilish smile, and something about his face dares me not to run away as his summoning spell proves successful and a waiter arrives.

"Flat white in a mug, and I'll have a long black," Flawless Executioner orders.

He turns to me.

"That's right, isn't it, Paige?"

I nod, and the waiter vanishes to do the bidding of Flawless Executioner, who now looks me up and down. He subtly licks his lips, and bites his lower lip softly before speaking again.

"And how is your War of Social Justice going, Paige?"

"Well, this morning I've had to fight against the preposterous notion that if we allow same sex couples to marry, it will be a slippery slope to non-monogamous marriages, or unions with inanimate objects, and animals..."

"Nobody really believes that, though," Flawless Executioner quips. "You're getting fired up over nothing."

"Actually, those opposing Marriage Equality are using those as genuine examples, and people have proven receptive."

"I've a war of my own, because I like to push boundaries."

"Oh?"

"You're intrigued," Flawless Executioner tells me in his mellifluous voice.

"I am," I confirm, though he clearly needs no reassurance.

"One of my talents is for finding the line," he tells me, returning to the point in the conversation where he'd mentioned boundaries.

Because I don't know where this is going, I've nothing to say.

"It's one of my favorite things to do at work, finding that line. Once I find it, I like to dance to the edge, then dip my toe into the other side."

"Sorry, it sounds like you're saying you sexually harass the people you work with?"

Flawless Executioner laughs, throws back his head and flicks his hand in a dismissive gesture.

"Not in any way they can ever prove," he sings smugly. "I'm very clever, and even more cautious."

"Oh, okay," I say, suddenly overcome with an inescapable feeling of vulnerability.

"One girl did report me, but she hasn't been able to prove anything. It's just harmless fun."

I don't agree, but I can't vocalize my sentiment. I've two strong desires; for this date to be over, and for Flawless Executioner to play a wrong move, leading to some long-deserved punishment. To reclaim a little power, I write a follow-up to my dating blog.

THE BLOG POST, ENTITLED:
"Could You Date a Woman Like Me? Part Two"

The second part of this three-part post is really all about the physical side of following statement that I was sure I just came up with, but it sounds really familiar, so perhaps someone else actually coined it first.
¯_(ツ)_/¯

"To date a trans woman, is merely to date a woman, and that is just to date another human being."

Pretty [Average] Woman

Every woman I know is subject to unwelcome scrutiny when it comes to her appearance.

For a woman like me, that same scrutiny exists, but with an additional layer on top. Hands are one of the first things people gawk at when hearing the news that I've transitioned to female form. Mine are fairly average and slender, meaning I sit within the hand size norms for a cisgender woman. Time for a fun, handy fact!

During film school we did an exercise where we went around shaking the hands of our classmates. We then formed a circle, and each took turns being blindfolded. The blindfolded person had to work around the circle and guess who everyone was, based purely on touching their hands. 100% of the students guessed me as one of my female classmates; they knew they were touching female hands, but didn't yet know that I was female.

My feet are slightly smaller and daintier than the average woman of my height, though I wear Doc Martens everywhere, giving the appearance of slightly larger feet when I'm not nude. With my overall shape, again I'm average for a woman, somewhere between pear and hourglass in that I'm widest at my hips and smallest at my waist, but around the chest area it depends on how much body weight I have at the time of measurement. The breasts that I grew myself (not that it is anybody's business) have varied a lot over the years, as my weight has fluctuated, and I have aged. Probably, they're just a little perkier than the average woman my age, because they developed a few years later than most.

With regard to other things like body hair, again, I'm overwhelmingly average, with or without taking my specific mix of ancestral lines into account.

What does all this mean? There are many cisgender women with bigger hands and feet, with far more body hair, smaller hips, and broader shoulders. None of these less feminine cisgender women are more female than me, nor should they be considered less female. This is just the diversity that exists under the umbrella term "woman". I guess, in a way, I am just lucky that I was born with a body that was ready for stealthy transition to female as a young adult.

So very lucky.

Much fortunate.

Wow.

The Unsealed Section

Many men have tried to convince me that they don't need to use a condom with me, because there's no risk of pregnancy if we have sexual intercourse. Some of those probably knew what they were doing, but for the naïve few, my God, if you're going to have a sex life please educate yourself. Condoms are not just to prevent pregnancy! That said, in a long term monogamous relationship, I personally prefer my partner to go without because things tend to work a little easier and feel a little better when there isn't that artificial barrier.

Since we're down here…

If you closely examine my vulva as well as the vulvas of nine cisgender women, you would notice some differences between all ten. Whether or not you could tell which one was made on an operating table, I don't know. Maybe. I guess it would depend on who the other nine belonged to (I've seen a few variations in my time). The differences between theirs and mine certainly aren't enough to cause someone to change from "this is genitalia I want to engage with" to "this is genitalia I do not wish to engage with".

Then there's function, which is what people always seem to be curious about.

A combination of reading and real life experience has led me to the conclusion that my function is standard for a woman, and you can skip to the next section if you don't want more detail.

I was overjoyed when I was able to confirm that the surgery hadn't left me with urinary incontinence, which was one of many possible side effects I deemed worth it. A good few months following surgery I worked out that I was able to reach climax (on my own). And it was surprising when I realized I was able to engage in sexual intercourse without assistance… sometimes, with some people. The seamlessness and requirement of things like lubricant have differed with every partner. This seems to have had more to do with level of attraction, age, number of previous partners, and technique. Things that could affect cisgender women. It's rarely been anything trans-specific.

Package Unlabeled

Let's forget for a moment that I never select trans as a gender option on a form unless there's a medical reason to. In most cases I tick either woman or female because I usually don't want or feel the need to differentiate myself from cisgender women. I never considered myself a boy, nor was I a young man. I was a girl with a male body, then a woman, and eventually I was able to adapt my outer shell to reflect me as I am now. The label trans has never felt right for me in part because my identity never changed.

When it comes to online dating, I avoid those tick boxes for a whole other reason.

It all goes back to fiction.

Mainstream audiences see nothing but trans sex jokes, offensive trans clichés, and pornographic trans tropes. Do you remember that sweet love story about the man who fell in love with the woman who was assigned male at birth? No, of course you don't. That is unless you've read my books that included a few romances from my own life, or you've seen or read something in a subsection within queer media. Although these beautiful romances exist in real life, they're not really showcased in works of fiction. Especially not in the mainstream where heterosexual trans people often live their lives.

Unless someone has been friends with or had a relationship with a trans person, they've little more to go off than the awful misrepresentation in mainstream media.

Not Your Exotic Fetish

When someone with no real experience approaches me because they're seeking out a trans person, it's almost always because they've seen some kinky porn and figure that I will be just like that. Or (and this is equally incorrect) that I'll be super feminine and submissive because I'm overcompensating for my birth sex. Typically, these people want to sneak around with me in the dark, and do not respect me as a person at all. It took me far too long to realize that there are a lot of people who will gladly have sex with me, as long as nobody else knows about it. Screw them, but not in the fun way.

What I've found, is that romance works much better for me with someone who realizes they are interested in me before they know of my gender history. With those, back in the day after we had the talk and worked through any confusion or concerns, we were able to slip under the radar as a normal cisgender couple. Back then, there was rarely any reason for us to disclose my past to anyone in their social circle. These days, though, dating me is a bigger commitment because I no longer hide in the shadows allowing the assumption that I am a cisgender woman…

— 12 —

*This year serves as proof
that I don't need alcohol to cause me to
walk down the wrong path.*

Previously…

MY BLOOD SEEMED TO RUN COLD a lot back then.

I wasn't entirely sure what I had been expecting the search engine to return.

But it wasn't that.

Vulpine Foe wasn't bluffing in what he'd put in writing.

He'd survived worse.

He must have had a very good legal team.

There was no reason he wouldn't still have.

If anything, he had probably gained even better resources.

I was completely fucked.

Now…

EMBARRASSINGLY WET-EYED, I tap away on the display panel until I see the word *CONNECTED* obscuring the face of a tutor who exists in a room at The Southern Teaching Hospital. With an especially flawed mask of joviality, I turn to the group of students and smile.

"Anything else I can help you with?"

The students all either shake their heads to answer in the negative, or ignore me entirely. Not in a way that seems rude, but rather in a way that makes them feel like low maintenance wards. I swiftly exit the tutorial room, return to my office, sit at my desk, and release. A tear forms, and rolls down my cheek.

People are such f█cking c█nts, I think.

"Paige, is everything okay? You seem upset."

Horrified, I breathe in quickly, freeze my emotions, and give Compassionate Ward a wooden smile. What comes out of my mouth is less like a word spoken by a human, than the sound you get if you tightly pull flat the opening of a full balloon, and allow the air to slowly escape to a shrill soundtrack.

"Yep," is the word I try to squeeze out.

Compassionate Ward stands hesitantly in my doorway. Their face tells me that they're experiencing inner conflict. In this context, it's most likely about whether they should try to help with my distress, or accept my obvious lie and return to the tutorial. They make their choice.

"Okay, Paige. Thanks for your help!"

When Compassionate Ward is gone, I close the door, lean back against it, and sob. I feel scared. My fear is not so much about my current work situation—though I do feel overwhelmed with the unknown at work—but the idea of the countless unknown future complex issues I will be required to navigate. I'm terrified by whatever it is that's lurking just around the corner. I worry about demons that will confront me months, or years down the track.

It feels in this moment that my life, from the beginning, has been a war. Every phase of life has been its own battle. Discussion surrounding the vote on Marriage Equality is just the current battle. The end of the war will be my death. There is no other way this plays out.

By the time Compassionate Ward walks casually past my office after the tutorial, I've calmed down, and my jovial appearance is near authentic. Compassionate Ward momentarily decreases momentum, glances in my direction, then speeds up and away.

I'd love to tell Compassionate Ward all about why I'm upset. Not specifically them, but any student, really. Not any, but many. Discussions at the medical school level would be helpful later, when the graduates all face their first LGBTIQ patient. Also for the sake of the medical professional, but mostly for the sake of the patient. What I want, is for them to be adequately prepared.

Compassionate Ward starts to drop by my office on a regular basis. We chat about the part of the curriculum they're currently studying, and their experience at Satellite Hospital in general. Every now and then, I'm asked about my volunteer work. Increasingly, I feel I'm sinking into a situation that is complicated.

The circumstances at Satellite Hospital differ to The Southern Teaching Hospital with respect to how I can relate to the students. I was previously in an inaccessible office, and there were hundreds of students under my care. Because of this, almost all interactions with students were fleeting, and the relationships superficial. At Satellite Hospital, I've an open door, and there are less than 25 students under my care. What this means, is that my relationships with a lot of the students can be more substantial.

How I start to feel about Compassionate Ward, is like a friendship is developing. This feels nice, but as the non-friendship develops, I naturally want to disclose that I am a woman who was assigned male at birth. Because this is a truth that has made many people in my past uncomfortable, I feel that it is inappropriate to disclose to Compassionate Ward. I do not want to put a student who is under my care, in a position where they feel uncomfortable, least of all with me.

Enlarged and deep, Gallant Suitor's bright blue eyes team with an especially smug grin to convey pride and satisfaction. His first win was my surrender into a compromising horizontal position in the garden bed; a proposition I'd at first refused to entertain. His final success was the cause of my current pink, moist skin, and breathlessness. He brushes a lock of red hair from my face, then in what seems like the same movement, he slips his hand around to cradle my head, pulling me toward him until our lips are pressed against each other and we are kissing tenderly again.

It occurs to me that it's probably getting late, and I've a long train journey followed by a walk before I'm tucked safely away in Home Owner's bed by the bayside. I have only allowed myself to be out so late because Without A Tail and Set Of Lungs have already been seen to prior to the date. I still need to be mindful of getting to bed at a reasonable hour, though, because Without A Tail will wake me early so I can serve them their morning meal. I also need to let them out of the house early for bladder emptying purposes.

"Proof of evolution," Gallant Suitor tells me, bringing my attention back to him.

"What is?"

"How much better that feels with someone else."

Gallant Suitor delicately uses his fingers to touch the area made sensitive by his tongue moments ago, and I quickly brush him away. We both laugh, as a warm blush spreads over my body, and I quiver.

"You know, with this debate on Marriage Equality," Gallant Suitor says to me. "I think people haven't really considered how relatively new a concept human rights are."

My post-coital reverie starts to fade as he continues.

"I'm not saying that my gay friends don't deserve to marry, just that we can't just expect everyone to suddenly share the same rights. It wasn't long ago that slavery was considered acceptable. I think in some places it still is."

It annoys me that people tell me so casually that what I'm fighting for doesn't matter, or that we won't have the luxury of meeting success. So that my annoyance isn't obvious, I take a deep breath in and exhale slowly before I speak.

"Do you know what time it is? I should probably think about catching a train, so it's not too late when I get home."

"Near midnight," Gallant Suitor tells me casually.

My eyes fly wide open in a synchronous movement with my mouth as I realize the Cinderella moment I'm in.

"I have to go! I might miss the last train!"

"I'll come with you," Gallant Suitor says, pulling me to my feet, and helping me collect my bag and coat.

Following a hasty dash to the nearest train station, we both look up at the display with dismay. I've missed the last train by several minutes.

"Sht," I say.

"Damn," he adds.

We're both silent for a while, and I see him bite his lip.

"What will you do?"

"Um, I don't know," I say. "A single ride share out to the bayside will completely offset any money I've saved in rent."

A hotel room would do similar, and I'm not into the idea of falling asleep in a public space until the first public transport services of the morning. My type of homelessness is definitely still one of extreme privilege.

"I wasn't expecting this," Gallant Suitor starts. "But if you need to, you can crash at my place."

"I think I need to take you up on that," I vaguely accept.

"Cool, well I'll just need you to wait in the hallway while I tidy my room."

I laugh.

"Surely it can't be that bad," I say.

"It is, and I really wasn't expecting a visitor."

Following a night at Gallant Suitor's apartment that involves much less sleep than intended, I write down and post my final thoughts on dating.

The Blog Post, Entitled:
"Could You Date a Woman Like Me? Part Three"

The final part of this three-part post is really all about the social side of following statement that I was sure I just came up with, but it sounds really familiar, so perhaps someone else actually coined it first. ¯_(ツ)_/¯

"To date a trans woman, is merely to date a woman, and that is just to date another human being."

Meet the Parents

Once upon a time, a partner wouldn't experience much stigma from dating me.

Before my history was colorfully splashed all over the internet, and well-documented in a series of books, I remember the first time I met The Father of a man who, at the time, was my boyfriend. The Father and I met one on one for a meal while my partner was out of town. We shared laughs, and I was given the impression that this man would go to great lengths to please and help me, because I was the girl his son was in love with. He said some incredibly beautiful things to me as we ate.

During that same meal, he noticed someone walk by us. She was obviously a trans woman. That is, she didn't possess the right combination of physical characteristics to pass as a cisgender woman. The Father's words rapidly changed to graphic descriptions of how trans people should be tortured and murdered. While telling me how wonderful I was, he spoke in detail about how much he hated my kind. As someone who passed as a cisgender woman, witnessing this type of confusing dual love-hate firsthand was not uncommon.

Back then, I did whatever I could to keep my past hidden from my partner's family and friends, for fear of their safety and mine.

These days are a bit different.

Past the Point of No Return

Gone are the days when I could easily become involved in a partner's family and social network without any disclosure of my past. Obviously, a Google search of my name will reveal without a shadow of doubt, that I am a woman who has been through a gender transition. But even without that, these days it's far too easy for someone to stumble onto it by accident. The signal boost of social media is something I count on to assist with educating as many people as possible to reduce future stigma and consequent trauma.

What this means is, if you're to date me now, you will be exposed to some trans stigma backscatter.

Don't worry though, I can assure you that what you experience for liking or loving me has nothing on what I have experienced for actually being that thing. And because it's me, you can actually lead the appropriate people to literature I've written on the subject, and hopefully, just maybe, having a better understanding of my experience will give them a better appreciation. Perhaps they will even come around, like most of my conservative family have.

Free Samples

Something that makes it a little different dating a woman like me, is that people sometimes say and do things that illegitimize my gender. Again, this is on top of the discrimination and harassment experienced by all women, and it's likely to be a sore spot so I could seem oversensitive. That said, anyone you date could have a sore spot – this is just mine. Following are just two phrases that have caused me to feel marginalized, with a sprinkling of reasoning for good measure.

"You really ARE a woman."

If you break this comment down, it infers that the person has been questioning whether or not I was actually a woman. Not only that, but it also implies that my being a woman is dependent upon their validation. That is, I am only a woman if they think and state that I am. When I have heard this phrase uttered to me, I have immediately lost all respect for the speaker. This is a case of "it goes without saying" and in that case, keep your mouth shut, okay?

"I hate to say it, but all women experience that."

When I heard this one, I was quite shocked. For context, I'd been telling someone about something I had found difficult as a woman in the workplace. Further context, this was when I'd already operated as a woman in the workplace for a decade prior to anybody knowing about my gender history. At no point did I say anything about how I thought that it was related to the label trans. With the statement, in that specific context, this person made it clear to me that they saw me as trans before anything else, and also that they didn't think I understood what it was to be a woman. Naturally, I was offended.

The Fear

If we date, I will hold you a little more accountable for steering clear of words and behaviors that propagate transphobia. At the same time, if we're dating I've opened myself up to you a bit more than I do to other people, so when you do slip up, I'm probably going to be too sensitive to call you out on it right then and there. In these instances, I've been known to make up a reason to excuse myself, calm myself down, then put something in writing in a way that is as clear as possible, without placing too much blame.

Where this stems from, is a lifetime of trying to explain my emotions to cisgender individuals, and being told that they are invalid. See also: being told that I should just have a laugh, that it was just meant in jest, and I need to toughen up. The problem here, specifically with jokes of which trans women are the horrid punch line, is that these jokes reinforce that we are disgusting, that we should be hated, and it is these sentiments that lead to an astounding number of brutal murders every single year.

If your friends or family come out with something transphobic, I will most likely remain silent, and let you make the call on whether to set them straight.
Good News

In 2017, it's easier than ever to date a woman like me.

Stigma is at an all-time low for me.

This year, there has only been one person who decided they were no longer interested in dating me after I revealed my past. In my current workplace, not a single person has treated me disrespectfully, and in fact colleagues, doctors, and medical students have indicated overwhelming support for me when receiving the news of my past. Similarly, this information has spread throughout my extended social networks, with the percentage of negative reactions steadily decreasing. I'm loved and accepted as I am by the majority of my family, and have an amazing support network of friends and colleagues.

And instead of the opposite, I frequently witness actions that affirm that I am no longer someone you need to love in the shadows.

— 13 —

Triskaidekaphobia is defined as an abnormal fear of, or extreme superstition regarding, the number thirteen.

— 14 —

Whenever I act cowardly, life gives me opportunity after opportunity to be brave, and just sometimes, I take it.

Previously...

"WRITE IT AGAIN," Male Ally told me, and again I broke down into tears. "You need your response to line up exactly with what you're responding to. I know you want to defend your character, but it's important that you don't add anything unnecessary. You also want to avoid anything that will antagonize him further. Read his letter again, then try reworking your response."

"I need a break," I told Male Ally. "Please don't make me read it again."

We took a short break, then I told him I was ready to plunge myself back in to the next draft.

Male Ally pointed to one of the paragraphs I'd written.

"That whole section is unnecessary," he told me. "I do understand your desire to defend yourself, but we're trying to diffuse, so you should stick to the facts, and respond only directly, and as necessary."

"Okay," I said.

Male Ally pointed to another section.

"I would also take this out, as it could antagonize him."

I swallowed the saliva that had pooled.

"Okay, I think I need to read his document again."

I dreaded the thought.

Now...

NEAR THE END OF THEIR TIME at Satellite Hospital, Compassionate Ward visits to tell me that they will be in another town for their next year of clinical placements. The present moment will be one of the final times they'll have the opportunity to visit my office for a chat.

News that we're close to our final interaction of the year causes me to feel sad. It feels like an extended farewell from a friend who is moving away. I remind myself that they are not my friend, though. Rather, this is a professional relationship that is friendly. Maybe we will be friends when they graduate, but for now, that's not how we can relate to each other.

"That book," Compassionate Ward says, pointing at the copy of *Outer Shell* that Hospital Companion has returned. "Did you write it? Is Paige Krystal Wilcox your full name?"

My heart hits the turbo button, *and we're off and racing!*

"Oh, ha ha, yes," I tell them. "Sorry, I've got some work to get through."

"Of course, sorry," Compassionate Ward apologizes. They leave, then return on another day.

"I was talking to my mates about how you've written books, and we were discussing whether or not you would want to talk about it, and we decided that you would. It's an accomplishment you would probably be proud of."

I feel uncomfortable.

Compassionate Ward points to the visible copy of *Outer Shell* again.

"Can I have a look?"

"No, sorry," I tell them. "I get a bit self-conscious about it."

"Okay, no worries," Compassionate Ward says.

After some light banter that feels awkward for the first time, Compassionate Ward leaves. I start to think. Twice now I have missed an excellent opportunity. Because they initiated by expressing genuine interest, surely it would not have been inappropriate to let them take a copy to read. I curse myself for being cowardly, and make a commitment to myself.

The next time Compassionate Ward visits, I think. *I will loan or give them a copy of one of my books to read in their own time.*

Days pass, and it seems like I get visits from every student, with the exception of Compassionate Ward. I worry that I've made them uncomfortable, and also that I have missed my last opportunity to extend the reach of my message. Fortunately, on their last day at Satellite Hospital, Compassionate Ward visits my office to offer a third chance.

"It's my last day, so I had to visit," Compassionate Ward tells me from my office doorway. Not wanting to allow myself time to back out, I quickly reach for the copy of *Outer Shell* and hold it out to Compassionate Ward. I try to talk myself out of feeling awkward, by focusing on the fact that after they read it, they'll not be in a position to see me face to face for a while.

"Before you go, you're welcome to borrow or keep this. I've a few spares."

Compassionate Ward's eyes light up as they take the book from me.

They start to flip through it.

"Please don't flip through it in front of me," I plead, covering my face with my arm to make my sentiment more clear. Compassionate Ward closes the book, then reads the back cover.

"Is it autobiographical?"

"Yes," I say. "That's why I get a bit embarrassed."

"I'm really excited to read it," they tell me. "It might take a while to get through it, though. I don't get much time to read outside of study."

"Read it in your own time," I say. "I don't need you to return it."

Compassionate Ward smiles kindly at me.

"I actually have to come back next week, so I might have read some of it by then!"

I grimace.

"Great," I say.

Compassionate Ward looks quizzically at me.

"Well, I better let you get back to work. I'll see you next week hopefully."

"See you then," I say.

Compassionate Ward leaves, and the following week, returns.

"I just came to say goodbye, and to thank you for everything you've done for us," Compassionate Ward tells me. I stand up, and extend my hand to shake. Compassionate Ward pulls me in for a quick hug.

"It's my pleasure," I tell them. "I like helping people."

"I can see that," Compassionate Ward says. "I didn't read much, but I can see why you dedicate so much of your life to Intersectionality Advocates."

"CAN YOU USE ME to rehearse? I'd love to hear your talk," Hospital Companion tells me.

I shake my head violently.

"No way," I tell them.

"What? Why not?"

The fear I'm experiencing is irrational. This human sitting across from me has been nothing but supportive, yet we've had no in-person discussions about my past. Although I know they're a fan of my writing, I'm afraid that they'll exhibit negative physical signs as I speak candidly about what I've endured. For some reason, how they react matters a great deal more.

"Paige?"

"Well, I mean, I'll mostly speak off the cuff," I tell them in a dishonest non-lie. "I'm much better if I just have some dot points to guide me, and the freedom to explore each of them in a way that feels right in the moment."

Hospital Companion scowls at me. I'm unsure if they can see past my statement to my cowardice, or if they're just disappointed. They've read about my public speaking, but have never had the opportunity to witness it.

There's a way I can partially redeem myself, I think.

"Wait right here!"

Hospital Companion's eyes light up. I run back to my office, then back to Hospital Companion, bringing with me some paper, and a copy of *Inner Demons*.

"I'm going to start with my usual *Paige like in a book* gimmick, then say I'm very nervous, so I've made some notes."

I hold up the first piece of paper.

The First Note

Don't let them know you're nervous!

"I'll then say how I've already failed, because I started by telling them how nervous I was."

Hospital Companion silently laughs with their body as they grin at me. I hold up the second piece of paper.

The Second Note

Imagine the audience as potted plants.

"I'll then say how my original version of this note said something different, but I changed it after reading the updated *Sexual Misconduct Policy*."

An audible laugh escapes Hospital Companion this time.

"Then I'm going to read a chapter from this!"

I hold up *Inner Demons*.

"Speeches are so much easier when you have your own books to fall back on."

Hospital Companion gasps, and grabs the book out of my hand.

"You've got a book that I haven't read yet?"

"You've read every story that's in this book," I tell them. "Don't worry, you'll know as soon as I've published anything new."

Hospital Companion looks deflated. I wonder how many people would feel similar to Hospital Companion. Would there be enough to justify me writing another? It doesn't feel like anything of interest has happened in the past year. I've been too busy with work to experience anything worth writing about in a book.

"I hope your talk goes well, Paige," Hospital Companion tells me.

"Thanks," I reply. "I'm really nervous, but it's important. I feel very honored to give a keynote at the launch of a firm's new LGBTIQ policy."

When I exit the elevator, I'm immediately intimidated by the area that leads to the foyer of Another Law Firm. The floor is tiled with lustrous marble, the shine accentuated by a wall of cubes emitting a soft light. As I move to the foyer, there's minimal, expensive-looking furniture, a feature staircase of glass and plants, and a serious reception desk.

There's a short, professionally dressed Reception Boy behind the reception desk, and behind him, Another Law Firm is proudly displayed in bold lettering so large that it spans the entire wall. There is a soft glow behind each letter.

"Paige?"

The bubbly young Reception Boy bounces over to greet me with a flirty smile.

"We spoke in the phone," he says. "I'm Reception Boy. It's such an honor to meet you in person."

I probably go bright red.

"It's nice to meet you," I reply. "Thanks so much for inviting me to speak. This is such important policy to introduce to your organization."

My words are wooden, and I hope I'll be able to loosen up before it matters.

"Now, you're early, so there's nobody else here except Tech Woman, who's doing final checks in the conference room. I'll take you through so you can see where you'll be speaking!"

Reception Boy floats off smoothly to the right and gestures for me to follow.

"Hey, Paige, I'm Tech Woman!"

Tech Woman is a stocky blonde lady who thrusts her hand out toward me, initiating a firm handshake.

"I'm just checking that our interstate office will be able to see and hear you properly," she tells me.

"Interstate office?"

Reception Boy looks down at his feet.

"I meant to ask if it would be okay," he says. "Our interstate office was just so excited when they heard about you, and they didn't want to miss out on the opportunity of hearing you speak!"

"I don't think I could say no at this point," I laugh.

Reception Boy and Tech Woman join in the laughter.

"You'll need to stay close to the lectern mic," Tech Woman tells me.

"Oh, that's a shame," I say. "I was hoping to wander a bit as I spoke. But I can definitely confine my pace to a shorter distance."

Before the routine with the notes that I previously demonstrated for Hospital Companion, I add a more detailed introduction. I reprimand myself for not having had the courage to utter the words in front of Hospital Companion. Hopefully I will be presented with another opportunity soon, so I can redeem myself.

"My name is Paige, like in a book, but with an '*i*' in the middle, so not really like in a book at all. Speaking of i's in the middle of things, I coordinate medical student teaching at Satell-i-te Hosp-i-tal, and lead the Queensland branch of Intersectionality Advocates. I also just happen to be a woman who was assigned male at birth."

The audience is already engaged.

"Even though I've assumed you all knew of my past before I stood up here and announced it, I felt quite strong fear while uttering those words. This is due to thousands of negative reactions throughout my life, some of which occurred in the workplace."

I pick up the pieces of paper.

"I'm a bit nervous, so I wrote some notes."

I complete the routine almost word-for-word the way I did it earlier for Hospital Companion. Perhaps because it is a law firm, and this is a policy launch, the audience responds particularly well to my joke that has been changed since reading the policy on sexual misconduct.

"I'm going to read a chapter from one of my books that feels relevant for this launch, and then I'll talk through some other related experiences, and finally invite questions."

I pick up my copy of *Inner Demons*, flip through to the chapter *Inaudible Screams*, and clear my throat. I look up and scan the audience. I note the eager eyes all fixed on me.

"*I Googled you, she told me, immediately killing anything positive I was feeling,*" I read, striking a dramatic, crouched pose to set the mood.

— 15 —

*It surprises me how many years in a row
I've managed to escape death.*

Once...

WHEN THE FINAL DRAFT of my formal response was submitted, I returned to waiting, and worrying.
 "I've been through worse, so I'm fine," I joked with Male Ally.
 "Oh yeah?"
 While we waited, I filled him in on some of my history.
 He was surprised, and seemed impressed.
 He remained my unwavering ally.
 That a man was on my side, was of vital importance.
 That I could label a man *good* was also of vital importance.

Now...

ON MY THIRTY-FIFTH BIRTHDAY, I wake at 4:00 am to the sounds of a crying baby in the room above the one I'm crashing in for a few weeks in between house sitting gigs. I decide very quickly not to fight it, opting instead to use the extra morning time to write a post about how I feel about life on this particular morning.

THE BIRTHDAY POST

Well! Wow! I guess I made it to Half Seventy, hey.

Or Double 17.5, which sounds like a lesser achievement. So... Because I've woken up super early for no good reason, here's a slightly different birthday post that, really, is just as narcissistic as any other.

On this day, if I had a dating profile, it could read something like this...

Because I know I'm not for everyone, before you make contact please read the following profile that has been finely crafted [Appreciates Written Communication] over a period of several minutes in the early morning [Morning Person] to give you a clear idea of whether or not you'd be open to dating me [Values Honesty].

I'm Paige, like in a book, but with an 'i' in the middle [Awful Pun Lover]. So not really like in a book at all [Acknowledges Mistakes]. So. Well [Is Kinda Awkward].

A bubbly, compassionate, funny, eccentric storyteller, mine has been a life worthy of a book that begins with a page of content warnings [Has Lived]. Or three [Has Literally Written Books About It].

For cash I combine my two greatest passions of Medicine and Education by coordinating hospital-based teaching for medical students [Satisfyingly Employed].

Purely for heart-warmth, I lead the state team of a not-for-profit that assists young LGBTIQ professionals navigate the early stages of their careers through a mentoring program and networking events [Actively Trying To Change The World].

At the moment for shelter I look after homes, pets & children [Atypical Lifestyle]. After displacement in the 2011 floods, this time I've purposefully gone No Fixed Address in an effort to level my debts and I'm almost there [Determined With Bright Future]!

Also, when I was 19 I went through a complete gender transition, which mostly just means I'm a woman who can't have kids, and people label me 'trans' [...].

Though I don't drink alcohol, much of my limited free time is spent with close friends who do, while playing games and being mediocre at pub trivia. Also, wandering through the bush and along the river, writing, and reading [Wholesome AF These Days].

Romance is noticeably absent [Oh No!], so here's who I think I'm looking for.

Someone I can get lost in deep conversation with... intermittently engaging in childish banter [A Youthful Deep Thinker]. I'm not looking to build a home through the accumulation of material possessions, rather to create a path forward with someone who understands the personal sacrifices required to help change the world [Compassionate Companion]. A partner to travel and experience the world with [Adventurous].

In the unlikely event of you thinking we might be compatible after reaching this sentence, ask me an open ended question.

FOLLOWING A REFRESHING SHOWER, I slip into the green, floral jumpsuit I've purchased with this specific day in mind. Because it was to be new on my birthday, this is the first time I've put it on since confirming in the store that it is a perfect fit. In fact, I've had the thrill of unwrapping it this morning, but this quickly becomes something I regret not doing days earlier when I notice that the shop assistant has forgotten to remove the safety tag. Because the outfit is expensive, it has a big, black, round security tag that now hangs by my thigh as if to yell

"THIEF!"

I know enough about these tags to know that I should not try to break it off, lest ink saturate the fabric. There's also not enough time to unpick the seam, remove the tag gently, then sew it closed again. I also realize that I've no clean clothes, and I definitely can't wear dirty clothes on my birthday! I decide to wear the jumpsuit with the security tag for the day. At least it will be a talking point.

Even though I tell myself it doesn't matter, I spend longer than usual applying cosmetics to my face, and styling my hair. As strong and confident that I tell myself I am about being 35, I still feel as though I'm on the way down from the peak of youth and beauty that is used to measure a woman's worth in our society.

When I reach the ground floor of the house to make my exit, my face and hair are immaculate, handbag is slung over my shoulder, with the security tag hovering just below it. The baby is now sleeping soundly, and there are no other signs of life in the house. As I creep toward the front door, the security tag audibly slaps against my thigh, and there is then a clinking sound as its two parts collide with each other. I continue to walk with one hand on the tag, and use the other to stop the strap of my handbag from falling off my shoulder. It would be a gloriously awkward sight.

By the time I reach work, I've already indulged in a Danish pastry and a strong coffee. It annoys me that I'm alternating between awkwardly holding the security tag, and making a slapping, clinking noise as a I walk. Overall, though, I feel wonderful. It feels especially nice to be entering an office of the perfect temperature, and I'm looking forward to a visit from Hospital Companion at some stage.

Deciding that a birthday is an excellent excuse to buy a second coffee before I start work, I take a detour to the hospital café. While I'm waiting in line, I read through birthday messages and social media posts, which is how I see Parental Being calling, despite my phone remaining on silent, without vibration.

"Happy birthday, Paige!"

"Thanks, Parental Being," I beam.

"Are you at work already?"

"Yes, I'm just getting a coffee before I go to the office," I tell them.

"I'm visiting a patient at The Southern Teaching Hospital where you used to work. It's not far from Satellite Hospital, so I thought you might like to meet for coffee or lunch."

Ah, the typical amount of notice given about Parental Being having the capacity to meet in person.

"There's not really anything at the hospital, but perhaps you could drive us somewhere?"

"Wonderful, does around midday suit? I will text you when close," they tell me.

"Brilliant, love you," I say.

I arrive at my desk to a small, red ceramic pot. Inside the pot is a bonsai, and beside both are three small bags. I recognize the bags as the type I've used to collect the poop of dogs I've looked after. In two of the bags are small stones. Those in the first bag are tiny, and coated in a lustrous, vibrant pink. The second lot of stones are a little larger, also shiny, but black. It is the contents of the third bag that I am most fond of. It is filled with small pieces of bark. Noticeably absent from the whole package, is a note.

Hospital Companion bursts through the door of my office moments later, and erupts into a large, friendly grin.

"Happy birthday, Paige," they tell me. "You got my gift?"

"Oh, is it from you? There was no note," I tell them.

Hospital Companion points to the bark.

"Your favorite?"

I smile.

"All the options were great, but yes, that was my favorite," I say. "I love it, thank you."

"What else did you get?"

There's a childlike twinkle in Hospital Companion's eye, like I've seen in children opening gifts at Christmas time. I'm glad to have a friend like them at work.

"Nothing yet, I don't really do that," I tell them. "This outfit is new for today, and Parental Being is taking me for lunch."

Hospital Companion's lip shrivels ever so slightly for just long enough for me to notice, but then the flawless façade is back.

"How're things with Parental Being? I mean, because of your books... Sometimes I wonder about things, because of what I've read in your books."

I pause, and decide to let Hospital Companion in just a little more.

"Things are a bit weird, but they're okay," is what I settle on. Maybe at a later stage we'll have a more frank discussion, but not on my birthday.

"There's something else," Hospital Companion tells me, gesturing to the plant. "Come out to the tea room."

What Hospital Companion leads me to is a cake. There are a bundle of sparkly, rainbow-colored candles in the cake. I feel incredibly touched, and this is because I don't just feel as though I'm tolerated. I don't just feel like I'm accepted. I feel as though I'm being embraced. Knowledge of my past has not caused anything negative. This moment serves as a reminder that I have work to do. Everyone in my position should feel as welcome as I do to bring their whole, authentic selves to work.

At lunch time, Parental Being sits opposite me at a Korean restaurant that I have chosen because it wouldn't cost Parental Being much, and it's more a bonus that there's food on the menu that we will both enjoy. As I look at Parental Being, there's so much I want to tell them that I know I can't. I want to tell them about my positive experiences of coming out in the workplace. I want to tell them all about the difficulties and successes with my volunteer work.

"I'm really proud of you," Parental Being tells me.

Receiving these words is bittersweet, because I know they've also been heavily involved in political activity surrounding the vote on Marriage Equality. In direct opposition to me, they've been working just as tirelessly for the *No Campaign*, much of which has been through the spreading of misinformation about my gay and lesbian peers. Separate to the campaign, but directly related, I've had to work harder to support those in the community struggling with their mental health.

In that sense, in no uncertain terms, Parental Being and I are enemies. When the time comes, one of us will be out celebrating, and the other will be mourning. There is no way that this plays out in a way where we both win. In relation to the war, we will never truly be happy in the same moment.

"Thank you," is all I can say, having successfully destroyed anything good about the affirmation through my relentless inner monologue. I wonder if they saw me on television for the *Yes Campaign*, standing with Important Human behind more notable public figures.

After a lovely, low-key birthday lunch, the mood of which my mind has actively sought to sabotage, Parental Being drives me back to Satellite Hospital. Before I get out of the car, Parental Being looks at me, their face conveying utmost seriousness.

"You know," Parental Being tells me. "If we all died at age seventy, you'd be middle-aged today."

As I head back in to Satellite Hospital, I see that I have a message from Important Human.

Message From Important Human

We won. Love wins.

I weep with joy.

— 16 —

*Visibility and representation have
the power to change lives.*

Previously...

MY HEARTRATE ROSE due to the knowledge of the close proximity of the elevator.

I stopped suddenly.

The person I was with almost tripped over me.

"Do you mind if we use the stairs? I like the exercise."

It wasn't the worst lie I'd ever told.

I just couldn't get back in that elevator.

Not yet.

I couldn't even go near it.

"WHY DO YOU HAVE THE DOOR LOCKED?"

"Oh, I'm just concentrating on getting a lot done since I've got a bit of solitude."

"It needs to be locked for that?"

"Oh, that was just accidental when I closed it."

"Uh huh."

Now...

PARTIALLY UNDRESSED ON THE FERRY that is taking me by water from the hair salon to the annual Med Gala, I'm frantically sewing myself into my gown. There are several people on the ferry looking on cautiously. I consider how—despite giving myself more time to sew than last year—the final stitches are even more last-minute. At least I'm not drunk this time, so there's less chance that my dress will fall apart during the event.

When I pass the second last ferry terminal, I pack up my sewing equipment. I'm not finished yet, but I decide that I can find a public bathroom somewhere between the ferry terminal and the exhibition center where the Med Gala will be held this year. What this means, is that when I leave the ferry, I'm in a very interesting visual state.

How I'm dressed when I leave the ferry, is in a black singlet to protect my modesty, with the blue velvet bodice section of my dress hanging limply over the top of the skirt section that is red lace. It's hard to say why everybody is staring, between the unfinished gown, the sprinkling of sparkle, or the odd combination of black, with vibrant red and blue.

In the first public bathroom I can find, I rip off my singlet and examine the almost-complete ball gown. I realize that there's far too much fabric in the bodice, and there's no time to cut and re-sew at this late hour, so I decide to fold the excess fabric over, and tuck it into my bra. The end result is false advertising of epic proportions, as my breasts are pushed up and out to the extreme.

I'm not entirely comfortable with how large, perky, and visible my breasts are at the Med Gala, but I decide that the time has come to accept this as the completed gown. This will be a look that will definitely draw more attention, which is a good thing; #transvisibility was a major contributing factor to spending money on tickets, and putting in so much effort with creating a unique gown. I'm there to be noticed, and there's no way I won't be.

Within moments of entering the foyer, I've received a multitude of positive comments about my dress, and congratulations regarding the majority of the country voting in favor of Marriage Equality, as if it's somehow my achievement. Several people indicate that they've been excited to see me because they heard I've spent months designing and hand sewing my dress. We all laugh about how my initial *circulatory system* design was abandoned, and I instead look like a comic superhero version of a Disney princess.

"Nobody is getting photos on the red carpet by the wall," a photographer interrupts when I've taken a moment to be alone. "You look like you'd be up for getting the ball rolling."

I leap onto the red carpet confidently, and just as my brain catches up and I scratch my head, wondering how best to pose, the photographer snaps a photo.

"We'll have some photos inside," the photographer informs me, though I'm not entirely sure what they mean.

A variety of former colleagues arrive, and vulture-like I convince as many as possible to join me on the red carpet for a photo. Some oblige, some object, and the majority express their joy regarding the outcome of the Marriage Equality debate. It feels good to be so out, and proud. After a little mingling, I notice people start to head into the dining hall.

When I follow, I'm horrified by what I'm confronted with. Although the room is elaborately decorated, and looks spectacular, what takes my focus are the large displays that line the top of each wall. Larger than life, multiplied by six, is an image of me, alone, scratching my head, in a gown that leaves little to the imagination. The image changes, and it's me with a group of colleagues, and then me with someone else. Every now and then, there's a group of people without me. Well, I've certainly achieved my goal of visibility!

— 17 —

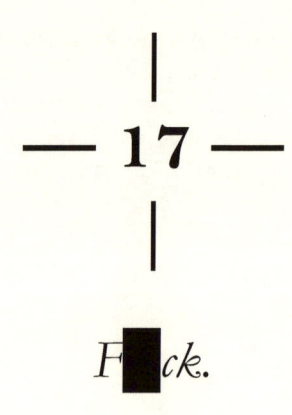

F█ck.

Once...

POSTAL DUDE STOOD BEFORE ME, holding out the next envelope, just as he had the first.
 I took the envelope from him.
 It was thinner and lighter than the last.
 Postal Dude left.
 I locked myself in my Safe Space.
 This was it.
 I would soon know of my punishment.

Now...

CHRISTMASTIME'S A CLUSTERF█CK EVERY YEAR, and my body has clearly decided to up the ante again. The hormonal cherry atop the sleep-deprived, moody cake that is me, is what more typical girls might refer to as period acne. It's hair follicles that have been plugged with dead skin cells and oil, leading to unsightly, red lumps around my mouth and chin.
 I'm too f█cking old for this sh█t, I think. *And I most definitely do not have time for it.*
 What my body is telling me, is what it's been trying to tell me for a while, and it is only now that I am staring at the acne in the mirror that the penny has finally hit me in the chin. I'm critically low on estrogen, because the pellet wedged in my abdominal fat is almost depleted. This is confirmation that my body has figured out how to process it in less than a year, as opposed to the 18 months I'd been hoping for. Still, it's far better than a daily pill or cream.
 In order to replace the depleted pellet, I'll have to make an appointment to see Nurture Essence to get a prescription. A scanned copy of the script

will need to be sent to a compounding pharmacy interstate, and I'll have to pay for it over the phone. I'll then have to send them the hard copy original, and upon receipt they'll post the pellet to me. Well, not me, because I don't have a fixed address.

The compounding pharmacy will send the implant to Important Human. During the busiest month of the year, I will need to find time to catch up with Important Human to collect the pellet, before I can go back to Nurture Essence for the procedure to have the pellet inserted. For safety, she'll use a stitch, which will need to be removed a week later. That's at least something I can do myself. Or maybe Hospital Companion, as they will be back from holidays by then. Anyway, my point is, f█ck Christmastime, and especially this year.

For the moment, I concentrate on getting ready for work. I then gather my bags, and leave them by the front door of Hospital Companion's house. This includes my sleeping bag that I used the previous night so I could wash Hospital Companion's linen, and put it back on the bed. Although it wasn't the most comfortable way to sleep in the summer heat, it feels worth it, because if they need or want to, Hospital Companion can pass out on a clean, fresh bed moments after they arrive home from their holiday.

Before I leave, I head back through the house for a final spot check. I've been up for hours, meticulously returning everything to a state as close as possible to the state I found it it in several weeks ago. I made time the previous evening to vacuum, and have spent the early morning completing all the quiet tasks, like wiping over every surface I've been near. Satisfied with what I've achieved, I grab my bags, and head off to Satellite Hospital.

It's an especially busy work morning, requiring meticulous planning to determine what I can achieve prior to the new year, in preparation for the new medical students who will arrive in my second week back in January. I realize that my first week is shortened by a public holiday, and I hadn't anticipated that several hospital departments would be closed when I need to be liaising with them. I feel a little anxious about my ability to get everything done.

How wonderful that I've no capacity for boredom right now, I think scathingly at my past self who put me here.

In what seems like no time at all, lunchtime has arrived, so I quickly catch up on messages relating to the Intersectionality Advocates Christmas Function that will finish off the busy day and week. I also confirm a house sitting gig for February, and make the first hormone-related appointment to see Nurture Essence. The work afternoon vanishes just as quickly, and I soon find myself sitting on the first of two busses to the home I'll be crashing at until the house sitting gig that will take me from Christmas through to New Years.

I change busses, then lug my bags up a hill. When I arrive at the security gate, I'm confronted by a panel requiring a code for entry. I can't remember it, and Home Owner won't be home. As I stare at the panel, I notice that there are five buttons that are more weathered than the rest; four numbers, and the # key. I punch in a sequence that seems like a nice pattern, and the gate opens. Phew!

Quickly bounding up the stairs to stash my bags, I whip out the ball gown from the Med Gala, and a little bag of silver fabric, safety pins, and battery operated tea light candles. As quickly as I can, I cut the silver fabric into squares, wrap each one around a tea light candle, and pin it to the dress. In record time, I've a unique gown for the Intersectionality Advocates Christmas Function! As I catch myself in the mirror, I laugh at how I look more like a decorated tree than a person.

There are a few very emotional words exchanged at the function. While it's a celebration that we've finally achieved Marriage Equality, a lot of people have been seriously mentally injured by the brutal fight that came before. Following a few heartfelt conversations, and a lot of photos, I notice that most people are passing the point of tipsy. This, as a sober person who feels worn out by the year, seems like a good time for me to leave. So I leave.

"POLITICAL CORRECTNESS GONE MAD," are the words I'm slapped with in one of the first emails I read when I return to work. I note the lengthy list of recipients. The email has been distributed to every Medical College Ally, and then some. The pain caused by the words is stronger; still fresh in my mind are several heartfelt conversations with members of the community who were injured during the disrespectful debate on Marriage Equality. My emotional reaction confirms for me that I've found another way to be a mother.

Not wanting to be too hasty committing anything to writing, I jump up from my desk, and take a fast-paced walk through Satellite Hospital. When I return to my desk, I see that there have been a few, cautious replies. I consider how much of the positive feedback on my writing and public speaking is with regard to how raw it is. So, I throw caution to the wind, write from my heart, and hit *send* before I've even proofread it.

My Email Entering The Discussion

Dear colleagues,

As someone whose identity is represented on the resource in discussion, I have been in two minds about whether or not it is safe for me to join in. I've decided that it's worth the risk, for the value I feel my perspective can add.

I'll point out that since commencing the typing of this email, my heartbeat has steadily increased in both speed and strength, the skin on my arms and face has become warm and red, and I'm having to drink from my water bottle using two hands to steady the shaking.

This violent physical reaction is due to decades of language and behavior that reinforced that my truth is a negative one. For those who don't know, that truth is that I am a woman who was assigned male at birth, and who underwent a complete gender transition in her late teens to authentically represent herself to the world.

I'll add that I personally dislike the label "transgender" as it has often been used to invalidate my gender, disclose my personal history without consent, and outside the context of receiving healthcare, it is a label that I view as completely unnecessary. Referring to me as female, woman, girl, chick works fine socially and at work.

When looking for employment after transitioning to female almost 20 years ago, I faced a difficult choice. It was between disclosing that I'd undergone gender affirmation, and pretending I had no history of work or education. I decided that it would look more favorably to hide the gender stuff. In 2017, I sadly feel that this would still be the case for job applications outside of The Medical College.

Despite that, between then and now, I've progressively become more open because:
- *workplace gossip and internet searches have disclosed my past in undignified ways;*
- *hiding had a long term severe, negative impact on my mental health (and sick leave required);*
- *the effort to hide my past was detrimental to the quality of work achievable; and*
- *I want to prove to young trans people that they can be themselves AND thrive.*

With respect to the above, the workplace journey to 2017 has been nothing short of harrowing. However I'm now in a place where most of my colleagues know of my past, and I'm treated with dignity and respect. This is something I hadn't dared to fantasize as possible.

Diversity and inclusion has never been an easy journey, but I can assure you that any difficulty associated with learning new and emerging terminology has nothing on the daily struggles of those who can benefit from an environment where people have made the effort to include them.

Best wishes,
Paige

I don't receive a response from the person accusing the program of going over the top with asking people to use respectful language. I do however receive quite a few replies from other people. Some of the emails are from people who thank me for the opportunity I've given them to learn. Undoubtedly, my email has been the correct approach to take. In my workplace at least, things are getting better.

— 18 —

It is no longer possible to deny that all parts of my life intersect.

And finally…

MALE ALLY TOOK THE ENVELOPE from me.
 He slipped the letter out.
 His face was wooden as he read.
 When he'd finished, he looked up at me.
 "Are you happy with this outcome? They've essentially just told him off, and not to approach you again."
 "Yes," I said. "All I wanted was assurance that it wouldn't happen again. To me, to someone else. I see this as a win. At least they clearly believe me."
 Male Ally smiled at me.
 "Well then, I'm happy for you."
 And for a while, I was too.

Now…

IT'S MORNING ON THE EVE OF CHRISTMAS EVE. I've woken far too early to blinding summer daylight, in a pool of my own sweat. I consider this only a little less disgusting than being drenched in the sweat of someone else. Although it's only been half a year, it feels an eternity since I've woken up beside someone at all, sweat drenched or otherwise. This thought leads me to the realization that the year will end exactly as it began; with me alone, in someone else's house, caring for their beloved pet. So not entirely alone.
 Aside from the sturdy iron security bars on the windows, the large room of stained wood and brick that I'm in is quite pleasant. Cozy, even. It's

almost like an entire apartment under the main house, and even includes a decent sized bathroom. That'll be handy if I get locked in, which is something Home Owner has informed me is a possibility if I close the door, which I have done. It was the only way to escape Affectionate Darling.

Affectionate Darling is a big, brown labradoodle, who I've come to know as one of the most beautiful people I've ever met. My only issue with him, is that if we're in the same room, he will ensure I have at least one hand on him at all times. If we're *not* in the same room, we're only separated because there's a closed door preventing us from being together. That is why I've woken behind a closed door, with a risk of isolation until someone can break in to save me.

I recall I was once stuck in a studio apartment for half a day. Legitimate One—which is a name synonymous with True Love—had come to my aid with a friend. This was after he had already shapeshifted into The One Who Got Away, and the act of removing the front door of my apartment served as further evidence of just how good a man I had lost. In the present, calling on him is not an option I have.

Surely if I'm stuck, I could summon someone else though, I think. *I can reach any number of people with my phone, that is…* I turn to look at the bedside table, and find relief in the sight of my phone. That relief is a temporary guest, and it takes flight the moment I allow further thoughts on the matter.

They'd have to make it through to the front yard first, I think. *This place is like a fortress, with a fence and gate high enough to make it very difficult for unwelcome visitors to get to the front door. The gate is closed for the night, and openable only with a small remote control. That remote control is locked inside the house, inaccessible to my potential liberator. If I am stuck, I can't let them into the property to sneak them a key through the window, and allow them to enter the house to retrieve me.*

Quite suddenly, the thought of being trapped in the room seems much more likely, and even more terrifying. This truth causes me to panic. I jump out of bed, lunge for the door handle, push down hard, and relief visits again when the door flies open to reveal a startled Affectionate Darling.

"Good morning, my dear," I greet him. "I'm very sorry about the sudden movement. I hope I didn't scare you too much."

Affectionate Darling leaps up at me the moment he realizes there's no longer a barrier between us. As if to confirm his acceptance of my apology, he rests a paw on each of my shoulders, and presses lovingly against me with his face. I give him a cuddle, and smooth back the long, curly hair that's covering his eyes. Although the hair on his body has been shaved short, the hair on his head has been left untrimmed. It's a grooming choice of the owner that I don't understand.

"It's going to be a stinking hot day," I sing to Affectionate Darling. "So how about we go for a walk now, hey?"

Affectionate Darling promptly drops to the floor, and sprints to the base of the stairs by the front door. All I'm wearing is knickers and a singlet, so I return to my room, slip into the only pair of trousers I own, then step into the only pair of shoes I own; sturdy, black Doc Martens. As I pull the laces tight, then tie them together in large, evenly sized bows, I think about how nice it is to feel free to dress as I please. No longer do I feel it necessary to dress feminine to justify my female identity.

I drag my feet up the hallway, and as I pass a shelf full of a stranger's collectables, I take two small plastic bags intended for the collection of something more disposable. Further along, I grab a leash. Affectionate Darling is watching me patiently. When I get close, he tilts his head back, to give me better access to his neck while I attach the leash. He then moves closer to the door.

"Patient, Darling," I tell him.

Before I open the door, I grab Home Owner's house key, and a small remote control. I pocket the key, and press a button on the remote control. There's a grating sound, made by the large security gate to the property as it scrapes across the ground as it opens. I open the door, and Affectionate Darling pulls me outside the stranger's house in a jerky movement.

With Affectionate Darling, I wander through a stranger's neighborhood. Together we strut down a street of luxury apartments and expensive houses. I scan the beautiful man-made structures, and Affectionate Darling sniffs about for what nature left him to discover. I feel my body heat up from the sun, but as we reach the river, a gentle breeze cools me. I tie Affectionate Darling's leash to a park bench with plenty of wiggle room, and sit.

"I'm going to miss you fella," I say to Affectionate Darling. "We've made quite a good team."

Affectionate Darling rubs against me, then notices something under the bench, so he abandons me to investigate. He reappears upon hearing a human approaching.

"Oh, he's so cute!" a female stranger exclaims. At the end of her leash is a small designer dog. It's one of those breeds that look adorable at the expense of their quality life.

"Yeah, I'm very lucky," I tell her.

"What's his name?"

"Affectionate Darling," I say to the stranger.

"Oh my God! Honey," she calls over her shoulder.

"What's up?" asks a male stranger who seems to have appeared out of nowhere. It's suddenly much less peaceful here, and I wonder how many more people will populate the river before I leave.

"This is that dog from puppy school earlier this year!"

I smile politely as the strangers gush over Affectionate Darling. It doesn't surprise me that he's so memorable, and I feel even more fortunate to have him under my care. A sudden pang of sadness attacks me, as I realize how little time we have left together. Still, the time we've had has been wonderful, and soon enough I'll be doting on someone else's pet. And then another. *Rinse, and repeat,* as they say.

It's evening on the eve of Christmas Eve, and I'm standing in a room full of people I'm related to by blood through Parental Being. Unlike the rest of my day, not one of the people who surround me are strangers. With the exception of Parental Being and My Sibling, they all feel like strangers though. If Parental Being and My Sibling left, I'd be in a room filled exclusively with people who have not seen me since my psychotic breakdown in front of them several years earlier.

It seems a dream—or perhaps a nightmare—that we sat and stared at a large screen displaying old images of a Pre-Paige identity. The form I refer to as Outer Shell, who was a person people called ▮▮▮▮▮, or Blank. That's not the name that was really used; it's just the least traumatic way to speak about an appearance I was forced to fake for the first half of my life. I remember that as we all gazed upon his image, a dark cloud grew around me until I could no longer see. Hopefully that occasion is not on anyone else's mind. It's still a source of embarrassment for me.

It's literally been years since I've shared space with anyone here other than Parental Being and My Sibling, and the last has gone by like no time at all. As I look around the room of faces that make up my extended family, I feel more alien than ever. They're emotionally close to each other because of a shared religion, and fierce intolerance of the LGBTIQ community, of which they surely must realize I am a part.

As on my birthday, I can't shake the dark thoughts about this group of people who are smiling and laughing, with and around me. They've spent the year fighting brutal battles against a cause I've made continual sacrifices to fight for. All year, these people have spread lies about individuals in my community. All I can hope is that they don't realize they're lies.

It could have been worse; none of their action has been to my face. I made sure of that through purposeful avoidance during the Disrespectful Marriage Equality Debate. Now that it's over, here I am. I feel a little bad that I've avoided them, and have had a lot of to tell them about with regard to how different my life is now. Sobriety, Satellite Hospital… Pibling (Parent's Sibling) seems particularly interested in the atypical living arrangements.

"He's house sitting at the moment," Pibling tells My Cousin. "He told me he's down to living out of one suitcase, a laundry bag, and his handbag! Isn't PK crazy?"

It's not until I hear the nickname *PK* that I realize that the *he* and *his* that Pibling is referring to is me, confirming that this is not a space where I am welcome. PK was a nickname I offered at the beginning of my gender transition, for those who were not yet comfortable referring to me as a woman. It was a nickname that Pibling held onto and used with male pronouns to remind me that they did not accept my truth.

The strong guilt I feel regarding my purposeful avoidance of Pibling for the year, it packs up and leaves my person. Filling the void left by the departed guilt is a resolve to spend at least another year away from Pibling.

A sensation of panic starts to rise from within, attempting to drown me as I consider the unfortunate truth that we're again in a regional location I can't easily escape. While struggling to remain afloat of the intensifying panic, I feel a hot rash begin to develop around my neck, trying to choke me. I raise an arm and awkwardly rest my chin on a fist to obscure the rash from view.

"Paige, I was meaning to ask you about something," My Cousin says to me, then she turns to Pibling. "I'll bring her back in a minute."

It feels as though My Cousin has been especially bold, referring to me correctly by name and gender. They take my hand and pull me away from the crowd. In a daze, I walk with them into a vacant room in the house. I focus on breathing slowly, and I feel both the panic and rash recede. This time, I don't disappear into a blinding psychological storm. It is a small win, but a win none the less.

"Sorry," My Cousin says, as they rub my arm affectionately. I shrug, and force a smile.

"I've missed you this year, and of course I can't say this in earshot of anyone in there, but I voted in support Marriage Equality. When we were younger, I hadn't really considered that it was discrimination."

"Really?"

My Cousin nods, and I'd love to allow myself to feel happy, but I just can't.

"Do you think we could return to regular coffee dates? I'd really like to hear more about your volunteer work some time," My Cousin continues. "Particularly regarding anything that can help me better support students who identify in your community. I don't feel like we give them the support they need or deserve."

My heart explodes.

LATE AT NIGHT, on the eve of Christmas Eve, I sit by the river's edge, with Affectionate Darling by my side. Emotionally exhausted, I'm staring intently at the ripples in the water, upon which light appears to be dancing. It's beautiful, but my thoughts are not. I'm feeling troubled as I think back to the family Christmas event, and how nothing sweet ever seems to come from my family without a bitter component to spoil it.

While it's lovely to confirm that My Cousin is now on my side, I hate that they feel it necessary to keep that knowledge private. Can you even be secretly on a political side? I do understand the position they're in, however, having fought long and hard to be recognized as the woman I am. And apparently, as we head towards 20 years, that's not a battle I've fully won yet.

"I'm going to take a different approach next year," I tell Affectionate Darling. "There's so much work I still need to do, but I think I've been doing some things the wrong way around."

Affectionate Darling rubs his head against my leg.

"Okay, so partly it was because I was paying off debt, but I mostly didn't organize any travel this year because I was scared I would miss out on great house sitting opportunities. That seems a silly way to live now."

Affectionate Darling pulls against the leash, and I allow him to lead me along the river, as I continue my soliloquy.

"With the biggest debts out of the way, I can relax; give myself permission to pay them off slowly from here on out. I should live a little, and I think I should plan a few trips away, then work house sitting around that. Something always comes along, or if it doesn't, I've plenty of people offering temporary housing."

I stop, and take in a deep breath.

"I do hope we meet again, Affectionate Darling," I say. "Our evening walks have been quite wonderful, and it would be a shame not to return here with you in a year or two. I'll be different then. I always am."

With a stranger's dog, I wander back to a stranger's house, considering the year ahead. I seem to have a handle on this leader business now, and I've achieved a level of visibility I'll need to capitalize on somehow. Upon returning to the house, I sit at a stranger's desk, and write down some ideas in preparation of the most epic year of my life yet.

And then, quite literally, an opportunity falls at my feet.

Volume III
2018

The Book That Lives and Bleeds
(Memoirable Book 5)

Warning and Advisory Statements and Declarations

THERE'S GOING TO BE A LOT TO UNPACK in this somewhat fictionalized reality, and not all of you are going to make it. For those who dare, there are clues at every corner of darker truths. For those who don't, you're welcome instead to take the content of this book at face value. Both statements also apply to all previous books in this series, and if you didn't realize that before, by all means, return to my origin story with a more suspicious eye.

On the topic of unsettling content, some of this is going to be overt, and for that I feel obliged to warn you. As we sort through my baggage, we'll find references to cancer, sexuality, assault, and mental illness, inclusive of addiction, suicidal ideation, and the lingering effects of trauma. Where possible, these themes are explored superficially, but in some instances a deeper understanding is necessary. Fear not, I confronted this all in the first instance and survived; reading about it second hand can't be so bad.

The phrase *somewhat fictionalized* was used above. Although everything you will read has occurred in some form, adjustments have been made for reasons of law, ethics, and protection. This has been done by writing collectively about people, switching dates and locations, and at times exploring emotion associated with an experience, rather than providing details that could be used to identify a real place or person.

Just in case the above doesn't quite sell it, I now explicitly state that the thoughts and ideas expressed in any book that I write are my own, and have absolutely nothing to do with any of my employers, past or present. Additionally, no character descriptions should ever be considered as accurate representations of real people. None of the content explored in this book should lead you to feel negatively about any specific person, with one exception; me.

Before you progress past this page to start zipping back and forth through time, unpacking the puzzling, disturbing, and inspiring parts of my life, it's important that you have understood the words above. If that is so, then it's almost time to dive into the thick of it. But first, a few words from… elsewhere.

-V-

IT WAS AN ACCIDENT, the first time she did it, and at that point, of course she hadn't looked into the relevant legislation. These are not words in her defense, by the way. Rather, it is an attempt to draw attention to the lack of brilliance on her part. There had been no brainstorming sessions leading to great, abstract ideas. I had simply slipped from her grasp, causing an opportunity to quite literally fall at her feet, before her very eyes.

That opportunity, was me, and we'll become acquainted soon.

The next admission, is with regard to what she was doing moments before the mishap. She'd be a little embarrassed, because despite appearances, she's never been comfortable with the sales and marketing aspect of being an artist. Nor of social justice. She had, however, finally surrendered to the truth that in order to fulfil her World Changing Goals, it was necessary for her to succeed in the arts. And to succeed in the arts, she needed to sell two things.

She had to sell herself, and she had to sell me.

Part One

(Package No. 1 to No. 9)

1. Cottage
2. Virgins
3. Tokens
4. Atypical
5. Green
6. Shells
7. Clubbed
8. Sleeve
9. Evidence (a)

Cottage

(Package No. 1)

Containing a premonition,
something urgent,
and a recipe.

THIS WILL BE THE FUTURE I ASKED FOR, and this is what I should be expecting. It will feel surreal, standing in that room in one of the old colleges of The University. It will be a room lined with portraits of great academics long gone, and filled with great professionals still living. My existence will be somewhat dissociative, like that of childhood; my insides an active battlefield hidden behind a flawless, calm façade.

Only one thing could make this more awkward, I'll be thinking.

Important Human—a close friend who volunteers with me for Intersectionality Advocates as my deputy—will then look up at me suddenly from the event program that they are holding, and they will erupt into an enormous smile. There will be a shimmer beaming from all parts of their face, which will be conveying pride, excitement, and… Although I can't quite put my finger on that third sentiment, it will be there to keep the other two company.

"Paige, have you seen this?"

Following their question, Important Human will hold up the documentation in their hand so that I am confronted with what will seem to have become everyone's favorite professional photo of me. I will see myself on the red carpet at the Med Gala of the previous year, scratching my tilted head, looking mildly confused at the camera. Against a black backdrop, my vibrant electric orange hair and bold blue velvet dress will demand to be the single part of the picture that is most eye catching. Both will lose out to the amount of pale skin showing.

Below the photo I will see my own words that will have been hastily thrown together in a café while waiting for a plane home from Canberra. Hastily written because of the knowledge I will have lacked when writing them.

"I didn't think it would travel so far," I will tell Important Human.

"Do you regret it?" they will ask.

I will consider that question deeply before giving Important Human my answer. The article certainly will have dramatically changed the situation, and really, if I have to pick a specific point in time that caused life to veer off in this direction... Why, I do believe it started when I was in desperate need of a visit to the toilet.

-V-

MY URGENCY STEADILY INCREASING, the person on the other side of my work desk at Satellite Hospital remained consistently oblivious. Their cheeks were flushed, their eyes wide, with the skin between them temporarily crinkled. Their words were flowing without filter, but were charged with maximum passion. They stopped to breathe, and I noticed a change around their temples and upper lip, that became firm moments before quivering commenced. History told me that the movement was a visual signal that the floodgates were about to open.

I dropped my gaze to the tissue box on my desk, then returned to the visitor's oceanic eyes. They reached for a tissue and dabbed around their chin, cheeks, and then eyes. They grabbed another tissue and pressed it against their neck. I reached under my desk, retrieved a wastepaper basket, and held it out to them. They screwed up their tissues then dropped them in it, and I returned the bin to its home at my feet.

"Thank you for listening," they told me. "I'm sorry to dump all that on you."

"That's quite alright," I said.

"Visitors like me must really take a toll on you."

I swiveled in my chair and pointed to the wall behind me. It was covered in photos that were predominantly from events organized by my team at Intersectionality Advocates, the not-for-profit organization I was leading at a state level outside of my day job at the hospital. Some of the photos were of me speaking from the heart to a captive audience. They were proud moments fondly remembered.

"I do this a lot for my volunteer work," I told them. "So I've developed the skills to listen, and then let it go."

They smiled at me, and something about their body language made me wonder if they believed that I would carry their pain around along with my own, as my own. There was a small seed of doubt within me that also wondered if I would.

"I'd best get to clinic," they told me. As they stood, they grabbed a chocolate from a small bowl that was next to the tissues on my desk. "One for the road."

I smiled, they left, then I immediately locked my computer, raced out the door, locked that, and sprinted up the hospital corridor in the direction of the nearest toilet. Before I was able to go in, I heard the loud familiar voice of a Handsy Man who worked elsewhere in the hospital.

"Paige! Haven't seen you in a while," Handsy Man bellowed at me from a distance.

"Maybe I've been avoiding you," I said, partially as a joke that made him laugh as he rapidly reduced the space between us.

"It's been a busy work month," I added as Handsy Man became close enough for me to feel the warmth of his body. He gently placed his hand on my shoulder, and gave my upper arm a brief rub.

"I love that hair," Handsy Man told me, reaching up and almost touching the hair he apparently loved. "And you always dress so well."

On the way down, Handsy Man's hand brushed lightly over the curve of my left buttock, and instinct shifted me slightly closer to the toilet door.

"Sorry, busting to pee," I said, backing myself into the toilet as quickly as I was able.

Once inside, I leant back against the closed door for a moment, but the feeling of urgency returned. I barged into the only available stall of two. Not long after, I let out a loud sigh. The feeling of urgency had passed, and I could relax. I could also take a moment to think about what had occurred just outside the toilet.

I suppose I should have seen the butt touch coming, I thought to myself. *Now that I think about it, every few interactions he has progressed things. Before the shoulder rub, it had just been a brush against the shoulder a few times, and the few times before that, he'd been standing progressively closer as we spoke.*

As I reached for toilet paper, I realized none was there. This lack of toilet paper business was nothing new to Satellite Hospital. We had a regular visitor who removed all toilet paper from this specific toilet. Every time prior to that, I'd checked for toilet paper before sitting. On the frequent occasions there'd been none, I'd either moved on, or come back via my office with tissues.

Perhaps it's time to upgrade and stash emergency tissues in my bra, I thought. *Good future planning, though I do still need to deal with this situation.*

"Excuse me," I called out hesitantly. "There's no toilet paper. Are you able to pass some through, please?"

"Sorry," came a terse reply. "All used."

"No worries," I lied to them.

Well this is a bit shit, I thought to myself.

There was the sound of the toilet flushing in the cubicle next to me. Then I heard the stall door being unlocked, someone punching the soap dispenser, then the sound of running water inconsistently hitting the basin because it was interrupted by moving hands. There was brief silence, then I heard two pieces of hand towel being removed.

Hand towel!

I waited to hear the door close after the stranger had left, then—squatting with my underpants around my ankles—I hastily waddled out of the cubicle. With cautious haste, I waddled past the other stall, careful to avoid spillage on the floor or, perhaps more importantly, my clothes. I took enough paper towel and then some, and returned to the safety of the cubicle.

When I returned to my desk, I saw that the work day had finished, and if I didn't hurry, I'd miss the hourly bus to the cottage that was my temporary home. On that day it was important to get home on time, because I had a stranger's dog to walk before receiving a special visitor who I would be cooking for. I promptly left the office, and tried to notify the *SafetySpace* app that I had done so.

NOTICE FROM SAFETYSPACE APP

You Have Not Been Checked In.
Check in is not available at your current location.

"Stupid, pointless thing," I muttered.

-V-

THE STRANGER'S KITCHEN WAS QUAINT, and what I mean by that, is that it had this country cottage feel to it. From my vantage point of the kitchen sink, I had a view of a backyard garden partially obscured by white lace curtains that hung from a lightly stained wooden curtain rod. On the other side of the glass was a natural collage of varied green shades, shapes, and textures.

"Who is Hospital Companion?"

The question had come from Friendly Entity—my close gender-fluid friend—who was sitting, unseen, behind me. I caught their reflection in the window, and assessed their overall appearance. They were wearing a binder over their breasts that day to appear more masculine, but would still prefer the gender neutral pronouns of *they*, and *them*.

"Hospital Companion is my friend at Satellite Hospital," I told Friendly Entity. "They know all about me, and I'm being something of a mentor to them, to help them be a better ally. Why?"

"*They*, and *them*? Is Hospital Companion like me?"

"Oh, no, I just refer to them without gender in anecdotes for de-identification. They're actually several people rolled into one."

"Dear God, so you've degenerated to speaking in the voice of your books even in person. Like that's not unhealthy…"

"Whatever. Anyway. Why did you mention Hospital Companion?"

"They've sent you some photos. Of their hand."

I swiveled to face Friendly Entity who had picked up my phone. They held up my phone so that I could see the message previews that could all be interpreted as a variety of photos of the same hand if you didn't understand the context.

"Ah," I told Friendly Entity. "I found an old plant pot at Satellite Hospital that I wanted to use to grow something edible from some seeds I was given, but the pot didn't have a tray to collect water. Hospital Companion mentioned they had some spares at home. These photos are of different tray options, and the hand is just there so I can pick the right size."

"I'm confused," Friendly Entity said as they screwed up their face. "I thought The Medical College were just sending you to work at Satellite Hospital for a few weeks, as some sort of three-way temporary job swap, and it just got extended a few times to cover someone's sick leave. That is what you told me, right?"

"Yeah, I was, but then both the other people involved resigned, and I got asked to stay on at Satellite Hospital indefinitely."

Friendly Entity studied my face.

"I'd congratulate you, but you don't look all that thrilled about it…"

"It's complicated," I muttered.

"Surely nothing is too complicated for you to talk through with me…"

"Well, part of it is that there are a few men there who get a bit handsy with me, and although it makes me feel really uncomfortable, I don't feel confident enough there to call them out because I'm already a bit of an outsider."

"That's awful," Friendly Entity said. "Doesn't The Medical College have policy protecting you from that?"

I exhaled loudly.

"I'm not sure, because none of the men are students, but none of them are colleagues either."

"Is there nobody who works for The Medical College that you could ask?"

"Yeah, but I'm hesitant to ask because they might pressure me to explain why I'm asking for the information, and I don't want to be pressured to pursue any kind of formal action."

"Would that be a problem?"

"I've not really talked about it except with one person who indicated that I should feel flattered that the men clearly just see me as an attractive woman. And you know, I'm still a bit too vulnerable to have a rational discussion where I might have to prove that I'm a victim again."

Friendly Entity nodded sadly, then looked at me quizzically.

"Is that all?"

"There's also… actually I don't really feel like going into it right now. I'm seriously looking at leaving, though. Like, The Medical College, not just Satellite Hospital."

Friendly Entity offered me a halfhearted laugh.

"How does that fit in with your World Changing Goals? Don't you need to be connected to the medical field?"

"I've decided that it's time to go bold, and then move on. And anyway, I've adjusted to all parts of my current life, so I've just sort of been aimlessly coasting at the same intensity for a bit longer than I'm comfortable with. It's time to take action."

"I see," Friendly Entity chuckled.

I pointed at the pantry.

"Could you please find the coconut cream, brown sugar, and fish sauce?"

"Sure thing."

I turned away from Friendly Entity and returned my focus to the sink that was filled with Swiss Brown Mushrooms. To the right there was a pile that had been destemmed, as well as had the skin torn off. I continued to add to the pile, as I elaborated on my thoughts for the year ahead.

"There's this medical student I've been thinking about making contact with because I feel like they might be a good place to start."

"Is that not a conflict of interest?"

"Well, the line is a little blurred there. Firstly, they're not a student under my care, but also they've approached and connected with me outside of The Medical College because of my affiliation with Intersectionality Advocates."

Friendly Entity arrived at my side with the requested ingredients. I pointed at a blue bowl to my right.

"Could you please pour the coconut cream into that bowl, then add a tablespoon of brown sugar, a teaspoon of fish sauce, then stir?"

Friendly Entity wandered over to the blue bowl and did as directed.

"It sounds like you're not quite sure enough to make the move," Friendly Entity told me.

"Yeah," I agreed as I rinsed, then started to slice the mushrooms.

"Where's the bathroom?"

"Third door down the left side of the hallway," I told Friendly Entity. I started to carefully place the slices of mushroom on top of two stacks that each consisted of Hokkien noodles that sat on large squares of baking paper, that sat on squares of foil slightly larger than that.

Friendly Entity returned.

"Why are all the doors in this house closed? Is that how they were when you arrived?"

"No," I said. "On my first day in a new place I usually work out which spaces I will be going in and out of, and then to reduce maintenance, I close everything else up for the duration of my stay."

"Okay, then, weirdo. So what else can I do here?"

"There are two salmon steaks in the fridge. Could you please rinse them?"

"I've been meaning to ask you," Friendly Entity said casually as they wandered over to the fridge. "That suspected basal cell carcinoma on your face... since your debt is more manageable do you have any plans to seek treatment?"

I winced as I started to pluck the stems off baby spinach leaves and place them on top of the mushrooms.

"Dermal Saviour is on leave right now, so I'm just waiting for him to return."

"Wouldn't it be worth just getting it out now by a different doctor, before it grows deeper?"

I shrugged.

"It's changing pretty slowly, and if I went to someone else, I would have to go through my history, probably get biopsies, and I don't even know how many people do the treatment I'm looking for. I've got it in my calendar to call again soon to see if he's returned."

"I really think you should do something sooner..."

I groaned.

"Okay, okay. I'll make the call from work first thing in the morning."

"Good."

Friendly Entity handed me a salmon steak that they'd rinsed. I placed it on top of one of the stacks while Friendly Entity rinsed the other piece.

"Whatever, you're totally overreacting."

I stood back to look at the mess that was to become our meal.

"When you're done just add it to the other pile," I directed. I focused more intently on the stack I was working on, pulling up the sides of the foil to create a bowl shape. I grabbed the blue bowl and drizzled the liquid over the salmon steak, allowing excess to gather around the Hokkien noodles.

"Want me to do the same with that too?"

"Yes please," I told Friendly Entity. "I just need to look up how long we need to cook these for."

"Cool. Then maybe you can talk me through the specifics of your big, bold plans before your exit from Medicine."

I rinsed and dried my hands, then picked up my phone.

"Hah," I exclaimed. "Guess I don't need to worry about a conflict of interest after all."

I held up my phone so Friendly Entity could see the email I'd received that would propel me faster and farther toward a future my younger self would never have dared imagine.

Virgins

(Package No. 2)

Containing a nightmare, and a conversation.

WHERE I AM, I WISH NOT TO BE. *Sometimes I'll lay awake for hours wishing to be here, alone, with my body shut down for the night in order to recharge. But sometimes when sleep arrives, I am transported to this place, which is a place of torment. On this occasion, Parental Being is here with me, looking mournfully in my direction. Parental Being is the person who gave birth to, and raised me. My Sibling and I share Parental Being. Sometimes people tell me that looking upon my face is eerily like looking through time at a young Parental Being. For whatever reason, nobody could say that about My Sibling.*

When I am, Parental Being is approaching the Middle Age, which is much older than I ever expected to be, even after I stopped trying to leave Earth early. When I am, the last incomplete suicide was no more than several months ago, and it will be years until I try again, but I will.

"I always thought you were going to be a wonderful father," Parental Being is telling me. *"That's why we got you that operation when you were a child."*

In my mind, that surgery is completely irrelevant. I felt female long before I'd learned to read well enough to understand that the body I resided in had a developmental problem 'down there'. This truth is something that I so desperately want to voice right now, but in my heightened state of vulnerability, I'm unable to articulate any thoughts aloud at all.

Parental Being looks broken, and it is me who has broken them, because I'm not what they expected, and it's taken me until my late teens to tell them. When I wake, many years older than expected, I'm different yet again. When I wake, I am essentially a book.

-V-

BEING A BOOK THAT IS ALIVE technically isn't an experience that is new to me, but it sure as heck feels that way. Earlier in life there had been a rehearsal specifically for this moment, in addition to a host of preparation undertaken much less purposefully. Although it shouldn't, everything in this moment feels brand new; I do not feel the confidence of adequate preparation I'd hoped for.

How I am a book that is alive, is obviously not like Vivacia being a ship that is alive in the fantasy trilogy *The Liveship Traders*. Much less magically, as an authority on the topic of gender diversity, medical students have been allowed to reserve time with me to ask related questions. How it is that I became a book in the first place, is a story for a little later. For now, I need to focus on the medical student who is nervously sitting opposite me, as I struggle to find balance between gazing too intently, and avoiding eye contact altogether.

"Hey," he utters softly.

Before I know his name, from his physical characteristics alone, I have a pretty good idea about where his family is from. It is a region that spans the west of Asia to the northeast of Africa, and is commonly referred to as the Middle East. The medical student before me would commonly be described as Middle Eastern.

"My name is Culturally and Linguistically Diverse," he tells me with a subtle accent that provides me with a little more information about him.

From the way he's speaking English, I know that he's lived in Australia since childhood, and that he's still required to to regularly communicate in his first language. I smile warmly at him, and before I have time to give a return introduction, he adds to his.

"But you can just call me CALD," is what he adds.

In any other situation, I would feel bad for CALD; feeling pressure to offer up a shortened version of his name, presumably because so few Australians can pronounce it in full. Today though, my vulnerability makes me much more self-focused. As I think back to the rehearsal for this interaction, I'm forced to confront more than one bias that I'd prefer I didn't have.

That CALD is visibly male, is a contributing factor to me being more nervous than I was when I rehearsed with his female classmate. That CALD's family is from the Middle East, adds to that. He's no control over either of those things, nor has he behaved in any specific way to reasonably cause any emotion even approaching fear. My reaction to him really has nothing to do with him at all. It's about widespread, damaging stereotypes, and to a lesser degree, a connection with others of a similar profile.

"Did you have any specific questions you'd like to ask?"

CALD looks nervous, and doesn't say anything. I realize that he's more nervous than I am. Probably, this is because he doesn't want to cause offense. What this tells me, is that I really need to push past my bias, and treat him as an individual that I have met, who's been nothing but respectful. In turn, he is deserving of my respect.

"If you'd like," I offer. "I can give you a brief overview of why I'm here, and we can go from there."

"That would be good," CALD tells me, his face showing subtle signs of relief.

"Well," I start. "When I was born, the doctors looked at me, and based on what they saw…"

I pause, and gesture in a hybrid movement somewhere between the Auslan action for *continue*, and the waving hand of Queen Elizabeth. This involves a circular twisting motion of the hand with fingers almost entirely extended, with the palm at first facing myself, and ending outward to face CALD. He moves forward ever so slightly, and raises his eyebrows, interested to hear the next words out of my mouth.

"Because of what they could see, down there, they assigned my gender as male."

CALD nods gently to let me know that he's understood. There are no visible signs of judgement, just a desire to know more about my situation. That is, how it is that I grew up to be the woman who is sitting in front of him. A slender, feminine woman exhibiting no visible signs of having previously existed as any other gender. I take a deep breath in, slowly let it out, and continue.

"That never felt quite right for me," I tell him. "As a teenager, I found out about a doctor I could see to talk about these feelings."

CALD raises his hand to seek permission to speak.

"Yes?"

"What about before you were a teenager?"

"Oh," I say. "Well I knew something was wrong with me, but it felt important to keep my thoughts private. I was scared of what might happen to me if anyone found out, so it became a secret I carried with me. Hiding felt like safety."

CALD nods again. He looks sad.

"So, I was diagnosed with gender dysphoria by this doctor, and went through a complete gender transition."

We're both silent for a moment. I wonder what he's thinking, and how our perception of this conversation differs. It feels so strange to be sitting here, as I think back to my earliest thoughts and feelings. Back then I was alone, convinced that I was the only person who ended up in the wrong body. Today, I am surrounded by supportive people, and I'm connected to many individuals who've had similar experiences with their identity. I'm mindful that CALD doesn't have much more time with me.

"Is there anything specific you would like me to speak about in more detail?"

CALD manipulates his face so that he has a furrowed brow; very serious, and contemplative. His next facial movement is to raise his left cheek that pulls his firmly closed mouth to one side and causes skin to gather under his eye for a temporary wrinkled effect.

"Well," CALD begins, swallowing saliva that has pooled in his throat. "I'm quite interested in how you communicated this to everyone. What did you say to your family and friends?"

CALD has surprised me with yet another unexpected question. My assumption had been that every medical student would have only an interest in the clinical elements of my story. Already assumption has made me a fool. In fact I am a fool several times over.

"A distinction I would like to make, is between disclosure before and after my transition, as these were two very different things."

CALD nods, and looks off to the side as he thinks deeply about something he hadn't considered earlier.

"I don't think I did a very good job in the beginning," I confess. "Talking about it was a new experience, and I found it difficult to use the right language."

"What do you mean?"

"Because I had only spoken about it fairly briefly with one friend and a doctor, I think the way I told people to begin with, it made it sound like I was changing who I was as a person. What I had to do, was I had to explain that I wasn't changing myself, just that I was changing what they could see. I would still be the same person, but my form would be more comfortable for me."

"I understand that," CALD tells me. "Are there any things you regret?"

"Yes," I say, allowing a little bitterness to shine through. "Because I expected it would be difficult for people to adjust, I offered up a temporary neutral nickname of PK, and gender neutral pronouns of *they*; and *them*. I really regret doing that, because even this past Christmas I had someone refuse to refer to me correctly, and it was quite traumatic. I'm 35 now, and I thought I'd be past that well before I turned 20."

"Oh, I'm sorry."

Again, we are both silently reflective. All I can do is guess what he's thinking.

"I'm interested to know specifically how you told people. Did you arrange to see them in person?"

"With my friends, for some I wrote to them, and at college I sat in a circle with my classmates to tell them all as a group after checking first with the teacher, who had more experience with it than I did. Some people were a bit weird, and cruel, but I also got a lot of support. It was a very confusing time, because by then I was already adjusting to different sex hormones."

"What about after your transition?"

"Well, I hid my past for a long time, and only disclosed it to romantic partners."

"I'm curious about how you got here from that. You seem to broadcast your past very widely now."

I laugh.

"Yes, well, it's been a bit messy. One of my partners got angry after I told him. He put it on social media in a way that I wasn't happy with, that made it seem like I was something to be ashamed of. I decided to take control by writing about it in my own words, and putting it out there myself, refusing to be ashamed. I got a bit fatigued by the backlash from that, so tried to disappear for a few years, but people in my personal and professional life kept finding out about it and bringing it up."

"I would hate that," CALD states. He seems annoyed on my behalf.

"Yeah, I did too. A particular workplace incident prompted me to write an open letter that explained who I was, what I had been through, and I included some boundaries. For a while the only way I disclosed was to direct people to the open letter…"

Ding ding ding!

"Oh, I guess I have to put you back on the shelf so someone else can read you," CALD jokes. "I wish we had more time."

I reach down into my tote bag and retrieve a copy of *Outer Shell*, my first book.

"You're welcome to have this, if you'd like to know more. I have a few spare copies. It explores my life up until the gender transition."

CALD takes the book.

"Thank you," CALD says. "I'm glad I came."

When CALD leaves, I slide down into a slouched position to reflect, and recharge before my next reader. I allow my mind to travel through time to a more pleasant location, which just happens to be on the flight where the year began.

Tokens

(Package No. 3)

Containing a recapitulation, and a visit to Sydney.

THE FLIGHT SYMBOLIZED A NEW BEGINNING. It had been about 15 months since I last had a fixed address, and the plan was to go at least another 12. Amongst other things, the adventure had begun as a way to eliminate substantial debt, and on that front I'd met largely with success. Having made commendable headway, I was in a position to relax the purse strings. There were also other ways in which my situation had changed.

When I began, the emphasis was on finding house sitting gigs that were as lengthy as possible. That more naïve version of myself had thought it would all be over in 12 months. My childish hope, was that the cost of freedom from debt would be looking after 4 houses, for 3 months each. Acknowledging that it was unlikely that the dates would line up exactly, I came prepared with a solution. For the few days between these 4 anticipated housesitting gigs, I would rely on friends who had offered up their spare rooms and couches.

Seemingly suddenly, it had been about 15 months, and I'd lived in as many homes. There had been cats, succulents, birds, herbs, dogs, children, uninvited snakes, grandparents, incidental rodents, and even a small patch of grass. I'd stayed for 2 months, 6 weeks, 3 days, and overnight. Some people had booked half a year in advance, and some cancelled the night before.

The beginning of the journey saw me with 13 bags, and 5 big debts. Very quickly, the 13 bags became 10, 5, and then I was moving about with 1 suitcase, 1 backpack, and 1 handbag. Less quickly, it took almost a year to level the 2 scariest debts that were with the tax office. Interrupted only by healthcare, I found myself in the position of being merely several hundred dollars away from having only 2 debts remaining.

All of the above is true, but it doesn't tell the whole story. Going sober helped with debt elimination on two fronts. Firstly, and obviously, alcohol is expensive, and as far as cost, nothing took its place in my life; at first. Secondly, and perhaps less obviously, I avoided a lot of social events when I remembered how taxing they were without alcohol to act as a social lubricant. This further reduced outgoing expenses.

Another detail that's missing, is that I had a big office at Satellite Hospital where I worked, and had stashed a bunch of my other stuff. There were also bags and boxes with assorted friends, but I'd not thought of any of those possessions since downsizing. I was very much just living out of a suitcase, backpack, and handbag.

This minimalism thing had started to feel comfortable. The clothing I carried around could be washed in a single load, and there was enough to last me a week; longer if I didn't wash them after every use. Several times a busy schedule forced me to wear outfits twice between washes. This was then deliberately repeated to save on the resources of time and washing detergent. The thought of going back to a full wardrobe had come to repulse me, for little more than the ability to accumulate more than one cycle worth of washing.

In those first 15 months, I barely left Brisbane. To begin with, this was so that I could plough through the debt elimination more quickly. When I realized that a lot of great housesitting gigs were offered to me at the last minute, it became the predominant reason I dared not plan any time away. In the blink of an eye, more than a year passed, and I felt I had done little more than work, and move house many times.

At the end of that year, I decided that it was time to flip the situation. This would allow me to explore the country, connect with fellow Intersectionality Advocates volunteers, catch up with interstate friends, and help with a Secret Project. Very quickly, I identified the best weeks of each month to arrange leave from work, and I planned out the different cities I would live in for each of them. That, my dear readers, was why I was on that, my first flight of the year.

-V-

WHEN I TRIED ON SYDNEY, IT WAS JANUARY; nearing the end of a Dry Hot Australian Summer. With the help of a 737-800, I slipped in from above until the city's embrace was all-encompassing. By the time I left the airport to expose myself unprotected to the cool night air, however it felt in Brisbane was a distant memory; I didn't look back. It wasn't until I was in the vehicle of a stranger I'd summoned through the RideShare app, that I caught up with messages that had been sent to me after my flight's departure.

I saw that my first ever HomeShare app host had given me the code to a lockbox for key access. They did this because they'd decided to go to bed, rather than stay up to welcome me as intended. The changed plans pleased me immensely, because I'd been a little stressed by the idea of meeting a stranger in a foreign city, in their home where I'd be living for the weekend. Why it stressed me, was the intersection between introversion and being the T in LGBTIQAP+.

That morning I had risen early to move out of the cottage I was looking after, and I'd spent all day interacting with students, doctors, and administration staff at Satellite Hospital. After work, I'd caught up with Intersectionality Advocates volunteers over the phone, and then made some light chit-chat with someone on the plane. After all that, the last thing I wanted to do was to awkwardly fumble through the minimum required conversation to avoid offending my host before sneaking off to bed.

Something I also worried about, was that when I was tired I didn't 'pass' as cisgender. I also worried that the host had somehow stumbled onto my past and in either case would confront me about it. It was a fear firmly founded on past experience, and I thought back to several occasions when strangers in bars looked at me suspiciously as they told me my voice was deep for a woman. And there was that one stranger who leaned in close to whisper something that effectively ruined the rest of my night.

Night Ruining Whisper From Stranger

I know what you are.

If that stranger could tell, then others could. Perhaps strangers who hated women like me, and were less inclined to exercise self-control while intoxicated, and in a dark environment. What that had meant for me, was that I was potentially in physical danger. After several minutes of glancing repeatedly over my shoulder, I'd decided to go home early.

"You alright?"

Back in the present the driver's eyes were dancing between me, the GPS, the road ahead, and the rearview mirror. Their overall appearance was masculine, so it felt more likely that they could be a threat. Clearly, this judgement call was somehow evident in my face.

"Sorry, I'm not trying to be intrusive," they added. "Just want to make sure you're okay because you seem not okay."

It wasn't something a threatening person would say, but I also didn't need to elaborate.

"Yeah, thanks," I lied. "Big day, very tired."

I yawned to sell my statement.

"You're almost home," they told me in a friendly, singsong way. They gestured to the GPS.

"Can't wait to sleep," I mumbled, instead of correcting them. They didn't need to know how far I was from home or people I knew.

"Which place is it?"

Because I didn't want to let the driver know I was in unfamiliar territory, I pretended to know my accommodation by sight, and directed them to drop me off. When I was finally standing alone in the dark, able to look up the address privately, I realized I had a lengthy walk ahead. I was on the wrong side of the road, and had to find a gap between construction on the new lightrail, which seemed to be the new name for what I'd previously known as trams.

When I woke the next morning, it was early. Outside I could hear work on the lightrail that had kept me up later than desired, and had probably been the reason I'd woken so early. I decided to get up and leave the house straight away, to avoid navigating conversation with my host at a time I'd rather be alone with my thoughts.

I took a long, scenic stroll to a café that was recommended by a possible romantic interest. There I sat to handwrite a chapter of my next book. Handwriting is often a part of my creative process. I feel that the work I produce is always more interesting, and by the time I've typed words on an electronic page, it's already a second draft. Because this paragraph was written in its entirety on a computer, I shall promptly end it here.

-V-

AFTER TAKING CARE OF MY SECRET PROJECT, I set off in search of the café where I'd be dining with a few members of the National Executive of Intersectionality Advocates. I wove in and out of the streets, taking much longer than necessary. This was in part because I was going to be very early, but was also to take advantage of being in a city where I was anonymous, and the sights were unfamiliar. I'd forgotten how good new experiences were as a writing muse.

Even with the purposeful dawdling, I was the first to arrive at the busy inner city café. The Spark arrived shortly after, and she wasted no time, slipping quickly into the seat beside me.

"Hi Paige," The Spark said. "I'm The Spark. Do you still have availability in your itinerary? I'd like to catch up with you alone."

"I'm actually free for a bit tomorrow," I confirmed.

The Spark gestured to my phone.

"I'll add my number so we can work it out later. There's something I want to discuss privately with you."

When my phone was returned, I noted a message from Friendly Entity.

MESSAGE FROM FRIENDLY ENTITY

Hey Paige, got any time to catch up this weekend?

As The Spark slid out of the chair and moved to the other side of the table, I sent a rushed reply to Friendly Entity.

THE RUSHED REPLY

Hey, sorry, in Sydney. Talk soon!

When I looked up from my phone, the CEO of Intersectionality Advocates entered with a small entourage that were the other members of his team. We all greeted each other, chose our seats, and commenced chatting to those beside and immediately across from us. For me, this unfortunately no longer included The Spark. Interest piqued, I couldn't help but want to be a part of whatever conversation she was involved in.

"I've actually got something I wanted to speak with you all about while we're all together in person," the CEO announced. "At the end of the financial year, I'll be stepping down from my role as CEO of Intersectionality Advocates."

There were a few gasps, and disappointed murmurs.

"For the moment, this is just between us. It will be announced next month, then we'll open applications internally, and I'd urge any of you to apply."

The CEO's eyes made contact with everyone at the table, finally resting with me.

"Even if you don't think you're qualified."

I considered how it was a shame this wasn't happening a year later. With an additional year I could have developed strong enough leadership skills to apply. In that moment, I didn't view them so positively, and there were other skills that a CEO needed that I didn't possess. Not that I knew what those were. Still, I figured the next CEO would probably just last a few years, so I decided to do some research later that day.

After the dust settled from the unexpected news, we all exchanged recent triumphs and challenges from our volunteer work. It was refreshing to learn that many of my struggles were shared by other volunteers. I realized that I'd allowed myself to be fooled by the social media versions of their lives, where they could choose to only ever have their best foot forward. I made a mental note to remind myself to reach out to offer and seek support, instead of making assumptions.

While I had their ear, I used the opportunity to mention the benefit of appointing Important Human, who had been invaluable as my deputy. They'd been instrumental in filling my performance gaps to ensure continued forward momentum in our state when my ability had been impaired by work stress, frequent moves, medical appointments, demanding pets, and long commutes.

When the crowd dissipated, I joined a few of the volunteers for a spontaneous trip to a local Queer fair. Together we chatted excitedly about the year ahead, and who we thought might rise to the challenge of CEO. We agreed that they'd need to be a strong leader, creative thinker, and especially compassionate. These were qualities that I decided I could acquire within a few years.

That night, I took a trip to Bondi for the Queer Short Film Festival. While watching, I felt ashamed that these were not stories I ever went out of my way to watch. Although I'd put in a lot of effort to join the Queer community, I wasn't fully celebrating and supporting it as I should have, given my role with Intersectionality Advocates.

Something else happened, and it was quite unexpected. One of the short films was focused on a young trans woman and her gay best friend as they got ready to go out for a night of dancing. How the audience confirmed that the woman was 'pre op' was by being confronted with her slightly blurred genitals. Because of feelings about my own body that had been adjusted long ago, I found the unexpected image distressing. Unfortunately, it didn't stop there.

How the film played out, felt very much like sexual assault to me. Perhaps that said more about my life experience, than it did about the film I was watching. The gay friend went beyond flirty, to convince the trans woman to have sex with him. The point was stressed that she should do it while she had the chance. That is, she was not really a woman yet, rather, she was a man with breasts.

Because many people had treated me similarly, I was so offended by the film that I spent a good deal of the following hour silent, as I collected my thoughts.

"I really didn't like the trans film," I finally admitted.

"Yeah, we didn't either," my friends told me. "Are you okay?"

"It's put me in a bit of a weird head space," I told them. "I really wish I hadn't seen it."

"Us too."

-V-

I WAS INSANELY CURIOUS by the time I met with The Spark the following day, having spent a good deal of my private time wondering what it was they wanted to talk about without the other volunteers present.

"Thanks so much for meeting with me," The Spark said.

"That's quite alright. I've tried to be a little unplanned for this trip, so that I can be more open to opportunities that might arise in the moment. I think I've missed out on a lot of exciting things because so much of my life is planned down to the minute."

"The way you're living your life is so intriguing to me," The Spark said. "I've read a little bit of your work and thought you'd be good to confide in about some concerns I've had."

"Oh?"

"I'm the L in LGBTIQAP+, as you can see I'm not white, and as you can hear, English is not my first language."

I nodded.

"I've really disliked seeing how people have grabbed on to the phrase People Of Color as a catch-all. Similar to how people lump trans, intersex and gender fluid people in the same group. Like, you are both this label, therefore you must face exactly the same shit."

"Yeah, I've had some concerns about that, but I wasn't sure how, or even if I should voice them."

"Can I tell you a bit of my personal story?"

"Of course."

"I came to this country because I knew I liked women, and didn't like men."

I nodded for The Spark to continue.

"I knew that my family would never allow me to act on that, and it would be impossible to lead a double life in my culture, because we live so closely with our families."

There was a sadness in her eyes that made me feel closer to her. Although she hadn't yet told me, I knew we had both shared some negative family experiences.

"I fell in love with an Australian girl," The Spark told me, a brightness appearing in her eyes. "For a long time I hid her as a part of a double life I was able to and felt I had to live here."

The Spark stopped to consider how best to tell the next part of her story.

"To keep up appearances I had two Facebook accounts. I had one for family and work, where I hid my sexuality, and then a personal one, where I could be myself."

It wasn't until The Spark looked me directly in the eyes that I realized she'd been avoiding eye contact. Something new seemed to show in her face, but I couldn't quite put my finger on the exact sentiment.

"Then I found Intersectionality Advocates, and I saw how people had thrived at work after coming out, and I saw people who were living authentically in all aspects of their life, and I decided I wanted that, too. I also got to see the hurt of people who, like me, were hiding. I took my girlfriend to my family and it was really difficult, but I did it. Some of my family won't accept it, and are not talking to me now."

The Spark stopped speaking, and the silence made the pain in her eyes more prominent.

"I had no idea," I said.

"My story is very specific to me. Some things were more difficult because my understanding of the English language is different. You can be a Person Of Color and not have that problem. You can also be a POC and not have the pressures I had with family. I feel like Intersectionality Advocates has been insensitive in the way they've tried to include us. We can't just have token POCs on a panel, or in videos or photos, and say that we're being inclusive. That's just tokenism. Not once has anybody asked me what it is that I need, and there are people who are more vulnerable than me who go unnoticed. Do you understand what I'm saying?"

"I do," I say somberly. "Is there anything you think we can immediately do?"

"Yes. We need to ask a variety of people what they perceive their specific barriers to be. We need to hear voices from a variety of people who've experienced difficulties because of their culture, and their language skills. Where possible, we need to give those people a microphone, and step back to be available for support."

"I'm so sorry that we're not yet where you need us to be," I replied, because I wasn't sure what else I could say.

"Will you find a way to help? Can you help more of us get our voices heard?"

"I'm not sure how to go about it, but I will," I promised.

But it wasn't something I could do alone, or even with the help of people within my social network.

Atypical
(Package No. 4)

Containing a nightmare,
and an interview.

AGAIN I'M IN THE MOST UNSAFE OF PLACES. This time, My Sibling is here with me, looking devastated as they consider my poorly constructed explanation of why I have commenced a gender transition. Their view is somewhat tainted by Parental Being having beaten me to the punch.

My Sibling and I are on a park bench, except that the bench is on a dark grey cloud, and everything else is a black expanse. When I am released from slumber, these physical circumstances will help me separate these events from memories of how things really went down; slightly different, spanning years, not minutes.

"Have you ever noticed," My Sibling is telling me. "We all have this darkness, in our family."

Their words are like a large, sharp knife, and I find myself thinking of another. I recall when we were both children, I saw them clasp one with both hands, the sharp end aimed toward their chest. Witnessing their incomplete action, had helped me get much closer to completing my own. I struggle to keep back tears.

"None of us is quite right," they tell me.

This isn't just about about suicidal ideation, nor my obsession with the number 3. It is not about the times I've felt anxious and depressed without obvious reason. What My Sibling is trying to tell me without stating anything overtly, is that being transgender is wrong. Though different to mine, and not requiring childhood surgery, they've also grown up a little different, and they are not transgender, therefore I am not legitimate. They will not accept my truth.

"This is about who I am," I plead. "Your opinion doesn't come into it at all."

The black expanse starts to shimmer, as heavy rain falls.

"Maybe it's my fault, for dressing you up like a girl."

That they feel they caused me to be this way, that they feel that there's something wrong who who I am, that they feel guilty for who I am. All of this breaks my heart, but I've had too few discussions to articulate the truth. Instead, I shut down, I turn my back, and I walk away.

-V-

MY NEXT READER IS PETIT, and her skin is a snowy landscape adorned with thousands of tiny freckles that go all the way to the edge of her fine, copper, pixie-styled hair. Beneath thick, black eyelashes, her sapphire blue eyes seem fierce, as though capable of calling me out for bad behavior and following up with appropriate discipline. She flashes a purposeful smile, showcasing perfectly aligned white teeth decoratively framed by peach lips.

"I'm Connie," she tells me at a pace that makes the two words feel like one. "Which is a shortened form of Confident, which is what my parents really named me, but I stopped using that when I started associating it with negative subliminal influence. People often confuse confidence with arrogance when it comes from women."

"Hi Connie," I reply at my normal pace, which comparatively seems closer to that of a snail. "I'm Paige, like in a book…"

"I know," Connie interrupts me. "Except you spell it with an 'i', and in this case you actually *are* a book, and I know all this because I specifically came here to read you."

It takes a little longer than usual for my brain to catch up to the words that have been so swiftly spoken. Connie doesn't wait very long for a response, because she has more she would like me to know, and she is aware that her time with me is quite limited.

"My background is in psychology, by the way, so I already know all about gender dysphoria, and more problematic historical diagnoses like gender identity disorder."

This time Connie gives me a firm smile without teeth, and she keeps her mouth closed to allow me to speak. It seems to take some effort on her part, to the point of seeming painful. That she's successful in curbing her compulsion, should be commended.

"What specifically would you like to learn from me?"

"Drugs," Connie states. "I'd like to know what medication is needed to keep you going."

"Well, that will take a little bit of explaining," I tell her.

"What do you mean by that?"

"There's not a single best option for all people, and what we need during different phases of life is also different."

Connie brings her left hand up, rests her chin on the palm of her hand, then curls her fingers around to clasp her chin as if it is a large diamond in a ring.

"Why don't you start with the options you were presented with first," she offers. Or perhaps she is directing me. It feels more like she's directing.

"When I first went to a doctor about gender identity issues, my blood was tested to assess naturally occurring sex hormone levels. Surprisingly, no problem was found, so, as required, I proceeded to seek approval from two separate doctors in order to get a prescription for hormones associated with the first stage of a male to female gender transition."

Connie narrows her gaze. I wait.

"What specifically were you prescribed?"

"The first was spironolactone, which directly blocks androgen signaling, and acts as an inhibitor of androgen production."

"Oh."

"As you might expect, it helps to reduce body hair, induces breast development, causes some feminization, and stops, er, the physiological response to sexual stimulation."

I blush, but Connie doesn't seem awkward at all, so I quickly move on. Well, quickly for me, but still slowly compared to Connie.

"The second drug was a mix of cyproterone acetate and ethinylestradiol. They worked with the spironolactone to maintain levels of estrogen more consistent with that of an adult ciswoman."

Connie raises her eyebrows.

"What is a ciswoman?"

"A woman who was assigned female at birth. It's essentially a label for someone who is the opposite to trans. I think it's a fairly recently adopted term."

"Interesting," Connie says, her eyes arbitrarily fixed on a space nearby as the thinks deeply. "So back to the drugs. I assume this is just maintained until there's a problem, or the physical situation is changed."

"More or less," I say, as I sense visitation by Self Doubt, who I figure is a complete stranger to Connie.

"Well is my assertion correct or not, Paige?"

"I'm not a doctor, and it's been a while since I've studied Medicine, so I'd just use this conversation as a starting point for your own research."

"You studied Medicine?"

I look down at my feet.

"I always wanted to be a doctor," I confess. "A few years ago, I decided to teach myself for a while, and I had planned to apply to Med School after I had solid foundational knowledge, but… life took a turn."

"Hmmm. Okay," Connie accepts. "You're supposed to be an expert on matters of gender and sex diversity though, so it would be worth your while maintaining medical knowledge pertaining to that area."

I grimace, because I agree.

"So the situation changes. Then what?"

"There are a few options," I tell her. "After lower surgery… I won't bother going into much detail, because it's similar to management of a post-menopausal woman."

"I…"

Even though I've only known Connie a few minutes, it seems out of character for her to exhibit signs of being unsure. Beneath the white backdrop of her skin, and very slowly at first, cloudy patches of red seep through from behind the white, obscured in parts by freckles. These red clouds move to slowly morph into larger shapes that I could fancy as silhouettes of other things if it wasn't rude to stare.

"I don't know how post-menopausal women are managed," Connie finally states, bringing her left hand up over her mouth and nose as a shield.

"Oh, well I'm specifically meaning how post-menopausal women need hormone replacement therapy to prevent osteoporosis."

Connie looks even more insecure.

"Why? What's that?"

I find it confusing that Connie would lack knowledge that I view as rudimentary.

"You don't know about osteoporosis?"

Connie's red facial clouds catch fire, and completely obscure any previous whiteness of her skin.

"I'm two months into my medical degree, Paige," Connie says, her voice wavering.

I can't think of how to respond, but fortunately Connie has more to say first.

"And aside from the entrance exam, my previous study was psychology," she adds gruffly.

I can see the rise and fall of her chest as her breathing is deep, and deliberate. She's distressed.

"Oh, of course, sorry," I say. "I guess I'm used to talking to students who are near the end of their training."

"Mmm."

I feel bad that I've bruised Connie's ego, so I start with a little self-deprecation.

"Again, because I'm not a doctor I'd just use this as a place to start your own research, but inadequate levels of estrogen increase bone resorption, decreasing overall bone mass, which leads to an increased risk of fracture."

"Okay."

Connie's dermal fire recedes, and the clouds begin to dissipate, returning the freckled background to porcelain.

"As far as forms, what's available?"

"Generally the options are a pill, a patch, or a cream."

"Is there much difference between them?"

"The patches and cream tend to be favored over pills, because they enter the bloodstream directly, whereas the pill is processed by the liver."

"Which did you choose?"

I slump in my chair as I confront the reality that when it comes to my healthcare, things are rarely straightforward. There are a few current things I know I need to take care of, and I try to push those thoughts aside. Perhaps it would be wise to take some action in the morning, but it's pointless entertaining any related thoughts while I'm confined to being a book.

"My situation was different," I tell her. "When my blood was tested after surgery, it was identified that on those standard doses my levels would be inadequate. That is, I would leave myself open to osteoporosis."

"Oh, I know about that!"

Connie flashes me a toothy grin. I feel relieved.

"So I could either return to the high dosage from before surgery, or take a supplement to help protect my bones. I chose the higher hormone doses."

"Interesting. And that's what you're still on now?"

"No."

"Of course," Connie exclaims. "Your situation is different."

I consider whether I want to be telling a current medical student the next part of my story. This hesitance is because of words of concern spoken to me by Hospital Companion when I first told them I was going to be a book.

Words of Caution From Hospital Companion

I worry about how this event will affect your relationship with the medical students.

"What?"

I remind myself that this is all a part of my *go bold, or go home* mantra as I potentially head toward the end of my time with The Medical College. I take a deep, slow breath in, then let it out even more slowly.

"I ran into problems that I think were associated with alcoholism. See, I was sick, vomiting a lot, so that affected the number of days pills were effective. On top of that, my memory became quite bad, and I'd swing between skipping pills for days, and taking possibly several in one day. I also sustained stress fractures in both tibias, that took years to heal, and although I had been eating poorly and exercising excessively in unhealthy footwear, I think hormones also had a part to play."

Connie nods, and thinks for a moment before asking her next question. I notice a slight movement to the side of her lower lip. She's biting it from within.

"How did you solve that one? I imagine patches would be easier to remember than cream, because it's on your skin."

"There was another option that I chose, that isn't as common because it leaves scarring."

"Of course there is."

"Estradiol is available as a pellet that can be implanted into the abdominal fat. For my required dose, it's not available locally, but I just have to get one made up by an interstate compounding pharmacy once each year, then book in to have it inserted. It's been transformative."

Ding ding ding!

"Anything else you want me to quickly run through?"

Connie shakes her head.

"No, thank you Paige. This has been really informative."

We smile at each other in silence for a moment, then Connie nods, stands, and walks away.

During my break—in order to fully emotionally recharge before the next student—I send my mind through to an unrelated time and place. Where my mind lands, is the open wooden door of a friend's home.

Green

(Package No. 5)

Containing a memory,
a letter,
and a consultation.

IT WAS EARLY EVENING WHEN I RETURNED to the city I technically lived in, a month after returning from Sydney. Because my Melbourne trip didn't line up exactly with the next housesitting gig, I'd arranged to spend a few nights at what would become a regular crash pad for the year. The crash pad was the permanent residence of Green Energy, a woman who had entered my life in a professional capacity, but had then transitioned into the social space due to mutual friends and common interests.

Green Energy met me at the door.

"How was Melbourne?"

"Unexpected," I told her. "Thank you so much for letting me stay."

Green Energy looked around and behind me.

"Where are your other bags?"

"It was only four days, so I just took the backpack and my handbag," I told her. "My suitcase and the rest of my things are at Satellite Hospital, so I can bring back some clean clothes tomorrow. I'd bring the whole suitcase, but I've got a doctor's appointment right after work, followed by a mentoring workshop I designed for Intersectionality Advocates. I don't want to lug it around with me."

Green Energy smiled.

"Have you eaten?"

"Yes, but can I sit with you while you eat?"

"Of course. I'll give you the tour first."

Green Energy waved me in to the main living area. There was something very calming about the way the space was styled. It took a while for me to notice that it lacked a television. Later I would find out it was also without Wi-Fi. It was the absence of modern technological clutter that made the room feel like some kind of mindfulness sanctuary. It was a type of minimalism that was different to the kind I was living.

After showing me the bathroom and kitchen, Green Energy ushered me to a small room on the side of the apartment. The room was modestly furnished with a single bed, table, chair, shelf, and lamp. I instantly loved the simplicity of the room. It felt like a space that was designed specifically with me in mind. If I decided to return to a fixed abode, I fancied it could be to a space like that room.

While Green Energy ate, I lay on the floor, telling her about my trip to Melbourne. I told her that I felt like it was time I tried to prompt action that could improve the standard of healthcare provided to the LGBTIQAP+ community. The outcome of the conversation was a letter that I wrote before going to bed. When I woke, I proofread the letter and sent it before fear could prevent me. I also forwarded it to Hospital Companion, along with an invitation to catch up over lunch.

THE LETTER I WROTE AND SENT

Dear Relevant Academic,

I hope the year has begun satisfactorily for you. It seems to be shaping up to be a pretty big one already, and this email is also likely to be big.

A recent chat with a friend made me think I should flick you an email about some of the things I do outside of Satellite Hospital. There are potentially other ways I can and would like to be of help to The Medical College. I'm always keen to take on new projects, and assist with pilot initiatives if there's some way we can improve things for students and their future patients.

I hold the volunteer position of Queensland Director of Intersectionality Advocates, which is a not-for-profit organization that seeks to help young LGBTIQAP+ professionals navigate the early stages of their careers. This is largely achieved through a free mentoring program, where we match LGBTIQAP+ students with those in the community who are established in their careers. We also organize a variety of events, and I mention this for several reasons.

This work has led me to connect with a few LGBTIQAP+ medical students, who continue to express concern about our medical program not adequately preparing their colleagues to deal with patients within the LGBTIQAP+ community. There's also been mention of a sexual health case that's problematic and offensive to certain members of the community.

As a leader in the LGBTIQAP+ community, I also frequently get to hear from patients who confirm the above. That is, they have bad experiences with healthcare professionals who they don't feel have been trained to deal with them, for what they felt were simple needs. Their bad experiences cause them to avoid seeking medical attention where necessary.

Last year, Intersectionality Advocates hosted our first 'LGBTIQAP+ Medical Issues' event. Despite it purely being a panel of clinicians, the event was very popular. Because medical education has been a lifelong area of passion for me, I'd like to get bigger and better. Ideas for the future include an LGBTIQAP+

Healthcare Master Class and an Objective Structured Clinical Examination style event.

A student union group have approached me about being a Live Book for an upcoming event next month, which is exciting and a bit daunting. At this event students will have the opportunity to ask specific questions about my place in the community. In case you're not aware, it's that I'm a woman who was assigned male at birth, and went through a transition in my late teens.

Organizations often call on me to speak about my lived experiences related to going through a gender transition. I've become quite good at speaking off the cuff if given a general direction, ranging from health concerns, workplace issues, and more personal topics. It helps that I've written several books on the topic that I can defer to. I would definitely be happy to speak as a part of a medical course, if ever given the opportunity.

With all that in mind, if there is anything you feel I could assist with, you're welcome to email, visit, or give me a call. I would love to chat about any way I can ensure we're doing the best we can by the LGBTIQAP+ community, in preparing graduates to interact with them.

Yours Sincerely,
Paige

-V-

WHEN I ARRIVED AT SATELLITE HOSPITAL, I watered my potted plants before I did anything else. I was pleased to see that my long weekend away hadn't caused them to suffer. This wasn't because they were particularly hardy, but because Hospital Companion had dropped by to water them in my absence. Half a day later, I was again standing by the potted plants, this time merely inspecting them.

"Afternoon, Paige," I heard Hospital Companion call.

We sat down either side of a table by the potted plants, where my lunch was already waiting. Hospital Companion looked at the small collection of spinach and lettuce leaves that were on the plate in front of me.

"Fruits of your labor?"

"Yes," I confirmed.

"I see it caused your water to break," Hospital Companion said with a cheeky smirk.

"What?"

Hospital Companion motioned to my dress.

"Oh," I said, pointlessly wiping a large wet patch. "When I pulled the watering jug down from the cupboard I found out the cold way that someone hadn't completely emptied it the last time it was used."

Hospital Companion snorted.

"And how are your little babies?"

"They've a lot more growing to do, but hopefully I'll eventually have enough for a daily salad."

Hospital Companion snorted.

"You've clearly got a green thumb, but it's not a real salad if it's just a few different leaves with tomatoes."

"It's a salad if I say it is! Anyway, thanks for coming and watering them while I was away. You're super helpful these days!"

Hospital Companion narrowed their eyes and this time shot me a snide smirk.

"Surely you've noticed people walking on eggshells around you since you started immortalizing your life in books…"

I was shocked, and felt defensive. I'd spent a good deal of energy trying to avoid that truth.

"But everyone is de-identified," I said in my defense. "And most characters are an amalgam of people. You, for instance."

I looked sheepishly at Hospital Companion before continuing. Their eye contact didn't waver.

"Some of the things people did are even toned down."

Hospital Companion peered at me with an intensity that made me worry they could see through to my inner most desires. I felt naked, and I didn't like it at all.

"Be that as it may," Hospital Companion said cautiously. "People could still be hurt by reading about mistakes made that they recognize as their own."

There was an uncomfortable silence as Hospital Companion continued to seemingly gaze trancelike right into my soul.

"Anyway," Hospital Companion said, snapping us both out of it. "How are the kids?"

"I quite like the current medical students, and the ones who witnessed the jug incident today were cautiously entertained! There are some really nice characters about the place at the moment, and a few have needed my help with extra things."

"You're such a mother. On another topic… how's your sex life? I haven't heard any dating stories for a while."

"I'm not nearly as popular as I used to be, back before my history was splashed all over the place."

I looked down at my feeble salad glumly.

"And I guess…" Hospital Companion's continuation of my own thought was delivered cautiously. "Since people started realizing that their bad behavior could end up in a book?"

In silence, I scowled.

"Green with envy at the version of yourself that existed before all this?"

"Huh?"

"I was trying to talk like one of your books," Hospital Companion explained. "What I'm specifically asking is, *do you regret it?*"

"Well, not entirely. I mean, most people who've known have still been okay about having sex with me as long as it's in secret, but I'm not so keen on that anymore."

"Sounds like a good thing that you've excluded people like that," Hospital Companion spat. "If they want you in secret, I'm not sure they do actually want you at all."

"Mmm. I think though that I've also pushed away people who are genuinely interested, but who don't want to become a story in one of my books, or to end up in the spotlight some other way."

I chewed on a piece of spinach while I considered where I wanted to take the conversation.

"We all make mistakes," I acknowledged. "And I think people are scared of making those mistakes under public scrutiny. Perhaps if I was in their position I would feel the same."

Hospital Companion jumped out of their chair and clapped their hands together loudly.

"Oh, this is another intersectionality thing! This is something that anyone in the public eye would face, but yours also has the gender element to it!"

Hospital Companion did a little dance, then sat back down at the table, grinning like a maniac.

"Considering how green you were just a short while ago, you've become an amazing ally," I commended them. "I'm really grateful for your measured curiosity and ability to re-learn."

Hospital Companion shrugged, but didn't say anything further. I was curious about what thoughts they were hiding from me, but decided to respect their clear desire to keep them private. Perhaps they were scared of saying the wrong thing, and having their words immortalized in my next book. I pushed aside the feeling of guilt about ruthlessly sacrificing the feelings of those close to me for what I perceived to be the greater good.

"I've been thinking about the sex and romance in my books, actually," I confessed. "I think I've explored everything I wanted to."

"I don't know what that means," Hospital Companion stated flatly.

"Well, in my earlier books, I specifically chose stories that would help normalize romantic and sexual relationships with trans women, and to explore a few different disclosure situations to help people understand what we go through. Anything further would just be revisiting the same content, so it might be a good time to bow out and focus more on everything else."

Hospital Companion grinned at me.

"Good luck with that," they said.

"What does that mean?"

As I swiftly felt defensive again, I wondered whether the emotional transition was due to something unresolved. I decided I should make an appointment to speak about it with a professional.

Hospital Companion raised their eyebrows and leaned in close. I could tell that they were amused by something.

"Well, Paige, I actually don't think you can help yourself."

-V-

SUDDENLY SEVERAL BILLION HEARTBEATS was a milestone that was a whole lot closer, but I reminded myself that there'd never been any guarantee that I would last until then anyway. Life offered us all many different ways to check out long before our bodies expired from old age. Perhaps skin cancer would finally overtake, or irreparable damage to my liver would reveal itself to be the bringer of my end. Murder by someone else's hand felt more likely by the day; it was just part of being a woman who was known to be assigned male at birth.

Sitting in the waiting room of Take Two—yet another new General Practitioner—I couldn't ignore the reality that life offered an impressive smorgasbord of options for early check-out. Perhaps Take Two would help me dodge a few of the more likely causes of early death, but I was feeling quite negative about him. Yet more bias for me to deal with.

"Yeah, I'm good thanks," I told Take Two flawlessly when he cautiously asked how I was.

"What brings you here today?"

I remembered that I was there as a patient, and his questions had not been social pleasantries. I thought about less helpful things like the greater context. My long term treating physician Dermal Saviour was no longer available, and the search for a suitable replacement was ongoing. Also, I wasn't in the office I had planned on.

"I had an appointment to get my skin checked by your colleague," I finally said. "But they left the practice for the day just before my appointment with them, so the receptionist booked me in to see you instead."

Although I couldn't be sure, Take Two seemed bruised by my explanation, and had he known a little more, he'd have even more reason. I'd chosen his colleague because they were young, and I had this notion that they'd be an easier person to come out to. That this doctor was an old man was the reason I was so many heartbeats closer to my last.

"Is a skin check something you would be able to do?"

Take Two nodded, and took my hand. He squeezed the skin on the back of my hand to see how it gathered. Similarly to witness reaction, he pulled against each side to stretch it out. He then rolled a finger along the surface to assess the texture.

"Your skin is very sun affected! Did you grow up near a beach?"

"Yes," I told him, but of course it's never a straightforward answer with me. I corrected myself.

"Well, I grew up in a few different places, but spent a decade living seaside up north."

I felt Take Two's finger stop.

"Wound?"

"Yeah," I confirmed. "I look after pets."

"Another?"

"That was one of the skin cancers," I corrected.

Take Two pinched the scar tissue.

"It's very deep."

I laughed, and lifted up my shirt.

"This one," I said, pointing to the large, red keloid scar across my abdomen. "Was severely dysplastic. Over a year and it still looks like that."

Take Two gasped.

"Or maybe that was the one on my back."

I swiveled, to show a similar scar across my lower back.

"Anyway, they've both left pretty decent scars so the countless other ones seem somewhat insignificant now."

Take Two stopped the physical exam and started to type, asking questions as he did so. My answers told him that I'd been badly sunburnt many times, but not in years. I'd been a smoker until age 21, and although my red hair was artificial, it occurred naturally in some of my blood relatives. I told him about how the scar under my ear was a reminder of my first squamous cell carcinoma, found and removed when I was a teenager, and pointed out the former locations of as many basal cell carcinomas as I could remember.

"Have you had any other surgery?"

"Gender affirming surgery, many years ago," I stated.

"Ah," he said, and perhaps I was just oversensitive, but from that point on, Take Two seemed cold.

For what seemed like far too long for so few words exchanged, I watched the wall behind Take Two as he typed in silence.

"Best you go to a dermatologist," Take Two told me when he had finally finished typing. "That seems to be your main concern, and your skin is rather sun affected. I've written you a letter that will be available at the front desk."

I decided that I would only see Take Two again if absolutely necessary. It was important to me that I replace Dermal Saviour with a doctor who wasn't just knowledgeable about skin. I needed someone who was friendly, and it was vital that I find someone who didn't make me feel uncomfortable about my gender.

Chapter Six

IT'S STILL RAINING IN MY DARK PLACE, except in the cylinder of light where I'm standing opposite Outer Shell—my pre-transition form—who is eighteen years old. Behind Outer Shell, I see the black rain shimmer, and a new form slowly emerge. A thin, blonde twenty-year-old woman becomes visible to me, but not to Outer Shell. The Blonde Woman holds her finger up to her lips, silently telling me to keep her presence a secret from Outer Shell.

Blonde Woman, who is also my younger self, runs her fingers through the long, wet curls that sprout from her head. Mascara is running down her cheeks, and it looks wildly sexy. She runs her other hand down her body, closes her eyes, and moans. She slips her hand behind her back, then swiftly brings it back holding a knife. She plunges it into Outer Shell.

Before my own eyes, my young self stands in front of the lifeless body of Outer Shell to hide it. A stranger appears, and looks Blonde Woman up and down. Then another, and another. A stranger appears behind the body of Outer Shell, and drags it out for everyone to see. I'm tapped on the shoulder, and I turn to face a woman who is me at age Twenty Eight. She has dark brown, blackish hair.

"Everyone knows," Twenty Eight tells me, crying. "But this... the details are wrong. It's all wrong."

I turn back to the strangers.

"It's not right, and I need to do something," I can hear Twenty Eight telling me.

I see strangers throwing black bubbles at Blonde Woman. Others are linking arms in solidarity. Blonde Woman sustains bruises from the black bubbles, and some of the strangers gently stroke the bruises that are more obvious.

-V-

"HOW IS IT THAT YOU CAN YOU BE SO OPEN," the woman who is my next female reader asks. "When you know that it increases your chances of being discriminated against?"

"I wasn't always," I tell her, as I watch her slide gracefully into her chair.

"I'm just like you," she tells me. "Not in that I was assigned male, or anything. Just... Stealth Privilege is my name by the way," she tells me, delicately presenting her hand to offer a handshake. "But please, just call me Espy."

"Pleased to meet you," I say, shaking her hand.

More than anything else in this moment, I want to ask her about her name, however I know that it's likely to be a question she gets frequently. Having my own experience of growing tired from the curiosity of others, I make the decision to let it go. After all, the whole purpose of this conversation is to answer her questions about me, not the other way around.

"I know," Espy says, grinning. "You probably weren't expecting my name to be Stealth Privilege, because with my skin color…"

Espy makes a joke about the blackness of her skin.

I bite my lips closed to prevent a loud cackle. Something I appreciate is when people can take power back through humor about a part of themselves that is the cause of discrimination or harassment. Similarly, something I despise is when power is taken away from those same people through the same means by others. There are plenty of ways to make people laugh without taking stabs at minority groups.

As Espy watches my invisible cogs working, she smiles widely, exposing her pearly teeth.

"That is a joke I can make, but you can't," Espy confirms. "I'm sure this is something you'd appreciate, as it would never be appropriate for me to make a joke at the expense of a trans identity."

I smile gratefully and nod.

"Regarding my earlier question and comment," Espy says, dipping her head slightly. "It ties into my own situation. You've now seen my skin, heard my voice, and know my name. Like you, there are certain situations where I have the privilege of not having to disclose one of the parts of me that is the cause of discrimination. In my case, I'm talking about the color of my skin."

I nod, momentarily distracted by the immaculate tight braids that cover her head. I remember reading an article about how painful the process could be.

"What you won't know," Espy tells me. "Is that before I got into Medicine in Australia, I had another career. The nature of my career is not really relevant to the story, but what I would like you to know, is that whenever I applied for jobs, I deliberately chose to never include a photograph. If I wasn't shortlisted for an interview, I wanted to know that it was because I lacked the necessary skills or experience. I didn't want to wonder if it was a matter of racism."

"I see," I say, starting to see the reason for her initial question that I realize I haven't answered.

"Also, whenever possible, I elected for phone interviews, rather than in person or via videoconference. Like you, I have in the past actively hidden that part of myself that can be the cause of discrimination and harassment."

I cut in.

"My stealth goes further though," I say sadly.

"Yes," Espy confirms. "Not to belittle your struggles at all, but you do have the luxury of walking down the street without people knowing that you were assigned male at birth. I do not have that luxury."

"You don't have to be delicate about my privilege," I tell Espy. "I'm well aware of it, and it's one of the things I try to acknowledge in everything I write, to set an example for other people who could do more good if they did the same."

Espy again shows off her immaculate teeth with a smile. I remember that it's been some years since I've been to the dentist for financial reasons, and one of my back teeth has partially disintegrated. Hopefully I'll remember to make a note to make an appointment in the next break between conversations.

"May I tell you a little about what I know," Espy requests. "Before I quiz you?"

"Go for it."

"Of course people of color in general were far worse off than white people across all areas, but I was devastated to read about the effects of anti-transgender bias in the US when I was doing research for this conversation. I understand it's a little different in Australia, but it's a little more difficult to come by solid information about that."

"It sounds like you're here to teach me," I say sheepishly. It's not the first time I've felt less than adequately prepared for this event.

"This is presumptuous, I realize, but my reason for being here probably differs from the other medical students," Espy tells me. "I've read some of your work, and just thought you'd be an interesting person to speak with. There are actually plenty of online resources for trans healthcare if you're willing to put in a little effort to sift through the ever increasing trash on the internet."

This time I make no attempt to stifle my laugh.

"If all medical students were like you, I imagine we'd improve the situation pretty quickly."

"One of the research papers that I was reading included a survey where over sixty percent of transgender respondents had experienced a *serious act of discrimination*. That is, something that had a major impact on the person's life. Again, it was from the US. I would have spent more time looking for Australian statistics, but I'm set on going home after I graduate."

"I don't suppose you recall what the specific acts were?"

Espy pulls out a piece of paper, and hands it to me.

"I made you a list of ten things I found that were a direct result of bias against their gender. You do like lists, don't you? I wasn't sure how much of you as a character in your book was fictional."

I chuckle.

"I reveal less of myself than the typical reader would assume," I tell Espy. "It wouldn't be wise to fully arm strangers with the ability to manipulate me."

My amusement quickly fades as I read the list that Espy has given me.

THE LIST FROM ESPY

1. Lost job
2. Eviction
3. Forced to drop out of school
4. Teacher bullying
5. Physical assault
6. Sexual assault
7. Homelessness
8. Lost relationship with partner or children
9. Denial of medical service
10. Incarceration

"I personally know people who've experienced all of these things," I say sadly. "People are constantly reaching out to me, and often I can do no more than listen to them complain."

"Well, you can't be everything to everyone, and listening is also important," Espy says. "Something I found more alarming than that list, was that more than twenty percent had been affected by at least three of those things."

"I wish I was surprised."

"Back to my original question from when I first met you," she says. "Even with the little knowledge I have…"

"…which evidently is far more than I…"

"…I know that women like you are discriminated against, ridiculed, and abused at alarming rates. I see that the community in general are surprisingly resilient and determined with regard to actively fighting barriers to healthcare, employment, and housing."

And here I am, employed full-time, and able to pay for private health cover. Sure I don't have a fixed address, but I'm never stuck for accommodation, and will soon be completely free of debt. When that time comes, if it feels right, I could actually choose to return to renting a place. Something about that idea makes me feel uncomfortable.

"Then there's you," Espy says. "You have the ability to escape most of that, yet you are one of the most actively out of the closet people I've ever heard of."

"I call it *aggressively out*," I tell her.

"Aggressively out," Espy laughs. "I love it. So you would know that you are not only missing out on opportunities because of that, but also facing bigger hurdles, and more frequently. Yet you still do what you do… How?"

I look down at my feet, ashamed.

"In fact for many years I actively sought to hide it. But I suppose you already know that from reading my books."

"I've only read *Outer Shell*, and some of your articles. That would be something you cover in your later books? Anyway, the point is that you don't hide it now."

Ding! Ding! Ding!

"Oh, our time is up," Espy says.

"If you're okay with it, I would like to keep talking through the rest break," I offer.

"I'd like that, if you feel you're up to it."

"I do. In answer to your question, it was progressive," I tell her. "I played it relatively safe once I started taking back my story that had been inaccurately told and distributed without my permission. I started with videos and written posts. And before I went full throttle, I worked hard to build a solid support network of allies. And not that it wasn't a huge risk, but when I first came out at work, The Medical College Ally Program helped me feel that I would at least have some support, and well I obviously can't give you specifics, but I did need to call on that support network."

"Yeah, I get that it would be inappropriate to disclose to a current medical student."

Espy touches her ear, and avoids eye contact as she considers something deeply personal. I brace myself for a potentially intrusive question.

"Do you ever feel like going back?"

This is where I go bright red, because of the strong shame I'm feeling. I look down at my feet as I contemplate how to respond.

"Often," I confess. "I'm painfully aware of privilege related to my appearance. But that same privilege is a power that I can use for good."

"How so?"

"It doesn't seem to really be acknowledged as much as it should be, but one of the reasons I'm so widely accepted by heterosexual cisgender people, is that I seem like one of them."

A lightbulb shines through Espy's face.

"Oh, of course!"

"People don't have to put any effort in to remember my pronouns, for starters, because I look how they traditionally consider a woman should. Then there's dating. If someone is dating me, people in the street wouldn't need to know the person was holding the hand of a woman who was assigned male at birth. A lot of these people, they wouldn't be so accepting if I was less able to slip under the radar."

Espy looks down at her feet this time.

"It's for those people that I press on. All I am really, is a stepping stone. I'm helping potential allies get their head around gender being something different to what they have been raised to believe."

Espy opens her mouth to speak, then closes it again, and finally decides to speak after all.

"Do you think you would ever do a lecture for medical students? It would be really useful, have a much wider reach, and be less resource-intensive than this event. I really appreciate you talking through your rest break, by the way."

"I would actually love to," I tell her. "I just don't know how to go about that. Well, I sort of did make an offer to a relevant academic person, but I'm not sure it's going to go anywhere. I think I need to find a way to prove myself worthy."

"I'm sure a lot of us here would be happy to endorse you, if you really would like to do that."

"We'll see," I say. "Perhaps I'll just write about it. I find it amusing that you think I should give a lecture to medical students, yet you haven't asked me anything medical."

"It's mostly discrimination I was curious about," Espy tells me. "As I said, there are resources on trans healthcare for anyone willing to put in a bit of effort to find them. I think I would have felt guilty asking intrusive questions I could have found the answer to online."

"If only most people felt that way! Well do you have any more non-medical questions for me?"

Espy looks up at the ceiling.

"Is there anything I could do as an ally, to help reduce or prevent discrimination?"

I smile at Espy.

"What we still really need from allies, is for them to show visible support, either through social media posts, or with things like wearing a rainbow badge with the words ally on it. Something that I also think is important, is calling people out when they say something that promotes discrimination or harassment."

"This is good. What else?"

I feel stuck for ideas in the moment, so I reach down to my bag and pull out a copy of *Outer Shell*.

"You could pass this on."

Espy takes the book.

"I've found it pretty good for giving allies a more intimate understanding of what someone like me could have gone through. Medical students and doctors especially seem to respond well to it."

"I'll introduce someone to it," Espy says.

Ding! Ding! Ding!

"Sorry, guess that's your break finished. I really hope I get to hear a lecture from you one day."

"Me too."

Quite naturally, as I watch Espy walk over to her friends, my mind slides back to my final night at my favorite Book Club.

Clubbed

(Package No. 7)

*Containing first a refusal,
and then an invitation.*

"It's Black Privilege," White Noise said heatedly. Every single book club attendee stopped; stunned into silence. I felt my body try to melt into the wall as means of escape. White Noise broke the silence with what I supposed was meant to be something of a defense.

"Well that's what it is. I'm just calling it as it is."

After several months of non-attendance, I'd arrived at book club early to secure myself a dark corner so that I could observe more than participate. The book we were there to discuss was *The Hate Race*, a memoir by Maxine Beneba Clarke. It was unusual for us to choose a memoir, and I was very glad that we had. I'd loved the book, and had been surprised by the many childhood experiences I could identify with, though for reasons other than race.

From my cozy corner of the wine bar, I felt as invisible as a fly on the wall. Unnoticed by White Noise and her husband Chewie, I glanced around the room at all of the other attendees, except for the two either side of me. I didn't want to draw attention to myself with a head movement, disallowing my preference to continue in the role of a spectator.

White Noise looked to Chewie for validation. He nodded at her and held her hand.

"Black privilege isn't a thing," Book Clubber said finally. White Noise huffed.

"Oh, really? So you're telling me that she hasn't made a name for herself and money because she's black?"

White Noise held up her copy of the book.

"This book is proof. It's all about her being black."

A few of the attendees glanced in my direction. I could tell that they wanted me to use my own situation to argue against White Noise. I had faced hardship, and had chosen to write about it in an attempt to improve the situation for others like me. Regardless of the fact that I had made a few cents per copy, showcasing *Outer Shell* to the world had come at great cost. No profit had been made.

Instead of accepting the silent request of the other people at book club,

I remained still and quiet. I didn't feel safe entering the conversation and making myself vulnerable to direct attack. I could tell that White Noise and Chewie were not safe people to disclose to, and I doubted my ability to lead them to reason. In this situation, I perceived the risk to outweigh the potential benefit.

Book Clubber decided to speak up instead.

"The author went through a lot of terrible, unnecessary experiences before she chose to speak out publicly for the greater good. It's so clearly not a money-making popularity exercise!"

I shrank back into myself, and considered my own situation. I remembered the person who had told me how lucky I was that public discussion of trans issues had put a spotlight on me. Because of that, writing and speaking opportunities had landed right in my lap, putting me in a more privileged position than many ciswomen. I recalled the overt comments about how I'd only been appointed as the Queensland Director of Intersectionality Advocates because of my gender history. I'd also been told to be thankful that difficulties I'd faced in childhood had given me content to flesh out my books.

"There weren't even that many examples of discrimination and harassment," White Noise continued. "In my own life I've had more occurrences than she wrote about."

My skin flushed red, and although I kept my mouth closed, I now had a strong desire to enter the debate. I wanted to tell White Noise that when writing a memoir, an author is generally required to write about the single occurrence that best explores the topic. Whatever that thing is, it probably happened repeatedly in many forms, maybe more than daily. That was something I'd done with my memoirs, because I could have filled an entire book with a single week, but it would make for a boring, exhausting read. Still, it seemed too risky to say so.

"And anyway," White Noise added. "I often experience discrimination because I'm a Christian."

Book Clubber looked utterly pissed off.

"And how is it that strangers in the street know that you're a Christian?"

"Well, it comes up in conversation, obviously," White Noise said.

"So you tell them you're a Christian."

"Well, yes," White Noise said hesitantly.

"That's not comparable to what someone experiences because of the way they look. They can't just take their skin off."

From my hiding place in the corner, I again thought about my own situation. As far as things like walking down the street, I was in a similar situation to White Noise. If I didn't feel like going into battle on any given day, I could just choose not to disclose that I was assigned male at birth. Partially because of my ex, and more so because of my own recent actions, there were less spaces in which I still held that privilege, but those spaces were still there.

I thought about the many trans people who wouldn't ever pass as cisgender. For them, leaving their home was in itself an act of bravery. For them, the only way to hide was to avoid being seen in public at all. Although my life was more difficult because of the trans label, my challenges had nothing on those who had absolutely no control over disclosure. For them, I decided that I needed to try even harder.

-V-

"Are you going to get that?"

Sitting by my thriving garden at Satellite Hospital, Hospital Companion watched me as I watched my phone silently ring. It was a local number. Probably not a bad phone call, and if it was, at least Hospital Companion was with me. I decided to answer the call.

"Paige speaking," I said.

"We have a referral here for you to see one of our dermatologists," a woman said on the other end.

"Oh, yes, can I make an appointment please?"

"Unfortunately that dermatologist is no longer taking any new patients."

"Oh, okay," I said.

"We can make you an appointment with someone else, though. What's your availability?"

"One moment, please, I just need to grab my planner."

I bolted into my office, and returned with my rucksack. From my rucksack, I pulled out my planner, and flipped to the current month. I then retrieved my stationery bag that was filled with meticulously chosen colored highlighters and pens. Before I explain my reasoning, I would first like to tell you a little story.

The Story That Is A Flashback

By happy coincidence, Hospital Companion and I realized that I was on leave for what would be their final week in Australia. I was sad to be losing them from Satellite Hospital, but we found a way to defer those feelings.

I had decided that during my week off, I would visit several cities. This was to include some I'd never been to. As with my interstate travel earlier in the year, this would allow me to catch up with friends, fellow Intersectionality Advocates volunteers, and broaden the reach of my Secret Project.

At this stage, flights hadn't been booked, and Hospital Companion indicated they already planned to visit one of my listed cities. We agreed that we should spend a few days gallivanting around it together.

It was a good month later, after flights were booked, that I realized a problem while comparing written notes and my phone's calendar. Halfway through my grand tour, I was committed to looking after a pet in Brisbane. My tickets were non-refundable, however I was fortunately able to transfer them to a voucher for flights later in the year. This of course attracted a fee, and the new flights for the shorter trip were more expensive. It was important that I put something in place to ensure a mistake like that didn't happen again.

What I landed on, was a Month to Opening planner. Within the planner, was each month spread over two pages, with each day of that month clearly defined within a large square. I then had to work out a coded system for recording information, so that I could get a feel for the whole month at a glance. Despite my color vision defect, I chose to use color, and here's what I came up with.

Day of Month Real Estate

The left side of each square was designated for vacation and travel. The center of the square would be for recording events. The lower right corner is where I would put housing details.

The Colors I Chose

A line of purple highlighter indicated that I had approved leave from Satellite Hospital, and line of turquoise highlighter told me that I would be traveling outside of Queensland on that day. Purple marker was to indicate a work commitment, turquoise marker was for recording housing details, orange marker told me of volunteer commitments, leaving black pen for anything else.

As well as ensuring I didn't book travel at times I was required back in Brisbane, it made it easier to confirm/reject house-sitting requests, plan Intersectionality Advocates meetings and events, and realistically RSVP to social invitations.

When I finished with the phone call, and had recorded the appointment in my planner, I noticed that Hospital Companion was watching me with curiosity.

"Your appointment, is it a gender thing?"

"What? No, it's skin. Hey, I told you about the stuff up with my flights right?"

"Yeah, I'm a part of your grand tour, remember?"

"Of course," I said. "Well this is planner is how I'm going to prevent a repeat."

Hospital Companion laughed.

"You don't think it would be easier to just live in one place?"

I rolled my eyes, but said nothing.

"All these cute pets you become attached to as you nurture them. Doesn't it make you long to have one of your own?"

"This isn't me complaining, just problem-solving. I'm quite happy with this lifestyle, thanks very much."

"You sure you don't long for less transience in your life?"

"No," I objected, without really giving it any thought. "It's quite good to be able to give them back sometimes, especially when they're really naughty."

"Oh, like the dogs who got into the treats, then pooped and puked everywhere?"

I shuddered.

"The sofas, the bed… there was just so much."

"That can't have been as bad as when you found out that house had four cameras continuously recording, and the owners only told you about one of them…"

I considered the things they'd have seen me do because I was under the false impression of having privacy. Even months later the thought made me feel sick. It was the last time I did a job for someone who wasn't a personal recommendation from someone I knew.

Hospital Companion looked at their watch.

"I best be off. Hit me up for coffee when you get back from… is this trip Melbourne or Canberra? I can't keep up with all your movements."

"Canberra, this time. I just got back from Melbourne."

"Okay, well we've only got so many opportunities left, so let me know when you're back."

When Hospital Companion was gone, everything seemed deathly quiet. The medical students were all up on the wards, and nobody else had any reason to be nearby. After sitting alone by my work garden for a few minutes, I decided to return to my office, which is when I saw an email that caused me excitement. It was an email I'd been expecting from Markety Mark, of the Medical College Marketing Department, because of a conversation I'd had with Medical College Ally.

EMAIL FROM MARKETY MARK

Hey Paige,

I work with Medical College Ally and they gave me your deets as you could be keen on being in a short video to be shared on The Medical College social media on Saturday 31 March for Transgender Day of Visibility.

Given the short timeline to get these videos completed we're hoping to film next Wednesday morning before midday. We've roped in a few other people already, so we will only need you for about 30 mins anywhere after 9am. Is there a time on Wednesday morning that suits? Or if Wednesday doesn't suit we could potentially do Thursday after 10:00am too…

Our idea for the video is Q and A, with everyone answering the same three questions. We'd cut their responses together.

The questions we were thinking of are: 1. What are your experiences of being trans, both in our workplace, and just generally in Australia? 2. What message would you like to pass on to cisgender allies about how they can be more inclusive of gender diversity? 3. What specifically does the transgender day of visibility mean to you?

No stress if you've any concerns, or wouldn't feel comfortable answering any of the questions, just please let me know and we will alter accordingly.

Look forward to hearing from you.

Markety Mark

By the time I'd reached the end of Markety Mark's email, my excitement had already faded. I quickly fired off a response.

Reply to Markety Mark

Hi Markety Mark,

Just wondering if the full message got passed on? I indicated that I can only participate either out of office hours, or if someone comes to Satellite Hospital where I'm based.

Cheers,
Paige

A day passed before I received a response, and unfortunately, the content of the response wasn't what I'd been hoping for.

Unfortunate Response from Markety Mark

Hey Paige,

Sorry mate, I didn't get that part of the message. Just that you were willing to participate. What hours outside of office hours would suit you? I think that's more likely than being able to get to Satellite Hospital... that looks a bit tricky on public transport.

Thanks,
Mark

As I read the email, I became annoyed. I whipped out my planner that confirmed what I had hoped wasn't the case. Before a flight to Canberra at the end of the week, there was a change in housing, and two meetings for Intersectionality Advocates. It wasn't possible to fit anything else in outside of work. With sadness, I sent my final reply.

Desolate Reply to Markety Mark

Hi Mark,

It looks like I won't be able to make time. I'm juggling a lot of commitments at the moment. If similar is done again with a bit more notice I'd be happy to coordinate participation.

Cheers
Paige

It felt especially disappointing having to turn down the offer of spreading my message further, after spending so much time and effort being aggressively out at work. Surely there was something that I could do to contribute. Some way I could help prompt positive change in people I was yet to reach. I realized that there was. There was definitely someone in my own life, who was potentially unaware of quite a lot, but I just couldn't bring myself to do it.

Sleeve

(Package No. 8)

Containing a trip to Canberra, and some more emails.

It was nearing two a.m. when our Boeing 717-200 set us down in Canberra. Maybe because I was exhausted from an especially long day, or perhaps because of our hours spent roaming the sleepy Brisbane airport prior to boarding, but I felt a strange attachment to the strangers around me. I smiled and waved at Jack, who'd shared a power source with me so I could charge my phone. The memory caused me to glance at my phone, and I saw that a message from Friendly Entity had come through.

Message From Friendly Entity

Heya Paige, don't suppose you're up for a coffee some time in the next few days?

My Regretful Reply

Sorry mate, but you have the worst timing! I'm in Canberra. Just landed.

Their Immediate Response

At this hour?! Okay well see you soon hopefully.

My Reply

Up late for a school night...

Their Reply

Just finishing up at the pub. Was feeling a bit agitated.

I wondered if there was anything to worry about, but decided I should focus on getting myself safely to the accommodation.

My Final Response

Alright, well hope you feel alright in the morning! Gotta find my way to a bed now. Talk soon.

Outside the airport, the cold, dusty air worked with lifeless visuals to create a strong feeling of isolation. I felt as though I was the sole survivor of a zombie apocalypse. Not that I've a tendency to let my imagination dramatically carry me away.

"Hey," I heard in a deep voice. So I was not the sole survivor after all. "Is this where we wait for our RideShare?"

How was I to know? This was a city I'd not been in since childhood, and back then I never saw the airport. The Man Who Was A Stranger wouldn't know that, though.

Actually, I thought. *It's best that he doesn't know that.*

A quick glance told me that he was likely strong and large enough to overpower me, if that was what he decided he wanted to do. Obviously the best thing for me to do was to pretend to be a local, or at the very least, a regular visitor with someone already on the way to pick me up. I noted a nearby sign that said *Wait for* RideShare *Here.*

"Yeah mate," I bellowed as gruffly as I could. "Just by that sign there."

I headed in the same direction, as if that had been my intent all along, and I stealthily summoned my own RideShare. Together, we waited in silence, and I barely took a breath until I was in the car with another stranger that was a man.

"Are you okay?"

"Yeah mate," I breathed to the new male stranger I was alone with. "Just a bit later than expected, and I'm looking forward to getting home."

It seemed like my lie was believed.

Near the end of my trip, yet again fear caused me to confirm the incorrect drop-off location to avoid outing myself as a vulnerable visiting woman. Unlike the time in Sydney, once I was standing alone in the dark, I was relieved to confirm that I was a short walk from my accommodation.

The hosts of my my HomeShare had left me a series of photos with instructions, because, fortunately, they knew they wouldn't be home even before I knew I was four hours later than anticipated. The instructions came with photos, and as a way to let go of earlier fear, I fancied the experience as an especially exciting treasure hunt in a foreign land.

The first photo led me to their garage, where I was directed to stand at the back, and face the street so that I could see a specific pile-on, behind which was a lock box. When the keys were in my hand, I was led to two doors, and the key unlocked the one on the left. Inside and also to the left, was a winding staircase up to an area with a dresser between two doors. On the right, I found my room.

How I spent my time in Canberra was how I had spent it now in

Sydney, and in Melbourne. Time was split between friends, Intersectionality Advocates volunteers, the Secret Project, and traveling on foot to the local theatre, gallery, and library. By the end of the trip I felt completely recharged, and ready to take on the world.

As was custom, I headed to the airport several hours early, to make absolutely sure I wouldn't have to rush. I set up camp to write, read, and catch up with work emails. It pleased me to see a new, promising email from Markety Mark.

The New and Promising Email From Markety Mark

Hey Mate!

Was really sorry you couldn't be part of the video for TDoV, but! I was having a chat with a colleague who was wondering if instead you would be interested in writing a blog post for The Medical College? Aim would be for publication to coincide with TDoV. Let me know if you're interested.

Cheers,
Mark

No doubt it was Medical College Ally who had again made an effort to include me. Overjoyed, and not having to give it any thought at all, I responded immediately.

My Immediate Response Oozing Overjoyedness

Hey Mark!

Regarding your email below, I've been on leave (returning tomorrow), but definitely keen to write something (probably adapted from previous writing). Are you able to give me more details please?

Cheers,
Paige

Markety Mark must have been sitting at his desk, because by the time I'd caught up on a few other work emails, he'd managed to write a detailed reply.

The Surprisingly Detailed Reply From Markety Mark

Hey Mate,

Stoked! Yeah, no worries, feel free to adapt something you've previously written! Have posted a bit of a blog brief below. Any idea when you reckon you could get me something by? I'd love to publish it ahead of the day coz there's not a lot of people reading the blog on a Saturday morning. Fridays however…

For word-count we're looking at 800 words, but I can work with as little as 400, and up to 1200.

For style, can you write in the first-person? No need to write like an academic paper or like you're going for a job interview. Just use your usual tone… Oh, and it totally doesn't need to be some big ad for The Medical College. But do include at least a sentence about your role here, which can even be as part of your little author profile. No need to write a lot of positive stuff about campus or anything like that. Actually, if there's something you think we could be doing better, mention it…

With pics, please include some! People love pics, so the more, the better. Could be your office, just yourself, pets, mates… you about campus. Anything you think is relevant. No stress if you're uncomfortable with that, coz we can definitely fall back on stock photos. Just need some key words or themes. Oh, and links to video are welcome too!

Ummm… so, links. If you've got a researcher's page, website, social media account… anything like that you want to promote, link me up.

Alright, finally, with editing, your blog doesn't have to be perfect. Once you give me a first draft, I'll make sure there's no spelling or grammatical errors (yeah don't use these emails as an indication of my skills!). I'll also ensure it's readable by a wide audience. After I've done all that I'll show it to you again before we hit publish so you get final say.

Any more questions?

Cheers,
Mark

My Next Immediate Response

Hi Mark,

I can have something done in the next few hours probably. I'm in Canberra and have a few hours to kill before my flight. :)
Have attached some photos of my office for the moment. There should be three. Let me know if you don't get them.

Cheers,
Paige

Markety Mark

They've come through perfectly! Travel safe!

Me

Please see below draft for your comments.

Markety Mark

Paige, that is bloody brilliant! Will lay it out ASAP.
Any links you want me to include? Will link to Intersectionality Advocates, The Medical College Ally Program, etc. but if there are any other places... twitter, LinkedIn... let me know. Also, did you want us to include any photos of you, or just stick to the office photos? Also, can link or embed videos or audio if you've ever done a podcast or similar...
Thanks for sharing your story mate. Once upon a time I did reporting in regional Queensland where I grew up... so I'm familiar with the... horrifying attitudes. Stoked you've overcome that small town thinking.

Thanks,
Mark

Me

Thanks Mark :) Glad I could use this time productively.
I've attached some photos that could work. Happy to scrounge around to find others. I'm just a bit hopeless on my phone.
You're welcome to include any of the following. Just check them out first to ensure they're appropriate :)

Me, Again

Hi Mark,

I also realized there's this video for Intersectionality Advocates that's definitely very relevant. Let me know if there's anything else I can do.

Cheers,
Paige

Markety Mark

Brilliant. Laying it all out now. Also started following you from The Medical College twitter account... let me know if you'd prefer we didn't, or if you don't want to be tagged when we tweet about your blog. It's mostly monitored by me, and we just use it to re-tweet positive stuff happening across campus. I promise we're not watching you, big brother style!!!

Although, did see on twitter that you saw Love, Simon. *How great was it? I was lucky enough to go to an advance screening and the whole cinema was crying and cheering.*

I didn't hear from Markety Mark again before my flight, which turned out to be completely uneventful. Upon landing, as soon as we were given permission to deactivate flight mode, I logged into my work emails. I was pleased to see yet another email from my new work pen pal, that included a link to the blog post draft. It occurred to me that I had no idea what he looked or sounded like, and then, that it was quite odd that I was known intimately by many people I'd never met.

Markety Mark

And here we go… That's just a preview link, so don't share it too widely because the story is not live yet… Have changed a word or two in the main body for clarity, so have a read and let me know if any of the changes don't feel right.

Also, I created a headline and standfirst, which is an introductory part under the headline. Let me know if you're happy with what I've come up with, or you can rewrite… And I hope you don't mind, I got a pic off your author page as well. :)

Me

That all looks really great, thanks. :)

Happy to be tagged etc in anything, as I feel the signal boost is important for the whole concept of visibility. Had a little chuckle with a friend about the line you've used for the standfirst because I write and speak about that aspect of myself more than anything else at the moment.

BTW I thought Love, Simon *was excellent. Trashy rom coms have always been something I enjoy so it's nice to see one that represents some diversity. I'd actually love to do one with a trans woman but I don't think we're quite at that point yet!*

As I waited for a train to my next temporary home, not fully appreciating what I'd done, I felt immensely pleased. Slowly, but surely, I was ensuring a better environment for younger versions of myself. And really, I was ensuring a better future for me.

This is perhaps a bit selfish, I thought.

But with how things would play out, I would realize that it most definitely was not selfish. And it definitely wouldn't make life easier for the version of myself that existed in the future.

Evidence (a)

(Package No. 9)

Containing a package within a package, the contents of which you will find out shortly.

THE WEIRDEST REQUEST OF MY LIFE came on a Wednesday. It was one day after the second most unexpected phone call of my life. The Tuesday phone call would have taken home the award for first place, had it not been for the Debt Collector who had called on behalf of the Tax Office several years earlier. The terrifying conversation with the debt collector had been the primary reason I'd fled the rental market, embarking on a No Fixed Abode adventure that saw me flitting between house-sitting gigs and couch-surfing stints.

Even though some years had passed, I still remembered the call like it was yesterday. I had been sitting in my office at The Southern Teaching Hospital, considering how there was no realistic way of crawling out of such substantial debt without finding a way to increase my budget. But earning more money was something I had considered impossible, what with my gender history splashed all over the internet to spoil the appetite of any potential employer. In the Australian workplace outside of The Medical College, those who opposed people like me flourished, supported by the likeminded.

It was Medical College Ally who had called to seek my permission for something unexpected on that Tuesday afternoon. The action they would only take at my command was to nominate me for a Diversity and Inclusion Award as an Inspiring Person. The reason they were asking first, was because in order to nominate me, they would need to pull me out of the closet in writing, to a panel of complete strangers. If I won, I'd be forced out of the closet to an immeasurable audience of strangers, and likely also people who were connected to me.

The cocktail of emotions I felt, included ingredients such as surprise, pride, humility, and gratefulness. More than anything, it warmed my heart to have tangible evidence that progress had been made since the days when people would often tell my story without my consent. Medical College Ally didn't just assume that they were able to tell my story just because their motive was good, which was an excuse many people had previously used to justify disclosure. Medical College Ally clearly understood that regardless of their reason, my approval was still required.

On the Wednesday afternoon, just as I was reaching for my phone to notify the *SafetySpace* app of my departure from Satellite Hospital, I received a follow-up email from Medical College Ally.

The Email I Received From Medical College Ally

Dear Paige,

I'm currently working on our application for you for the Diversity and Inclusion Inspiring Person Award. The application requires that I collect evidence of your achievements, and I was hoping you could assist me with that. My sincere apologies if you've already sent some of it previously; I've lost a bit of time looking, so thought I'd be more efficient by going directly to the source.

I don't suppose you have a copy of the presentation slides you provide to students at the start of the year for orientation? What was the book that you provided to senior leaders in your work area? And do you have any written feedback from them? Also, I'd appreciate any other tangible evidence of the work you do toward your World Changing Goals. Evidence could include emails, photos, and presentation slides. Anything at all that could serve as proof for the submission.

We need to submit the application pretty soon, so if it is possible for you to please send me anything you may have within the next few days, that would be amazing. After I work out what can be used, I want to get it sent off, so I can get back to focusing on a few other things. Really sorry to ask, and that it's so last minute!

Kind Regards,
Medical College Ally

My immediate emotional response to the request was repulsion. I already hated how much I had to talk up my achievements in order to be visible enough to prompt the change in the world that I wanted to see. This request seemed like a whole new level of self-promotion that felt... Well, the single best word I can think of is *ugly*. So instead of replying, I shut down my computer, locked the office, and set off for the bus stop.

Because I was back to living in the home of one of my best friends who had two small children, instead of heading straight home, I decided to take myself out to a quiet dinner. I chose a reasonably empty dumpling restaurant, and scanned the menu as I considered Medical College Ally's request. What I landed on as far as decisions, was spicy chicken dumplings to start with, and a short email that I promptly wrote and sent to Medical College Ally.

My Email To Medical College Ally

Dear Medical College Ally,

I'll forward a few emails shortly and tomorrow. It feels a bit weird. It is I hope obvious that I don't do any of these things with the intention of gathering evidence, rather it's to prompt the change I'd like to see in the world. There are, however, a few things that I can provide you with.

Attached is a photo of Outer Shell. This is the book that I provided to the Organizational Unit Head, as well as several staff of Satellite Hospital where I am currently working. I'm actually heading to your campus to field gender identity related questions this Thursday evening, and could drop a copy of the book off for you before that.

If you'd like me to, please let me know, what is the latest time, and where do I go? I've got to be at the event by 5:30.

Cheers,
Paige

While I was waiting for my food to arrive, I remembered that Hospital Companion had sent me a text when they had finished reading *Outer Shell*. I found the text, took a screen shot, and it became the next piece of evidence collected. Then I remembered two different doctors had written me letters of endorsement that included my involvement with the LGBTIQAP+ community. These were easy to find and add to the collection.

"Your spicy chicken gyoza," a young Japanese woman told me as she gracefully slid a tray of food onto the table in front of me.

"Thank you," I said.

As I struggled to pick up the first dumpling with chopsticks, I recalled that I'd been photographed while speaking on a panel on Intersectional Feminism. The photo had been posted on social media by a mutual acquaintance, so I dropped the dumpling and scrolled through their account to find the image, then added it to my mounting evidence. I whisked up the dumpling again and quickly popped it in my mouth, before returning to social media where I found myself tagged in an assortment of other relevant photos.

List of Other Relevant Photos

1. *Networking for Intersectionality Advocates*
2. *Speaking on LGBTIQAP+ Mentoring*
3. *Moderating a Workplace Diversity Panel*
4. *Celebrating at a Pride Festival*

I dropped my phone for a moment to focus on eating the next dumpling more slowly. The texture was pleasing; soft and almost rubbery on the outside, with crispy bits where it had been pan-fried. The meaty center was reminiscent of mince rissoles that Parental Being had made me on many occasions. I felt a pang of sadness that this whole side of my life was a secret I kept from Parental Being, because I feared it would upset them, rather than bringing them joy. Perhaps if I won the award, I could help other parents be prouder of having a child that was a bit different. There was a third dumpling that I left to cool.

I then trawled my work emails. I found the one where I'd come out to my former supervisor, and asked permission to do the same with the rest of the team. Then of course there was a positive reply, my email to the team, and several beautiful responses from my former colleagues. When I searched through a different account, I found an email with a copy of the medical student orientation presentation, where one of the slides noted my LGBTIQAP+ ally status.

Then I remembered the email from a medical student who approached me about being a *Living, Bleeding Book*, and their related social media post that included a photo of me. I was then confronted with my retaliation email to the person who had emailed a large number of staff about gender language education being *Political Correctness Gone Mad*, and finally the letter I'd sent to Relevant Academic about the medical curriculum.

"I've been more active than I realized," I said aloud.

"Can I help you with something else?"

"Oh, could I have more of the same, please?"

While I waited for my next round of spicy chicken dumplings to arrive, I sent off all my evidence to Medical College Ally, feeling temporarily confident that I was doing enough to help the community. Well, almost enough. I couldn't shake the feeling that I wasn't being honest enough with my family. Goodness knows, they never missed an opportunity to tell me all about the work they did for The Church.

When I logged in to my emails the following morning, I saw that I had a new email from Medical College Ally, to which I replied immediately, because something occurred to me that caused panic.

The Email From Medical College Ally

Thank you Paige!

That's really great. I understand completely, and know that you don't have that intent or disposition. I feel incredibly awkward asking, because I feel like I am making work for you, as well as creating the overall awkwardness! Hopefully it is all worth it and you get recognized by this award. You definitely deserve it! :)

Medical College Ally

My Immediate Response to the Email From Medical College Ally Because I Felt Panic

Good morning Medical College Ally,

Sorry for all the emails last night. I trust your discretion with not widely distributing emails people have sent me. If there's anything you need me to make sense of, let me know. I thought it also worth showing you my office space (attached) and breaking down the strategy behind it:

The pile of books at the front are where visitors sit. One book is a copy of my first book Outer Shell which is about my life leading up until gender affirmation surgery. It includes intimate thoughts surrounding identity confusion, denial, and the medical treatment journey required. Several students and clinicians have prompted conversations because of it being there, and gone on to read the book. This is the same book I've provided to several academics, as well as professional staff. Everyone has returned in person to express appreciation for broadening their perspective.

The wall behind me is what visitors see while chatting to me. Apart from the obvious LGBTIQAP+ Ally poster and rainbow watercolor skeleton that was painted for me by a medical student, there are photos, including a lot from my work with Intersectionality Advocates. This also prompts some conversations – sometimes even weird questions like 'what does the Q stand for, because I thought queer was a slur?' There are also copies of my other books (Inner Demons, Synthesis and Isolated Moving Human Target) that explore the many different parts of life after transitioning, including health, travel, family, dating, and work.

There are so many little, sustainable things we can do to our offices as allies to go a bit beyond visibility, and to welcome discussions that really need to be happening. I really feel that my office has become a genuine safe space where people feel comfortable to be themselves, leaving social masks at the door.

Thanks again for considering me for this. Hopefully it will lead to helping many more people who don't yet feel adequately supported or able to be their authentic selves at work! :)

Cheers,
Paige

"I'm going to do what I should have done long ago," I said aloud for nobody to hear. And with that, I wrote a more honest update about my life, and sent it to My Immediate Family; Parental Being and My Sibling.

Email to My Immediate Family

Dear Parental Being and My Sibling,

I'm still happily bouncing around from house to house looking after pets, which feels much more natural to me than sticking to one place. These days I live out of a combination of a suitcase, and a rucksack. Sort of cheating though, as I have some things at work, but I've never needed to access them. Something that has changed is that I've got a Post Office Box so that people can get in touch the old fashioned way if they need to (which banks and the Government seem to feel is important hahaha). If you ever need to post anything to me, see below –
Ms Paige Wilcox
PO Box ▮
City ▮ *QLD 40*▮
With work, things are very different now, and I don't know how much you know or I've told you.
At Satellite Hospital, I've worked hard to create a safe, inclusive environment so medical students there feel well supported, particularly in relation to their mental health. This includes a 'Wellness Station' outside my office where they can color in pictures of hearts and bones to relax, or read through literature about mental health and seeking support when struggling. It feels like a really beautiful thing to be a part of, and students have expressed their appreciation through cards and gifts, so I know it's working! I've attached a photo so you can see what it looks like.
As far as volunteer work, I am doing a lot to help improve things for women like me, who have grown up different and struggled through issues with identity, health, and social transitions. I'm now the Queensland Director of a not-for-profit organization that has a free mentoring program, so people like me for example, can provide guidance to someone younger, and hopefully navigate these issues with less pain for all involved. It's been incredibly rewarding to be a part of nurturing people who can be 'outsiders' to society, often forgotten about or mistreated.
Joining both The Medical College, and my volunteer work, I've been doing a few different things. Firstly, working with a Relevant Academic to address issues in the medical curriculum. This evening I will be a 'Living, Bleeding Book' for medical students, who can 'borrow' me to have important discussions about providing sensitive, responsible healthcare to people like me. Next month I will be meeting with a General Practitioner to have a similar discussion, which is something I've done with a few different doctors now. I've also been invited to speak on the topic a few times at different events.
As you can probably see, I am leading a rich life, and feel no disadvantage for having no romantic partner, home, or possessions. :)
Looking forward to seeing you all later in the month.

Cheers,
Paige

It felt especially brave putting myself out there in this way, particularly with the knowledge of how hard My Immediate Family had fought to prevent Australia from achieving Marriage Equality. That in mind, I was incredibly surprised by the response that I received from Parental being.

Parental Being's Response

Glad you're keeping up the family tradition of helping people who are in need.

As in all similar occasions, my response was to weep, and to make another bold move. Although I didn't feel ready, and I doubted my ability to succeed, I gathered evidence that had been used for Medical College Ally's award submission. I then put together an application to be the new CEO of Intersectionality Advocates.

Part Two
(Package No. 10 to No. 18)

10. Aftermath
11. Mental
12. Evidence (b)
14. Slasher
15. Skin
16. Transpecific
17. Farewell
18. Promise

Aftermath

(Package No. 10)

Containing...

...consequences.

IT'S THAT DEBILITATING NAUSEA you get when you're experiencing severe fear, and it comes with sweat, which for me is rare. The sweat that is; I'm frequently in situations that cause me severe fear. For just a moment, I can't move. I'm just staring at the computer monitor, reading the words over and over. Just two words, and words that have never before been the cause of emotion like this. But here we are, and there they are.

'It's live!'

As I read the words again, I realize there are more words that probably should have more of an impact on my emotional state. It's the following words that cause me to realize something I naively hadn't thought of earlier. They're the words of Markety Mark.

'We'll start pushing it on our social media accounts shortly,' Markety Mark has told me in an email.

My phone lights up with a notification.

'I had no idea you were doing that,' Friendly Entity is telling me. 'I'm really proud of you.'

Little time passes before there's another.

'Oh, Paige, that is such a brave thing to do,' Bosom Buddy informs me.

'I'm sure you're very busy, but I just wanted to tell you that I admire you. What you're doing is so important, and I understand how much of a sacrifice it is.'

That last one is from Simmering Spectacle, and it brings a modest tear to my eye, moments before the torrent begins. For once the word torrent isn't describing full-fledged tears. What I'm referring to, is contact based on the social media push. I flick back through the previous emails, and take a moment to read over the article I was asked to write a while back. Back when I was waiting for the plane home from Canberra.

THE ARTICLE FOR THE MEDICAL COLLEGE

My name is Paige. At age 35, I'm a Student Coordinator for the The Medical College at Satellite Hospital, the Queensland Director of Intersectionality

Advocates, and I live a life of sobriety, without a fixed address. As you might expect, the road I travelled to get here is not typical, and it is that journey I would like you to know about in more detail. Perhaps 'need' is a better word than 'like'.

I'll point out that since heading toward the next paragraph of disclosure, my heartbeat has steadily increased in both speed and strength, the skin on my arms and face has become warm and red, and the device upon which I'm typing is gripped tightly using two hands to steady the shaking. This violent physical reaction is due to decades of language and behavior that reinforced that my truth is a negative one.

Here goes...

Because of my rural-Church upbringing, I suffered with an unknown condition until age 19. I finally sought medical advice after moving to Brisbane, and was diagnosed with gender dysphoria. Essentially, this means I was raised as the opposite gender (male), and at 19 I went through a series of psychological, pharmaceutical and surgical treatments to become visibly female.

You may have heard this simplified to the labels 'trans' and 'transgender'.

For several reasons, I generally don't label myself in this way. Those terms have been used in the past to invalidate my gender, disclose my personal history without my consent, and there has been a lot of stigma attached to them. Who I am is far more than the gender transition I went through once, and outside the context of receiving healthcare, the trans label is one that I view as completely unnecessary. Referring to me as female, woman, girl, chick works fine socially and at work.

I'm simply a woman who had a slightly different journey to get here.

When looking for employment after transitioning to female almost 20 years ago, I faced a difficult choice. It was between disclosing that I'd undergone gender affirmation, and pretending I had no history of work or education. I decided that it would look more favorably to hide the gender stuff. In 2018, I sadly feel that this would still be the case for job applications outside of The Medical College.

Despite that, between then and now, I've progressively become more open at The Medical College because:

workplace gossip and internet searches have disclosed my past in undignified ways;

hiding had a long term severe, negative impact on my mental health (and sick leave required);

the effort to hide my past was detrimental to the quality of work achievable; and

I want to prove to young trans people that they can be themselves AND thrive.

With respect to the above, the workplace journey to 2018 has been nothing short of harrowing. However I'm now in a place where most of my colleagues know of my past gender transition, and I'm treated with both dignity, and respect. This is something I hadn't dared to fantasize as possible. I feel strongly that it would not have been possible without the tireless efforts of the The Medical College Ally Program and The Medical College in general actively promoting diversity and inclusion.

Now that my words are out there, specifically pushed in the direction of people who are only connected to me through work, I can't help but consider each sentence that could be more eloquently phrased. My heartbeat takes over with a solo drum performance, and I'm momentarily transported elsewhere as the world around me seemingly falls away. I slowly manage to progressively take longer, deeper breaths, reality returns, and my mobile device takes focus.

The device continues to light up with messages of support from friends, colleagues, and acquaintances. Social media notifications become unmanageable, and emails begin to trickle in. Although I don't see and respond to everything, what I receive seems to be exclusively positive. At a glance, I don't notice anything negative whatsoever. This has both a warming and calming effect on my heart.

Before I can overthink it, I write and send an email to Parental Being and My Sibling that includes a link to the article. It's important that I continue to shamelessly push for them to view me as I am, and for them to recognize my efforts and resultant achievements of which I am most proud. After all, they've never expected any less from me.

Time starts to move at an unusually fast pace, as I juggle my workload with positive attention about the article. This attention is all from a distance, through emails, messages, and social media. Viewing in solitude from my desk at Satellite Hospital, I'm reminded of the time I sat in front of a television watching my home being swallowed up by a brown ocean. None of it feels real.

"Hey Paige," a medical student says, startling me.

A day has somehow passed as though it has been no time at all. I see that the student is standing hesitantly in the doorway, awaiting permission to cross the threshold into my office.

"Oh, hi, come in!"

"I don't need your help with anything," they say quickly. "I just wanted to say that I saw your article last night. What you've done is really brave. Also, I would really like it if I could borrow one of the copies of *Outer Shell* I've seen in your office."

Of course I'm beaming as I seamlessly swivel, reach out, pick up a copy of *Outer Shell*, swivel back, and present it to the medical student. I recall how bashful I had been the previous year when students had asked about my writing. What had once seemed terrifying, I realize, is now... exciting. And this realization, it is nothing less than wonderful.

"I might not get a chance to finish it before I leave," the student admits as they flip through the pages. Again, witnessing this action is a positive experience that once was the cause of anxiety.

"You're welcome to keep it," I offer. "Or pass it on when you're done. I've a few spare copies."

"Thank you," they tell me, then they leave.

Several days later, I meet in person with Relevant Academic regarding LGBTIQAP+ representation in the curriculum. My energy restored, I send what feels like a brave follow-up to ensure I will be appropriately utilized by The Medical College. Not for my career, but to creep even closer to my World Changing Goals.

The Next Letter to Relevant Academic

Dear Relevant Academic,

Thank you for taking the time to speak with me this morning.

To reiterate what was discussed, I will gladly be on any review committee for tutorial cases and other medical program resources. I agree that LGBTIQAP+ and Mental Health content should be represented throughout various parts of the curriculum, as there is some crossover.

If there is any opportunity for practical workshops, I'd love to offer my experience gained from clinical examination planning and coordination, as a Simulated Patient for Paramedics, with LGBTIQAP+ and Mental Health issues, as well as training design and facilitation. The biggest notable gap in my ability is that I'm not a medical doctor.

Regarding the 'office foyer' that I mentioned, I've attached a photo that is in two parts:

1. Pictured at the top is outside my office. It's a small desk that promotes seeking help, offers a variety of support options and contacts, as well as some anatomical adult coloring to calm nerves while people wait. The increasing colors on paper, and mention of it by students when they visit, is confirmation that this is a part of the Satellite Hospital Student Experience that has been appreciated.

2. Pictured below is inside my office, next to my desk. I've a selection of things for people to fidget with and look at while they chat to me. There are also things like tissues and chocolates to complete the welcoming, safe feel of the environment. Students have expressed that they enjoy stopping by for a casual chat, and feel welcome to voice concerns that I can either address, or forward on as appropriate.

It would be worthwhile seeing if spaces like this could become standard across all clinical sites to change the culture of perceiving seeking help as something that is scary, or bad in any way (for example, a sign of being a weak student). After initial set up, there is very little maintenance required. Since creating these spaces, I do think more students have felt that they are welcome to reach out, and that The Medical College will support them when they do.

If there's anything else you think I can be a part of, please do let me know. Until then, I'll await contact regarding the above that I've already put my hand up for. Although I'm confident it can fit in with my current workload, I'm also willing to volunteer time, as there is some cross-over with what I already try to achieve outside of The Medical College. That is, involvement in this area fulfils both professional and person goals.

Thanks again for your time, it was really great to catch up.

Yours Sincerely,
Paige

There's a gentle knock on my open office door, followed by the equally soft voice of an elderly woman.

"Hello, Paige?"

I look up from my computer to see a Satellite Hospital employee that I frequently see in the corridors. She never fails to smile at me, and I've always wondered if she would still be so friendly if she was aware of my past. Something that has stopped me from disclosure, has been an awareness that she shares a religion with Parental Being. It is that religion that has been consistently used as a reason to reject who I am.

"Oh, hello," I say warmly, though I feel slightly panicked. "What brings you down my way?"

"I get The Medical College Newsletter," she tells me. "So I came to congratulate you on your article. It's very well written."

"Thank you," I tell her, surprised by the knowledge of yet another avenue of distribution.

"I can't stay, but I wanted to let you know that. You should be very proud."

As soon as she leaves, I notice yet another email that's been prompted by the social media push. This particular email has come in from someone with a familiar name, but familiar for what reason, I can't recall. I think I'll call them… Surprise Ally.

The email from Surprise Ally begins with mention of a heartfelt written piece I had distributed the year before to everyone in The Medical College Ally Program, of which Surprise Ally is a member. The body of the email provides details of conversations they have had with their family because of my brave, assertive words, and I am commended for my efforts in general.

It isn't until I reach the final sentence of Surprise Ally's email that I know of their motive. The email has been leading up to an invitation to give the Keynote address at a mentoring event at the main campus of The University. Surprise Ally tells me that there will be representatives not just from The Medical College, but from all sectors of the wider University. What Surprise Ally would like, is for me to speak about using intentional storytelling as a vehicle for mentoring. With my specific experience, it will be a speaking gig that will fit me better than anything I've ever done before.

As fate would have it, not only is the mentoring event timed with one of my pre-planned long weekends, but I've not yet booked any flights. I promptly accept the invitation, feeling pleased by how life is going, at least in terms of movement toward my World Changing Goals. There's still this feeling though that I could be doing more in terms of improving the healthcare situation for people in the LGBTIQAP+ community. I lean back in my chair and allow my mind to travel back in time to the event where I had been a *Living, Bleeding Book*.

Mental
(Package No. 11)

Containing a nightmare,
and a conversation.

A CHROME ELEVATOR APPEARED IN THE DARK PLACE. On the other side of me, a shadowy dog-like being named Vulpine Foe materialized. Snarling, it backed me into the elevator, and we were suddenly locked in together. Vulpine Foe advanced in a threatening manner, its teeth bared, saliva gathering. When the doors opened, it gave me a firm nudge with its snout, and I involuntarily shuddered.

The elevator transformed into a thick, black smoke before it vanished, and Vulpine Foe followed suit.

Standing alone in the dark place, I saw that in my hand a letter had appeared. It was a formal report of events that had occurred. Official Officer appeared before me suddenly, took the letter, then vanished, only to reappear some distance from me. I saw Vulpine Foe appear, and hold up a paw to Official Officer, who tapped the paw in reprimand. Vulpine Foe shot a look in my direction, then sauntered off in the other, howling mournfully.

Patches of black smoke started to appear in several directions, from which other shadowy dog-like beings materialized. They moved in on me, snarling and barking. Official Officer appeared, and the shadowy beings vanished. Official Officer vanished, and the shadowy beings reemerged.

In the distance the large pages of a year calendar flipped, indicating the passing of many months as the beings continued to threaten me whenever Official Officer was not present.

As time passed, I started to shrink, becoming smaller, and smaller, until I was a puddle of water.

-V-

I WAS RECOVERING FROM A WAVE of exhaustion when my fourth reader had extended his hand to greet me, and I remember I had almost replied with:

> 'Sorry! Can we chat in the break? I'm due to be read by another student just now.'

It was fortunate that my tiredness had caused me to become too slow to speak before he did. In my tired state, I was likely to transform a mildly awkward situation into one that was quite uncomfortable.

"Hey Paige, it's a pleasure to meet you," he said warmly in an accent that reminded me of the part of my childhood that took place in North Queensland. "I'm The Fourth."

Rather than responding with words, I stood to shake The Fourth's hand, then gestured for him to sit down. His movements were slow in a way that was relaxed, and how he looked at me was with measured curiosity. In his presence, I felt calm.

"Sorry if I'm vague at all," I apologized. "All these conversations are starting to tire me out, and I missed my last break."

My thoughts felt disjointed, and I knew that he could tell. I'd heard that the eyes of some men could indicate high intelligence, and it felt to me that The Fourth served as proof of this. His intelligence, I could tell, was not purely academic in nature. I watched his silent consideration that came before the spoken word.

"Well," he said slowly. "I had been considering some pretty heavy questions, but you're welcome to pass on any of them."

"I appreciate that," I said, smiling weakly. "What would you like to know?"

"Considering the mental health needs of transgender patients, mostly," The Fourth told me.

Mental health was a topic close to my heart, and I was faced with a dilemma. Conversations about mental health were important, especially with medical students who could in turn educate their friends. I was mindful though, that with tiredness my emotional state had become more vulnerable. I took a deep, slow breath in, then let it out even more slowly, in an attempt to get a little more oxygen to my brain. It was a technique that I'd used to continue to perform well during moments of anxiety.

"Um, okay, well something you might not realize," I started. "Is that it's typical for mental health issues in transgender patients to be more substantial by the time they're first in a doctor's office."

"I'd heard that," The Fourth said thoughtfully. "Do you know why that is?"

"Humans have a long history of pathologizing diversity," I said snidely.

"Pathologizing?"

"It goes back to gatekeeping," I said. "There's a lot of upcoming change in this space, but... take me for example. Actual mental health issues aside, when I spoke to a doctor about how my gender identity didn't match my assigned sex, I was diagnosed as having the mental health disorder *gender dysphoria*."

The Fourth silently considered what I'd told him, before making his confusion known.

"I'm not sure I understand the problem," he confessed.

"Well it can feel like your whole identity is pathologized, like you're permanently broken from your core. Really, there's this discomfort with the disconnection between our identity and our body, and we just need to find that physical sweet spot. For me, it included hormones, a social gender transition, and surgery. But am I still considered unwell? I still don't identify with my birth sex, so is who I am a terminal illness?"

"I sort of understand," The Fourth said softly. "I'll do some reading about this on my own later."

The Fourth retrieved a small beige notepad and a pencil from the pocket of the dark tan leather jacket he was wearing. He made some private notes, then slipped the paper and pencil back into his jacket pocket.

"Anyway," I continued. "Resultant mistreatment can cause us to be reluctant to seek help, particularly if it's for reasons of mental health. By the time we do, things have usually progressed quite far."

The Fourth nodded.

"Yeah, I've had my own setbacks," he told me. "It's why I'm in med school so late in life. I probably wouldn't even be here now if it wasn't for help with a place that was only open to Aboriginal and Torres Strait Islander people."

"Ah," I said. "Is that difficult?"

The Fourth grinned at me.

"The mental health, the age, or the race aspect?"

"So many intersecting identities at play," I laughed. "Age is what I was asking about. Don't worry, I won't ask you anything about your health, mental or otherwise."

"All good," The Fourth said warmly. "Sometimes it can be a bit isolating, because I've got more family responsibilities, and I don't drink like a typical med student. My peers tend to exclude me a bit because of that, but it allows me the time and energy I need to focus on maintaining good grades."

The Fourth looked down at his feet before continuing.

"I feel like there's a bit more pressure on me to prove my worth than those who took a more typical pathway into Medicine."

"I understand," I said, nodding. "People tend to assume you only made it so far because you used a diversity card that caused someone more deserving to miss out…"

"Yeah, you get it," he said, mimicking my nod.

"Anything else you'd like to know about my situation?"

The Fourth again took out his notepaper. He studied it for a while, then slipped it back into the pocket that was its home.

"I've written a note about trauma-informed primary care. But I'm not sure where I was going with it."

"Ah, well that's essentially an understanding that a patient can present with complex trauma histories with interpersonal, social, and medical…"

"Oh," he said, cutting me off. "Yeah I won't waste your time with that one. Are there any mental health concerns that tend to be experienced by a lot of transgender patients?"

"Okay, so of course this is in addition to the background rates of common mood disorders that are seen in the general population, but off the top of my head, generalized anxiety, post-traumatic stress disorder, substance abuse…"

How long have I been sober? Has it been two years yet? Going strong, yet I've still found myself in situations I'd previously blamed on intoxication. Still I seem unable to keep myself safe from some men… and myself.

"Alright," The Fourth said, interrupting my downward mental spiral. "Something a bit lighter. Maybe this is working backwards, but I'm curious about transgender patients having that first discussion with a doctor, when they realize that their identity doesn't align with the sex they were assigned at birth."

"First things first," I said gratefully. "Is they've got to come out. This is something that can be pretty challenging for the patient."

The patient. Why am I othering it?

"How so?"

"Remember they may have come out to a lot of people with our without their consent. Their anxiety could be about that, rather than you as a person. It's typical that from a distance they've seen negative feedback about transgender people in the media and online. They've likely also had related experiences where they've been mistreated, harassed, marginalized, or been subject to intrusive questions and violence. It's important to be mindful of all that."

My eyes started to sting.

"What can a doctor do to make a patient feel safe and comfortable when they come out?"

A dam in my throat was causing saliva to pool.

"You could reinforce their self-identification, confirm their pronouns, clearly and sensitively explain why certain anatomical information is needed, prior to asking for it. And be honest early about knowledge gaps, which might mean finding someone to refer them on to."

The Fourth nodded thoughtfully.

"Say I was a General Practitioner, and one of my regular patients just happened to be transgender. What sort of mental health stuff should I be thinking about with routine check-ups?"

Has the temperature in the room increased?

"Screening for co-occurring mental health conditions, past treatments, and history of suicide and self-injurious behaviors… And, uh, substance use and symptoms of posttraumatic stress…."

There is surely less air in the room than before.

"Really," I force out. "I think any primary care provider should be well equipped to handle the basic mental health needs of transgender patients like depression and anxiety, just as they would any other patient."

My face is becoming red, I can feel it.

"I agree with you completely, Paige. This is all really helpful."

I took a deep breath in, and let it out slowly. My face started to cool, and I could see The Fourth carefully considering his next question. I wondered if he had also done the *Mental Health First Aid* course I'd completed a few years earlier.

"And what about other mental health stuff? The things that aren't so basic?"

"It's best to be honest, and refer them to a clinician who is experienced with both mental health and transgender health. Sometimes a patient will be able to provide a name, but it's worth having your own list ready, or to know where to look quickly."

"From what you've said, it seems as though a lot of mental health problems in transgender patients are directly related to stigma. Are there other things that transgender people tend to experience that could affect their mental health, besides stigma?"

"Well, they're more likely to live in poverty, be victims of violence, lose their family, and home."

They are more likely? We are more likely.

"Statistics change a bit based on their intersecting identities, and there's not that much data available for Australia. I guess that could be traced back to stigma too. Anyway, it's a good idea to assess for housing, food, financial, and safety concerns, both in living and work environments."

Tears began to build in my eyes as I thought about aspects of my life that had been especially difficult because of the stigma attached to my past. I felt angry that every single part of my life had been affected at one time or another, and some still were.

"Keep going," I whispered, because although it hurt to talk about it, I knew the conversation with The Fourth was important. He would become a compassionate doctor who could help, and he immediately proved himself by swiftly and smoothly producing a new line of questioning.

"For initiating hormone therapy, is there some sort of process that needs to be followed?"

I wiped away a stray tear that was the product of both Hope and Pain fighting to simultaneously reside within me side by side despite their differences.

"Yeah, basically informed consent these days I think. Previously standards of care required the presence of formally diagnosed gender dysphoria, and endorsement from a psychologist, but there's a bit of change going on in that area. In any case it's still important that the patient be fully aware of all risks, so they can make an informed choice. Their health literacy obviously comes into play here, but you might find that trans people have a better understanding of their health than the rest of the population, because they feel like they have to…"

I stopped myself short to make an important correction.

"*We* feel like we have to."

"Why is that?"

"Lack of adequately trained medical professionals. Even with simple things like misgendering and deadnaming…"

"That's something I was wondering about," The Fourth said. "I sometimes see posts about it on social media and I've never been sure of why it's such a big deal. Am I right in thinking that deadnaming is using your birth name?"

I nodded, and took a deep breath.

"For me, until I was 19, I had to go by a name and gender that felt wrong to me. That hurt every moment of every day that it came into play in social interactions. After I finally came out as female, and chose a name that felt right, being incorrectly referred to hurt even more. Especially when it was a deliberate refusal of my identity, but even when it was done accidentally. It's strongly associated with 19 years of feeling traumatized by something I couldn't fully understand. A struggle in which I was completely alone in facing. I've been so deeply affected that even in my books, I had to censor the name ▮▮▮▮▮▮▮ (pronounced: Blank)."

Tears started to fall from my eyes, and I could see that The Fourth was hesitant to continue. His hand disappeared into his jacket and this time he retrieved a small pack of disposable tissues. He offered them to me.

"Please ignore my tears," I begged as I took a tissue and dabbed below my eyes. "I do really want to talk to you about all this, because I feel that these conversations are important in helping us get to a better place."

The Fourth nodded, but didn't say anything for a while. He noticed a wastepaper basket within his reach, so shifted it to my side. I dropped the used tissue in.

"Do you have any advice," he said finally. "For dealing with a patient who may have been through all of this?"

I took a moment to think. The Fourth was waiting for my response with patient eagerness.

"Something we really need, is to ensure that most doctors, at the very least, have enough training in the area to communicate with us with respect, honesty, and compassion."

I looked into The Fourth's eyes, and something occurred to me.

"You listened, respectfully sought clarification, patiently kept us moving forward, and redirected when you noticed me struggling. I really don't think you'll have a problem dealing with someone like me as a patient."

By the final word, my pain had faded to a point of me wondering if I'd really been all that upset in the first place.

"If I was in a position to help others…" The Fourth started. "Are there any specific areas you think need addressing more urgently? People within your community who have a more difficult time?"

I smiled at The Fourth.

"People with different abilities, like those who are confined to a wheelchair, who might need a caregiver with that same basic training. And people who have difficulty with communicating articulately, whether for reasons of health or linguistic diversity."

"Anything else?"

"People in regional areas. In the city we complain about having to seek out doctors we know will deal well with us, but in many parts of Australia, travel to another town or city is required."

Ding ding ding!

"Alright, Paige," The Fourth said. "Thank you for being so obliging. I'll definitely do what I can to help your community, and see if I can urge some of my peers to do the same."

We shook hands, and he left me to sit alone in a warm, appreciative glow. I was blushing.

Evidence (b)

(Package No. 12)

*Containing a premonition,
and a reflection.*

"Do you regret it?"

I am too stressed in the moment to be amused by how often I am on the receiving end of this question. Does it say more about me or the general public that it's the first thing so many people now think to ask? I ponder the question deeply, and consider how my response will affect Important Human. The article certainly has changed the situation.

"Not in the slightest," is what I decide to say. "Although I do wish I'd spent a bit more time on writing and editing it."

Important Human gestures to the other staff members in the room. There are some familiar faces, but most of these representatives from every institute and faculty across the university are strangers to me. Most of them already know who I am, and those who don't are about to. Intimately.

"Is it weird for you that some of these people in the room are finding out about your gender history right now, while you're standing here?"

"A little bit," I confess.

It's not entirely a new situation for me though, I think, considering the times I've been approached about my past at parties and nightclubs, by people who had been told by attendees and patrons.

"It doesn't feel as unsafe as some previous social situations though," I add. "At least coming out on stage doesn't seem like such a big deal."

I look around the room and notice someone glance at me, then back at the piece of paper they are holding. I notice them repeat the motion. I note that most people are just chatting to each other, taking advantage of the social aspect of a work event that has brought together a broad collection of colleagues. As my eyes continue to scan the room, I consider how, just a little further into the future, all of these people will be my audience.

Only one thing could make this more awkward, I think.

And then, like the complete opposite of serendipity, I see what I had hoped desperately that I wouldn't. That one thing that I had thought could make this situation even more uncomfortable for me. I see skin that—as some private joke that I don't think either of us remember—I'd previously described as The Instigator in a blog, and then a book series.

"Excuse me," I tell Important Human, suddenly anxious. "There's someone I need to talk to."

"Okay, I'll find us a seat," they tell me.

As I approach, The Instigator spins to face me. Her face is as radiant as the time she'd drunkenly confessed to carrying out an internet search of my name. I think back to my heated drunken reaction, and the letter of apology that started all this and caused me to name her The Instigator. I push aside my pointless feelings of shame, and The Instigator and I simultaneously open our arms then wrap each other up, squeeze, and release.

"Hey!" I shriek.

"Paige! I get to hear you speak!"

I gulp down the saliva that has built in my throat.

"About that," I say. "I'm reading from a chapter in one of my books."

The Instigator seems suddenly even more excited.

"Oh, which one?"

"It's…" I hesitate, and like the sign for *continually* in Auslan, I gesture with my hands in a repeated circular back and forth motion.

"…the story of us."

"Oh," she murmurs.

"I have a backup," I offer. "But it's not as good an example of intentional storytelling, which is what I've been asked to speak on."

We stand together in silence for a moment, and my body temperature steadily rises until worry causes me to break the silence lest I explode.

"But I'll only tell our story if it's okay with you."

Of course I have a preference, and hope that she will be obliging, but… *You must respect her preference here*, I scold myself.

"Did you want to point me out in the audience?"

The Instigator's response causes me to let out something between a laugh and a gasp.

"No! Of course not. I just don't want to make you too uncomfortable. It's an intense story."

"Read it, it's fine," she confirms.

Just a little further into the future, Important Human and I sit together in the front row. We listen to an acknowledgement of the traditional custodians of the land, which is followed by a short spiel about how the event will unfold.

"There'll be a keynote talk on intentional storytelling, a series of 3 minute talks on how different fields are approaching mentoring, then specialty break-out groups to bring ideas together and create."

Important Human nudges me when my name is called, prompting me to scoop up my battered copy of *Inner Demons*, jump up from my chair, and dance awkwardly onto the stage to tell the story of a defining moment in my life. On stage, my eyes are immediately drawn to The Instigator, and I find I have to work hard to find balance between staring and obviously avoiding eye contact altogether.

My interest is piqued by an email upon return to work. It is the first of a second round of emails from a doctor—a General Practitioner—who was told about me through one of her patients. I think back to the first email I'd received, and how I'd agreed to arrange to meet her for a discussion.

In the first round of emails the GP and I hadn't managed to arrange to meet due to being two very busy people. They seem intent on trying again, which is fortunate because I realize that my social life has become entirely reactive. There's also an imbalance I've not previously noted. Because the only people I see are those who've reached out to me, I've mostly been meeting with extroverts and people in crisis.

Returning to the GP's email, I note the presumptuous nature and chuckle. Curiosity causes me to read the middle section again.

Middle Section of the General Practitioner's Email

My daughter will also be with me. She's 9, has ASD, and is the archetypal absent minded but super-excited professor. Now, I figure for warned is for armed, so you need to know my daughter will ask you about medical and surgical gender transitioning. I know because she has already quizzed me about it at length. It goes back to the story in the book Rebel Girls *with the transgender girl. The story does talk about surgical transitioning and so my daughter naturally asked me every question relating to that. I figure if a child is asking a specific question then I should answer that question. So my kid now knows about medication that can be used to stop puberty until 16 years of age, and then a person can decide which gender they want to go through puberty as, and also about surgical gender reassignment. My daughter loves life and people, is super curious, and loves to learn. Just sometimes that can result in socially awkward moments and discussions. I feel like I am one indemnity clause after the next. I really hope you aren't too scared!*

By the time I reach the end of the email the second time, I can't help but think back to my childhood. How much pain could we all have been spared if Parental Being had been educated like this doctor? Even though we're heading toward a better place now, thoughts about difficulties with my family start to overshadow everything else. Before long, there are tears in my eyes, and I'm desperately trying to think of a way out of my despair.

Naturally, I think of the final email I'd received from Medical College Ally regarding submission for the Diversity & Inclusion Award.

Previous Email From Medical College Ally

Dear Paige,

Please find attached the draft award submission for the Diversity and Inclusion Award as an Inspiring Person. Please let me know if there is anything that you want changed or added. I am just waiting on one more reference who will be getting it to me tomorrow and then we are ready to submit tomorrow.

Kind regards,
Medical College Ally

Again I sift through the draft award submission, and look at evidence that was collected from elsewhere. All over again, I'm touched to be surprised with written endorsements by people I was unaware had been inspired by my work. Included was a woman I hadn't expected to remember me at all. I'd considered her to be quite brave when we had spoken on the same panel years earlier. Reading her words, I weep, but this time I'm feeling joy.

I read over the response that was sent not that long ago, though it feels that a lifetime has already passed.

Previous Email to Medical College Ally

Dear Medical College Ally,

Goodness, I couldn't get through that without a few tears. Some of the appreciation in that was quite a surprise (the CEO of Intersectionality Advocates for example!). It was a bit of an overwhelming read, so I'm really not sure what could be improved or adjusted.

Side note: I've since been a Living, Bleeding Book, and got to have 8 intensive discussions one-on-one with medical students about what being a trans woman means in terms of healthcare. We've got some incredibly compassionate, open-minded doctors headed for graduation in the next few years. Soon I'm going to write up fictional accounts of several of the conversations so people who weren't there are able to learn from them. It was an amazing event to be a part of.

Also this morning I got this funny email below from a General Practitioner that I plan to meet soon to help improve how she deals with patients who are trans women. The medical students felt like a really good practice run! I could forward you the email thread if you like. Not sure if it would count as mentoring?

Sorry for being so blabby! I'm just so excited that after so long I'm starting to feel like things are really starting to have an impact. :)

Cheers,
Paige

I lean back in my chair, and consider some of the things I've written to Medical College Ally and the General Practitioner. It feels as though I've had good intentions that I've gone nowhere with for quite some time. Surely there's a way that I can build on what was achieved with the medical students. There must be some way to boost my signal, and to reach more of the people who are in a position to create the change that our community needs.

Like a figurative lightbulb switching from dark to light, the idea is there, and I feel stupid for not having started on it sooner.

13

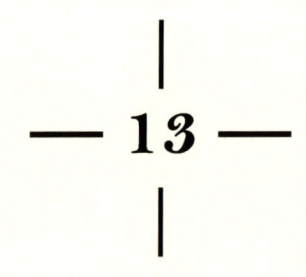

Slasher

(Package No. 14)

Containing a nightmare, and a conversation.

SHUDDERING IN THE DARK PLACE, *I was cowering in a vast expanse of nothingness, completely alone. It was painfully silent.*
   My own booming voice broke through.
   "You're obsessive."
   My eyes became moist.
   "You're an alcoholic."
   Tears formed.
   "You'll never be a real woman."
   Tears dropped.
   "And the majority will always see you as a freak."
   I flooded the dark place.

-V-

"IT'S AN ABSOLUTE HONOR, PAIGE," I heard my second last reader say confidently. "I'm Final Girl, and I'm sure it pleases you to know that we're almost at the end of the event."

Final Girl's beauty was describable as severe, yet enticing, but also dangerous. She made me think of Lucy Liu's character in *Kill Bill*, except with a dash of kindness seeping through her tough exterior. This was a woman capable of slicing her way through to whatever future she deemed worthy of her.

"Hi Final Girl," I said timidly, starting to sit.

"Do you mind if we stand? I've been sitting so much tonight, and I figure if we're standing, it's a lot more like a casual, social conversation. You'll find that much less threatening. Or intimidating. People say I'm both, but I don't mean to be."

I stood back up, and pushed my shoulders back in an attempt to seem confident in her presence.

"Sure thing, and you're right. I'm very much glad we're almost done. This has been far more taxing than I could have anticipated."

Final Girl made a clicking noise as she tilted her head. She manipulated the muscles of her face into an over the top expression of sympathy. The look more accurately said *incredulous*.

"Well, I'm sure you could have anticipated that, Paige," Final Girl teased. "It's not like you've never been assaulted with questions about this topic from a lot of strangers before."

I could tell that nothing false would ever wash with Final Girl, and felt envious of her apparent strength. She had the ability to go places I'd not dare to dream of. Perhaps with an attitude or manner like hers, I could move beyond roles that were merely support for more esteemed individuals.

"I hope I don't disappoint," I said weakly. "You seem like someone who would have prepared well for this conversation."

"I did a little digging," she confirmed.

Final Girl manipulated her fingers into the shape of a handgun, tilted it by about 45 degrees, then leant into it with her chin. Her final powerful pose was to rest her chin in her hand, with her elbow supporting from just above her hip. I marveled at how close it was to Connie's pose that had instead seemed delicate, reserved, and fearful.

"What is it you think I could talk you through?"

"I'm going to be a surgeon," Final Girl boasted. "Not sure exactly what kind, but definitely surgical."

Surgery was the direction I might have gone in, had there not been so many barriers preventing it. Sometimes when I hand sewed elaborate gowns, I fancied it was preparation for suturing skin. Aside from several camping emergency situations, I'd resigned to the unfortunate truth that my gowns were likely to be as close as I'd ever get. Final Girl disallowed my indulgence in self-pity through continuation of speech.

"I deliberately didn't research trans surgeries before this, because I'd like to hear what you have to say, and tailor my reading to knowledge gaps I identify by the end of our discussion. I'm a little worried about less specific searches returning pornographic results."

I was hesitant to say anything at all in reply. I wondered how many potential allies had come to me for information, for the very same reason. Perhaps I had been too hard on them for wanting to open up my wounds instead of taking to the internet to find answers without my help. Final Girl again tore me away from my relentless inner monologue.

"Why don't you start more… philosophically. I suppose."

"Sure. Uh…"

"Can you tell me about the relationship between… your community… and surgery that is directly related."

I appreciated that as a person who had a very direct communication style, Final Girl was putting a lot of effort into attempting tact. She was doing a better job than a lot of people had in the past, and my feeling of appreciation made it easier to be obliging.

"The first thing I would say," I told her. "Is that there are two major streams of surgeries. Essentially, surgery associated with a transition from male to female, and surgery associated with a transition from female to male."

Final Girl stared blankly at me, and I figured she was working hard to hold in the word, *obviously*. There was a teneseness around her eyes that I thought was perhaps an indication of struggle against an eye roll. I could tell that it was indeed a struggle that was real.

"On top of that, not all trans patients want the same surgeries, and some don't feel the need for any at all. There are many reasons for seeking surgery and they can include easing discomfort, meeting requirements for changing identification documents, and… safety."

Final Girl nodded at me to continue.

"For me—and this is the case for many women transitioning from male to female—the first surgery was a tracheal shave; removal of what people call an *Adam's Apple*. In my case, when I was required to present as female full-time to prove my authenticity in order to progress to the next stage, it had been the prominent neck feature that I felt was the only visible indicator to strangers that I'd been assigned male at birth."

Breathless, I rapidly filled my lungs to allow me to continue. Instead, it prompted a little dizziness that was at least short-lived.

"After the surgery, I was a lot less worried that strangers could tell. Beyond reactions that made me feel bad, it was a safety issue."

Final Girl scanned my face and body silently.

"Around the same time, to assist with social transition, other women elect to have various facial feminization surgeries. It could include shaving bone around the brow or jawline, or rhinoplasty if they perceive their nose to look male. My feelings about it are quite conflicting."

"How so?"

"So much of stuff like this is about how strangers perceive you. I think that's a problem. Those things shouldn't matter."

"Yet they do," Final Girl said. "And it's not limited to trans women. There are many ciswomen who undergo a variety of surgery for no reason other than appearance."

"It's more often a safety concern with trans women, though," I fought. "We're less likely to be physically assaulted when strangers can't tell."

Final Girl bit her lip, then swung her index finger from side to side, in the vague direction of my chest. I chose to answer the question she wanted to ask, but had held back. As with all readers previously, I deemed satiation of her curiosity to be of utmost importance.

"Some trans women choose to get a breast augmentation, but I didn't feel that the benefit would be worth it. These are just what grew there. Not quite the same size, and not the biggest, but I can pump them up with the right bra if I want to. Like many ciswomen, really."

Final Girl looked me directly in the eyes.

"Are you comfortable talking about lower surgery?"

I held her gaze.

"Yes," I said, and dove right in before I could chicken out. "There are a few different methods that involve an orchiectomy—or removal of the testicles—and a vaginoplasty, which is usually inversion of the penis."

Final Girl looked stunned by my brazen approach to answering what would normally be considered an invasive question about a sensitive topic. I boldly pushed forward while I still felt confident enough to do so.

"It's quite impressive how they work with what's there to create everything from labia to a working clitoris," I said, as if I was mentioning a marvelous operation that could have been performed on any human.

Final Girl gulped. I refused to feel shame, and maintained steady eye contact with her.

"Indeed," Final Girl said. "Though I imagine there is substantial risk, and some or all parts might not work out as hoped?"

"Correct. I was fortunate that the only issue I have is a little scarring, and you need to be staring at it under good lighting to really notice. Anyone in that position would have already seen my more prominent scars that are completely unrelated."

"So fortunate," Final Girl laughed. "I'm glad you're able to admit your privilege within a marginalized group."

"It's helpful for understanding how to help those who need it most urgently," I explained.

Final Girl broke our eye contact to look at someone else in the room. I was reminded that we were in a room full of people who were either medical students like Final Girl, or *Living, Bleeding Books*, like myself. This was my seventh discussion, and each time it had been as though we were conversing with complete privacy. We weren't though, and I had to force myself to block out the other voices in the room that had started to attract my attention.

"Is there something else along these lines that you'd like to know about?"

"Yes," Final Girl said, her mind still partly elsewhere. "You can't just go out and get these surgeries, can you?"

"Things have changed a lot since my day, but I'm certain you still need a team of doctors to assess your suitability. Like, not to just confirm that you're definitely trans, or to ensure that you have the money and your body parts are useable. But also that you're mentally capable of making an informed decision, that you're aware of what's irreversible, and have a thorough understanding of the risks involved. For me it required formal letters, and a lot of appointments—many of which were interstate—over a long period of time. It's not as difficult these days."

Final Girl squinted at me.

"So, I won't ask specifics of your surgery, but are there… can you tell me about any variations?"

She grimaced as she finished her question, seemingly regretting not censoring herself.

"Well, say there's not enough tissue in the area to work with," I said. "Sometimes a vaginal lining can be created from skin grafts, which could be from the hips or thighs. I've heard of surgeons using a section of colon, too."

A glint in Final Girl's eye told me she'd remembered something once forgotten.

"After care! That's…"

Final Girl bit her lower lip, and with her palms facing toward me, thrust her hands violently downward into a V shape, tapping against her upper thighs. It was jarring.

"I mean," she said. "There's no way you could just get up and walk after all that cutting up and sewing!"

It was my turn to grimace, as I remembered the debilitating pain that no doctor's warning could have ever prepared me for. Nothing in my life had neared that level of pain, and definitely not for so long uninterrupted. Something that had made it even more uncomfortable, was the need to stop taking hormone medication in the weeks leading up to the operation, causing an undesired slide back toward masculinity.

"It was excruciating," I said. "They packed it full of stuff while I was asleep, to keep it from healing closed. For hygiene reasons I had to change that packing regularly until I was fully healed, and each time I did so there was a spike in pain. I was very tempted to just let it close over."

Final Girl seemed to struggle with what I was saying. It wasn't quite repulsion, but what she felt was definitely along those lines.

"And yeah, I was mostly in bed for a few weeks, even after the stitches came out."

Final Girl sighed loudly.

"Is that basically it, in terms of surgery for trans women?"

"Yes," I confirmed. "I know a little less about what's required for men."

"That's fortunate, because I think we're almost out of time. What can you quickly run me through?"

"Depending on how big their breasts are, they might choose to have a mastectomy to remove most or all of their breast tissue. It seems pretty standard for them to get a hysterectomy, too, removing all or part of their uterus."

"To stop menstrual cycles, mostly?"

"Also so they don't have the physical and social discomfort of pap smears, and to eradicate the primary source of estrogen production."

Ding ding ding!

I stopped breathing to allow shortening of the duration of and space between each of my next words.

"There doesn't seem to be much desire for facial surgeries but as far as lower external surgery it's called a phalloplasty or metoidioplasty…"

"Awesome, I'll look those words up later," Final Girl said. "Thank you for being so obliging."

"No worries. Good luck with your pathway to surgical training!"

As soon as Final Girl turned to leave, I collapsed into my chair, and into my mind.

Just one more student, I told myself. *You can do this, and then you can return to thinking and talking about everything in life unrelated to your gender.*

Little did I know that my gender was soon to be focused on more than ever before, with most other parts of my life deemed unimportant or irrelevant.

Skin

(Package No. 15)

Containing a medical appointment, followed by a reunion.

IT'S COLD WHEN I ARRIVE in the CBD, especially early for the first appointment with a dermatologist named The Potential. Cold for South East Queensland, that is; it's still more than a few degrees above freezing. Part of my being early is that I plan to come out to the new doctor, and I'm worried that anything negative I do will reflect poorly on the transgender community at large. It's not uncommon for people to use a single example of someone from a minority group as an example of how they expect that group to always behave. Especially when it's something negative.

Excellent, I think. *This gives me time to indulge in coffee and breakfast while I complete some life admin.*

"Triple shot latte?"

I'm momentarily disappointed that Regular Barista has only remembered half of my preferred order. I realize, though, that the past few times I've been here, Regular Barista has only asked if I would like *the usual*, so I've probably been drinking lattes for quite some time.

Why stop now and risk unnecessary awkwardness?

"Yes, please," is all I say at first, then I realize there's been a much longer silence than necessary. "Sorry, my brain will hopefully start after I've had coffee."

As Regular Barista rushes off to bring me the legal drug I depend on, I whip my planner out of my rucksack. I smile fondly upon the words *Interview for CEO of Intersectionality Advocates*, then take note of the specific details of The Potential, and find the referral letter I'll be required to present upon arrival. My eyes skip straight to the jarring words *lower gender surgery* that for some reason Take Two has deemed important enough to include in a referral about treatment of my sun damaged skin.

Although I think it seems completely unnecessary for a skin consult, I talk myself into putting a positive spin on it.

You no longer have to worry about how to disclose your gender stuff, I coach myself. *And in turn, you don't have to witness whatever reaction they have to the information.*

To further improve my mood, I make light of the situation on social media. I joke that a new doctor will be checking *my transgender skin*. It is a joke most people won't fully understand. In case you don't, I'll explain.

It's about how I identify. I have never identified as a transgender woman; honestly, you can check everything I've ever written about myself. My current identity is *woman*, and was once *girl*. I just happen to be in a body that was male, and it is my body that went through the transition, not my identity.

Anyway, because I indulge in a leisurely second coffee as I flip forward in my planner to prepare for the month ahead, by the time I arrive at the clinic I'm no longer early. It's a mad dash for me to fill in the medical questionnaire and return it to the receptionist prior to the time of my appointment. When I do return it, I feel incredibly self-conscious because my voice is affected by a cold.

"I've got a cold at the moment," I tell her, for no reason other than to say, *it's not because of my gender history, if that's what you were thinking*.

These deeply ingrained negative thoughts are evidence of internalized transphobia, a natural development arising from near constant reminders of associated stigma. This is why it's important for young trans people to see a woman like me out of the closet and thriving. Visible role models don't just give hope; they help young people circumnavigate near irreparable emotional damage. Perhaps this is also why I so fiercely reject the label *transgender*.

I find a comfy corner in the clinic waiting area that feels both cozy, as well as prestigious. I reflect on the medical questionnaire that had asked what I was *known as* instead of for a *preferred name*. The specific phrasing makes me feel as though people at this clinic might be accepting of me as far as my female identity, rather than viewing it as a preference or choice. This feeling of confidence is shattered as I notice the two receptionists suddenly engage in animated whispers.

Is it gossip about me?

"Paige?"

I note that The Potential has the same color eyes as Hospital Companion, and a similar face to a former colleague from many years ago. As well as this visual familiarity, they also seem especially warm in manner, so my paranoia quickly fades. I happily follow them into their exam room.

The Potential starts to verbally confirm my medical history with me, by working their way down the medical questionnaire I'd hastily completed only moments ago. They type as we converse, and then seamlessly stop before reaching mention of gender affirmation surgery. This causes dual thought processes, the first being that they clearly haven't read my referral letter yet.

Off in a different direction, my thoughts are about The Potential's flawless transition to a change of topic. This relaxes me, because it feels as though they're both adequately trained and experienced to reduce any awkwardness surrounding the topic of my identity. I know that they're aware, that they know it could be a source of social discomfort, and trust that they'll bring the topic up only if relevant to current medical needs.

"Okay," The Potential announces. "Pop behind that curtain, undress to your bra and undies, then take a seat on the examination bed."

As directed, I duck behind the curtain and remove my dress, tights, and boots. For a while I just stand behind the curtain, trying to remember all the abnormal skin I want to point out. There was my face, my neck, and a small patch on my leg. The patch on my leg had been there a while, and I recall that Dermal Saviour had told me to let him know if it didn't go away.

"Paige?"

"Oh, yes, sorry, I'm ready," I call out.

The Potential opens the curtain.

"Can you take a seat on the bed, facing me?"

The Potential takes my right hand, first looking with their eyes and then with some kind of magnifying glass with its own light source. The Potential moves it along my extremity to examine my forearm.

"Do you know what fluorouracil is?"

"No," I tell them.

"It's the main ingredient of a cream I'd like to prescribe. I'll give you some written information to take away, but all of these precancerous skin lesions you can see are sun damage, and the cream can destroy the abnormal cells so that when you're in your eighties, you're not covered in skin cancers."

It feels odd to hear someone speak of my potential to reach such old age. I didn't think I'd even reach thirty! Goodness knows how much I'll be able to achieve if given another few decades. The Potential continues.

"What I'd recommend, is that this winter we focus on your hands, as that's where the most substantial damage is. Next winter we can do your arms, and then we can work through the areas that are most sun affected."

"Okay," I say, more than a little overwhelmed.

"I'd also like to start you on nicotinamide, which is one of the forms of Vitamin B3. It's been recently shown to reduce new non-melanoma skin cancers."

"I'm happy to try that."

"Alright, lie down on your back, please."

"There's a patch above my eyebrow that Dermal Saviour was going to use photodynamic therapy on, but they went on leave before I was able to save up enough money, and then they never came back."

"Dermatologist?"

"General Practitioner with a special interest in skin, so I'm also looking for a new GP. Aside from their skills with skin, we had developed a really good rapport. I've tried two other GPs since, but we didn't connect at all, so I'm still looking."

"I can give you the names of some that are spoken of fondly by my patients, if you like. Where you do you live?"

"Oh, I'd prefer someone central. I don't really live anywhere in particular."

The Potential stops for a moment, but doesn't say anything. I break the silence.

"I look after homes, pets, and sometimes children. Very rarely children, and it's just babysitting when I do."

The Potential nods and continues to look over my face. Something embarrassing comes to mind.

"Oh, that patch on my chin, by the way," I say. "It's where I burnt myself waxing the other day. Just, it's not some lesion to worry about."

"You still get hair there?"

"Just enough to be annoying," I confirm. "It's thick and blonde, so laser won't work on it."

"I can prescribe you a cream that I sometimes use for post-menopausal women when they develop new facial hair. It's called eflornithine, and you just apply it to the area."

"Yes, please! I didn't realize there was such a thing."

Yet another thing that naturally occurs in women that we're supposed to pay to change, I think. And then, *What a happy benefit of being out of the closet to my doctor.*

When The Potential has finished examining my face, there is a circle around the spot above my eyebrow, and another around a mole on my chin that they suspect is also a Basal Cell Carcinoma.

"It's worth noting," The Potential says casually, as they work their way down my body. "That your genital area is skin too."

I wonder if they mean me specifically because of my gender history, I think. *Or if this is all women.* But I don't seek clarification.

"Did you want me to examine the area, or are you happy enough doing that yourself?"

"I can look," I say, feeling as though I've exposed myself enough for one day.

"Okay, well make sure you're checking thoroughly for any visible change. It's rare, but it does happen."

More likely for me, I think. *Due to the solarium reaching skin on the inside, that was once on the outside.*

"How often have you had your skin checked?"

"For a while I was on 3-monthly recall, but then I went back to yearly, except for the past few years because I was waiting for Dermal Saviour to return."

"If it's okay with you, I'd like to see you twice a year."

"That's fine."

"I'll also get you back soon to excise an irregular mole I've found on your back, a BCC on your shoulder and… do you have health insurance?"

"Yes."

"Good. I'll biopsy these two spots on your face. Depending on what they come back as, I might refer you to a cosmetic surgeon I often call on. In that case, you could choose to get them to also do the one on your neck. Right now, I'll freeze that spot on your arm."

I feel incredibly overwhelmed.

"So freezing forearm, two biopsies from face, and I'll book you in for 2 to 3 excisions as soon as possible. I'll also prescribe you fluorouracil for your hands, eflornithine for your chin, and give you information about nicotinamide, as well as a list of GPs."

Although I still feel overwhelmed, I have a strong sense of being in good hands. I'm pleased that being open about my past has led to a possible benefit, and because all of this will be expensive, I feel validated in my choice to continue to live rent-free, and to take a risk to seek higher-paid employment.

-V-

ON THE OTHER SIDE OF THE AIRPORT'S glass walls, it's raining. I'm staring at the outside world waiting for Hospital Companion, my dominant thoughts about how we will part ways in about sixty hours from now. I whip out my phone in an effort to distract myself. The weather app tells me to expect intermittent stormy weather until then.

While I wait, I catch up on messages, emails and social media. Distraction from thoughts of future loss aside, this is also in an attempt to pull myself out of the painfully vivid world Holly Ringland has created for *The Lost Flowers of Alice Hart*, which is a book I've been reading for my new book club. One of the messages I read is about that very book, and naturally I am once again focusing on the overpowering presence of loss in that world, and my own.

After this weekend together, Hospital Companion and I are unlikely to be in the same country again for years, let alone the same city, or workplace. It occurs to me that distance isn't the only way in which our relationship will be irreversibly different to what can now be referred to as our past. My feeble and unsuccessful attempt to put a positive spin on the loss of Hospital Companion from my workplace is to rename them Future Pen Pal.

My thoughts wander down a depressive trail, reflecting on the excess of transience in my life. The pets that I nurture, I come to love before handing them back to their owners. With students I develop rapport, then take back their locker keys as they bid me farewell. And of course there's the rapid turnover of Intersectionality Advocates volunteers. As far as colleagues at Satellite Hospital, Future Pen Pal—formerly known as Hospital Companion—has been the closest thing I've had to one, not to mention being an eager ally-slash-mentee.

I spot Future Pen Pal driving toward the pick-up zone in a campervan they've been using for the Pre-Paige portion of their final Australian vacation. After a quick dash through the rain, I jump up into the passenger seat, then, legs dangling out of the campervan, I awkwardly wriggle out of my rucksack. The rain on my lower legs is cold. I pull my legs back in, the door closed, then lean over the substantial gap between the seats to give Future Pen Pal a side-hug.

"Future Pen Pal!"

"What happened to your face… P-Face?"

"Biopsies to check for skin cancer."

"Is that a trans thing, needing to get checked so frequently for skin cancer?"

Future Pen Pal's facial expression tells me that they are serious, and I know they don't mean offense.

"No," I say. "Pale skin, badly burnt as a child…"

"Oh, okay."

Future Pen Pal looks from me to my rucksack, and back again.

"Um, Paige, did you forget your handbag?"

"Nope," I say excitedly. "I threw it out, and now I just take my rucksack with me everywhere I go."

"Why…"

"Well I'm so often on the move that a rucksack is much more consistently convenient, and really I was just hanging onto the handbag as some symbol of womanhood. Don't feel the need to try so hard these days."

"Fair enough," Future Pen Pal says, an amused smile on their face. "Alright, we've got to drop this bad boy off, then my friend will drive us to our loft!"

"I'm so excited," I say, suddenly unable to stop myself from breaking into an oversized grin. Future Pen Pal hands me a piece of paper, and points to an address.

"Punch that into your phone, would you, Bookface?"

I do as directed.

"So," Future Pen Pal says. "I'm done with organizing stuff for this vacation. It'll be up to you to tell me what we're doing all weekend."

"Oh," I say, taken aback. When with others, I have a tendency to just tag along, so as not to be the reason someone else misses out on their desired activities. "Well, one of the things I like…"

The GPS interrupts me.

"Turn left in one hundred meters."

"Oh, oh, oh," howls Future Pen Pal. "Your phone is a British man-boy! I feel like there's something in one of your old books about this."

I blush, then continue.

"What I was about to say…"

"Turn left."

"I'd really like to…"

"Continue straight for one kilometer."

Future Pen Pal erupts into jovial laughter.

"Oh, for f■ks sake," I spit. "I'll shut up until we're there."

"What!" Future Pen Pal exclaims. "We're going to have silence at least for a kay now."

"Okay," I say warily. "So…"

"You will reach your destination in…"

"NOPE!" I yell. "I'm out!"

Transpecific
(Package No. 16)

Containing the memory of the final conversation as a book.

My jaw figuratively dropped at the sight of my final reader; Mister Beige. It wasn't until the moment he slid into the chair in front of me, that I realized he and Connie had been the only readers who shared my fair skin complexion. Unlike Connie and I, Mister Beige's hair was a dusty blonde, and I noted he had dark brown eyes. Overall, I found him boyishly cute.

I wondered how the diversity of my readers compared with that of the entire student population. Due to entrance requirements (or: barriers) I figured it was unlikely to be similar, leading me to a conclusion. That was, the majority of people who had gone out of their way to read me were people who'd similarly experienced additional obstacles because of parts of themselves over which they had no control. They were naturally more sympathetic to people who were different.

"Hey Paige," Mister Beige said casually. "Please let me get this all out."

I nodded.

"I just wanna start by sayin that as a healthy, young, white, straight guy who was born male to a wealthy family, I know there are a lot of difficulties I haven't had to deal with. And I know that has given me a bit of a blind spot. So if, no, when, I say something that offends, I'm really sorry. I hope you will feel comfortable pulling me up on it, because I'm here to learn."

"Wow," is all I could think to say.

Mister Beige scrunched his face up.

"I also wasn't sure if I should announce my pronouns to you, because they're *he*, and *him*, which is what you'd expect from looking at me anyway."

I smiled.

"That's quite the disclaimer."

Mister Beige looked panicked, or at the very least concerned. His entire body was rigid.

"I'm sorry if I…"

"No, you're fine. I'm just surprised, pleasantly so. Thank you. I'm glad you're here."

Mister Beige let out a relieved sigh, and his body very quickly fell into a relaxed pose.

"No worries, Paige."

"So I take it you already know about my situation? Why I'm here?"

Mister Beige nodded furiously.

"Yes, and I read your first four books to prepare for speaking with you today."

"Oh, wow. And you still have questions? I thought I'd been very thorough."

"I'm sorry," Mister Beige said. "I didn't mean to imply that you didn't do the topic justice. But yes, I have just one question really."

"Big time commitment for one question," I laughed. "Let's hear this question. Let's hope it's actually something I can answer considering I've not covered it in a book yet!"

Mister Beige subtly swung his head from side-to-side and scrunched up his nose as he weighed up something invisible. It was adorable, and I had to actively mask an increasing attraction. The silence started to feel awkward from my side, but fortunately Mister Beige made a decision about what to voice, and how.

"Something that you've mentioned quite a bit is that outside the context of healthcare, you view the trans label as something that's completely unnecessary."

He waited for me to say something.

"Correct," I confirmed. "I've mentioned that a lot, and do indeed still hold that view. Though I've realized that my strong rejection of the label is an indication of issues within myself that need to be addressed. Sorry, you don't need to know that last bit."

Mister Beige hesitantly laughed.

"All good. So, in the context of healthcare, aside from gatekeeping and assisting with a transition, when is it actually necessary for a healthcare professional to know about your situation?"

This time my jaw literally dropped, and I let out a soft gasp. It had not once occurred to me to follow up with an explanation of the flip side of my frequent statement. Every single Medical-Student-Turned-Paige-Reader had blown my mind, right up until the very last one that sat before me.

"I've had so many questions over the past two decades," I said to Mister Beige. "But nobody has ever asked me that, and I've never thought to address it."

Mister Beige looked really pleased.

"I wanted this to be worth both your time and mine," he said through a toothy grin. "I'm guessing you got a lot of questions tonight that you've already answered in great detail in your books."

I laughed.

"You've no idea, though I have more of an appreciation now of why some people approach me rather than digging around the internet for an answer."

"Rule 34?"

Mister Beige grinned.

"Mmm," I murmured as I considered the ways I could address his question without undertaking further research.

"Okay, well I had an amusing situation with a doctor who had asked me about periods. It made sense for them to know why it was that I didn't get them, and why it wasn't actually a problem."

"I think I read about that appointment in one of your books," Mister Beige told me. "And along that same line, you've now made me think it would affect things like pregnancy, and certain routine screening."

"Correct again," I told him. "I'm unable to get pregnant, and rather than screening for cervical abnormalities, I'll eventually need to get my prostate checked like most men do."

Mister Beige smiled appreciatively.

"It's nice to hear you speak so candidly," he said. "I know you've previously felt a lot of shame about how your body differs from other women."

"Yeah," I acknowledged. "I've still a ways to go, but I'm getting there."

"So, what else? I'm keen to know!"

"A physician told me a story about a routine physical exam they used to quickly do on men when they worked in the emergency room."

"Yeah?"

"It involves a quick check for testicular issues, and they were really stumped when a transman came in. The way they found out was by reaching to check with their hands for what was not there."

"Oh," Mister Beige gasped. "That would have been awkward for both sides…"

"From what I heard, it was, but they were able to have a chat about it afterwards at least. I think they both learnt from each other, and hopefully can prevent a worse situation happening to someone else."

"Are there any other situations you think warrant a trans patient coming out to their doctor?"

"It's worth knowing what medication they're on, in case there's a need to prescribe something that is contraindicated by different trans-related medicine. Like, I remember being told that when I was on antibiotics, the oral contraceptive pill would be less effective. That was with the assumption that I was a ciswoman who was using the pill to avoid pregnancy. It could have been helpful to know whether it would have an impact on a woman with my specific anatomy, taking it for my specific reasons."

"So really, a lot of this is about having a thorough patient history just in case it becomes relevant. It doesn't seem like it's in play often."

I pondered his assertion.

"To get solid, current information, I'd suggest searching for *Standards of Care for Transgender Patients*. There are so many other situations that I'm not familiar with, like puberty suppression, or coexisting health issues."

"So… say I was in a position to help improve healthcare for trans, and gender diverse patients. Any areas you think it would be good to focus on?"

On the spot, I found it difficult to think of anything specific. Really, I should have been prepared for this question with an elevator pitch.

"Clinical guidelines and associated research," I blurted out. "Barriers faced by people in rural areas, as well as the culturally and linguistic diverse. Using language that's respectful and inclusive."

Mister Beige opened his mouth to speak again, but I cut him off as an idea occurred to me.

"Actually, I think every medical school needs to address this, so that every single junior doctor is at least a little prepared in terms of communicating with patients in a way that makes them feel safe under their care."

Mister Beige smiled at me.

"Also, there are some online and local courses on treating transgender patients. It would be worth finding details, and passing them around to people you think might be interested."

"Easy peasy," Mister Beige said. "Anyone can do that."

"So true."

Farewell

(Package No. 17)

Containing sadness and frustration.

WHILE FUTURE PEN PAL COMPLETES paperwork for the return of the hire car, I wander around the facility. I sit down on a lone bar stool, whip out a copy of *Outer Shell* from my rucksack, and slip it under my butt. I then stand casually, and wander over to a couch where I sit and wait for Future Pen Pal to join me.

"Okay grumpy," Future Pen Pal says. "You have my undivided attention now."

I decide that I'll provide them with full details of my Secret Project, so retrieve another copy of *Outer Shell*, as well as an introduction card. Future Pen Pal's eyes grow wide, but not for the reason I'd hope.

"You've brought only your rucksack, and it's full of books? What exactly are you planning to wear on this trip, Facepage?"

"There's enough in here, although I do plan to do a small load of washing partway through the trip."

"Oh, well I suppose it saves a lot of space that you only have that one pair of boots for footwear…"

"They're all I ever need to wear. I don't need others. They look fine with all my outfits, and I can walk as far as I like, as often as I deem necessary."

"Well, I mean, your dresses aren't cheap, and you could do them more justice if you wore them with nice shoes."

I thrust the introduction card into Future Pen Pal's hand. On the card, below a photo of me at a Med Gala, there are gold, embossed letters that read:

PAIGE KRYSTAL WILCOX
she, her, herself

Author
Medical Education Coordinator
Human Rights Leader

See Also
A woman assigned male at birth

"Human rights leader? Really?"

Future Pen Pal looks at me incredulously.

"Well, I suppose you can put whatever you want on them. They're *your* cards…"

Can I not call myself that? I wonder. *Because my efforts have been indirect, leading other people to change policy and legislation, should I not get any credit?*

I can't tell if I'm being oversensitive, or if Future Pen Pal is being more antagonistic than usual. I try to ignore their negativity, and continue disclosing details of my Secret Project.

"In each capital city, I leave a few of these cards and books for strangers to stumble upon. Sometimes it's in a café, a book swap, or a place like this. I imagine the copies of *Outer Shell* to be living, waiting excitedly to find out who will be the stranger to stumble onto them."

I point to the lone bar stool that's now showcasing a lonely copy of *Outer Shell*. I continue.

"But always, I go to the state library and art gallery, then leave some nearby. Usually I would spend a bit of time in the library, handwriting parts of my next book, but since I'm not alone for this trip I'll just drop off a book as quickly as possible, and then move on."

Future Pen Pal laughs and shakes their head. I can tell that they don't take my Secret Project as seriously as I do.

"You're often alone in your free time, aren't you?"

"Yes. I was alone as a child, and it's when I'm by myself that I feel most safe."

"Perhaps I should just leave you here," Future Pen Pal jokes. There's a bitter undertone to their words.

"Oh, no, I didn't mean to imply that I don't also value social time! It's just that I'm frequently so vulnerably articulate with people for my volunteer work that in my personal life I want a break, but because people can see that it takes up so much of my life, it tends to more often be what they want to ask me about…"

"Take a breath, Paige, I was joking. Anyway, it's a funny little project you've got going."

I feel annoyed. Future Pen Pal is in an unacknowledged position of privilege where they don't quite understand how important one single new ally is. They don't quite grasp just how bad things still are for the majority of people who are trans and gender non-conforming. Most of their experience is with me, with my cis-passing, traditionally attractive privilege, being paid to work for an employer that celebrates diversity and actively promotes inclusion. My situation is far from what is standard for a trans person.

At the front door of our loft, we're faced with a juxtaposition that makes me feel like we're in *J. K. Rowling's Wizarding World* rather than our real *Memoirable World*. The door itself, like the wall that surrounds it, is severely weathered and uninviting. Below an aging brass doorknob, there is a sleek, shiny black panel.

Future Pen Pal glances at their phone, then waves their hand over the black panel. There is a ripple, and lights in the shape of numbers progressively appear, from top to bottom. Future Pen Pal punches in a sequence, then a small padlock-shaped light at the bottom of the panel. There's a crunching noise, and the door falls inward.

All I can see is a dusty corridor, with a short set of stone stairs halfway, then a wooden set at the end, presumably leading around the corner, though for a moment I do wonder if we're expected to lunge at the wall like you might expect in a book set in the aforementioned world.

We walk to the wall, then follow more steps up to the right, suddenly in a wide open space filled with art and furniture from every time period imaginable. There are colorful oil paintings, a white plastic cuckoo clock, gold sequined cushions, a whimsically shaped bookshelf, and several sofas. We trek up one more flight of stairs to stand on a mezzanine level that hosts a double bed, and beside that, an air mattress.

"I'll take the air mattress," I tell Future Pen Pal. "I slept on one of these for years back in the day."

After resting briefly in the loft, we venture out in search of gelato.

"Gelato is like my new alcohol," I tell Future Pen Pal. "I eat far more than a healthy amount, but it's like all these things everyone does in excess despite knowledge of adverse health effects."

They roll their eyes at me.

"You're so open about your alcohol struggles now," Future Pen Pal comments. "Do you… I was just thinking about your books, and how they could… make someone feel closer to you than they really are. Is it weird for you?"

"It was necessary," is all I say at first. "People often feel compelled to share with me after reading. It can be a bit annoying sometimes, and some people get stalkerish, but sometimes I actually like it."

I give Future Pen Pal a warm smile.

"Our resultant conversations, I think… they've been beneficial for both of us."

In our loft apartment, all night in a light slumber I can hear rain pattering on the roof, wind whistling through cracks, and intermittent rattling windows. My dreams consequently have me on a small island—a small coral quay in fact—nestled somewhere in the Great Barrier Reef, where I wait patiently for years for fate or chance to lead a stranger to my doorstep.

When I return to the real world it's very early in the morning, because

I'm in a different time zone to usual. Rather than trying to get back to sleep, I choose to head downstairs and re-enter the world of Alice Hart for the few hours it will take for Future Pen Pal to rise and join me.

"Good morning!"

I look up from my eReader to see Future Pen Pal grinning at me.

"This book is really sad," I blurt out.

"Got it. If you look upset, it's the book."

On the way to our chosen brunch spot, we pick up a takeaway coffee, like we did regularly once upon a time at Satellite Hospital. It's different now, though. In part because the coffee is delicious, and we're no longer required to confine conversation within the strict boundary of what is workplace appropriate. This freedom is not lost on Future Pen Pal, who crosses the threshold to probe me with deeper questions than ever before. Clearly, these things have been playing on their mind a lot. This whole time, they'd been secretly exercising restraint.

After we eat brunch, Future Pen Pal helps me to find the perfect spot to plant the next copy of *Outer Shell*. From the expression on their face, I can see that Future Pen Pal now has an appreciation for the magical experience of planting a book for a future stranger to stumble upon.

From a distance, we both look at the copy of *Outer Shell* that is leaning on a windowsill, as if to gaze with melancholy at the drizzle outside. There's something enchanting about the sad, lonely book, about a girl who is just as alone, looking out at a world that cannot see her. It occurs to me that before now, I have done this all on my own. As with many things in life, the experience is far better shared. It would be worth my while to lose the first word of the phrase *Secret Project*.

Perhaps, I think. *I should also think about opening myself up to romance again.*

On a whim, Future Pen Pal and I visit a small, local arts center. We wander in silence until we stumble into a room filled with the most recent paintings of Casper Fairhall, who just happens to be standing in the center of the room.

"Come in," Casper says, giving us a welcoming wave.

We join a small group of emerging artists for a discussion on the art pieces that surround us. I'm surprised by the amount of scientific research that has been untaken before Casper has planted his first brush stroke on canvas. I feel foolish under-appreciating the preparation that goes into a work of art like a painting. Or a book.

AUTHOR LOOKS DIRECTLY AT YOU AND SAYS:
"It took many boring articles and tedious conversations to get to this sentence that you are now reading."

-V-

THE FOLLOWING DAY, FUTURE PEN PAL and I wander to the train with our takeaway coffees and head into the city center to visit the state library and art gallery, and of course to drop of more copies of *Outer Shell* as well as my introduction card. When we get to the gallery, we part ways to wander alone in silence. After an hour or so, we reconnect near the gallery shop.

"Did you see the section up there?"

Future Pen Pal looks up to the second level where I am pointing, and shakes their head.

"You should," I say. "I'll be here when you're done."

While Future Pen Pal checks out the exhibit, I sift through the small selection of items for sale that are decorated with indigenous art. I stop at a collection of small bags. Having lost a few pockets since ditching my handbag, I've been wanting some small internal bags to more neatly store pens, keys, and phone accessories. I also want to find different ways of supporting the traditional custodians of the land I continuously wander over.

As Future Pen Pal approaches, I hold up my two bag preferences.

"Which one? I can't decide."

"Not that one," Future Pen Pal says. "It has cars on it, and you don't even drive."

My heart feels bruised. I put that bag down, and pay for the bag with a painting of the *Star Dreaming Story of the Seven Sisters*, which is a story that covers more than half the width of the continent, and travels through many different language groups.

"Paige, that was really awful," Future Pen Pal tells me about the exhibit I made them look at. "I had no idea."

"What's been done to the First Peoples is abominable," I say, unable to sound emotionally neutral. "More of it is acknowledged now, but we've still a long way to go before any real reconciliation is possible."

Future Pen Pal holds up a flyer for a local production of a play entitled *Hir* (pronounced *here*).

"What do you think? Are you up for some gender-bending comedy?"

I groan, and at first violently oppose the suggestion. I think back to the Queer Short Film Festival. More specifically, the trans film that I found to be a traumatic experience. After some consideration though, I decide that going to the theatre will be a nice end to our time together. We wander to the theatre to purchase tickets, which leads us to our next gelato stop.

"Your phone is ringing," Future Pen Pal says between gelato licks.

I stare at my phone. The display tells me that an unknown caller is trying to reach me. Of course it is not audibly ringing or vibrating, so it's no bother to patiently wait for it to ring out.

"Shit," I say, suddenly regretting the decision. "What if it was important? It might have been about the CEO position. It was about a week ago that I submitted my test scenarios as the final stage of the application process."

"They can leave a message," Future Pen Pal says.

"No they can't," I argue. "I don't have voicemail!"

"What? Why not?"

"Stalkers," I state matter-of-factly.

Future Pen Pal looks skeptical, which annoys me. I realize that they've been getting on my nerves a lot, and I've just worked out why. Most evenings I am alone with people's pets, which gives me a regular vacation from the tiring role of educator. Suddenly I'm appreciative of Friendly Entity, who requires no training, allowing me to completely relax. Because I know I'll be busy and forget as soon as I'm back in Brisbane, I send them a message to arrange a catch up.

Future Pen Pal draws focus back to them.

"Surely it would be less of an issue now?"

"What?"

"Your apparent stalkers…"

"Maybe," I say. "And maybe I should put voicemail back on."

It's not like people can't anonymously harass me on the internet anyway, I think. *And my phone number is slightly less accessible to those types.*

-V-

"THAT. WAS. BLEAK," Future Pen Pal mutters as the stage lights dim at the end of the play. "I need to go do something. This can't be the end of our trip."

I agree.

"Let's catch the train back and get more gelato on the way to our loft."

"Splendid idea," I say.

We spend a little time on the train trying to debrief. I express that in parts I felt the play was making fun of the community, rather than accurately representing it. Future Pen Pal disagrees, stating that it was more taking stabs at uninformed people who use their voice. Something we both agree on, is that it was mislabeled as a comedy.

Future Pen Pal's eyes grow wide when they hear an announcement of the next station.

"You've not seen the city lights from the park!"

"Oh, that's a shame," I say. "It sounds like I'm missing out on something pretty spectacular?"

Future Pen Pal nods.

"If you want, we can get off at the next station and walk. I know the distance won't bother you, though it is getting late…"

"Let's do it."

"Yeah?"

"Yes!"

We wander through a sleepy suburb of closed restaurants, and I wonder about the people who live and work there. So many lives that may never intersect with my own. After about half an hour, we reach the edge of the park. Future Pen Pal retrieves their phone and looks up the exact location of the lookout. It'll be a lengthy walk through the park in the dark to get there.

"It'll be a lengthy walk through the park in the dark to get there," Future Pen Pal states.

I look into the darkness ahead, and shudder.

"That's not something I want to do," I say firmly. "Maybe we should just go back to the train."

"Or..."

We summon a car through the RideShare app, then—because it's late, I'm tired, and we don't want to wait for another car in the cold darkness—Future Pen Pal requests that the driver wait for me while I take a quick peek and snap a few photos. I do, and we then leave.

In the morning, although we're not leaving the city together, we share a car to the airport. I'm fairly silent in the car, processing everything from the past few days. I suspect I'll want to keep in contact with Future Pen Pal if they're up for it. I know that from here on out we'll be physically separated, but I feel we've still got so much to learn from each other. If the past few days have done nothing else, they've highlighted that Future Pen Pal still has potential for growth as an ally.

"Are you okay, pal?"

I smile at Future Pen Pal, who, of course, has always meant well from the very beginning.

"Yeah, mate, I'm just tired."

After a little too much silence, just before I head through security, we embrace quickly and wish each other wonderful lives.

"Oh, I don't think I told you," Future Pen Pal calls as I am walking away. "I've passed on a copy of *Outer Shell* to my parents!"

"Thank you!"

My face erupts into a joyful red as I think about my message being spread across another continent.

Promise

(Package No. 18)

Containing hope.

IT'S NOT THE TEAR-FILLED EYES that make it seem like Friendly Entity is a stranger. I recall how I'd reflected the year before, when I'd realized more than a year had passed without any travel unrelated to work. Those thoughts had led me to attempt a correction, my approach being to plan out a year of regular long weekends, and for each to book flights to different cities. Although it had caused debt to weigh me down just a little longer, it was worth it to have felt as though I was living a full life.

Yet again though, I find myself in a position to feel regret about the way I've caused my year to play out. In this moment, I know I've got a decision to make soon. Although I'm not sure what, one of the parts of my life will need to be excised. It obviously can't be my day job, but the volunteer work? My writing? Or perhaps I'll have to farewell the nomadic pet-filled lifestyle I've come to adore. Surely not that. *Anything* but that.

Friendly Entity opens their arms, and I fall into a tight, extended embrace. They feel warm and soft. Although I can't be sure because it's been so long, they don't seem quite as soft as they once did. Similarly, perhaps, no I'm sure, they feel a little warmer than they used to.

"It's been a while," I say into their neck. "I'm so sorry I let so much time slip away again."

"I know," Friendly Entity tells me as they squeeze me tightly enough to cause me to expel air. "I knew back in that little cottage that you would lose another year."

"I'm still sorry."

Friendly Entity releases me and steps back. They hold both hands up to their heart to guide my eyes there, then they drop their hands down and outwards, landing in a shrug. Without words, Friendly Entity is ensuring we address the elephant in the room. That they are the one prompting this, is important. It wasn't my place to draw attention to a change that could be associated with pain.

"I did wonder," I acknowledge.

Friendly Entity rubs the stubble on their jawline. The stubble is one of a few visual changes I've missed out on because of the way I've chosen to live. A way that is unsustainable, and so requiring a big life change.

"I don't know if you can tell in this t-shirt, but I don't need a binder for my chest anymore," they tell me proudly.

I smile and struggle to hold back tears. How could I have missed that Friendly Entity had taken steps to permanently transition? I think back to the advice I'd given many allies; it's important that I not make this interaction about me. After what they've gone through, I shouldn't pressure them to make me feel better about my absence. It is I who must ensure that their…

"So, your pronouns now…"

"He, and him," Friendly Entity announces. I witness the most genuine smile I've ever seen on him. *Him*. It's clear that Friendly Entity had also been in need of a big life change, and this was his. *His*.

"I should be fine adjusting," I tell him. *Him*. "But if I slip up, of course you're welcome to correct me."

"I'd bloody well hope so, Paige."

Friendly Entity pokes out his tongue, and I can't help but throw my arms around him again, but this time I quickly release.

"Guess I should get more hugs in while I'm able," he says. "They'll be using skin from my forearms to create a phalloplasty, which'll leave me dodging cuddles for a bit."

I'd never have asked, but it's nice that he feels comfortable confirming his lower gender surgery intent.

"Oh my god, that's so exciting!"

"Hey Paige," Friendly Entity says, sporting a confusing, cheeky grin. They tap their ear, leading me to touch mine.

"Oh!"

"Flashy looking wireless earphones, Paige. Aren't you trying to level your debts?"

"Pets kept chewing the cords," I say as I remove the two earpieces. "This was actually a cheaper solution."

There's a coughing sound that draws attention to a waiter, who is a tall, thin, bored person. There aren't enough solid indicators for me to assign them a gender, so I don't. It's unlikely to become necessary for the success of our interaction today.

"Do you need more time?"

Friendly Entity and I both laugh, and sit down.

"Yes, sorry," I say. "We haven't looked at the menu yet."

"I'll come back."

Friendly Entity smirks at me, and waits until we are alone before he speaks.

"You need to see the menu?"

"No," I admit. "But I thought you might."

"What do you get when you come here?"

"Spicy chicken."

"Sounds good for me too," Friendly Entity laughs. "Oh, sorry you didn't get CEO of Intersectionality Advocates after all the effort you put in through the test scenarios and whatnot, but congratulations on your award for activism!"

"Hah! Thanks," I gush.

"Kind of amusing for you to win Trans Activist of The Year," Friendly Entity says. "Considering you resist the trans label."

"Yeah," I say. "In my head, it refers to my efforts in aid of the trans community, rather than a label on me that separates me from other women."

"I liked what you wrote for Intersectionality Advocates about hosting the event," Friendly Entity tells me. "Nice of you to give them free content."

The Article That Friendly Entity Has Just Referenced

In a handmade dress representing the measured way we're allowed to be out at work, this year with Nevo Zesin, I hosted the 57th Annual Queen's Ball Awards; the longest running event of its kind in the world.

As someone who has been active for many years within the Queer community, I have long been familiar with and appreciated what the Queen's Ball embodies and does for LGBTIQAP+ youth. So when Brisbane Pride approached me to be a host this year, I didn't hesitate to accept.

On the night I was excited to take home the Trans Activist of the Year award, and I am incredibly grateful for the committee's and the community's love and support.

Yet among the fanfare, what I'm most proud of is the event's approach to diversity and inclusion this year.

That as hosts they chose Nevo—who identifies as non-binary and trans—and, me—a woman assigned male at birth—was important, because even within our own community our voices are often taken away, and our authenticity debated. To see that the ceremony included a Welcome to Country, as well as Auslan interpreters, was heartwarming.

This year, the Queen's Ball also saw the introduction of awards to ensure recognition went to Aboriginal and Torres Strait Islander people, as well as intersex and trans people.

It reminded me of why I joined Intersectionality Advocates several years ago. As a community we've been through so much, and we can achieve so much more when we work together by ensuring all voices within our community have the opportunity to be heard.

I often speak at events about my past gender transition and have written in depth about my lived experience. Although I know firsthand that it can be quite

> painful, I persist with sharing my story and encourage others who feel they are able, to do so as well.
>
> Hosting the awards this year helped me further appreciate the importance of role models and shared experiences, especially to those who are at the start of their LGBTIQAP+ journey.

"Thanks," I tell Friendly Entity. "I still find it difficult to sell myself in this context. I know it's necessary, but it never feels comfortable."

"Part of your charm," Friendly Entity says, and I'm not sure what he means. "Thanks for putting me on to Nevo Zesin's memoir, by the way. It really helped me work through a few things that I was unsure of. How were they as a co-host for the awards?"

"They're pretty much my only celebrity crush," I tell him. "Cannot speak highly enough of them as a colleague, and as a decent human being. I knew when we were interviewed on the radio that they were awesome, but meeting in person, and working together... it was unexpectedly great."

Friendly Entity grins.

"What else have you been up to? There's been a bit too much social media action for me to keep up with! It really is your time, Paige!"

We both laugh jovially.

"Ummm, well Markety Mark from The Medical College interviewed me about the event, so it'll be interesting to see the consequences of that when it's published. Also had a nice chat at a community event for queer youth, and was one of two guest speakers at a national queer student awards ceremony. Oh! And I reached out to someone at The University about stepping up into a more challenging role outside of The Medical College. They've agreed to meet me for a chat about how that might look!"

There's a coughing noise that we've both heard before.

"Have you decided yet?"

"Two times spicy chicken, please," I request.

"That all?"

"Yes, thanks," I confirm.

"Won't be long."

"So, Friendly Entity," I say, suddenly embarrassed by being the dominant topic of conversation. "Is there anything about your recent life that you'd like to share with me?"

"Not for the moment," Friendly Entity says. "Most of life has been transition related, and I'm grateful for a break from that topic."

"Understood."

"How's your next book going?"

"Splendidly," I gush. "Did I tell you my plan with it?"

"Nope."

"Well aside from being a continuation of my memoir series, the focus is on healthcare. The hope is that I can get it to students at every medical school across Australia, and that by the end they'll not just feel compelled to do something to improve the situation, but that they'll have some idea of what area they can focus on, and how to go about it."

"Sounds ambitious."

"Guess we'll see!"

"What's your next project then, after that?" Friendly Entity asks. "I know you well enough to assume it won't end there…"

"Of course it won't," I tell him, unable to prevent warm excitement rising from within to burst through my pores. My cheeks puff up, and I bite my lip to make my smile at least a little more subtle.

"Go on, then," Friendly Entity presses. "Tell me what your idea is."

"No," I say with a cheeky grin.

"Aw, come on, Paige!"

"Can't!"

"Paige, come on! Tell me!"

"Well, I could show you…"

Friendly Entity's eyes grow wide in an instant.

"I'm intrigued! That's something you haven't made me feel in a very long time!"

I giggle as I jump up from the table, and jump back to give some distance between. I throw my hands out, gesturing to the space around me.

"There is silence, and the stage is completely dark," I tell Friendly Entity. "Suddenly the silence is broken by our narrator!"

Friendly Entity gazes up at me, amused, but also captivated. I choose to focus on his captivation to motivate me, and ignore the amusement that detracts.

"*I was 19 when I found out that I wasn't alone*, the narrator tells us."

I see a pang of sadness in Friendly Entity.

"*Before that, if I squint with my brain, I can travel as far back as the late 1980s, to regional Queensland, Australia, where the air is hot and dry.*"

The sadness in Friendly Entity starts to fade.

"*There I exist as virtually nothing but inner monologue; unvoiced thoughts. Somewhere in my fifth year of life, there seems to be a lot of darkness.*"

I grin at Friendly Entity, who is beaming and exhibiting signs of recognition on his face.

"*Is there actually an absence of light? Or is that just the way my memory is processing the lack of available information?*"

Friendly Entity's gaze is unflinching.

"Cautiously, I wander into the spotlight. Barefoot, I'm wearing only a black singlet and black shorts. I look at the wooden stool, then sit down next to it and cross my legs."

I stop to take in the image of Friendly Entity, who becomes aware that I am staring at him. Self-conscious, he looks down at his plate.

"There's still work to do," I say. "But I've had enough of being a book for the moment."

"Well of course, so the Memoirable Paige is going to become a play!"

Paige Krystal Wilcox is an Australian actress, author, and award-winning activist. Assigned male at birth in Toowoomba, Queensland, Paige spent her earliest years living in nearby rural communities before moving north to a coastal town to finish primary school. She moved to Brisbane in 2000 to attend high school, followed by a private college where she studied Film, Television and Theatre Acting. Upon graduating, Paige worked several casual jobs to pay for the required medical treatments to complete a gender transition and adjust her physical appearance to accurately reflect her female identity. Paige initially rose to online prominence after releasing a YouTube series about her transition from male to female.

Manufactured by Amazon.ca
Bolton, ON